CONTENTS

THIS IS A CARLTON BOOK

Design and map copyright © Carlton Books Limited 2010
Text copyright © Richard Overy 2010
Imperial War Museum photographs © Imperial War Museum

This edition published in 2010 by Carlton Books Limited. A division of the Carlton
Publishing Group
20 Mortimer Street
London
W1T 3JW

Printed in China

All rights reserved

A CIP catalogue for this book is available from the British Library

ISBN: 978 1 84732 658 4

ACKNOWLEDGEMENTS

I am happy to acknowledge the extent to which this book has been a real team effort. The book's editor Gemma Maclagan has played a key part in getting the book together and keeping me on schedule. Russell Knowles and Steve Behan are responsible for the book's strong visual content and layout. Philip Parker and Terry Charman have between them made sure that the history is as error-free as it can be and I am grateful to them for their scrupulous monitoring of the text and captions which has made this a better book.

INTRODUCTION

The Second World War was the largest and costliest war in human history. Its scale was genuinely global, leaving almost no part of the world unaffected. At its end the political geography of the world was transformed and the stage set for the emergence of the modern states' system. It is possible to exaggerate the break represented by victory in 1945, but the change between the pre-war world of economic crisis, European imperialism and militant nationalism and the post-war world of economic boom, decolonisation and the ideological confrontation of the Cold War was a fundamental one.

It is worth remembering that no-one at the start could be certain what direction the war might take or could anticipate the degree of destruction and violence that it would draw in its wake. A number of different areas of conflict coalesced, like separate fires growing into a single inferno: the European conflict over German efforts to break the restrictions imposed after her defeat in the First World War; the conflicts generated by an expansionist and ambitious Fascist Italy whose leader, Benito Mussolini, dreamed of re-creating the Roman Empire; and the war for Asia fought in the east by Imperial Japan, determined to assert the right of non-white peoples to a share of empire; and in western Asia by an alliance of anti-Communist states grouped around Hitler's Germany which launched a crusade against the new Soviet system in 1941.

As the war grew in scope all the major powers were drawn in. It is often asserted that the entry of the United States in December 1941 made victory certain for the Allied powers through sheer economic weight, but the outcome was not pre-ordained. Germany and her allies had large resources and captured yet more. German and Japanese forces fought with high skill. To win the war the Allies needed to improve fighting power, to co-ordinate their activities and to keep their populations, even in times of tribulation, committed to the cause. The idea that the Axis powers, and Germany in particular, lost the war through their own ineptitude distorts the extent to which the Allies had to learn to fight with greater effectiveness and to exploit their own scientific, technical and intelligence resources to the full. It is a measure of the significance they all gave to the war, not simply as the means to their own survival, but as a way to impose one world order or another, that they made the sacrifices they did. There was a powerful sense that this really was a war that would shape the way history would be made.

The Second World War: The Complete Illustrated History is the story of that conflict from its roots in the post-war settlement of 1919 to the final victory of the Allies and the re-establishment of a more stable world order. It starts with the early years of more limited war, when German armies conquered much of Europe with relatively low casualties and with lightning speed. In just 19 months Germany had conquered an area from Norway to Crete, the French Atlantic coast to Warsaw. It is little wonder that Hitler and the German leadership felt confident that they could now build a New Order on the ruins of the old.

It follows the war's progress as the Axis states pushed out into the Soviet Union, South-east Asia and the Pacific and almost to the Suez Canal. In the Soviet Union only exceptional efforts staved off defeat, but with losses on an extraordinary scale, any other state would have sued for peace. Stalin's ability to keep his people fighting was a vital element in 1941 and 1942 when the Western Allies were struggling to avoid defeat in the Pacific and Atlantic, and could do little to hinder the German advance. For the Allies these years turned into a holding operation in which they tried to avoid anything worse happening. For their Axis enemies the tantalising prize of a new world order seemed still within their grasp – German soldiers were in the Caucasus, Japanese soldiers a short step from Australia and German and Italian forces deep inside Egypt.

However this was not to be. Slowly but surely on land and sea and in the air, the tide of war began to flow the Allies' way. It became clear that Axis forces, which had once seemed all but unstoppable, could be defeated in open battle. Victory in the desert war paved the way for the reconquest of the Mediterranean; victory in the Solomons opened a small doorway into the defensive frontier of the Japanese Empire through which the Allies poured overwhelming naval, air and military strength; victory at Stalingrad demonstrated to the world that the Red Army had come of age and the period of easy German victories was over.

The Struggles of the end of the war were the costliest of the entire conflict. Most Western, German and Japanese casualties date from the final 18 months of combat. The sight of distant victory did not make the war easier to wage but called for the most supreme of efforts. The prospect of catastrophic defeat called for desperate measures of defence from the Axis forces. When the war was finally over in August 1945 the world had to take stock of the wreckage left behind. The changes provoked by the war were this time more permanent than in 1918. Nothing to compare with the Second World War has occurred in the sixty-three years since it ended, but its long shadow has extended down to the present.

RICHARD OVERY, 2010

OPERATIONS 1931–1941

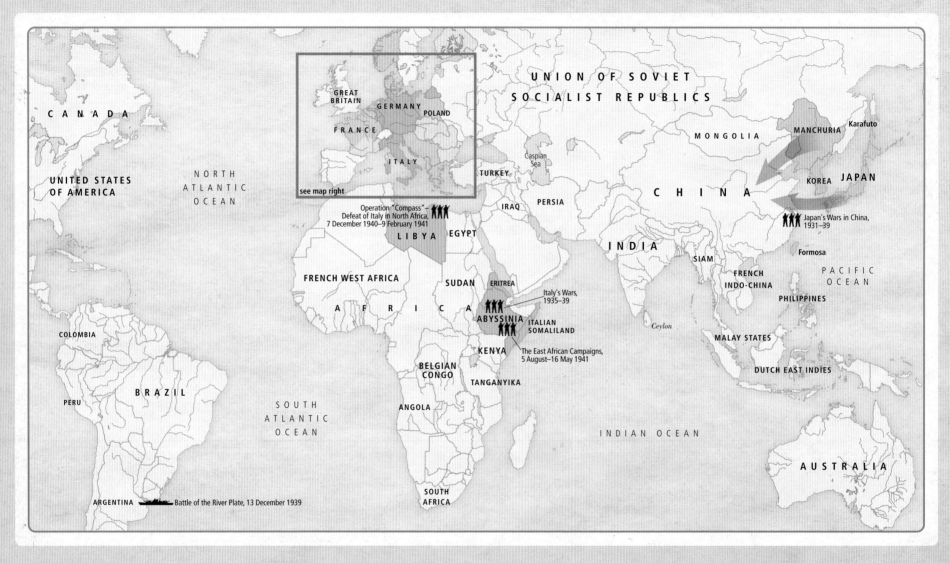

UNION OF SOVIET
SOCIALIST REPUBLICS

CANADA

UNITED STATES
OF AMERICA

NORTH
ATLANTIC
OCEAN

GREAT
BRITAIN

GERMANY POLAND

FRANCE

ITALY

see map right

MONGOLIA

MANCHURIA Karafuto

KOREA JAPAN

TURKEY

Caspian
Sea

CHINA

PERSIA

IRAQ

Operation "Compass" –
Defeat of Italy in North Africa,
7 December 1940–9 February 1941

LIBYA EGYPT

INDIA

Japan's Wars in China,
1931–39

COLOMBIA

FRENCH WEST AFRICA

SUDAN ERITREA

Italy's Wars,
1935–39

ABYSSINIA ITALIAN
SOMALILAND

KENYA

The East African Campaigns,
5 August–16 May 1941

SIAM

FRENCH
INDO-CHINA

Formosa

PACIFIC
OCEAN

PHILIPPINES

Ceylon

A F R I C A

MALAY STATES

PERU BRAZIL

BELGIAN
CONGO

TANGANYIKA

SOUTH
ATLANTIC
OCEAN

ANGOLA

INDIAN OCEAN

DUTCH EAST INDIES

AUSTRALIA

SOUTH
AFRICA

ARGENTINA Battle of the River Plate, 13 December 1939

GENERAL MAP KEY — TO SPREAD MAPS

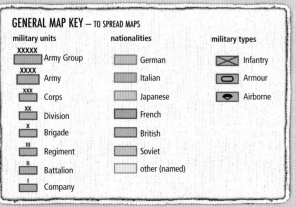

military units

XXXXX Army Group
XXXX Army
XXX Corps
XX Division
X Brigade
III Regiment
II Battalion
I Company

nationalities

German
Italian
Japanese
French
British
Soviet
other (named)

military types

Infantry
Armour
Airborne

WORLD MAP KEY

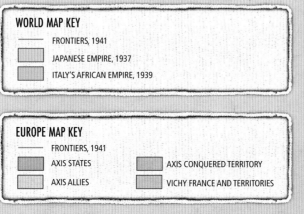

FRONTIERS, 1941
JAPANESE EMPIRE, 1937
ITALY'S AFRICAN EMPIRE, 1939

EUROPE MAP KEY

FRONTIERS, 1941
AXIS STATES
AXIS ALLIES
AXIS CONQUERED TERRITORY
VICHY FRANCE AND TERRITORIES

ABOVE & RIGHT Between September 1939 and May 1941 the Axis powers in Europe, Germany and Italy, came to dominate most of the European continent from Norway in the north to Crete in the south. The Allies had more success in the naval war and in sub-Saharan Africa, but by mid-1941 the British Empire, fighting alone, was under growing threat in North Africa and the Middle East and, in eastern Asia, from the expanding Japanese Empire, which by mid-1941 reached down deep into Chinese territory and was poised to threaten the eastern European imperial possessions from India to the Dutch East Indies.

ATLANTIC
OCEAN

NORWAY
· Oslo

FINLAND ᛭᛭᛭ Soviet-Finnish War
30 November 1939–12 March 1940

· Helsinki

· Leningrad

᛭᛭᛭ German Invasion of Norway,
9 April–9 June 1940

SWEDEN

· Stockholm

North
Sea

IRELAND

· Glasgow

· Edinburgh

UNITED

DENMARK

ESTONIA

· Tallinn

Baltic
Sea

· Pskov

· Riga

LATVIA

· Moscow

· Dublin

· Cork

· Liverpool · Manchester

KINGDOM

· Birmingham

German Blitz on Britain,
7 September 1940–
16 May 1941

London

NETHERLANDS

· Hamburg

· Bremen

· Amsterdam

· Rotterdam

· Hanover

· Berlin

LITHUANIA

· Vilnius

· Königsberg

Danzig

EAST
PRUSSIA

· Smolensk

· Minsk

SOVIET

Sinking the *Bismarck*,
24–27 May 1941

Battle of Britain,
July–October 1940

Dunkirk,
27 May–4 June 1940

· Lille

BELGIUM

Brussels

Germany Invades in the West,
10–27 May 1940

GERMANY

Elbe

· Leipzig

Oder

Vistula

Division of Poland under the
Nazi-Soviet Pact, 1939

· Warsaw

· Brest

POLAND

UNION

· Brest

LUXEMBOURG

· Frankfurt

᛭᛭᛭ Germany Invades Poland,
1 September 1939

Seine

· Paris

Fall of France,
4–17 June 1940

᛭᛭᛭

· Kraków

· Kiev

Bay of
Biscay

· Nantes

FRANCE

Rhine

Strassburg

Danube

· Prague

BOHEMIA

· Lvov

Dnieper

Dniester

· Bordeaux

Loire

SWITZERLAND

Berne

· Munich

AUSTRIA

SLOVAKIA

· Vienna

· Budapest

HUNGARY

· Odessa

· Oviedo

· Bilbao

Lyons

Rhône

· Milan

· Turin

I

· Genoa

German Invasion
of Yugoslavia and Greece
6–27 April 1941

· Belgrade

ROMANIA

· Sevastopol

· Porto

PORTUGAL

· Toulouse

Douro

SPAIN

· Zaragoza

· Madrid

Tagus

· Marseille

Corsica

T

A

Sardinia

L

· Rome

Y

YUGOSLAVIA

· Bucharest

Danube

BULGARIA

Black
Sea

· Lisbon

· Seville

· Barcelona

· Valencia

Balearics

Mediterranean

Sea

· Naples

Tirana

Italian annexation
of Albania, 1939

ALBANIA

Taranto, 11 November 1940

᛭᛭᛭

· Sofia

· Burgas

· Edirne

᛭᛭᛭ Italian Invasion of Greece,
28 October 1940

Salonika

· Istanbul

· Ankara

Sicily

GREECE

TURKEY

· Izmir

MOROCCO

ALGERIA

TUNISIA

Malta
(British)

Matapan,
28 March 1941

· Patra

· Athens

Aegean

Sea

RHODES

· Gibraltar
(British)

CRETE

German Conquest of Crete,
20 May–1 June 1941

OPERATIONS 1941–1942

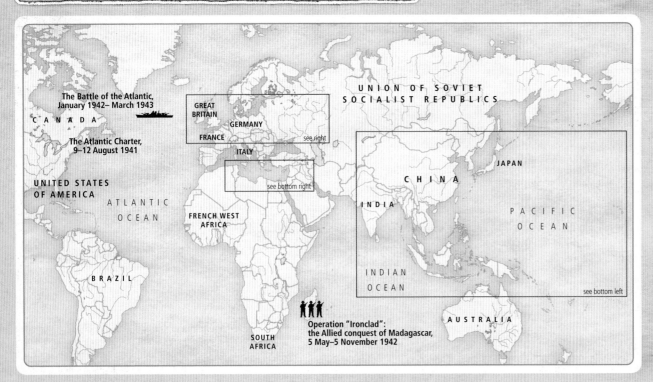

The Battle of the Atlantic,
January 1942– March 1943

The Atlantic Charter,
9–12 August 1941

CANADA

UNITED STATES
OF AMERICA

ATLANTIC
OCEAN

BRAZIL

GREAT
BRITAIN

GERMANY

FRANCE
see right

ITALY
see bottom right

FRENCH WEST
AFRICA

SOUTH
AFRICA

UNION OF SOVIET
SOCIALIST REPUBLICS

CHINA

INDIA

JAPAN

PACIFIC
OCEAN

INDIAN
OCEAN
see bottom left

AUSTRALIA

Operation "Ironclad":
the Allied conquest of Madagascar,
5 May–5 November 1942

IRELAND

Dublin

Cork

UNITED

KINGDOM

Glasgow
Edinburgh

Liverpool   Manchester

Birmingham

Plymouth

London

Portsmouth

Atlantic
Ocean

English Channel
Cherbourg

Brest

Caen

The Dieppe Rai
19 August 1942

Commando Raids:
from Norway to St. Nazaire,
3 March 1941–27 March 1942

Nantes

Seine   Pa

Loire

FRANC

GENERAL MAP KEY – TO SPREAD MAPS

military units		military types		nationalities	
XXXXX	Army Group	Infantry		German	French
XXXX	Army	Armour		Italian	Romanian
XXX	Corps	Airborne		Japanese	Finnish
XX	Division	Mechanised		United States	Vichy (named)
X	Brigade			British	Hungarian
III	Regiment			Soviet	other (named)
II	Battalion				
I	Company				

EUROPE MAP KEY

AXIS STATE, 1942

AXIS ALLIED STATES, 1942

AXIS OCCUPIED, 1942

LIMIT OF AXIS EXPANSION EASTWARDS, 1942

FAR EAST MAP KEY

JAPANESE EMPIRE, 1942

JAPANESE ALLIED STATES

LIMIT OF JAPANESE EXPANSION, 1942

MID EAST MAP KEY

FRENCH MANDATE, TO VICHY FRANCE

ABOVE & RIGHT From May 1941 to summer of the following year, the Axis powers ruled almost unchallenged over Western Europe. This permitted Hitler to launch an unprovoked invasion of the Soviet Union in autumn 1941, which after initial rapid advances stalled outside Moscow in the winter snow, and, despite reaching into the Caucasus the next spring, never quite succeeded in defeating the Soviets. In eastern Asia, the Japanese joined the conflict, launching a series of lightning assaults, pushing the paralysed British forces out of the Malay peninsula and capturing the vital strategic position of Singapore. The Japanese attack on Pearl Harbor in December 1941, however, brought the United States into the War, and, though Japan's forces pushed the Americans out of the Philippines and a series of other island positions in the Pacific, a serious naval check at Midway showed their over-extended perimeter's vulnerability.

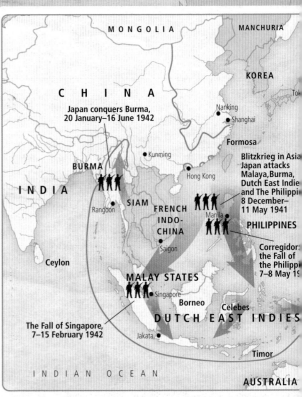

MONGOLIA   MANCHURIA

CHINA

KOREA

Japan conquers Burma,
20 January–16 June 1942

Nanking

Shanghai

Kunming

BURMA

Hong Kong

Formosa

Blitzkrieg in Asia
Japan attacks
Malaya, Burma,
Dutch East Indie
and The Philippi
8 December–
11 May 1941

INDIA

Rangoon

SIAM

FRENCH
INDO-
CHINA

Saigon

Manila

PHILIPPINES

Corregidor:
the Fall of
the Philippi
7–8 May 19

Ceylon

MALAY STATES

Singapore

Borneo

Celebes

The Fall of Singapore,
7–15 February 1942

Jakata

DUTCH EAST INDIES

Timor

INDIAN OCEAN

AUSTRALIA

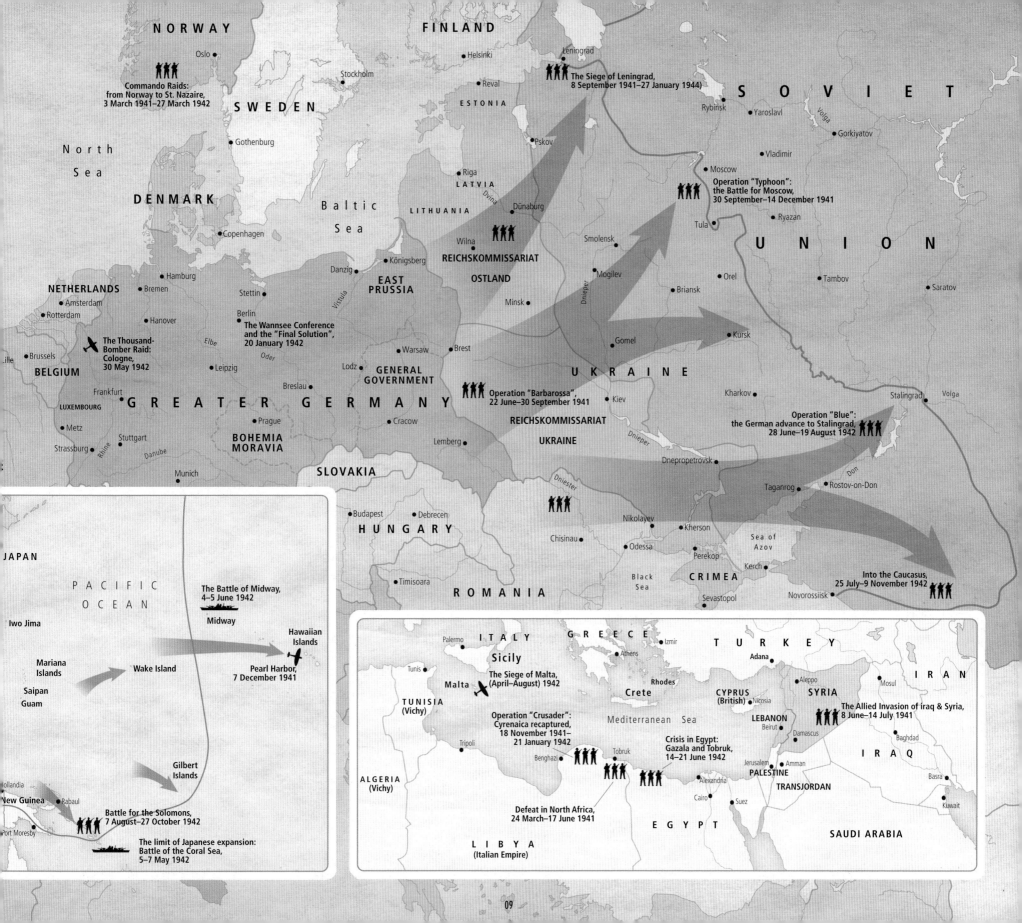

OPERATIONS 1942–1944

Battle of the North Cape:
the sinking of the Scharnhorst,
26–27 Dec. 1943

UNION OF SOVIET
SOCIALIST REPUBLICS

GREAT
BRITAIN
GERMANY
FRANCE
ITALY

The Casablanca Conference:
"Unconditional Surrender",
14–24 Jan. 1943

The Big Three:
The Teheran Conference,
28 Nov.–1 Dec. 1943

• Casablanca

see right

CANADA

UNITED STATES
OF AMERICA

ATLANTIC
OCEAN

FRENCH WEST
AFRICA

BRAZIL

• Teheran

CHINA

JAPAN

INDIA

PACIFIC
OCEAN

INDIAN
OCEAN

see bottom right

AUSTRALIA

SOUTH
AFRICA

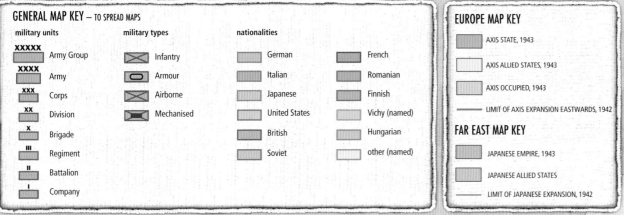

GENERAL MAP KEY — TO SPREAD MAPS

military units

XXXXX	Army Group
XXXX	Army
XXX	Corps
XX	Division
X	Brigade
III	Regiment
II	Battalion
I	Company

military types

Infantry
Armour
Airborne
Mechanised

nationalities

German		French	
Italian		Romanian	
Japanese		Finnish	
United States		Vichy (named)	
British		Hungarian	
Soviet		other (named)	

EUROPE MAP KEY

AXIS STATE, 1943
AXIS ALLIED STATES, 1943
AXIS OCCUPIED, 1943
LIMIT OF AXIS EXPANSION EASTWARDS, 1942

FAR EAST MAP KEY

JAPANESE EMPIRE, 1943
JAPANESE ALLIED STATES
LIMIT OF JAPANESE EXPANSION, 1942

ABOVE & RIGHT

The years 1942–1944 were the turning point of the war. In 1942 Japanese advances into south-east Asia, Burma and the Pacific islands created a large new area of Japanese imperial rule. In Germany, following a slowdown of the German attack in the winter of 1941–2, a renewed campaign in southern Russia brought German forces to the Volga and the Caucasus mountains. In North Africa by mid-1942 Axis forces were deep in Egyptian territory. From this point on the Allies began to organise an effective defence and then begin a slow programme of offensives in the Pacific islands, in the North African desert and deep inside Soviet territory which pushed the Axis forces back. Italy was invaded in 1943 and surrendered in September of that year, and the Red Army reached into the Ukraine by the end of 1943. By the middle of 1944 the stage was set for the final desperate struggle for Europe and the Far East.

IRELAND   U

• Dublin

• Cork

K I

Rationing:
the War for Food

Plymouth •

Atlantic
Ocean

Englis

Cherbourg •

Brest •

The French Resistance

Nante •

F

• Bordea

PORTUGAL

Tagus

• Madrid

Douro

Ebro

Toulouse •

Barcelona

SPAIN

Balearics

• Gibraltar
(British)

SPANISH MOROCCO

Oran •

Algie

Operation "Torch",
8 Nov.–Feb. 1943

MOROCCO

AL

AFRICA

SWEDEN

North
Sea

DENMARK

Baltic
Sea

**The Bombing of Hamburg:
Operation "Gomorrah",
24–25 Jul. 1943**

Copenhagen

Hamburg

Bremen

LATVIA

LITHUANIA

Riga

Dünaburg

Dvina

REICHSKOMMISSARIAT
OSTLAND

SOVIET

Moscow

Vladimir

UNION

Tula

Ryazan

**The Secret War:
spies, codes and
deception**

NETHERLANDS

Amsterdam

Rotterdam

London

Portsmouth
Channel

Birmingham

verpool
Manchester

TED
DOM

Brussels

BELGIUM

LUXEMBOURG

Lille

Caen

Paris

Seine

ANCE

Loire

Lyons

Rhône

Marseille

Turin

Genoa

Corsica

Sardinia

Cagliari

Palermo

Messina

**Anzio, 22 Jan.–
24 May 1944**

Rome

Anzio

**The Battle for
Monte Cassino,
17 Jan.–9 May 1943**

Naples

Salerno

Taranto

**Italy: Invasion and Surrender,
3–8 Sep. 1943**

**Operation "Husky":
the Capture of Sicily,
9 Jul.–17 Aug. 1943**

Malta
(British)

Stettin

Danzig

Königsberg

EAST
PRUSSIA

Berlin

GERMAN EMPIRE

Hanover

Elbe

Leipzig

Oder

Wrocław

Prague

BOHEMIA

Frankfurt

Strassburg

Stuttgart

Rhine

Munich

SWITZERLAND

AUSTRIA

Vienna

SLOVAKIA

Danube

**Dambusters,
7 May 1943**

Partisan War

Warsaw

Lodz

GENERAL
GOVERNMENT

Cracow

Lemberg

Brest

Minsk

REICHSKOMMISSARIAT

UKRAINE

Kiev

Dnieper

Dniester

Budapest

Debrecen

HUNGARY

Chisinau

Timisoara

Trieste

Po

ITALY

CROATIA

ROMANIA

Smolensk

Mogilev

UKRAINE

Gomel

Briansk

Orel

**The Battle of Kursk,
5–13 Jul. 1943**

Kursk

Kharkov

**From Kharkov to Kiev:
the Red Army Breaks Through,
23 Aug.– 6 Nov. 1943**

Dnepropetrovsk

Dnieper

Don

Saratov

Tambov

**Defeat at Stalingrad,
19 Nov.– 2 Feb. 1943**

**The Battle for Stalingrad,
19 Aug.–19 Nov. 1942**

Stalingrad

Volga

**The Soviet Counter-Stroke:
Operation "Uranus",
19 Nov.– 24 Dec. 1942**

Rostov-on-Don

Taganrog

Nikolayev

Kherson

Odessa

Perekop

Kerch

Sea of
Azov

Black
Sea

CRIMEA

Sevastopol

Novorossiisk

MONGOLIA

MANCHURIA

CHINA

KOREA

JAPAN

Tokyo

PACIFIC
OCEAN

**Operation "Longshot":
the Chindits in Burma,
8 Feb.–30 Apr. 1943**

Nankin

Shanghai

Kunming

Formosa

Iwo Jima

Midway

INDIA

BURMA

Hong Kong

**Japan's War in China:
Operation "Ichi-Go",
18 April–Nov. 1944**

Mariana
Islands

Wake Island

Hawaiian
Islands

**Battle for India:
Imphal,
8 May–3 Jul.;
Kohima,
4 Apr.–22 Jun. 1944**

SIAM

Rangoon

FRENCH
INDO-
CHINA

Manila

Saipan

Guam

PHILIPPINES

Truk

Marshall
Islands

**Island-Hopping in the Pacific:
The Gilbert and Marshall
Islands, 20 Nov.–17 Feb. 1944**

Ceylon

Saigon

MALAY STATES

Singapore

Borneo

Celebes

DUTCH EAST INDIES

Jakata

Timor

INDIAN OCEAN

Celebes

Hollandia

New Guinea

Rabaul

Port Moresby

AUSTRALIA

**Operation "Cartwheel":
the war for New Guinea,
30 Jun.–Mar. 1944**

Solomon
Islands

Gilbert
Islands

**Guadalcanal,
12 Nov. 1942–8 Feb. 1943**

Tunis

**The End of the Axis
in Africa: Tunisia,
19 Feb.–13 May
1943**

TUNISIA

Mediterranean
Sea

Mareth

Tripoli

LIBYA

Benghazi

Dera

**Second Alamein,
23 Oct.–4 Nov.1942**

El Agheila

11

EGYPT

El Alamein

**The Tide Turns in North Africa:
Alam Halfa, 13–30 Aug. 1942**

Alexandria

Nile

Suez Canal

PALESTINE

TRANSJORDAN

OPERATIONS 1944–1945

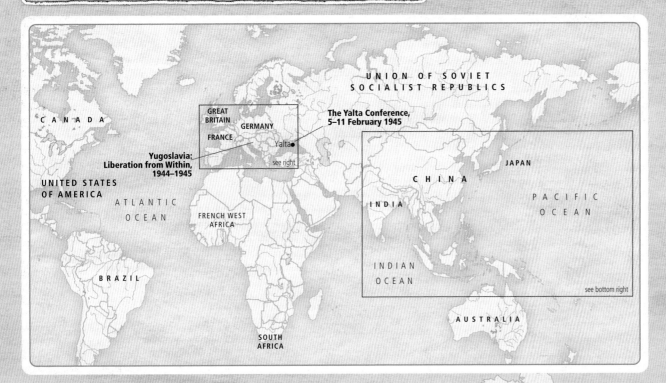

CANADA

UNITED STATES OF AMERICA

ATLANTIC OCEAN

BRAZIL

UNION OF SOVIET SOCIALIST REPUBLICS

GREAT BRITAIN

GERMANY

FRANCE

Yalta

see right

Yugoslavia: Liberation from Within, 1944–1945

The Yalta Conference, 5–11 February 1945

FRENCH WEST AFRICA

CHINA

INDIA

JAPAN

PACIFIC OCEAN

INDIAN OCEAN

SOUTH AFRICA

AUSTRALIA

see bottom right

IRELAND

Dublin

Cork

UNITED KINGDOM

Liverpool

Manchester

Birmingham

The V-Weapons Campaign, 13 June 1944–29 March 1945

Plymouth

London

Portsmouth

Dover

Atlantic Ocean

English Channel

Cherbourg

Lille

Rouen

Brest

Caen

D-Day, 6 June 1944

Breakout: Operation "Cobra", 25 July–25 August 1944

Battle for Normandy, 7 June–24 July 1944

Paris

Seine

The Liberation of Paris, 19–25 August 1944

Nantes

Loire

FRANCE

Vichy

Bordeaux

Lyons

Bilbao

Toulouse

Ebro

Rhône

The End of Vichy France: Operation "Dragoon", 14 August–14 September 1944

Marseille

SPAIN

Barcelona

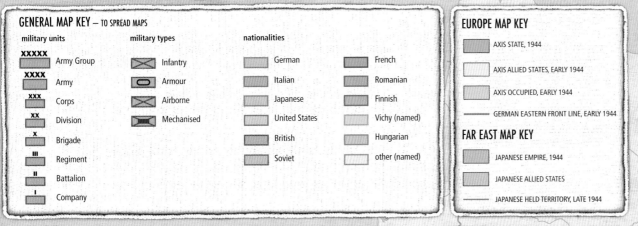

GENERAL MAP KEY — TO SPREAD MAPS

military units

XXXXX	Army Group
XXXX	Army
XXX	Corps
XX	Division
X	Brigade
III	Regiment
II	Battalion
I	Company

military types

	Infantry
	Armour
	Airborne
	Mechanised

nationalities

German		French	
Italian		Romanian	
Japanese		Finnish	
United States		Vichy (named)	
British		Hungarian	
Soviet		other (named)	

EUROPE MAP KEY

	AXIS STATE, 1944
	AXIS ALLIED STATES, EARLY 1944
	AXIS OCCUPIED, EARLY 1944
	GERMAN EASTERN FRONT LINE, EARLY 1944

FAR EAST MAP KEY

	JAPANESE EMPIRE, 1944
	JAPANESE ALLIED STATES
	JAPANESE HELD TERRITORY, LATE 1944

ABOVE & RIGHT

The last eighteen months of war saw the German and Japanese empires forced back on all fronts. The invasion of northern France in June 1944 opened up the path to the heart of German resistance. In Italy progress was slow up the narrow, mountainous peninsula. In the east, Soviet armies pushed into Poland by August 1944, and into Germany itself by the start of 1945. Berlin was captured in May. In the Pacific, Japanese resistance had to be worn down slowly, island by island. The army attacked through the Philippines, the US Navy through the islands of the central Pacific, finally seizing Okinawa by June 1945 and paving the way for possible invasion. Atomic bombs ended the war in the Pacific in August 1945.

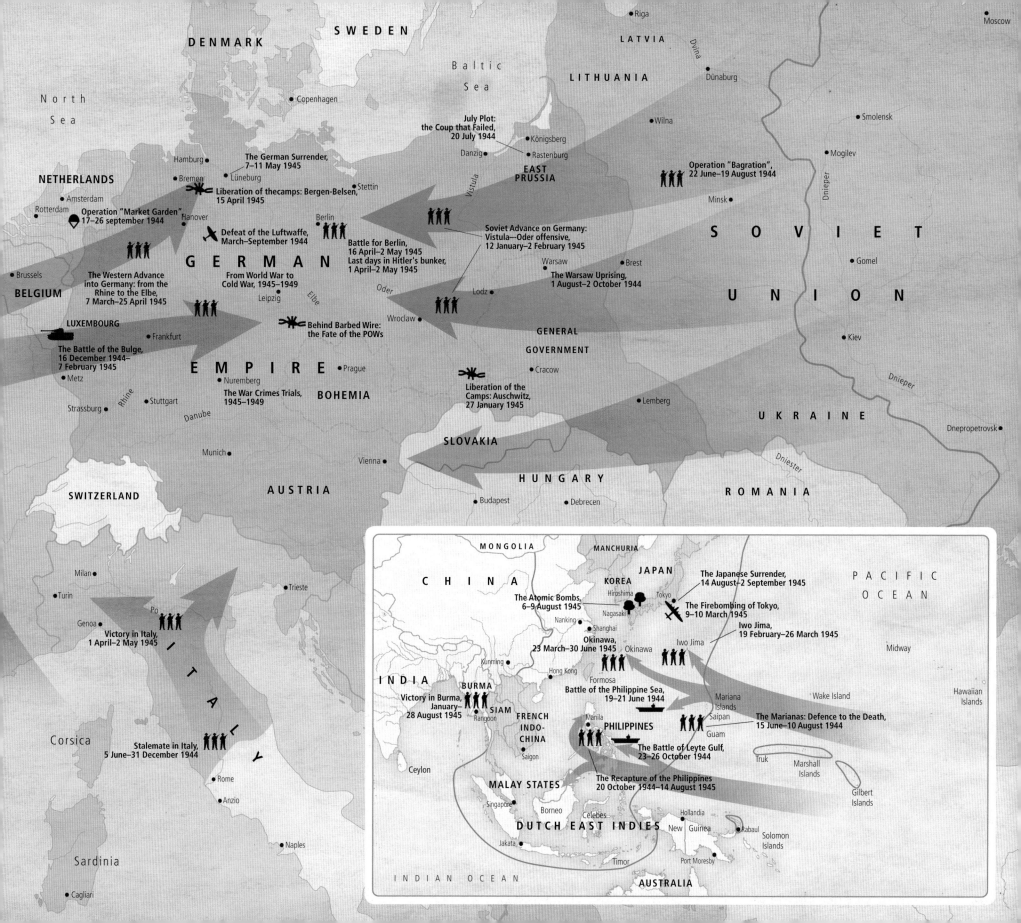

SWEDEN

DENMARK

North Sea

Copenhagen

Baltic Sea

LATVIA

Riga

Dünaburg

Moscow

LITHUANIA

Smolensk

Wilna

July Plot: the Coup that Failed, 20 July 1944

Königsberg

Mogilev

NETHERLANDS

Amsterdam

Rotterdam

Hamburg

Bremen

Lüneburg

The German Surrender, 7–11 May 1945

Liberation of thecamps: Bergen-Belsen, 15 April 1945

Stettin

Danzig

Rastenburg

EAST PRUSSIA

Operation "Bagration", 22 June–19 August 1944

Minsk

SOVIET

Operation "Market Garden" 17–26 september 1944

Hanover

Berlin

Defeat of the Luftwaffe, March–September 1944

Battle for Berlin, 16 April–2 May 1945 Last days in Hitler's bunker, 1 April–2 May 1945

Soviet Advance on Germany: Vistula---Oder offensive, 12 January–2 February 1945

Brest

Gomel

UNION

Brussels

BELGIUM

G E R M A N

From World War to Cold War, 1945–1949

Leipzig

Warsaw

Lodz

The Warsaw Uprising, 1 August–2 October 1944

Kiev

The Western Advance into Germany: from the Rhine to the Elbe, 7 March–25 April 1945

LUXEMBOURG

Frankfurt

Behind Barbed Wire: the Fate of the POWs

Wroclaw

GENERAL

GOVERNMENT

The Battle of the Bulge, 16 December 1944– 7 February 1945

Metz

E M P I R E

Nuremberg

Prague

Cracow

Lemberg

Dnieper

Strassburg

Rhine

Stuttgart

The War Crimes Trials, 1945–1949

BOHEMIA

Liberation of the Camps: Auschwitz, 27 January 1945

UKRAINE

Danube

Dnepropetrovsk

Munich

SLOVAKIA

Vienna

Dniester

SWITZERLAND

AUSTRIA

HUNGARY

Budapest

Debrecen

ROMANIA

Milan

Turin

Trieste

Genoa

Po

Victory in Italy, 1 April–2 May 1945

I T A L Y

MONGOLIA

CHINA

MANCHURIA

JAPAN

KOREA

Hiroshima

Tokyo

The Japanese Surrender, 14 August–2 September 1945

PACIFIC OCEAN

The Atomic Bombs, 6–9 August 1945

Nanking

Nagasaki

The Firebombing of Tokyo, 9–10 March 1945

Corsica

Stalemate in Italy, 5 June–31 December 1944

Shanghai

Okinawa, 23 March–30 June 1945

Iwo Jima

Iwo Jima, 19 February–26 March 1945

Rome

INDIA

BURMA

Kunming

Okinawa

Midway

Anzio

Victory in Burma, January– 28 August 1945

SIAM

Rangoon

Hong Kong

Formosa

Battle of the Philippine Sea, 19–21 June 1944

Mariana Islands

Wake Island

Hawaiian Islands

Saipan

The Marianas: Defence to the Death, 15 June–10 August 1944

FRENCH INDO-CHINA

Manila

PHILIPPINES

Guam

Naples

Saigon

The Battle of Leyte Gulf, 23–26 October 1944

Truk

Marshall Islands

Ceylon

MALAY STATES

The Recapture of the Philippines 20 October 1944–14 August 1945

Gilbert Islands

Sardinia

Singapore

Borneo

Celebes

Hollandia

New Guinea

Rabaul

Solomon Islands

DUTCH EAST INDIES

Cagliari

Jakata

Timor

Port Moresby

INDIAN OCEAN

AUSTRALIA

FORGING THE PEACE

The formal end of hostilities in the First World War on 11 November 1918 left Europe shattered by four years of the bloodiest conflict in history: more than 8,000,000 had been killed; twice as many maimed; millions more the victims of starvation or disease brought on by wartime conditions. There existed at its conclusion a widespread popular desire that this really would be "the war to end war".

The settlement arranged by the victorious Allies at Versailles between 1919 and 1920 was supposed to build the foundations of a durable peace. The principles behind the settlement were first declared by the American President Woodrow Wilson in January 1918 in the form of Fourteen Points. The most important of them committed the Allies to allowing those nationalities of Europe previously dominated by the pre-war dynastic empires of Germany, Austria-Hungary and Russia to establish independent nation states. Wilson hoped that all Europe's states would adopt a democratic form of rule. There was also a commitment to international collaboration through what became known as the League of Nations, whose members were to pledge themselves to the principle that all future conflicts between them should be resolved by negotiation rather than war.

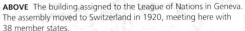

ABOVE The building assigned to the League of Nations in Geneva. The assembly moved to Switzerland in 1920, meeting here with 38 member states.

LEFT German statesman Gustav Stresemann who, as German Foreign Minister between 1924 and 1929, tried to pursue a policy of "fulfilment" of the terms of the Treaty of Versailles.

For all the idealism of the victor powers, the settlement was far from ideal. Self-determination was difficult to organize in practice because of the extensive ethnic mixing in central and eastern Europe. Many Europeans ended up living under the rule of a quite different ethnic majority: Germans in Czechoslovakia and Poland; Hungarians in Romania; Ukrainians in Poland. Britain, France and Italy refused to extend "self-determination" to their colonial empires. Britain and France took over control of former German and Turkish territory as mandates from the League, but then treated them as simple additions to their empires. The defeated powers, Germany, Austria, Hungary and Bulgaria, all lost territory as a result of the settlement and remained embittered and resentful at their treatment. Germany was treated with extreme severity: areas of East Prussia and Silesia were handed over to Poland; the Saar industrial region was internationalized; the Rhineland provinces were demilitarized; Germany was allowed only a tiny 100,000-man armed force for internal security; and a bill of reparations, finally settled at 132 billion gold marks, would have required Germany to pay out to the Allies until 1980. Disarmed, impoverished and shorn of territory, Germany had more reason than any other power to overturn the Versailles Settlement at the first opportunity.

The League of Nations was also flawed from the start. The American Senate rejected the Versailles Treaty in 1920,

THE "PEACEMAKERS"

The victorious powers met in Paris in the first half of 1919 to decide the fate of the defeated nations, Germany, Austria-Hungary, Bulgaria and Turkey. The discussions were dominated by Britain, France and the United States. Russia, recently plunged into revolution, was not invited despite the great losses suffered at German hands during the war. Italy and Japan were also victors, but felt cheated by the results of the conference. Italy failed to get the territory promised to her as the price of joining the war in 1915. Japan resented the second-class status accorded her as a non-white power. The final settlement, signed on 28 June 1919 at the Palace of Versailles, sowed the seeds of future crisis.

ABOVE A brigade of the new Red Army parades through Kharkov in 1920 during the Russian Civil War, which ended with Communist victory a year later.
LEFT Lloyd George, Georges Clemenceau and Woodrow Wilson at the Versailles Conference, 1919.

and the League opened its sessions in 1920 without the world's richest and potentially most powerful state, while Russia and Germany were excluded from the League. The organization was dominated by Britain and France, but it was never clear how the cluster of small states represented in the League could really prevent future conflicts, and general war-weariness meant that it was never really tested in the 1920s. In 1926, Germany was finally admitted, but remained resentful of the failure of other states to disarm as they had promised under the terms of the covenant of the League. These resentments were exacerbated by the problems of economic revival after the war; a brief American-led boom in the mid-1920s masked a deeper economic malaise. Hyper-inflation in Germany, Austria and the states of eastern Europe peaked in 1923–24, leaving an embittered and impoverished middle class whose savings were wiped out. Trade failed to reach pre-war levels and even victor countries in Europe were saddled with high war debts. Economic crisis provoked social unrest and political polarization which made it difficult to maintain democracy. In Italy, Benito Mussolini, leader of a new radical nationalist Fascist Party, was made premier in 1922 and had created a one-party dictatorship by 1926. In 1923, a coup brought a military dictator in Spain, General Primo de Rivera; three years later the Polish Marshal Pilsudski led an army coup in Poland. The newly-created Soviet Union was a one-party state almost from the start.

ABOVE Anxious shareholders stand outside the New York Stock Exchange on 24 October 1929, a few days before the disastrous Wall Street Crash which precipitated the world slump.

ABOVE LEFT Signing the Kellogg-Briand Pact outlawing war, Paris, 27 August 1928. Although Germany, Italy, Japan and the USSR signed the Pact they all resorted to war in the 1930s.

LEFT The veteran British pacifist George Lansbury pictured in 1929. He helped to lead the widespread anti-war movement in Britain in the 1920s and 1930s.

The shift to authoritarian rule was accelerated by the economic slump that followed the Wall Street Crash in October 1929. The crisis of the capitalist system was the worst the world had seen, throwing more than 40 million out of work worldwide. Within four years, a mass nationalist movement in Germany led by Adolf Hitler had become the largest party in the German parliament, arguing for an end to reparations and the overturning of the Versailles settlement. In Japan the slump provoked another nationalist backlash and, in 1931, army leaders launched a campaign in northern China to seize economic resources to aid the Japanese economy. The League did nothing to halt the economic slide or the emergence of a violent nationalism, and by the 1930s war was once again a strong possibility.

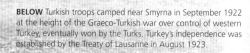

BELOW Turkish troops camped near Smyrna in September 1922 at the height of the Graeco-Turkish war over control of western Turkey, eventually won by the Turks. Turkey's independence was established by the Treaty of Lausanne in August 1923.

GERMAN DISARMAMENT

The Versailles settlement was supposed to produce a general disarmament even among the victorious powers. As the principal defeated protagonist, Germany was compelled to disarm. Its main arms and aircraft factories and naval dockyards were destroyed or converted to peacetime production. The large numbers of aircraft left over in 1919 were scrapped (shown above); German frontier fortifications were blown up. The German fleet had to be surrendered to the British even before the treaty was signed. Although Britain and France did reduce their military forces and budgets, they failed to honour the pledge to produce universal disarmament, provoking strong resentment at Germany's unequal treatment, and encouraging a wave of German nationalism.

JAPAN'S WAR IN CHINA

Between 1931 and the end of the Second World War in 1945, the Japanese army fought a vicious and intermittent war on the Chinese mainland. The whole 14-year war cost China more than 15 million civilian deaths. Japan's war for Asia was the last act of an epoch of violent imperialism and among the most savage. Hidden away from the glare of world publicity, the Japanese occupiers indulged in continuous and systematic atrocities against the populations under their control.

Japan had been an imperial power since the nineteenth century, annexing present-day Taiwan in 1895 and Korea in 1910. In May 1915, Japan began to encroach on Chinese sovereignty as China collapsed into political chaos, its territory fought over by competing warlords. In the 1920s a Japanese army – the Kwantung – was stationed in the northern Chinese province of Manchuria to safeguard Japanese economic interests. The military leadership was keen to increase Japan's imperial influence in China, and the rise of Chinese nationalism – directed at the Japanese presence – and the catastrophic effects of the 1929 world slump on Japan's economic prospects were used as excuses for the Japanese army, largely independent of the government in Tokyo, to embark on a programme of military expansion in Asia.

In September 1931, the Kwantung Army staged a clumsy fake attack on a Japanese-controlled railway near Mukden in Manchuria, and the incident was then used to justify the rapid Japanese occupation of much of the province. The incumbent Chinese

RIGHT A 1935 postage stamp from Manchukuo (Manchuria) showing Pu Yi, the last Manchu Emperor and the puppet ruler of the new Japanese-dominated territory.

LEFT Japanese soldiers fire from behind sandbag defences in the attack on the Chinese port city of Shanghai in autumn 1937 following a major amphibious assault on the coastline.

[Map]

Nomonhan, 1939 (Japanese-Soviet border conflict)

MONGOLIA — occupied by Japan, 1933 — MANCHURIA — Japanese puppet state of Manchukuo from 1932

Changkufeng, 1938 (Japanese-Soviet border conflict)

INNER MONGOLIA — JEHOL — Chihfeng — Chengteh (Jehol) — XXXXX NTH. CHINA

SHANSI — HOPEH — Peking — Tientsin — Gulf of Chihli — Port Arthur/Dairen

KOREA — Seoul — Pusan — Sea of Japan

Tsinan — SHANTUNG — Tsingtao — Yellow Sea

SHENSI — HONAN — Kaifeng — CHINA — KIANGSU — ANHWEI — Nanking — HUPEH — Hankow — Wuchang — Shanghai — XXXXX CEN. CHINA — Ningpo — CHEKIANG

HUNAN — Nanchang — KIANGSI — FUKIEN — Foochow — East China Sea

JAPAN — Sapporo — Akita — Tokyo — Osaka — Hiroshima — Nagasaki — Pacific Ocean

USSR — Tsitsihar — Taonan — Harbin — Yenki — Vladivostok — Kirin — Mukden — Antung — Sakhalin — Kurile Is. — Ryukyu Is.

Legend: Japanese Empire, 1930 | occupied by Japan, 1931 | attempted Japanese northern state puppet regime, 1935 | Japanese advances, 1937–39 | extent of Japanese advance to 1939

BELOW Two Japanese soldiers stand guard on top of a train in Manchuria in December 1931 to warn of the approach of Chinese bandit forces following the seizure of the province in September that year.

CHIANG KAISHEK (1887–1975)

At the end of the First World War, China was in chaos. The Manchu dynasty had been overthrown in 1912 and much of China was ruled by rival independent warlords. In 1924, the main nationalist movement, the Guomindang, established a regime based at Canton, but which controlled very little. By 1926, a young army officer, Chiang Kaishek, had emerged as the leading Guomindang figure and he began a decade of reunification. His early alliance with the Chinese communists was broken in 1927 when he destroyed the party in China's eastern cities. Step by step, he forced warlords to accept Nationalist rule from the new Chinese capital at Nanjing, and by 1936 was undisputed leader of around two-thirds of the country.

warlord, Chang Hsueh-liang, was driven out and a new puppet state of Manchukuo created in 1932, nominally ruled by the "last emperor" Pu Yi, while Manchuria's rich mineral and food supplies were brought under Japanese control. Although a member of the League, Japan's aggression was not reversed by the other powers, and in 1933 Japan left the organization. Over the next three years, Japan's army pushed down into northern China, taking control of the provinces of Jehol, Chahar and Hopeh, and stationing a garrison in the old imperial capital of Beijing.

Growing Chinese resistance sucked the Japanese army into further aggression: a small incident at the Marco Polo Bridge near Beijing on 7 July rapidly escalated. On 27 July, the Japanese prime minister, Prince Konoye, declared that Japan was now going to create a "New Order" in Asia. Within weeks, a full-scale war began between Chinese Nationalist and Communist forces and the Japanese army of occupation, which ended only with Japan's surrender eight years later. Using the railways and river valleys,

ABOVE Communist leaders Mao Zedong and Zhou Enlai during the Long March of Chinese Communists in 1934 to the Chinese interior province of Yan'an. Around 100,000 trekked the 5,000 miles to escape Chinese Nationalists.

Japanese forces spread rapidly into central China, capturing Shanghai in October 1937, the Chinese Nationalist capital Nanjing in December – after which Chiang Kaishek retreated to a new capital at Chungking – and Canton on the south China coast in October 1938. Communist guerrillas under Mao Zedong dominated the remoter regions of northwest China, but posed little serious threat to the Japanese invaders. By 1939, Japan dominated most of the major cities and arteries of communication, from the southern Yangtze River to the northern province of Inner Mongolia.

The sudden expansion of Japanese imperial power destroyed the unified Chinese state Chiang Kaishek had tried to create. It brought Japan into conflict with the Western powers, which tolerated Japanese aggression only because there was no effective way of expelling Japan's army except at the cost of a major war that they had neither the will nor resources to engage in. When Japanese expansion did pose a direct threat to Soviet interests in Mongolia, two short campaigns resulted, at Changkufen in 1938 and at Nomonhan in 1939, both won by the Soviet Red Army. Japan's government and armed forces preferred to look south to the rich oilfields and minerals of the old European empires for the next stage of the construction of the Asian New Order.

THE "RAPE OF NANKING"

On 13 December 1937, the Japanese army captured Chiang Kaishek's capital at Nanjing. What followed was one of the most horrific episodes in the long Sino-Japanese conflict. Japanese forces were allowed weeks of uninhibited violence against the defenceless population while their commander, General Iwane Matsui, proved powerless to stop them. Post-war estimates suggest that between 260,000 and 350,000 Chinese were murdered, most of them amid scenes of terrible cruelty. All 90,000 Chinese soldiers taken prisoner were killed, some in beheading competitions. Tens of thousands of Chinese women of all ages were raped and then killed. The Japanese army, Matsui told an American journalist a few days later, was "probably the most undisciplined army in the world".

RIGHT Japanese soldiers using stripped and bound Chinese men as live targets for bayonet practice after the capture of the Chinese capital in December 1937.

BELOW The destruction of the railway station in Shanghai during the Japanese attack in 1937. The Japanese used bombing indiscriminately in China, including poison gas.

ITALY'S WARS

ABOVE Medal awarded to Italian troops who took part in the Ethiopian Campaign.

Italy was the second League state in the 1930s to violate the organization's commitment to peace and "collective security". The Italian Fascist dictator, Benito Mussolini, dreamed of creating a new Roman Empire in the Mediterranean and Africa as an expression of the dynamism of the revolutionary Fascist movement. Once the Fascist regime had been consolidated by the early 1930s, Mussolini tried to turn these aspirations into reality. Italy was in his view one of the "have-not" powers denied economic resources and colonies by what Mussolini called the richer "plutocratic" powers of the West.

In 1934 he began to plan for an Italian invasion of the independent East African state of Abyssinia (Ethiopia). After he had, as he believed, won tacit approval from Britain and France – the main African imperial powers – Mussolini launched an attack on 3 October 1935 with three army corps of almost half a million men under the

RIGHT An Abyssinian soldier practises wearing a gas mask in Addis Ababa in October 1935 in anticipation of Italian gas attacks.

BELOW Abyssinians in November 1935 in the captured province of Tigre are forced to show their support for Mussolini, the "Great White Father".

LEFT Members of the Italian Thirteenth Motorized Regiment parade past Princess Maria José of Savoy after being presented with their new colours on 1 February 1936. Mussolini wanted Italian forces to appear thoroughly modern as befitted the new Fascist dictatorship.

TIME
The Weekly Newsmagazine

GENERAL ITALO BALBO

Volume XXI   Number 26

Circulation this issue more than 400,000

ITALO BALBO (1896–1940)

Italian Fascism liked to emphasize its modernity, and air power was the ideal instrument for demonstrating its propaganda claims for the power, speed and heroism of the Fascist revolution. No Fascist leader better exemplified this identification with the air than the flamboyant Italo Balbo. Fascist leader in the Italian city of Ferrara, he was promoted to Air Minister between 1929 and 1933 before becoming Governor of Libya, Italy's North African colony, in 1934 and Commander-in-Chief of Italy's North African forces in 1937. He was a skilful pilot and undertook a number of famous long-distance flights, the best known in 1933 from Rome to Chicago and New York. On 28 June 1940, two weeks after Italy declared war on Britain, the plane he was piloting was shot down by Italian anti-aircraft fire over the Libyan port of Tobruk.

command of General Emilio De Bono. The campaign against poorly armed Ethiopian troops was slow and in November De Bono was replaced with Marshal Pietro Badoglio, after which the pace quickened. To clear resistance, Italian aircraft dropped mustard-gas bombs on Ethiopian villages and soldiers. The decisive battle took place on 31 March 1936 at Mai Ceu on the road to the Ethiopian capital of Addis Ababa, where some 30–35,000 Ethiopian soldiers faced a mixed Italian and colonial force of 40,000. Heavy artillery and machine-gun fire left 8,000 Ethiopians dead against total Italian casualties of 1,273.

After Mai Ceu, the road to the capital was open. On 5 May 1936, the Italian army under Badoglio entered Addis Ababa. Four days later, Mussolini announced to an ecstatic crowd in Rome the creation of the new Italian empire in Africa. The result was Italy's international isolation: the League voted for trade and oil sanctions against Italy; but oil was still supplied by the United States, which was not a League member, and by Romania, which defied the ban. Mussolini now moved closer to Hitler's Germany, and in October 1936 the two states signed an informal agreement usually known as the "Rome–Berlin Axis". In November 1937, Italy also joined the German–Japanese Anti-Comintern Pact, so creating the trio of expansionist states that was to fight the Second World War under the general title of the "Axis".

In July 1936, army rebels in Spain launched an attempted coup against the republican regime in Madrid. At first Mussolini, who was sympathetic to the rebel leader, Colonel Francisco Franco, sent some limited assistance, but from December 1936 a full military force was sent to Spain, complete with tanks, artillery and aircraft, to help the nationalist cause. Italian propaganda made a great deal of Italian victories in Spain, but the conquest of Malaga in February 1937 was achieved against a weak and disorganized republican force. The next month, at Guadalajara, on the road towards Madrid, Italian forces

ABOVE A woman donates jewellery to Mussolini's "Gold for the Fatherland" initiative. The gold was melted down to form bars and distributed to banks.

LEFT A poster from the Spanish Civil War calls on supporters of the republican government to "Rise against the Italian Invasion in Spain".

LEFT The Garibaldi Brigade march to Guadalajara, March 1937.

ITALY IN THE SPANISH CIVIL WAR

Italians fought on both sides in the Spanish Civil War. To aid Franco's nationalist rebels Mussolini sent General Mario Roatta and 75,000 soldiers, airmen and militia. By 1938, there were more than 300 Italian aircraft in Spain. On the republican side, brigades of Italian anti-Fascists were formed, which fought against fellow Italians as part of the wider European civil war between fascism, communism and democracy. The most famous was the "Garibaldi Brigade" named after the legendary guerrilla fighter Giuseppe Garibaldi, who had helped to create the Italian nation in 1860–61.

¡ levantaos contra la
**INVASION ITALIANA
EN ESPAÑA!**

ABOVE The Italian dictator Benito Mussolini addresses crowds from the balcony of the Palazzo Venezia in Rome. This became his favourite place for announcing major victories to the Italian public.

ABOVE Italian troops occupy the Balkan state of Albania by bicycle on 7 April 1939, overthrowing the regime of King Zog, who fled first to Paris and then to London.

suffered a humiliating defeat. With 36,000 men, 81 tanks and 160 artillery pieces against a weak republican defensive line, the Italian commander Roatta attacked on 8 March. The Italian line broke and by 18 March retreated in disorder, a catastrophic blow to their prestige from which the Italian forces never recovered. Mussolini continued to aid Franco – over 75,000 Italians served in Spain – but the nationalist victory by March 1939 owed more to Franco's new Spanish army than to Italian assistance.

Mussolini saw a victory for Franco in Spain as essential for his own ambitions. In February 1939, he told Fascist leaders that Italy had to control the Mediterranean, which meant defeating or expelling the British and French. The first step was taken on 7 April, when Italian forces invaded and occupied the Balkan state of Albania. A few weeks later, Mussolini asked Hitler for a more solid agreement between them. The "Pact of Steel" signed on 22 May 1939 irrevocably tied Italy to standing side by side with Germany in any showdown with the Western powers.

GERMANY DESTROYS VERSAILLES

ABOVE German troops march across a bridge over the Rhine in Cologne on 7 March 1936 in defiance of the Versailles Treaty which had insisted on the demilitarization of the German Rhineland provinces.

Germany regarded itself as a victim of the international economic and political system. Hitler was dedicated to the idea that the "master race", in other words the Aryan Germans, should win its rightful place through conquest. "Empires are made by the sword," wrote Hitler in 1928.

Hitler was too shrewd a politician to act too quickly and so rearmament was carefully concealed while he consolidated his domestic position. Only in 1935 did Hitler feel confident enough to declare Germany's formal rejection of Versailles: on 16 March 1935 conscription was re-introduced in Germany, and the new German Air Force officially created. The following March, at the height of the crisis over the Italian invasion of Abyssinia, Hitler decided to remilitarize the Rhineland provinces along the French frontier, an action proscribed under the 1919 Treaty. On 7 March 1936, German troops re-entering the prohibited zone faced no international obstruction. Buoyed up by this success, Hitler began to look outside the borders of the German state or "Reich". In July 1936, he offered help to the Spanish rebel leader Franco, who needed planes to move his forces from Morocco to the mainland. A small number of aircraft and pilots, the Condor Legion, fought alongside the Spanish nationalists. On 26 April 1937, German planes bombed and destroyed the Basque city of

ADOLF HITLER (1889-1945)

Adolf Hitler was born in Braunau am Inn, a small town in the Austrian provinces of the Habsburg Empire. He tried unsuccessfully to enrol at the Vienna Academy of Art before moving to Munich in 1913 to avoid the Austrian army draft. In 1914, he volunteered for the German army, won the Iron Cross First Class, and emerged in 1918 embittered by the German defeat, the blame for which he placed on communists and Jews. Hitler became leader of the small National Socialist German Workers' Party in 1921 and two years later staged a coup in Munich against the Bavarian government. Imprisoned for a year, he wrote *Mein Kampf* and emerged to re-establish leadership of the Party. In 1933, despite having won only one-third of the vote in the November 1932 election, Hitler was appointed Chancellor. He became supreme leader or Führer in 1934, and Supreme Commander of the Armed Forces in 1938.

When Hitler was appointed German Chancellor on 30 January 1933 at the head of a Nationalist coalition government, it was by no means evident that he would survive in that post very long. Within a year, he had brought about a national revolution under his personal dictatorship: a one-party state was created; civil rights suspended; a secret police (the Gestapo) created; and the first concentration camps inaugurated. Any opponents of the regime were imprisoned or forced abroad. The first race laws were passed in 1933–35, driving German Jews from office and prohibiting marriage or sexual relations between Jews and so-called "Aryan" Germans.

One of Hitler's first ambitions was to rearm Germany in defiance of the Versailles settlement. He had no definite plans for war or conquest in 1933, but he wanted to tear up the Treaty, absorb the German minorities in neighbouring countries into the new German state, and at some point to create what was called "living space" (*Lebensraum*) in eastern Europe on which to settle German colonists and to exploit the region's natural resources. Like Japan and Italy,

GENERAL WERNER VON BLOMBERG (1878-1946)

General Werner von Blomberg was appointed Defence Minister by President Hindenburg at the same time as Hitler was offered the chancellorship. Hitler kept him on after 1933 and in 1935 his title was changed to Minister of War. He played a major part in rebuilding Germany's armed forces after the long period of enforced disarmament under the terms of the Versailles settlement, and represented Hitler's Germany at the coronation of King George VI in 1937. Leading National Socialists were jealous of his influence and schemed to remove him from office. In February 1938, he was forced to resign after his new wife was exposed as a former pornographic model.

ABOVE Hitler makes his way to the speaker's podium during the 1934 Nazi Party Rally in Nuremberg. He is flanked by members of the *Sturm Abteilung* (SA).

BELOW "The whole people say Yes on 10 April." A German poster to encourage support for a national plebiscite on the union of Austria and Germany. It was claimed that 99 per cent said "yes".

Das ganze Volk sagt am 10. April ja!

Guernica, an act which came to symbolize the horrors of what was now called "total war", a conflict waged against civilians as well as soldiers.

On 5 November 1937, Hitler called his military commanders together to tell them of his plans to unite his Austrian homeland with Germany in the near future, and to take action against Czechoslovakia, the only remaining democratic state in eastern Europe, and home to exiled opponents of the Hitler regime. In March 1938, after months of agitation by Austrian National Socialists, the Austrian Chancellor Kurt von Schuschnigg was compelled under the circumstances to accept the entry of German forces or risk bloodshed. On 13 March, the *Anschluss*, or union, of Austria with Germany was completed, and the enlarged state was now called "Greater Germany". Austrian opponents of *Anschluss* were murdered or imprisoned and Austrian Jews driven from their professions and businesses.

Throughout the period in which Hitler destroyed Versailles, the other major states did very little. Hitler took Germany out of the League in October 1933. Over the next four years Germany's growing economic and military strength was viewed with mounting alarm by democratic Europe, but although efforts were made to find some way of blunting the German threat by recognizing her grievances, no real concessions were made that

could satisfy Hitler. By 1938 his run of "bloodless victories" produced a wide popular consensus at home. What Hitler wanted now was a small successful war to bloody his troops and prepare for the struggle for "living space".

ABOVE An election campaign meeting in Graz, Austria on 1 April 1938. On Hitler's right sit Arthur Seyss-Inquart, later ruler of the occupied Netherlands, and Heinrich Himmler, head of the SS and the concentration camp system.

BELOW Prisoners in the notorious Sachsenhausen concentration camp on 6 January 1939. By the end of the 1930s there were 21,500 prisoners in the camps.

ARMING FOR WAR IN THE 1930s

If the 1920s were years of disarmament and cuts in military budgets, the 1930s saw rearmament on a scale that dwarfed the arms race before the First World War. This process took place across the developed world, and it began even before the threat from Japan, Italy and Germany became a serious one. World military spending was, by 1934, almost twice what it had been in the mid-1920s and the trade in arms also almost doubled between 1932 and 1937. The build-up of new military forces was a consequence of the breakdown of the world economy and the collapse of the League of Nations as an instrument of collective security, leading to the possession of military power once again being seen as the key to political survival.

At the heart of this arms race lay the massive military build-up in Germany and the Soviet Union. By the end of the 1930s, both countries were close to becoming the world's military superpowers. Germany in 1938 devoted 17 per cent of its national income to military spending, while Britain and France spent only 8 per cent. In 1939, the Soviet Union had the largest number of aircraft and tanks of any major power. German rearmament began even before Hitler came to power, with the so-called "black rearmament" carried out in

ABOVE The interior of an assembly hall in March 1936 which was part of the vast Krupp works in Essen, where many of the German army's heavy guns and armoured vehicles were produced.

secret by the German army, but real expansion was possible only after 1933. After three years of careful preparation and reconstruction, in 1936 Hitler ordered a rapid acceleration of military preparations. In October 1936, a Four-Year Plan was established with the air-force commander Hermann Göring in charge. The plan was to build up the material resources needed for war inside Germany to avoid the threat of blockade. By 1939, two-thirds of industrial investment in Germany went on war-related projects; one-quarter of the industrial workforce was working for the military.

Stalin launched the rearmament of the Soviet Union in 1932, before Hitler came to power, since the Soviet leadership was convinced that, according to Marxist theory, the economic crisis would usher in a new age of capitalist wars. Like Germany, the Soviet Union focused on building up the raw material and machinery base needed to produce

ABOVE A Soviet poster shows an urgent Stalin summoning aircraft from a Soviet factory in 1935. By 1932 the dictator had thrown his support behind a gigantic programme of rearmament.

FAR RIGHT The French Socialist premier Leon Blum at a mass rally for peace in Paris in September 1936. Blum's government in fact authorized a 14-billion-franc arms programme the same month.

MARSHAL MIKHAIL TUKHACHEVSKY (1893–1937)

After the Russian Revolution of 1917, a number of young officers from the former tsarist army were rapidly promoted to build up the newly formed Communist Red Army. Mikhail Tukhachevsky made his mark in the 1920s with new ideas about fast, mobile warfare conducted by thousands of tanks and armoured vehicles. He was appointed Chief of Armaments in 1932 to oversee the Soviet Union's rearmament drive, and in 1936 was made Deputy Defence Commissar. Perhaps jealous of Tukhachevsky's popular reputation and evident ambition, Stalin authorized his arrest and trial in June 1937. He was executed on 11 June along with seven other top military commanders.

finished armaments. The Third Five-Year Plan – started in 1938 – projected an increase in military spending of 40 per cent a year; two-thirds of industrial investment went to fuel the new military machine. Both Hitler and Stalin thought in terms of large-scale and long-distance war, and in January 1939 Hitler approved a "Z-Plan" for a new ocean-going battle fleet; four years before this, Stalin had approved work on a similar Soviet flotilla, which by 1939 involved plans for 15 battleships against the six projected by the German Navy.

The military build-up in Britain and France was more modest, though both countries already possessed a large military establishment even before the onset of rearmament. Britain began expanding its armed forces in 1934, and accelerated the programme in 1936. Emphasis was put on creating a large new modern air force, and the RAF received around 40 per cent of expenditure, so that by 1939 Britain

LEFT British troops cross a drawbridge into a fort on the Maginot Line in November 1939. The French fortifications were begun in the late 1920s and completed only by the outbreak of war.

ABOVE Prototype of the Supermarine Spitfire single-seater fighter in 1936. The aircraft became the standard RAF fighter and played a key role in the Battle of Britain.

MODERNIZING BRITAIN'S ARMY

The idea of using tank forces as the armed fist of the army, striking in mass against the enemy's front line was developed in the inter-war period by two British military thinkers, Captain Basil Liddell Hart and Major-General John Fuller. Efforts were made to develop a fast modern tank and to organize armoured divisions, but there was much conservative resistance to the idea. By 1939, Britain had only one armoured division ready for the war in Europe, and British tanks failed to match the standards set by the other major land armies. Here light Mark V and Mark VIA tanks of the 9th Queen's Royal Lancers are on manoeuvre in 1937.

was producing almost as many aircraft as Germany. In France, emphasis was put in the 1930s on the construction of a solid defensive wall – the Maginot Line – to face the German threat and provide France with real security against attack. In 1936, the French government authorized a large three-year rearmament programme, and began to build some of the best tanks and aircraft of the time. Political problems and disputes with labour held up progress, but France, like Britain, was better armed for conflict in 1939 than the myth of "too little, too late" suggests. Only the United States remained aloof from the arms build-up. Geographically secure and with a powerful pacifist lobby, there was no pressure to arm in the 1930s and its soldiers went on manoeuvres with dummy tanks.

RIGHT Soviet military motorcyclists parade through Leningrad before the coming of war in 1941. The Soviet Union had the largest armed forces in the world by the 1940s.

THE MUNICH CRISIS

After Hitler had taken over his Austrian homeland in March 1938, he began to make preparations to seize Czechoslovakia on the pretence that he was helping fellow Germans oppressed by Czech rule in the Sudeten areas of northern Czechoslovakia. On 28 May, following the "Weekend Crisis" of 20/21 May, when the Czech government, fearing an imminent German invasion, ordered the mobilization of its forces, Hitler told his military commanders to plan a short, sharp war against the Czechs for the autumn of 1938. "I am utterly determined," he said, "that Czechoslovakia should disappear from the map."

Hitler thought he could isolate the Czechs and reach a quick military solution before the other powers intervened. The military planning went ahead, reflecting Hitler's anxiety to wage a small, victorious war. In February, he had scrapped the War Ministry and taken over supreme command of the armed forces himself. The fight against the Czechs was a way of making his mark as a military leader, and an opportunity to improve Germany's economic and strategic position in central Europe.

ABOVE Commemorative medallion struck to mark Chamberlain's success at the Munich Conference in 1938.

ABOVE RIGHT Adolf Hitler signing the Munich Agreement in the early hours of 30 September 1938 after a dozen hours of negotiation. Behind him are Chamberlain and Mussolini, to his left Daladier.

TOP RIGHT Neville Chamberlain marches past an SS guard of honour at Oberwiesenfeld airport on his way to the Munich Conference on 29 September 1938 surrounded by National Socialist Party leaders.

EDUARD BENEŠ (1884–1948)

The Czech politician at the heart of the Munich crisis was a statesman of wide experience. Beneš had been active in the Czech independence movement during the First World War and was rewarded in 1918 with the post of Foreign Minister in the newly independent Czechoslovak Republic. In 1935, he became the country's president, by which time Czechoslovakia was the only genuinely democratic state left in central and eastern Europe. In 1938, he realized that his country was vulnerable to German pressure and had little confidence that his allies would support him. He went into exile abroad in October 1938 and returned to be president again between 1945 and his death three years later.

TIME
The Weekly Newsmagazine

Map:

GERMANY — Dresden, Breslau, Oder

SUDETENLAND

POLAND — Krakow

Elbe

Prague, Pilsen

PROTECTORATE OF BOHEMIA AND MORAVIA

Brno • German plebiscites, 1938

Danube

Passau

Linz

Vienna • Bratislava

SLOVAKIA

German military occupation, 1938

Kassa

RUTHENIA

Dniester

Salzburg

Danube

AUSTRIA — Graz

Budapest

HUNGARY

Debrecen

ROMANIA

	Munich Agreement, October–December 1938		Annexations, 1939	
Czechoslovakia, early 1938	to Germany	to Poland	to Germany	
	to Hungary	Czechoslovakia, Dec. 1938	Independent	
			to Hungary	

BELOW A weeping woman salutes the German occupation of the Sudeten German area in October 1938. For many Sudeten inhabitants occupation meant liberation; for Jews and socialists it meant persecution.

The crisis could not be isolated: as pressure built up on the Czech government to make concessions to the Sudeten German minority, Britain and France both acted to try to find a negotiated political solution. France had treaty obligations to help the Czech state, and the Soviet Union was also committed to intervening, as long as France did so too. In neither state was there much enthusiasm for the prospect of war. Britain, meanwhile, had no treaty obligations, but the Prime Minister, Neville Chamberlain, hoped to use his influence to bring about a negotiated settlement as part of his strategy of "appeasement" of Germany. In August 1938, the British politician Lord Runciman was sent on a League of Nations mission to the Sudetenland and returned arguing that major concessions should be made by the Czech government to the German community.

Hitler stuck to his guns. German leaders attacked the Czechs in the press and on the platform. By the beginning of September, it seemed likely that Hitler would launch the military campaign in the near future. To avert this, on 15 September Chamberlain took the dramatic step of flying to meet Hitler at his mountain retreat at Berchtesgaden. Chamberlain conceded the need for self-determination, while Hitler promised not to make war on the Czechs, but he had no intention of honouring his word. Chamberlain flew again to meet the German leader on 22 September at Bad Godesberg, and this time the atmosphere was quite different, with Hitler insisting that he would occupy the Sudeten areas no later than 1 October. Chamberlain returned home to a cabinet now determined not to concede. France and Britain both prepared for war and on 26 September, Chamberlain sent his personal envoy, Sir Horace Wilson, to see Hitler and on the following day he made it absolutely clear that German violation of Czech sovereignty would mean war.

On 28 September, Hitler, with great reluctance, gave in. Under pressure from his party leaders and aware that German public opinion was strongly against a European war, he accepted Mussolini's suggestion of a summit conference in Munich, to which the Soviet Union was not invited. Hitler was sulky and ill at ease throughout the Munich discussions, which ended on 30 September with an agreement for the cession of the Sudeten areas to Germany and a timetable for German occupation. Unlike Japan in Manchuria and Italy in Abyssinia, Hitler's plan for a short war of conquest was frustrated. Munich is usually seen as a humiliating defeat for the British and French, but in reality it was a defeat for Hitler's plan for war. His frustration was to make it impossible to negotiate away the next crisis in 1939 over the City of Danzig.

LEFT French premier Edouard Daladier is greeted by enthusiastic crowds on his return to Paris on 30 September 1938. "The blind fools" was his reaction to their welcome.

RIGHT Hungarian cavalry and light tanks on their way towards the town of Beregozasr on 1 October 1938. Hungary occupied and annexed areas of southern Czechoslovakia following the Munich Conference.

THE OCCUPATION AND BREAK-UP OF CZECHOSLOVAKIA

30 OCTOBER 1938
Poland occupies Teschen region of northern Czechoslovakia.

NOVEMBER 1938
Vienna Awards grant territory in Slovakia and Ruthenia to Hungary.

OCTOBER 1939
Czech university students demonstrate on the streets of Prague against German occupation.

Almost as soon as the ink was dry on the Munich Agreement, Hitler told his foreign minister, Joachim von Ribbentrop that he would march on Prague and smash the "Czech remnants" when the opportunity came. The Czech state was put under pressure to reach advantageous trade agreements to help German rearmament, and to concede the right to build a motorway across Czech land. In the Slovak areas, the Germans collaborated with the Slovak separatist movement, putting pressure on the Prague government to grant independence. Bit by bit, the Czech lands were being drawn into the German orbit.

The isolation of Czechoslovakia after Munich also encouraged its other neighbours to join in the search for spoils. On 30 October, Poland demanded the cession of the Teschen region and the Czech government complied; on 2 November, territorial concessions were made to Hungary in southern Slovakia. Germany then demanded that the Prague government turn Czechoslovakia into a virtual German dependency. It was only a matter of time before the remaining Czechoslovak area was broken up. On 12 January 1939, orders were issued to German army units to prepare

ABOVE German troops march into Prague during the occupation on 15 March 1939. Following the takeover the Czech army was disbanded.

ABOVE RIGHT German commemorative medal with a bar for Prague awarded to all those who took part in the re-occupation of the Sudetenland.

LEFT Enthusiastic Germans remove the frontier posts separating Germany from Czechoslovakia. The Czech lands became a Reich Protectorate, while Slovakia won its "independence".

ABOVE Emil Hacha, President of Czechoslovakia, talking on the telephone. He was compelled to invite German "protection" of the Czech state in March 1939.

to occupy the Czech lands, though no final decision had yet been taken. The immediate trigger for the actual invasion was the breakdown in relations between the Czechs and the Slovaks: in March, the Slovak government in Bratislava refused to abandon its claim for independence, thereby provoking the Prague government to declare martial law and send troops into Slovakia. The leader of the Slovak separatists, Jozef Tiso, fled to Vienna and then to Berlin, where Hitler encouraged him to call the Slovak assembly together, which then declared independence on 14 March.

The Czech president, Emil Hácha, took the train to Berlin to seek Hitler's advice, and in the early hours of 15 March, after Hermann Göring had painted a vision for him of German bombers over Prague, he invited Germany to occupy and "protect" Czechoslovakia. At six o'clock in the morning, German forces occupied the Czech provinces of Bohemia and Moravia, while the Hungarian army seized control of some Slovak provinces. The following day, the Czech areas were declared a German protectorate and the former German foreign minister, Constantin von Neurath, was appointed first "Reich Protector". Major Czech businesses, including the famous Skoda armaments complex, were brought under direct German control, and Czech military supplies helped to equip 15 German infantry divisions and four armoured divisions for the coming conflict. Slovakia was made an independent pro-German state under Tiso and remained a close ally down to 1944.

The occupation of the rest of Czechoslovakia tore up the short-lived Munich agreement. The British and French governments could do nothing to save Czechoslovakia, which had not actually been invaded but forced to "invite" German occupation, but the decision to incorporate non-German peoples in the new German empire prompted Neville Chamberlain on 17 March to make a powerful speech condemning German action. The Prague occupation had finally convinced him that there was no room for a negotiated settlement and he warned that if any nation tried to dominate Europe, Britain would resist "to the utmost of its power". A few days later, prompted by warnings from the security services of an imminent German occupation of Poland, Chamberlain offered the historic guarantee of Polish sovereignty in the House of Commons on 31 March. The Czech crisis had paved the way for the final countdown to war.

CZECHS IN THE SECOND WORLD WAR

Many Czechs who fled from German occupation in 1938–39 ended up in France and Britain. When war came, the skilled Czech workers took up jobs in industry or as mechanics in the British armed forces. A number joined the RAF and fought through the Battle of Britain. There were four squadrons of Czech airmen, one bomber and three fighter squadrons. A Czech armoured brigade of 5,000 men was formed and later fought in the north-west Europe campaign. Czech military intelligence officers who came to Britain also played an important role in the British counter-intelligence programme.

RIGHT An aerial view of the vast Czech Skoda armaments works. The firm was taken over by the Germans in 1939 and worked for the German army throughout the war.

FAR RIGHT Model 24 standard-issue Czech pistol.

LEFT Constantin von Neurath, former German Foreign Minister, on his appointment as Reich Protector of Bohemia and Moravia on 18 March 1939.

TOP Hitler greets leaders of the German community in Prague on 15 March 1939 in the Hradcany Castle following German occupation. To his right stand Himmler and the head of the Reich Security Service, Reinhard Heydrich.

TREARTMENT OF THE JEWS IN THE CONQUERED LANDS

German occupation of Austria in March 1938 and the Czech lands in March 1939 brought large Jewish communities under German control. Major Jewish businesses and shareholdings were seized to secure Austrian and Czech industry for the German rearmament effort. Thousands of small Jewish businesses were closed down or sold to "Aryan" owners; Jewish professionals were sacked and forced to abandon their possessions if they sought exile abroad. Other countries were reluctant to issue visas since there had already been a steady stream of refugees seeking asylum from National Socialism. Around 130,000 Austrian Jews were able to emigrate before the war, and 35,000 Czech Jews. Those who remained were almost all exterminated.

RIGHT Jewish shops in the Slovak capital of Bratislava destroyed the day before German occupation of the Czech areas of the country, 14 March 1939.

THE MOLOTOV–RIBBENTROP PACT

RIGHT Joseph Stalin greets von Ribbentrop during negotiations over the demarcation of Poland.

In 1939 both the Western democracies and Germany began to look to the Soviet Union as a source of support in the unstable international situation, and the British and French began to explore the possibility of using the Soviet Union to pressurize Hitler into good behaviour. On 17 April, the Soviet Union proposed a Triple Alliance which would guarantee the remaining states of eastern Europe and give the promise of military assistance if any of the three states were attacked by Germany. The West dithered, but on 25 May Chamberlain at last agreed to begin negotiations.

Unknown to the West, Hitler had also decided to open up links to the Soviet Union, despite his regime's strident anti-Marxism. After exploring the possibility of a trade agreement, the German Ambassador in Moscow was authorized on 30 May to begin negotiations for a political alliance. In these concurrent sets of negotiations, the Soviets trusted neither side. When the Western powers finally sent a delegation to the Soviet Union in August, there was little prospect of agreement. Between 12 and 21 August, the

ABOVE The British military mission to Moscow leaves from Cannon Street station, London on 5 August 1939. In the centre of the picture is Soviet Ambassador Ivan Maisky, to his left is Admiral Sir Reginald Plunket-Ernle-Drax, leader of the mission.

LEFT The Soviet Foreign Minister Molotov signs the Non-Aggression Pact in Moscow late at night on 23 August 1939.

Moscow and sign the treaty. Stalin agreed. Ribbentrop flew to Moscow and found the capital decked with swastika banners. It was, he said, just like being among "old party comrades". After a few hours of discussion, the treaty was ready and late at night on 23 August, it was signed in the presence of a smiling Stalin. A secret protocol divided eastern Europe into spheres of influence: Finland, Estonia,

two sides discussed military co-operation, but the failure of Britain and France to secure Polish co-operation to allow the Red Army to cross Polish soil could not be overcome. By then, Stalin had decided that the Soviet Union could avoid war more easily by reaching an agreement with his rival dictator and bitter ideological enemy, Adolf Hitler.

The two dictators had a common desire to avoid conflict with each other: Hitler needed Soviet neutrality to be sure of isolating Poland, his next intended victim, whose conquest was planned for late August 1939; Stalin wanted a guarantee that the Soviet Union would not be dragged into a European war. Early in August, the German Foreign Minister, von Ribbentrop, signalled the possibility of agreement. By 11 August, his counterpart Molotov had indicated a similar willingness, and on 17 August a draft non-aggression treaty was ready. With the planned Polish invasion only a week away, Hitler appealed to Stalin in a personal letter asking him to allow Ribbentrop to travel to

JOACHIM VON RIBBENTROP (1893–1946)

A former champagne salesman, Ribbentrop became the National Socialist Party's expert on foreign affairs after 1933. In 1936, he was appointed Ambassador to London, but he was generally snubbed or ridiculed and developed an intense dislike of the English. In February 1938, Hitler appointed him Foreign Minister, a choice conditioned by the Führer's wish to have someone he could dominate. Ribbentrop was a vain but ineffectual personality, who left most major decisions to Hitler. He was tried before the Nuremberg Tribunal in 1945–46 and sentenced to death.

ABOVE The American Communist leader Earl Browder at a rally following the Soviet–German pact. Like Communists everywhere he was expected to support the pact with the fascist enemy and to blame the war on British imperialism.

BELOW Molotov arrives in Berlin to be greeted by von Ribbentrop (far left) on 12 November 1940 for negotiations on a possible extension of the agreements reached in 1939. The talks proved inconclusive.

VYACHESLAV MOLOTOV (1890–1986)

Molotov was a Soviet Communist Party politician who was part of the favoured inner circle around Stalin. A dour, hard-working individual, he adopted the revolutionary name Molotov (meaning hammer) because of his reputation for driving home an argument remorselessly. In 1930, he became Chairman of the Council of People's Commissars (or prime minister) and in March 1939, was appointed Foreign Minister to try to keep the Soviet Union out of a European war. He was removed from office by Stalin in 1949, one of the longest survivors of his entourage, but returned to office after Stalin's death and finally retired from public life in 1962.

Latvia and parts of Poland and Romania for the Soviet Union; Lithuania and a share of Poland for Germany.

Hitler was delighted by the pact because he believed that Britain and France would not dare to defend Poland without Soviet help. A separate trade agreement also secured generous supplies of oil, food and raw materials for Germany. Hitler now dismissed any danger of Western intervention. "My enemies are little worms," he had told his commanders on 22 August, "I saw them at Munich." Stalin was pleased as well, for the Soviet Union had avoided war and might, he hoped, be able to pick up the pieces after a European conflict and then impose communism on Europe in its aftermath. To Stalin the pact was a necessary piece of diplomatic realism; for Hitler it was a piece of cynical calculation. A few weeks later, he told his party leaders that he would turn against the East when it suited him. Communism, as he later told his propaganda chief, Joseph Goebbels, was "enemy number one".

التعاون الألماني الروسي

ABOVE A poster by the Egyptian cartoonist Kem showing Hitler and Stalin in an uneasy three-legged race. The German–Soviet Pact reverberated round the world.

GERMANY INVADES POLAND

The German invasion of Poland on 1 September 1939 was the culmination of a plan codenamed "Case White" which had first been drawn up by the German armed forces on Hitler's orders in April. The war against Poland was not a conflict Hitler had initially expected. After Munich, he assumed that the Poles would be drawn into the German sphere of influence. He wanted them to readjust the status of Danzig, a city supervized by the League of Nations to allow Poland access to the sea, to become a German city as it had been before 1919, and to hand back the rich industrial areas of Silesia, which had been given to Poland after a plebiscite in 1919.

The Poles refused any concessions and Hitler, frustrated at not getting his small war in 1938 against the Czechs, decided to punish the Poles by seizing the areas by force. He argued to the doubters in Berlin that Britain and France would protest but would not intervene. After signing the pact with the Soviet Union, Hitler was certain that the risk was much reduced. A pretence at last-minute negotiation in the final days of August was designed to make it seem as if Germany had a legitimate cause for war, though in fact the SS – the elite National Socialist security force – planned to stage a frontier incident to make it look as if the Poles were the aggressors. An attack by Germans wearing Polish uniforms on the frontier station at Gleiwitz on the night of 31 August/1 September was the signal. The order went out for the 1.5-million-strong German army, supported by more than 1,500 aircraft, to move forward in the first test of what came to be known as *blitzkrieg* or lightning war.

BELOW A Polish mounted brigade in 1939. Poland still used cavalry armed with lances and sabres which were no match for modern German equipment.

ABOVE German tanks and armoured vehicles cross a bridge over a river as they advance into Poland on 6 September 1939.

The German plan was for a two-pronged assault from East Prussia in the north and German Silesia in the south aimed towards the Polish capital, Warsaw. In the vanguard were five Panzer divisions of fast-moving mobile troops grouped around 300 tanks, supported by dive-bombers and fighters. It was the first time this new form of swift battlefield attack, using modern weaponry, had been tried out. The Polish

THE BOMBING OF WARSAW

As German forces closed in for the kill, the German Air Force was ordered to begin the bombing of Warsaw. The air force commander, Wolfram von Richthofen, cousin of the famous "Red Baron" First World War air ace, wanted to "completely eradicate" the Polish capital. On 22 September, 7,000 incendiaries set ablaze the Jewish ghetto; three days later a massive attack with 400 bombers destroyed or damaged 50 per cent of Warsaw's buildings for the loss of only three aircraft. Heavy smoke from the fires made it difficult to aim, and some bombs fell on German troops in the north of the city.

— final Polish pockets of resistance   —— German-Soviet demarcation line, 30 September 1939

THE RED ARMY INVADES POLAND

On 17 September, Red Army forces began to roll across the Soviet-Polish border to occupy areas of eastern Poland agreed as the Soviet sphere of influence in the Molotov-Ribbentrop Pact. Stalin had been uncertain whether to act, but pressured by the Germans, he finally agreed. One million Soviet troops occupied the eastern provinces, and all Polish resistance ended by 28 September. Some 230,000 Polish troops went into Soviet captivity, including more than half the Polish officer corps, 5,000 of whom were taken to the forest of Katyn in April 1940 and murdered by a shot in the back of the neck. On 29 November, the Poles were officially made Soviet citizens.

LEFT Red Army armoured cars and a German rifle corps on parade in Brest Litovsk, September 1939.

ABOVE Polish 7.92mm WZ 29 rifle, based on the German Mauser 98K.

army, almost one million strong, resisted bravely, but was overwhelmed by the Germans' striking power. The small Polish air force of around 400 planes was eliminated, though the German air force suffered 564 aircraft destroyed or damaged. Within a week of the start of the campaign German forces were 40–65km (25–40 miles) from Warsaw, tightening a noose around the encircled Polish armies. A final Polish stand was made at Warsaw and the fortress of Modlin to the north, but following the heavy bombing of the capital, Polish forces there surrendered on 27 September. Around 100,000 Polish soldiers escaped across neighbouring borders but 694,000 went into captivity. The German forces had lost some 13,000 men, the Poles 70,000: the first test of the rearmed German forces was a complete success.

The following day, 28 September, German and Soviet commanders met to decide the demarcation line between them. A new agreement was reached, the German–Soviet Treaty of Friendship, which sealed the partition of Poland, granting Warsaw to the area occupied by the Germans. Jews were victimized from the start and in November 1940 they were forced into a sealed ghetto in the city. Behind the German armies, Hitler had sent special "action squads" (Einsatzgruppen) manned by security agents and SS men, who began the systematic killing of all Polish intellectuals, nationalist politicians and government elite in a pattern that was to be repeated across Europe in the grim years of German occupation. By the end of the war, more than six million Poles, including three million Polish Jews, had been killed.

ABOVE German troops raise a German flag over a ruin in the Westerplatte area of Danzig which surrendered on 7 September 1939.

RIGHT Polish civilians executed by German soldiers during the conquest. On Hitler's orders thousands of Polish intelligentsia, priests and politicians were murdered.

BRITAIN AND FRANCE DECLARE WAR

6 FEBRUARY 1939
Chamberlain pledges in House of Commons to support France militarily.

13 FEBRUARY 1939
Joint Anglo-French military staff talks begin.

14 AUGUST 1939
Franco-British delegation arrives for talks in Moscow on possible Three-Power Pact.

5 SEPTEMBER 1939
Roosevelt declares an embargo on arms sales to the fighting powers.

BELOW An artillery headquarters on France's eastern border in January 1939. Throughout the year French and British forces prepared for a war seen increasingly as inevitable.

At 11.15 on Sunday morning, 3 September 1939, the British Prime Minister announced over the radio from 10 Downing Street that Britain was once again at war with Germany. No sooner had he finished speaking than the air-raid sirens set up in the capital let out their mournful wailing noise. All over southern England people dived for bunkers, cellars or doorways. Neville Chamberlain was reluctant to leave his office but was finally persuaded to go down into the shelter prepared for him. It turned out to be a false alarm, but the initial panic reflected the profound fear that the new war would be won or lost by bombing with gas, germ warfare and fire.

Britain's decision to go to war was almost inevitable once German forces had crossed the Polish frontier. As early as February, Chamberlain had pledged Britain to defend France, and from March the British and French military worked on a war plan so that they could make advance preparations. They expected to face a three-year war of attrition, a repeat of the First World War in which German resistance would be sapped by economic blockade, food shortages and, if necessary, by the bombing of German cities. In France, opinion rallied to the idea of confronting fascism, though right-wing groups stuck posters up on the walls of Paris

ABOVE The British Ambassador to Germany, Sir Nevile Henderson (centre) talking with Field Marshal Hermann Göring at the National Socialist Party Congress on 7 September 1938. A year later it was his task to hand over the ultimatum from Britain which resulted in war.

BELOW A newspaper vendor in Paris carries news of the British declaration of war on Germany, 3 September 1939. The French ultimatum expired six hours later than the British at 5.00 p.m. on the same day.

NEVILLE CHAMBERLAIN (1869–1940)
Born into a family of Birmingham screw manufacturers, Neville Chamberlain was a hard-working and successful politician in home affairs but is remembered as a failure in foreign policy because of his attempt to "appease" the dictators in the 1930s. A Conservative politician, he made his reputation as a reforming Minister of Health in the 1920s and a successful Chancellor of the Exchequer in 1931–37, steering the British economy out of the slump. He became prime minister in May 1937, and tried to secure a "grand settlement" of European affairs in order to avoid the threat of a second world war. In 1939, he came to realize that Hitler could never be satisfied with concessions and prepared for war. His reputation suffered from not confronting Hitler sooner, but he was always sincere in his strong desire for peace.

BELOW Neville Chamberlain broadcasting to the nation. He was an early enthusiast for radio and newsreel talks, and announced the state of war over the radio on 3 September 1939.

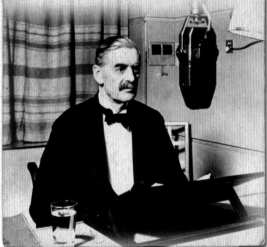

asking "Who Will Die for Danzig?". By August, Britain and France were mobilizing, ration-books were already being distributed to local authorities and millions of children and mothers prepared for evacuation away from the threatened cities. The British public steeled itself for the coming conflict "like the glassy sea when a hurricane comes", wrote the journalist Malcolm Muggeridge. Intelligence sources confirmed that German armies were moving into position. Although the British and French governments promised to help the Poles when war came, they privately agreed that assistance was useless and made no plans to do so. They hoped to restore a free Poland when the war was over and planned to hold tight on the western front.

In the last days before war there was a sudden flurry of activity. A Swedish businessman and friend of Hermann Göring, Birger Dahlerus, was despatched to London to see if the British could be separated from France by negotiating a

ABOVE Crowds watch as cabinet ministers pose for photographs outside 10 Downing Street on the day Britain declared war.

BELOW Londoners run for shelter minutes after the British declaration of war on 3 September when the first (false) air-raid alarm was sounded.

EVACAVUATION

Preparations were made before the outbreak of war in Britain, France and Germany for the mass evacuation of children and mothers from the vulnerable major cities. In Britain, official programmes covered evacuation of 1.75 million, with two million more expected to arrange private evacuation. Over 100,000 volunteers helped to organize the exodus and reception of the evacuees. The plan was activated on 1 September 1939 but only 40 per cent of those eligible took up the opportunity and 60 per cent of these had returned home by January 1940. In Germany hundreds of thousands were moved from the frontier zone after 3 September, but there too most had returned home by the start of 1940.

RIGHT During the 1930s "absolute" pacifists like the author Vera Brittain would not accept that any war was worth fighting. She campaigned with the Peace Pledge Union against war in 1939 and continued to write a regular *Letter to Peace Lovers* throughout the war.

deal. His mission was a blind, intended to confuse the British while Germany attacked Poland. At the last minute, after the German attack, Mussolini tried to intervene as he had at Munich, but the British and French governments, though willing to consider sensible proposals, were not prepared to allow Germany to occupy Poland. An ultimatum was delivered to Germany at 9 a.m. on 3 September by the British Ambassador, Sir Nevile Henderson, who found no one at the German Foreign Office except for Hitler's interpreter, Paul Schmidt, to whom he gave the solemn document. Schmidt hurried over to the Reich chancellery to read the ultimatum to a silent Hitler, who at the end turned to his Foreign Minister von Ribbentrop, and asked in harsh tones, "What now?" War could no longer be avoided. Chamberlain and the French premier, Edouard Daladier, would both have preferred peace, but could not abandon their commitment to Poland and to each other. The British ultimatum ran out at 11 a.m., the French later, at 5.00 p.m., and India, Australia and New Zealand declared war the same day. South Africa and Canada followed shortly after on 6 and 10 September respectively. In France, six million men were in the process of mobilization. The American Ambassador watched French troops leaving Paris: "The men left in silence. There were no bands, no songs," but only "self-control and a quiet courage".

THE SOVIET-FINNISH WAR

18 AUGUST 1939
Soviet negotiators offer Finland economic and military "aid". Finns refuse.

17 SEPTEMBER 1939
Molotov assures Finns that their neutrality will be respected.

29 OCTOBER 1939
Red Army ordered to begin planning war against Finland.

13 MARCH 1940
Soviet-Finnish ceasefire comes into force.

7 MAY 1940
Voroshilov sacked as Soviet Commissar for Defence.

The "Winter War" waged by the Soviet Union against neighbouring Finland was the first major test for the massive Red Army since the Russian Civil War in the early 1920s. The immediate cause was the Soviet search for greater military security in the Baltic region. Under the final terms of the German–Soviet agreements of 1939, the Baltic states lay in the Soviet sphere of interest. On 28 September, Estonia was forced to sign a treaty which allowed the Soviet Union to station troops there; Latvia signed on 5 October and Lithuania on 11 October, turning all three states into virtual Soviet protectorates. On 5 October, Finland was also asked to cede territory close to the Soviet city of Leningrad so that the Soviet Union could establish new military bases and make the country's second most important city more secure. The Finnish government refused and after the last meeting on 9 November, Stalin gave the final order for a campaign against Finland. Like the German war on Poland, the Winter War also began with a faked attack: the Soviet Union claimed that the "Mainila shots", named after a border village, were a Finnish provocation, when in fact the shells had been fired by Soviet artillery.

ABOVE British Volunteer Force badge.

FIELD MARSHAL CARL GUSTAV MANNERHEIM (1867–1951)

The child of a noble Finnish family at the time when Finland was still part of the Russian tsarist Empire, Carl Mannerheim joined the Russian army and became a successful cavalry officer. After Lenin's 1917 revolution, Mannerheim led the anti-Communist forces in Finland and imposed a harsh "White" terror on Finnish communists once an independent Finnish state had been established. From 1931, he was chair of the Finnish Defence Council and he took charge of the Finnish defence against the Red Army in 1939 after arguing with the government that it would be better to give in rather than fight. In 1944, he became President of Finland and succeeded in keeping Finland out of the post-war Iron Curtain bloc.

ABOVE Danish Volunteers badge. Danes were among many nationalities, including British and Americans, who volunteered to fight against the Russian invasion of Finland alongside the Finns.

ABOVE A group of Swedish and American volunteers for the Finnish army move to the front in 1940. Thousands of volunteers chose to fight against the Soviet threat to Scandinavia.

The Red Army attacked the Mannerheim defensive line across the Karelian Isthmus for a month. They used primitive tactics which allowed the Finnish defenders to mow down whole regiments of attacking infantry while well-directed artillery fire disabled the tanks. Some Finnish machine-gunners even suffered nervous collapse from the strain of killing row after row of Russian soldiers who ran head-on at defensive positions with no cover and no white camouflage suits. On Finland's eastern frontier, the larger Soviet force was harried and ambushed by the Finns, who moved quickly and silently. In the fighting at Suomussalmi in December and early January, the Red Army was annihilated. The Finns lost 900 men, but the Soviet dead numbered 27,500.

There was a limit to what the Finns could do, and by February the Red Army had brought up substantial reinforcements and was trying to refine its battle tactics.

One heroic Finnish force of 32 men still held off 4,000 Russians until overwhelmed by sheer numbers. By early March, the Soviet force numbered 30 divisions, 1,200 armoured vehicles and 2,000 aircraft. Faced with imminent defeat, the Finns sued for an armistice, which came into force on 13 March. When the fighting stopped, the Red Army had failed to break through the final Finnish line of defence. Perhaps impressed by Finnish bravery and fighting skill, Stalin did no more than take the areas of territory he had first requested. For a small area of Isthmus and a number of islands in the Baltic Sea, Soviet losses are estimated at anywhere between 125,000 and 270,000 dead. The Finnish army of 150,000 men lost 24,923 dead and 43,000 wounded. The international reputation of Soviet forces sank to new depths, and the Soviet Union was expelled from the League of Nations for her act of naked aggression.

ABOVE Houses destroyed by the Soviet air force in Finland during the Winter War. There was a marked disparity in air strength between the two sides.

BELOW A disabled Soviet tank and a pile of Soviet dead during the Soviet–Finnish war. The exact number of Soviet casualties has not been agreed. The official Soviet figure was 48,745.

Using this incident as an excuse, Stalin launched four armies, the 7th, 8th, 9th and 14th (and later the 4th), and 1,000 tanks against the Finnish defences. On 30 November, the Finnish capital Helsinki found itself under bomb attack. The Soviet regime was confident that Finland would be conquered as easily as Germany had overcome Poland, a view that was to prove a costly miscalculation. The Finns could mobilize a maximum of only 13 divisions to defend the country: no tanks, very few aircraft, and almost no anti-tank weapons. They did, however, have the advantage of experience in fighting in winter weather. Dressed in white suits, on skis, supplied with fast boat-shaped sleds filled with ammunition and supplies, and armed with the deadly "Suomi" sub-machine gun, Finnish soldiers proved themselves more than a match for an enemy that vastly outnumbered them. To fight against tanks, the Finns improvised the use of logs and crowbars to disable the tank treads. They also invented bottles filled with a deadly chemical and petrol mix that they christened "Molotov cocktails", which, when hurled against tanks and armoured vehicles, could inflict damage sufficient to slow them down, and sometimes to disable them.

MARSHAL KLIMENT VOROSHILOV (1881–1969)

An early member of the Russian Bolsheviks, the former metalworker Kliment Voroshilov worked on Stalin's military staff during the Russian Civil War. In 1925, with very little military experience, he was appointed Soviet Commissar for Military and Naval Affairs (from 1934 the Commissar for Defence). He was disliked by many of the generals, who regarded him as a military ignoramus, but he was too close to Stalin's inner circle for anyone to risk challenging him. The Finnish campaign finally persuaded even Stalin that Voroshilov was incompetent and he was sacked shortly after it, to be replaced by Semyon Timoshenko. He survived all Stalin's purges and emerged in 1953 as President of the USSR, a post he was forced to relinquish in 1960.

THE BATTLE OF THE RIVER PLATE

21 AUGUST 1939
Graf Spee and *Deutschland* set out into the Atlantic.

30 SEPTEMBER 1939
Graf Spee sinks its first ship.

30 SEPTEMBER 1939
Graf Spee sinks its first ship.

2 DECEMBER 1939
Graf Spee sinks *Doric Star*, which manages to send an emergency message before sinking.

ABOVE The cap worn by a German Naval Rating aboard the *Admiral Graf Spee*.

On 26 September 1939, Adolf Hitler ordered two German "pocket" battleships, *Deutschland* and *Admiral Graf Spee*, to begin intercepting and destroying British merchant ships in the Atlantic Ocean. The ships had been built in the early 1930s when Germany was still restricted to vessels of 10,000 tons. They were designed to maximize effective firepower despite the weight restriction and *Graf Spee* mounted six 280mm (11-inch) guns. The job of the pocket battleships was to destroy trade by what was called "merchant raiding", not to fight the Royal Navy, and the *Graf Spee's* captain, Hans Langsdorff, was under strict orders not to engage enemy warships. The German Navy High Command wanted no repeat of the disaster of the First World War, when a squadron under Admiral von Spee, whose name now adorned Langsdorff's ship, had been defeated off the Falkland Islands. Between September and 9 December, he sank or captured nine merchant ships but the wear and tear on the ship's less effective diesel-powered engines meant that a lengthy return trip to Germany became necessary for refitting. Before his departure Langsdorff decided to disobey his orders and find a weak British naval target to destroy. He sailed for Montevideo, where he was told a small British escort force would be leaving on 10 December.

LEFT The German pocket battleship *Graf Spee* on fire after being scuttled in the estuary of the River Plate, 17 December 1939.

BELOW RIGHT Damage to the heavy cruiser HMS *Exeter* after the 80-minute battle with the *Graf Spee* on 13 December 1939 which disabled the ship.

ABOVE Damage to the director tower of HMS *Achilles* after being hit by splinters from a 200-mm (11-inch) shell from the *Graf Spee* on 13 December 1939.

GROSSADMIRAL ERICH RAEDER (1876-1960)

Erich Raeder was Commander-in-Chief of the German navy at the start of the Second World War, a post he had held since 1928. Born in the port city of Hamburg, Raeder joined the navy in 1894 and rose rapidly through the ranks. He was not an enthusiast for Hitler, but recognized that under the Third Reich he could fulfil his dream of rebuilding a powerful German navy. He realized how weak his force was in 1939 when faced with the British and French fleets. The Allies combined had 22 battleships and 83 cruisers; Germany only 3 pocket battleships and 8 cruisers. Raeder told his commanders that they should know "how to die gallantly" when the time came. In 1943, after a series of naval disasters, he left office. He was tried at Nuremberg and sentenced to life imprisonment, but served only nine years before his release.

This would bring him a cheap victory and assure a triumphal homecoming to Germany.

Unknown to Langsdorff, British naval force "G" had been formed under Commodore Henry Harwood to hunt down the merchant raider. Even though one doomed merchant ship had managed to send out a signal with its position, tracking down the *Graf Spee* in an area as vast as the South Atlantic was extremely difficult, but on instinct Harwood decided on 9 December to make for the mouth of the River Plate. Early in the morning of 13 December, the German ship spotted the British force. Langsdorff ordered full steam ahead, and only too late discovered that he was engaging

ADMIRAL SIR DUDLEY POUND (1877-1943)

When war broke out, Admiral Dudley Pound was First Sea Lord, the Royal Navy's equivalent of commander-in-chief. He joined the navy in 1891, and served as a captain at the Battle of Jutland in 1916. He became Commander-in-Chief of the Mediterranean Fleet in 1936 before promotion to First Sea Lord in 1939.

Although in poor health, with a developing brain tumour, and often at loggerheads with his admirals, Pound worked well with Churchill. In 1943, his health forced him to resign and he died shortly after.

LEFT Captain Hans Langsdorff with the crew of the *Graf Spee* on a tugboat in Buenos Aires, Argentina, where they went to be interned on 18 December 1939. Langsdorff shot himself after his arrival.

one heavy and two light cruisers rather than the small escort vessels he had expected. Though outgunned, Harwood decided at once to engage the *Graf Spee*. While the heavy cruiser *Exeter* moved west to draw the German fire, Harwood took the light cruisers *Ajax* and *Achilles* – the latter manned largely by New Zealanders – northeast to attack from the other side. In a little over an hour of firing, *Exeter* was crippled and the two light cruisers badly damaged by the large 280mm (11-inch) shells from the German guns. But the determined British

attack produced 20 hits on the *Graf Spee* which left her in no condition to pursue the enemy or even to finish off the *Exeter*. Reluctantly, Langsdorff broke away and made off for Montevideo in neutral Uruguay.

Anxious that a stronger Royal Navy force was approaching and pressed by the Uruguayan authorities to leave, Langsdorff realized that his position was hopeless. He ordered the crew to leave the ship, set charges and sailed the ship out to sea where, at 8.45 in the evening on 17 December 1939, it blew up, sinking at once. Langsdorff ensured that his crewmen were interned in Argentina, which was sympathetic to the Axis, then wrote a suicide note accepting full blame for the disaster. Laying out his battleship's ensign, he shot himself.

Harwood was the one who returned home to glory. He was knighted and made a Rear Admiral, while his commanders all won high decorations. Winston Churchill went to Plymouth to welcome the damaged *Exeter,* which was later sunk by the Japanese in 1942. The Battle of the River Plate was Britain's first wartime victory and one of the few pieces of action throughout the so-called Phoney War which stretched from September 1939 to April 1940, when Hitler invaded Denmark and Norway.

LEFT Winston Churchill, First Lord of the Admiralty, hosts a lunch on 23 February 1940 at the Guildhall in London to honour the victors of the Battle of the River Plate.

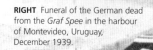

RIGHT Funeral of the German dead from the *Graf Spee* in the harbour of Montevideo, Uruguay, December 1939.

THE INVASION OF NORWAY

ABOVE German shield badge awarded to the German forces taking part in the 1940 Narvik campaign in northern Norway.

During the early months of 1940, both sides eyed Scandinavia as a possible area for military action. The Allies explored the possibility of cutting Germany off from her essential supplies of high-quality Swedish iron ore by mining Norwegian waters. The French government advocated the possible military occupation of the ore-producing areas. The German navy began to explore the idea of occupying Norway to protect the mineral resources and provide it with a springboard for attacks against Allied shipping in the North Atlantic. On 5 February 1940, Hitler ordered planning to begin for Operation "Weserübung", the possible occupation of Denmark and Norway.

The stakes were raised when Philip Vian, the captain of the British destroyer HMS *Cossack,* found the German tanker *Altmark* anchored in Norwegian waters. The German ship carried 299 British prisoners captured from ships sunk by the *Graf Spee*. To avoid offending the Norwegian government, Vian was ordered not to intervene, but he disobeyed orders, boarded the *Altmark* and rescued the British sailors. The exploit was well received by the British

ABOVE News of the invasion of Norway hits the streets of the City of London on 9 April 1940. The town of Kristiansand was heavily bombed on the first day.

LEFT British forces near the town of Trondheim on the north Norwegian coast during the attempt in May 1940 to wrest control from the German occupiers.

BELOW German soldiers gather on a beach on the western coast of Norway on 9 April 1940. Five major coastal towns were secured on the first day of the invasion.

BERNARD ARMITAGE WARBURTON-LEE VC

Warburton-Lee was Commander of a British flotilla of five destroyers ordered to Narvik on 9 April to stop a German landing. His ships arrived too late but the following morning in heavy snow he led them into the harbour where they sank two destroyers, damaged another and destroyed six merchant ships. Five German destroyers then appeared outside the port and opened fire. Warburton-Lee was killed and his ship, HMS *Hardy* beached. He was awarded a posthumous Victoria Cross.

ABOVE Narvik Harbour showing sunken German supply ships following the successful Royal Navy raid on the German destroyer force on 13 April 1940 by the battleship *Warspite* and nine destroyers. All eight German destroyers were sunk.

BELOW German soldiers deploy heavy artillery against Allied forces in May 1940 around Narvik, which the Allies captured on May 28 but abandoned 11 days later.

PARATROOPERS

German forces undertook the first invasion by paratroopers on 9 April when they were flown in Junkers Ju52 transport aircraft and dropped over airfields at Oslo and Stavanger. They secured the airfields quickly and German transport planes began to land vital equipment to allow the German forces to consolidate their grip in southern Norway and seize the Norwegian capital. The successful deployment of airborne forces was to be tried again with great success a few weeks later in the German invasion of Belgium.

BELOW The Norwegian royal family was forced to flee on a British ship on 7 June 1940. King Haakon is seen here on his triumphant return to Norway five years later on 7 June 1945 aboard the Royal Navy's HMS *Norfolk*.

LEFT British troops in northern Norway with a French Hotchkiss H39 light tank. The flow of military equipment was too slow to halt the German advance and after 10 May Allied priorities lay in France.

public, but it alerted Hitler to the real danger of British intervention, while Anglo–Norwegian relations reached a low ebb. In early April, Winston Churchill, as First Lord of the Admiralty, ordered the mining of Norwegian coastal waters, which began on 8 April, but Hitler had already decided on 2 April to launch a pre-emptive strike on his northern flank. Operation "Weserübung" began on the morning of 9 April, when two divisions of German troops entered Denmark almost unopposed. A large flotilla of ships made for the Norwegian capital, Oslo, and for the smaller port cities on the long Norwegian coastline. They were supported by a specially organized 10th Flying Corps, whose job was to ferry paratroops to Norway and to prevent the Royal Navy from intervening.

The German campaign took the Allies by surprise and succeeded within days in seizing most of Norway, despite the loss of a large part of the surface fleet and numerous smaller vessels, including the newly launched heavy cruiser *Blücher*, which was sunk by Norwegian shore batteries as it approached Oslo, carrying onboard the German administrators and Gestapo officials destined to rule occupied Norway. The new fast battle cruisers *Scharnhorst* and *Gneisenau* were also damaged in combat with the Royal Navy. On 8 April, the cruiser *Hipper* was holed by the British destroyer HMS *Glowworm*, which rammed the much larger ship, blew up and sank. However, an Allied expeditionary force which landed at Narvik on 14 April and near Trondheim on 18 April was pinned down by German forces, and by 3 May was compelled to evacuate from the Trondheim area, despite the destruction of most of the

covering German naval force. The battle around Narvik was hampered by continuous air attacks against British shipping, but by 8 June, with the Battle of France reaching its critical climax, Allied forces were evacuated, along with the Norwegian royal family and government, and with the Norwegian surrender two days later, German control of Norway was complete. King Haakon, however, insisted on maintaining a state of war from exile in London. German losses totalled 3,700 men, Allied forces the same number. The German navy lost a large part of the surface fleet, including three cruisers and 10 destroyers, and was never again in a position to mount a major operation. The Royal Navy lost an aircraft carrier, two cruisers and nine destroyers but remained a formidable force. Hitler secured the supply of Swedish iron ore and ordered Trondheim turned into a major German naval base. The remains of the vast concrete submarine pens can be seen to this day.

CHURCHILL TAKES OVER

3 SEPTEMBER 1939
Churchill appointed to the Admiralty.

5 OCTOBER 1939
Churchill begins a five-year confidential correspondence with US President Roosevelt.

7 APRIL 1940
Churchill gives the order to lay mines in Norwegian coastal waters.

15 MAY 1940
Churchill and the War Cabinet approve the bombing of German towns.

22 MAY 1940
Emergency Powers Act passed in Britain, giving Churchill exceptional wartime authority.

26 MAY 1940
Operation "Dynamo" launched to rescue British forces trapped at Dunkirk.

4 JUNE 1940
Churchill declares in House of Commons "We shall never surrender".

9 NOVEMBER 1940
Neville Chamberlain dies.

No figure so dominates the early history of the Second World War as Winston Leonard Spencer Churchill. He came to symbolize British resistance to Hitler, and his determination to fight on, whatever the odds, made him into a legend in his own lifetime. He had always harboured the ambition to be a great war leader but during the 20 years since the end of the First World War, Churchill had experienced increasing political decline and isolation and his choice as Britain's wartime Prime Minister to succeed Neville Chamberlain came through luck as much as ambition. Only in office did the full scale of Churchill's leadership abilities finally emerge.

There were many reasons why Churchill's parliamentary colleagues were dubious about him. He was flamboyant, intemperate and unpredictable – a larger-than-life personality who had spent a political lifetime making enemies. He was first elected to Parliament in 1900 as a Conservative, switched to the Liberal Party in 1904 and then back to the Conservatives in 1924. Churchill had strong views on empire and hated communism. He expressed himself forcefully, and followed his own instincts as much as political common sense. He was regarded as an unsuccessful Chancellor of the Exchequer between 1924 and 1929, and in the 1930s found himself in the political wilderness. During this time he wrote extensively, predominantly autobiography and history, including his famous *Life of Marlborough*, and he campaigned on issues that were far from popular. He was opposed to making concessions to Gandhi's Indian nationalists and demanded that Britain rearm as fully as possible to meet the likely threat from Hitler. His reputation as a warmonger and reactionary were out of step with the mood of pacifism and appeasement which prevailed up to Munich and even beyond.

ABOVE Winston Churchill side by side with the British Foreign Secretary, Edward, Lord Halifax, both contenders to succeed Neville Chamberlain in May 1940.

LEFT Churchill stands outside the Admiralty building in London's Whitehall on 17 September 1939, two weeks after his appointment as First Lord of the Admiralty, the same post he held at the beginning of the First World War.

CLEMENTINE CHURCHILL (1885–1977)

In 1908, Winston Churchill married Clementine Hozier after a whirlwind courtship. The granddaughter of aristocracy, Clementine was a staunch and loyal partner to a man who seldom had sufficient time in a crowded political life for his family. She organized canteens for munitions workers in the First World War, and during the Second World War chaired the Red Cross Aid for Russia programme. Though often in Winston's shadow, she played a major part in encouraging his ambition and in supporting his role as wartime leader. On 27 June 1940, she famously told him that his brusque and hostile manner was alienating his colleagues, telling him "you are not as kind as you used to be", and urging him to be more tolerant and approachable.

CHURCHILL IN THE FIRST WORLD WAR

Churchill began the First World War as he was to begin the Second, as First Lord of the Admiralty. Following the disastrous campaign against the Turks for the Dardanelles, Churchill had to accept a humiliating demotion. With almost nothing to do for much of 1915, he first took up painting, which became one of the great passions of his life. Finally, he went off to the Western Front expecting to be made a General but was forced to accept a Colonel's commission with the Royal Scots Fusiliers. He was in the front line, running daily risks, from January to May 1916, when he was recalled to London, becoming Minister of Munitions in July 1917. This was the last time Churchill was to see active service.

ABOVE Churchill, second from right, stands with officers of the French 29th Division at Nieuport in Belgium.

RIGHT Neville Chamberlain and his wife walk through St. James' Park in central London on 10 May 1940, the day of his resignation. Chamberlain remained a firm supporter of Churchill until his death in November.

BELOW RIGHT Churchill gives the famous V for Victory sign to a crowd outside the Sheffield City Hall in November 1941. The sign was first used by English archers in the Middle Ages to taunt their French opponents who used to cut off the middle fingers of English prisoners to prevent them drawing a bow.

Churchill was a powerful political figure nonetheless, and in September 1939 Chamberlain invited him back into the cabinet as First Lord of the Admiralty. Although Churchill oversaw the disastrous Norwegian campaign, it was Chamberlain who took the blame when the war went wrong, and the public mood then swung strongly against Chamberlain's handling of the conflict, meaning a successor as Prime Minister was needed. Churchill was not the first choice of the Conservative majority in Parliament, but he was a figure that the opposition Labour Party and the trades unions would work with. On 9 May, one day before German armies attacked in the west, Churchill was called to Chamberlain's office together with the Foreign Secretary, Lord Halifax, whom Chamberlain would have preferred as his successor. Churchill recalled in his post-war account that he said little, waiting for Halifax to speak. Finally, the silence was broken when Halifax announced that he did not feel he could cope with being a war leader. Churchill was left unopposed; he wrote later that at that moment, "I felt as if I was walking with destiny, and that all my past life

ABOVE One of the most famous photographs of Churchill, taken by Cecil Beaton in 1940, seated at his desk in No 10 Downing Street.

had been a preparation for this hour and for this trial…".

When Churchill arrived in the Commons on 13 May, there was no more than a ripple of applause, while the Lords greeted his appointment in silence. Within weeks, Churchill found himself the leader of a nation defeated in France and threatened with invasion. Although there were some British politicians who favoured a compromise with Hitler, from the day of his appointment Churchill never wavered in his determination to defeat Hitlerism and to rally British society to fight the war to the end. It is this defiance at a critical moment in the British war effort that moulded the Churchill legend. The public forgot his chequered past and rallied to his summons.

GERMANY INVADES IN THE WEST

On 10 May 1940 German forces launched a series of swift operations against the Dutch, Belgian and French armed forces. Hitler had wanted to invade in the West in November 1939 but bad weather prevented it. During the spring, German military planners prepared a campaign based on a rapid defeat of Allied forces by striking with armour and aircraft through the heavily wooded Ardennes sector of the front, where the French Maginot Line fortifications were weakest. The balance of forces between the two sides favoured the Western Allies in army divisions (144 to 141), artillery pieces (13,974 to 7,378) and tanks (3,384 to 2,445); German fighter and bomber forces were outnumbered on paper by the Allies (3,254 to 3,562), but both the French and British chose to keep large air forces away from the battlefield, defending the rest of France and mainland Britain.

The rapid German advance was based on a number of daring strategic strokes and the miscalculation of the Allies. The Western plan was based on a rapid movement of forces into Belgium and the Netherlands to counter the expected German attack. After German forces attacked the Netherlands and seized the key Belgian fortress of Eben Emael with the first successful airborne assault on 10 May,

LEFT German Army marching compass used in the movement west.

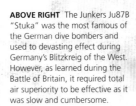

ABOVE RIGHT The Junkers Ju87B "Stuka" was the most famous of the German dive bombers and used to devasting effect during Germany's Blitzkreig of the West. However, as learned during the Battle of Britain, it required total air superiority to be effective as it was slow and cumbersome.

BELOW Despite the imminent Dutch surrender and the firing of red "abort" flares by Germans on the ground, Rotterdam was carpet bombed on 14 May, killing 800 and making a further 78,000 homeless.

BELOW German motorcyclists advance through a captured Belgian town, May 1940.

the Allies attempted to move forces into the Low Countries to halt the German advance. Dutch resistance crumbled and within a few days Belgian, British and French forces were in retreat. Unknown to the Western Allies, large German formations of armoured divisions, heavily protected by fighters, had by 12 May mustered in the Ardennes forest, considered virtually impassable by the French High Command, and stood poised for an historic breakthrough.

Under the command of General von Kleist, Guderian's Panzer divisions broke across the Meuse River on 13 May and, heavily supported by the Junkers Ju87 dive bomber and large numbers of medium bombers, unhinged the whole French front by driving a powerful wedge between two French armies, General Hutzinger's 2nd and General

GENERAL MAURICE-GUSTAVE GAMELIN (1872-1958)

Often regarded as the commander who lost the Battle of France in 1940, General Gamelin was in fact a successful and innovative soldier, who helped to modernise the French army in the 1930s and prepare it for the conflict with Germany. He was commander-in-chief of French forces in May 1940 when the Germans invaded. His plan to move French mobile forces rapidly into the Netherlands to stop the German advance fatally weakened the French line opposite the axis of German advance. He was sacked on 19 May as the Allied front crumbled.

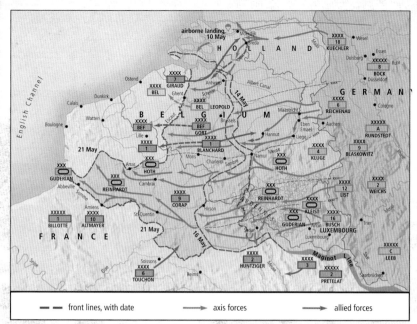

RIGHT A French gun firing at the advancing Germans during the defence of the Maginot Line, 16 May 1940.

RIGHT General Rommel, Commander of 7 Panzer Division, and his staff, plot their way through France, May 1940. They were known as the "Ghost Division" due to the speed with which they attacked.

Corap's 9th. "There has been a rather serious hitch at Sedan," reported Colonel Lacaille, chief-of-staff of the 2nd Army. The "hitch" turned into a rout. The French front collapsed and German commanders began the successful rush for the coast in the hope of encircling and destroying all the remaining Allied armies in the pocket. By 19 May Guderian's tanks had reached the Channel coast at Abbeville. A small number of counterattacks by French and British forces held up what was close to becoming a foregone conclusion. On 28 May, after a brave defence of western Belgium, the Belgian king surrendered. The Netherlands had capitulated on 14 May, following a fierce air bomb attack on the Dutch port of Rotterdam.

The rapid German advance created panic in the French leadership. British reinforcements were slow to arrive and the bulk of British air power remained in Britain to defend against a possible German air assault. On 16 May Winston Churchill flew to Paris where he was told that there was no French reserve left to hold up the German advance. The same day the French premier, Paul Reynaud, told the French parliament that only a miracle could save France from defeat. As the noose tightened around the trapped British and French forces in northern France, plans were made to try to hold the line of the River Somme, where more than 20 years before some of the bloodiest battles of the First World War had been fought. On 23 May the British

military Chiefs-of-Staff decided that the war in France was lost and prepared to abandon their ally. On 27 May British forces began to evacuate from the northern French port of Dunkirk. France was forced to fight on alone.

ABOVE Tank barriers in the Maginot Line. France spent nine years and three billion Francs building this line of defence only for it to be almost completely bypassed by the Nazis, who instead invaded by way of the Low Countries and the Ardennes forest.

ABOVE RIGHT Men of the Royal Fusiliers man a Bren gun position at the front near Saint Francois-Lacroix, 3 January 1940. By May 1940 there were 394,165 members of the BEF on the French/Belgian border. 237,319 of these were employed in front line duties.

RIGHT A mother leads her children to safety having been made homeless by a German attack, Belgium, May 1940.

GENERAL HEINZ GUDERIAN (1888-1954)

German officer who in the 1930s pioneered fast mobile warfare spearheaded by the use of armour, the famous Blitzkrieg strategy. He was Commander of Mobile Troops by the late 1930s, and led the 19th Panzer Corps during the invasions of Poland and France where his forces played a critical part in the breakthrough at Sedan which opened up the French front. He won spectacular victories in the Russian campaign in 1941, but fell out with Hitler, who sacked him in December. He was appointed Inspector-General of Armoured Troops in 1943, then Chief of Army Staff until Hitler dismissed him again in March 1945.

DUNKIRK

As German forces pressed forward into France they opened up a wide gap between the British Expeditionary Force in northern France and the bulk of the French army to the south. By the fourth week of May, German thrusts had also separated the BEF from the crumbling Belgian army, which capitulated three days later. There existed a very real danger that the entire British force would be encircled and captured, but on 23 May von Runstedt halted the armoured forces, and the following day Hitler, uncertain about the strength of the French army to the south, concurred. The German armour stopped in front of a network of water-courses surrounding the area around Lille and Dunkirk now occupied by the BEF and a substantial number of trapped French divisions. This pause allowed a rough perimeter defence to be established by the Allies. On 26 May, the British government ordered Lord Gort, the BEF commander, to evacuate as many troops as he could from France. The evacuation was masterminded by Vice Admiral Bertram Ramsay, who later, as Naval Commander, organized the shipping for the D-Day invasion. Given the codename Operation "Dynamo" – after the small dynamo room in the Dover cliffs used as the operational base – the saving of the BEF became one of the great legends in Britain's war effort.

The fighting retreat begun around 21 May was among the fiercest action of the campaign. The troops holding the British line at Arras were ordered to "fight to the last man and the last round". When German attacks resumed on 26 May, every mile of ground was contested. Under a hail of bombs from German aircraft, an estimated 850–950 small ships and larger naval and merchant vessels plied back and forth, carrying British troops between Dunkirk and the southern British ports. In addition to Royal Navy vessels and large steamers, there came lifeboats and trawlers. The Port of London Authority sent nine tugs drawing barges behind them. Fortunately, British fighter aircraft were able to reach Dunkirk from British bases and kept up regular sorties against German units, though 177 British aircraft were lost. When the weather was clear, German aircraft exacted

ABOVE British forces line up on the beach at Dunkirk waiting to be evacuated.

a heavy toll: on 1 June, three destroyers were sunk and Ramsay ordered sailings only at night.

During the eight days of the evacuation, an estimated 338,000 troops were rescued including 110,000 French servicemen, most of whom were saved only on the last two days after Ramsay was ordered to send back the big ships to rescue non-British forces as well. A mixture of British and French units continued to defend the pocket, and for many of them, including the 51st Highland Division, forced to surrender in mid-June, evacuation was not possible. Some 8,000 British soldiers went into captivity. On the evacuation beaches discipline was hard

ABOVE A British anti-aircraft gun abandoned at Dunkirk, June 1940. Most of the equipment of the British Expeditionary Force had to be left behind in France.

THE OTHER DUNKIRKS

Even as Operation "Dynamo" ended, there were more than 100,000 British troops still stationed in northern France, and as French resistance crumbled they fell back on the ports. On 13 June, 11,200 men were evacuated from Le Havre on the north French coast; 27,000 from St. Nazaire on 17–18 June. In total around 273,000 more British, French and Polish soldiers and airmen were evacuated to Britain between 13 and 25 June, a total not far short of the number saved at Dunkirk. On 17 June, a single German plane succeeded in hitting the overcrowded *Lancastria* in St-Nazaire harbour. The ship keeled over and only 2,477 of an estimated 6,000 crew and evacuees were saved. This was the worst disaster in British maritime history.

BELOW Motor vehicles on the quayside at Cherbourg during the evacuation, 13 June 1940.

ABOVE Officers of the Royal Ulster Rifles awaiting evacuation at Bray Dunes, about 8km (5miles) from Dunkirk.

FIELD MARSHAL VISCOUNT GORT, VC (1886–1946)

John Standish Vereker, Viscount Gort, was born into an Irish aristocratic family. He served in the Grenadier Guards and became a battalion commander in 1917. After a long army career, he was appointed Chief of the Imperial General Staff in 1937. He held that office until September 1939, when he was sent to France to command the British Expeditionary Force, where he was responsible for organizing the evacuation from Dunkirk. He later became Governor of Malta during the siege of the island, and was created a Field Marshal in 1943.

ABOVE French soldiers captured when the German army entered Dunkirk after the British evacuation, 4 June 1940.

ABOVE Shipping was an easy target for the German air force. Here the French destroyer *Bourrasque* is sinking off Dunkirk loaded with evacuees.

RIGHT Troops arrive back at Dover from Dunkirk, 31 May 1940. In total around 228,000 British forces were rescued in nine days.

to maintain and panicking soldiers were sometimes killed or beaten to keep order, while British forces also shot French soldiers suspected of spying or betrayal. On 27 May, a group of the Royal Norfolks was caught by the SS "Death's Head" Division, commanded by General Theodor Eicke, former commandant of Dachau, and 97 of them were murdered in cold blood.

The Dunkirk evacuation was both a victory and a defeat. It showed how important was British naval power and it also provided a taste of the conflict between the two air forces that later dominated the summer and autumn of 1940. German aircraft losses during the Battle of France were higher than in the later Battle of Britain. Yet Dunkirk did mean an ignominious end to Allied efforts to defeat Germany on land. Almost all the British army's equipment was abandoned or destroyed, and a new army had to be rebuilt over the course of the following years. "Wars are not won", Churchill remarked on 4 June, "by evacuations".

THE FALL OF FRANCE

10 JUNE 1940
Italy declares war on France and Britain.

14 JUNE 1940
Paris falls to the German army.

16 JUNE 1940
Premier Paul Reynaud resigns.

19 JUNE 1940
German army reaches Atlantic coast at Brest.

20 JUNE 1940
Japan forces France to agree to Japanese naval vessels in Indo-China.

1 JULY 1940
French parliament votes Marshal Pétain special powers, bringing the Third Republic to an end.

The surrender of Belgium and the British evacuation from Dunkirk left France fighting almost alone against the German advance. General Maxime Weygand, who succeeded General Gamelin on 19 May, organized an improvised defensive line along two rivers, the Somme and the Aisne, which had witnessed much of the fighting in the First World War. The German army reorganized into two major armoured spearheads led by von Kleist and Guderian, and attacked the Weygand Line on 5 and 9 June. After a few days of fierce fighting, the German forces reached the eastern edge of Paris. The capital was declared an open city, and on 14 June the German army entered almost deserted streets. The French government had fled first to Tours, where Churchill flew on 11 June to try to rally French resistance, then to Bordeaux. In the days before the German arrival, thousands of Parisians fled by car, train or on foot in what became known as l'exode, "the exodus".

Following the breakthrough to Paris, resistance began to crumble despite the existence of large units of the French army and substantial numbers of aircraft not yet defeated. German armoured forces pushed forward at high speed, reaching Brest on the Atlantic coast by 19 June, Nantes by 20 June and as far as Bordeaux by 25 June, when the armistice, sought by the French government on 17 June and signed five days later, finally came into effect. In the east of France, the Maginot Line was penetrated in several places while German forces swung south to encircle what was left of the Second French Army Group under General Prétalat.

French forces were forced to surrender piecemeal, but by 22 June French resistance towards the Germans was over.

On the Italian-French frontier in the south, however, hostilities continued. Mussolini declared war on France and Britain on 10 June, anxious not to miss any advantages he might gain from a peace settlement. Eleven days later, the 22 Italian divisions on the Italian-French frontier, totalling 300,000 men, were used to attack the southern French defences where they were held up by only six French divisions of approximately 85,000; the French strength had been greatly reduced following the redeployment of General Olry's forces to the north to face the German threat there. After four days of fighting, the Italians had gained almost nothing in the face of entrenched defences in difficult terrain. The Italian forces lost 1,258 dead and 2,631 wounded in the campaign; only 20 French soldiers were killed, and 84 wounded. On 24 June, an armistice was signed, ending what had been a brief, pointless and inglorious campaign. The battle to the north cost the French an estimated 90,000 dead and the

ABOVE The French SE MAS 1935 sub-machine gun. Ordered for mass production in 1940, the gun, designed five years earlier, only reached the French army in small numbers before the armistice. It was later used by the Germans and the Vichy regime forces.

MARSHAL PHILIPPE PÉTAIN (1856–1951)

To many Frenchmen Marshal Pétain was both a hero and a villain. In the First World War he commanded the defence of the French fortress of Verdun and was hailed in 1918 as one of the victors over Germany, for which he was rewarded with the title Marshal of France. In 1940, the ageing hero who had been ambassador in Spain in the 1930s and from May 1940 vice-premier, was called upon to bolster French morale in the crisis weeks of June 1940. On 16 June, as French resistance collapsed, he became prime minister and called for an armistice. He established a new authoritarian government in the small town of Vichy in central France from which his regime took its name. He was forced to collaborate with the Germans, including in the campaign against the Jews, and at the end of the war he was arrested and later sentenced to death. He died in captivity on the Île d'Yeu.

LEFT A French anti-tank mine.

ABOVE LEFT A French Char B tank in action during the Battle of France, May 1940.

LEFT French infantry surrender to the advancing German army in June 1940. Hundreds of thousands of French POWs were later made to work for the German war effort.

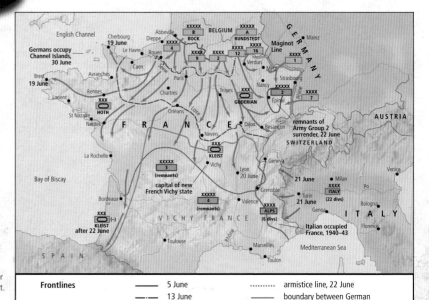

Frontlines		
—— 5 June	·········· armistice line, 22 June
—·— 13 June	—— boundary between German occupied and Vichy France
—— 17 June	

THE CARRIAGE AT COMPIÈGNE

Nothing so symbolized German humiliation at the end of the First World War as the railway carriage in the small French town of Compiègne where German delegates were compelled to sign the armistice that ended hostilities on 11 November 1918. When Marshal Pétain asked for an armistice from the Germans on 17 June, Hitler insisted that it should be signed in the same place as in 1918. The French General Charles Huntzinger led a delegation to meet Hitler on 21 June, and the armistice was signed the following day in the railway carriage. Its 24 articles were dictated by the German side rather than negotiated. The armistice came into force on 25 June following a second armistice signing in Rome to bring Italian-French hostilities to a close.

LEFT General Charles de Gaulle seated at his desk in London, c.1940. He escaped from France during the evacuation and was recognised by the British government as leader of Free French forces on 28 June 1940. In 1940 he took part in an attempt to capture Dakar in West Africa from the Vichy regime.

BELOW German troops parade through Paris following the occupation of the French capital, which was declared an open city on 13 June 1940 to avoid bombing attacks.

loss of 1.9 million men as prisoners of war; German losses were 29,640 dead and 163,000 wounded.

For other Frenchmen the war continued beyond the armistice. On 6 June, the French premier, Paul Reynaud, had appointed the young General Charles de Gaulle as Under Secretary for War. He wanted to continue the fight and on 16 June encouraged Churchill to offer France a union of the two countries which he did with the backing of his cabinet. The French government refused, but de Gaulle smuggled himself out of France in an RAF aircraft and in London on 18 June made an historic appeal to a "Free France" to continue the fight against the German enemy. De Gaulle and the small number of supporters he gathered in England formally established the Free French forces on 7 August; they numbered only 2,240 officers and men. The newly formed Vichy government of Marshal Pétain declared them to be traitors but they formed the nucleus of what was to become a large and effective fighting force later in the war.

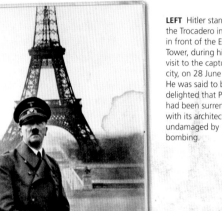

LEFT Hitler standing at the Trocadero in Paris, in front of the Eiffel Tower, during his only visit to the captured city, on 28 June 1940. He was said to be delighted that Paris had been surrendered with its architecture undamaged by bombing.

GERMANY'S NEW ORDER

3 OCTOBER 1940
The Jews of Warsaw are forced into the ghetto which is sealed from the rest of the city.

23 OCTOBER 1940
Spanish leader Franco refuses to join the Axis after meeting Hitler.

16 JULY 1941
Hitler orders savage repression of European resistance.

3 OCTOBER 1941
Hitler declares the launch of the New Order in Berlin.

10 JUNE 1942
340 Czechs are killed in Lidice in revenge for killing of Heydrich.

11 NOVEMBER 1942
Vichy France occupied by the German army.

5 OCTOBER 1943
Germany absorbs Italian alpine territories and port of Trieste into Reich.

19 MARCH 1944
German forces occupy Hungary.

The German conquest of much of Europe opened the way to the construction of what was popularly called the "New Order". There were no clear German plans before 1939 for what such an order would look like, and in its brief five years of existence it remained a confused patchwork of different forms of political association or occupation administration. The programme to create the German New Order was finally announced by Hitler in Berlin on 3 October 1941 at a time he believed the Soviet Union was close to destruction. The whole enterprise depended, like Napoleon's European empire, on the extension of military power.

The reorganization of German-dominated Europe followed no clear lines, but there was a division between those areas that became allied or associated with Germany (Hungary, Romania, Bulgaria and the new puppet states of Slovakia and Croatia); those defeated states allowed some degree of autonomy under German supervision (Belgium, the Netherlands, Norway, Denmark and France); and those remaining areas directly ruled by German political or military authorities (Poland, the Baltic states, the territories of the western Soviet Union, Serbia and Greece). In southern Europe, Germany had to share rule with the Italian regime in the former Yugoslavia and Greece, but when Italy surrendered in September 1943, these areas were also taken under direct German control.

The object of the New Order was to re-centre the politics of the continent on Berlin, which was to be redesigned by Hitler's favourite architect, Albert Speer, as the capital of a

new empire to rival that of ancient Rome. A triumphal route was planned through the centre of the city which would end at a vast People's Hall with a capacity of 200,000 people and whose dome was to be seven times larger than that of St Peter's in the Vatican. In the east, the creation of a colonial system was planned, in which German garrison cities would govern the vast Russian countryside while an army of labourers produced food and raw materials for the German master race. The process of constructing this empire began in 1940 with the dismemberment of Poland and the start of expulsions from the area. The conquest of the western Soviet Union laid the way for a large-scale reorganization of the region, known by the term "General Plan East" (*Generalplan Ost*). The surplus population was to be driven eastwards where it would disappear from starvation or disease; the remainder would work as virtual slaves for the Germans, who would provide the administrators, engineers and experts to run the empire. "Russia", Hitler was reported as saying, "will be our India."

At the core of the New Order was a system of economic exploitation. As early as July 1940, the German Economics Minister, Walter Funk, announced the creation of a new

LEFT Walter Funk (1890–1960) was chosen by Goering as Minister of Economics in February 1938. In January 1939 he became President of the Reichsbank, and in these two roles played a key part in the attempt during the war to build a European economy centred on Germany.

RIGHT Joseph Goebbels (1897–1945), Minister for Propaganda and Popular Enlightenment in Hitler's cabinet, played an important role in spreading propaganda across occupied Europe to show that Germany was resisting "Jewish Bolshevism" and "Jewish international capital".

BELOW Dutch recruitment poster for the German Waffen SS, 1942. More than 200,000 Europeans joined during the war.

The German New Order

Atlantic Ocean
NORWAY
SWEDEN
FINLAND (pro-Axis state)
Leningrad
Moscow
UNION OF SOVIET SOCIALIST REPUBLICS
North Sea
UNITED KINGDOM
DENMARK
REICHSKOMMISSARIAT OSTLAND
IRELAND
NETH.
London
Minsk
furthest Axis advance into USSR
Berlin
Warsaw
GERMAN EMPIRE
Alsace-Lorraine absorbed into Germany
BELGIUM
Paris
GENERAL GOVERNMENT
Kiev
Stalingrad
FRANCE
BOHEMIA & MORAVIA
REICHSKOMMISSARIAT UKRAINE
SLOVAKIA
SWITZ.
HUNGARY
VICHY FRANCE Occupied by Germany, Nov. 1942
BANAT
ROMANIA
Transnistria to Romania, 1941
CROATIA
Italian occupation, 1940–43
SERBIA
Black Sea
SPAIN
ITALY
MONTENEGRO
BULGARIA
Istanbul
PORTUGAL
Rome
former Yugoslavia jointly occupied
ALBANIA
TURKEY
Sardinia
Mediterranean Sea
GREECE
Sicily
ALGERIA (Vichy France)
Malta
Crete
Cyprus
SYRIA (Vichy France until 1941)

	German Empire		Italian Occupied		Neutral
	German Occupied		Axis Satellites		

EUROPE'S SS

All over German-occupied and allied Europe, propaganda recruitment campaigns were launched to encourage local volunteers for the Armed SS (*Waffen-SS*), the military wing of the Nazi Party's elite SS organization. By the end of the war, an estimated 152,000 Europeans from western and northern Europe had joined the *Waffen-SS*, including 800 from neutral Switzerland. Among Germany's allies in eastern Europe, Hungary supplied 22,000 volunteers, Romania 54,000, Bulgaria 21,000. Many were attracted by the idea of fighting on what appeared to be the winning side, but hatred of communism or hostility to the Jews also played a part.

Uw plaats is nog vrij
IN DE WAFFEN SS

European economic system based on a common currency, the German mark, with Berlin and Vienna as the twin commercial and financial centres of the continent. The German authorities and German businesses took over the major industries of much of the conquered area. Most prominent was the giant German holding company the *Reichswerke* "Hermann Göring", which bought up or expropriated the heavy industry of Austria, Czechoslovakia, Poland and the Soviet Union. At its height, the organization had a workforce of more than one million and assets four times larger than those of any other German business. Over the course of the war, European states contributed around one-third of the cost of the German war effort; seven million foreign workers were labouring in Germany by the end of 1944, while an estimated 20 million others worked on German orders in the occupied and allied lands.

The Germans extended their racial policies over the whole area. Blond-haired and blue-eyed children were taken from

MAJOR VIDKUN QUISLING (1887–1945)

Major Vidkun Quisling (whose real name was Abraham Jonsson) was the founder of the Norwegian fascist movement, the National Union Party. Although the movement had only limited support he launched a coup in Oslo on the day the Germans invaded and was then made prime minister by the German authorities. His ambitions were regarded cautiously by the German Commissioner for Norway, Josef Terboven, but on 1 February 1942 he was finally made Minister-President of Norway and embarked on a programme to make Norway conform to the fascist model. He was deeply hated by many Norwegians and at the end of the war was tried and executed as a traitor. His name has become a synonym for collaboration with the enemy.

LEFT A driver and "death cart" in the Warsaw Ghetto, August 1942. From 1940 onwards Jews were herded into ghettos and transit camps. In the spring of 1942 a programme of mass extermination began of all the Jews in New Order Europe.

ABOVE A French Anti-Semitic poster of 1942 announcing 'Enough'. The Vichy regime was one of many New Order governments to encourage anti-Jewish policies based on pre-existing prejudices.

their families and placed with foster-parents in Germany, or sent to one of the special children's homes set up to produce model "Aryan" children. The Jewish population of Europe was rounded up and deported to the extermination centres in the east or murdered by security men and soldiers. At the same time, German race officials scoured the occupied areas of the east looking for people of German ethnic origin and shipped over 600,000 of them back to the Reich. A racial hierarchy was imposed which saw northern Europeans as honorary racial "Aryans", but placed the Latin races and the Slav races lower down the racial scale. By the end of the war, around five million Europeans had been screened for their racial profile and in many cases recommended for "Germanization".

The New Order represented an extraordinary ambition. German victory would have produced a radically different Europe from the one that emerged in 1945. Although it has sometimes been likened to an early experiment in European union, German domination rested on military power, economic exploitation and a murderous racial policy. When Germany collapsed in 1945, the New Order disappeared without a trace.

RIGHT A hanging in German-occupied Yugoslavia. Thousands of Europeans were murdered by the German occupiers for acts of sabotage and resistance. Thousands more disappeared into concentration camps under the notorious "Night and Fog" Decree.

THE BATTLE OF BRITAIN

10 JULY 1940
German air force begins attacks on Channel convoys.

17 JULY 1940
Britain closes the Burma Road supply route to appease Japanese.

3 AUGUST 1940
Italian armies invade British Somaliland.

13 AUGUST 1940
"Eagle Day" launches the German attack of airfields.

25/26 AUGUST 1940
The RAF bombs Berlin.

27 AUGUST 1940
US Congress approves conscription by a majority of one vote.

2 SEPTEMBER 1940
"Destroyers for bases" deal signed with the US.

4 SEPTEMBER 1940
Hitler announces switch to bombing cities.

7 SEPTEMBER 1940
The German Blitz on Britain begins.

15 SEPTEMBER 1940
Major German attack on London with high civilian casualties.

ABOVE Shoulder badges of British Commonwealth and Empire pilots that fought in the Battle of Britain. By September 1940 Fighter Command had become a multinational force.

O n 18 June 1940, Winston Churchill told the House of Commons that "the Battle of France is over. I expect the battle of Britain is about to begin". Over the following four months, the German air force attempted to destroy the RAF and undermine British military capability to an extent that would make the German invasion of southern England a possibility. It was the aerial duel fought out over the southern counties of Britain that became the Battle of Britain.

There were no clear dates for when the battle started and ended, but after it was over, an official Air Ministry pamphlet dated it from 8 August, when the air assault began to intensify and ended it on 31 October, when air attacks by German fighters petered out. German attacks began on 5–6 June, before the final defeat of France, and continued intermittently over June and July. These were probing attacks designed to lure Britain's RAF Fighter Command into combat and to destroy ports and communications. Only in August did the German air force commander-in-chief Hermann Göring order an intensified campaign following Hitler's directive, issued on 1 August, "to overpower the English air force". Air Fleet 2 under the command of General Albert Kesselring and Air Fleet 3 commanded by General Hugo Sperrle began a sustained attack on the airfields, supply depots and radar stations in southern England. By mid-August, Göring was confident that Fighter Command

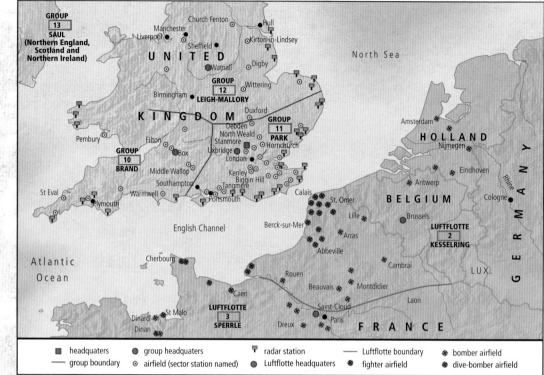

■ headquaters	● group headquaters	📍 radar station
— group boundary	⊙ airfield (sector station named)	📍 Luftflotte headquaters

— Luftflotte boundary
● Luftflotte headquaters
✦ bomber airfield
✦ fighter airfield
✦ dive-bomber airfield

BELOW When the approach of enemy 'planes was reported, RAF squadrons were "scrambled" to intercept them. Here pilots of No.19 Squadron, RAF based at Fowlmere in Cambridgeshire, are delivered by lorry to their waiting aircraft at the height of the battle.

ABOVE The badge awarded to Czechoslovak pilots on qualification. Squadrons 310 and 312 were Czech fighter squadrons although the top scoring Czech Battle of Britain Ace, Sergeant Josef Frantisek, flew with Polish Squadron 303. He gained 17 "victories" in 28 days.

ABOVE The Supermarine Spitfire became the symbol of Britain's struggle in the air. Here a group of Mark 1A Spitfires from No. 610 Squadron, based at Biggin Hill in Kent fly in formation, July 1940.

AIR VICE MARSHAL SIR KEITH PARK (1892-1975)

One of the key roles during the Battle of Britain was played by the New Zealand airman Air Vice-Marshal Keith Park who commanded No. 11 Group, Fighter Command, in south-eastern England. An artillery officer in the Great War, he was wounded at the Battle of the Somme and subsequently joined the Royal Flying Corps. After 1918, he became a career RAF officer and in 1940 was posted to command No. 11 Group. His squadrons organized the air defence of the Dunkirk pocket, and then took the brunt of the German attack in the autumn of 1940. Park was a shrewd tactician who watched German operations carefully and adjusted the tactics of his own force to maximize the damage done to incoming German aircraft. His flexibility and tactical imagination were vital qualities in winning the air battle. He was later posted as air officer commanding Malta in 1942, where he organized the air defence of the island, and ended up as Allied air commander, South-East Asia in 1945.

ABOVE A still from the camera-gun film of a Supermarine Spitfire Mark I as it attacks a formation of Heinkel He 111 bombers which have just bombed the Supermarine aircraft factory at Woolston, Southampton, 26 September 1940.

REICH MARSHAL HERMANN GÖRING (1893-1946)

The commander-in-chief of the German air force, Hermann Göring, was a well-known pilot from the First World War who briefly commanded the famous Richthofen Squadron following the death of the "Red Baron". He became an enthusiastic supporter of Hitler's National Socialist Party in the early 1920s and head of the Party's paramilitary SA until he was forced to flee abroad after the failed Hitler Putsch of 1923. After his return he became a Party deputy in the German Reichstag of 1928, and became one of Hitler's right-hand men. In 1935, he was made commander of the newly created air force, and in 1940 promised Hitler that he would smash the RAF prior to a German invasion of Britain. His failure was the first major reverse for German forces and contributed to his political decline. In 1945, he was put on trial as a war criminal and on the night before his planned execution, 15 October 1946, he committed suicide.

was on its knees and he ordered a final blow. The main attack was scheduled for Eagle Day (*Adlertag*) on 13 August, though poor weather on that day blunted the full scale of the assault. Between 12 August and 6 September, there were 53 main attacks on airfields, all but two of them against the bases of No 11 Group led by Air Vice-Marshal Keith Park. The raids against radar stations were not sustained and only three of Park's airfields were put out of action and then only temporarily.

The German side assumed that the RAF was close to extinction, but the reality was very different. On 23 August, Fighter Command had an operational strength of 672 Spitfire and Hurricane fighters; by early September the figure was 738, more than at the start of the battle. Fighter Command losses totalled 444 aircraft between 6 August and 2 September; German losses were over 900 for the whole month, including bomber aircraft. Great attention had been paid by the Commander-in-Chief of Fighter Command, Air Marshal Hugh Dowding, to conserving RAF strength, training pilots and building reserves. Though hard-pressed in August and September, Fighter Command never came close to collapse. As the battle went on, it was the German air force that suffered levels of loss of aircraft and pilots that became in the end impossible to sustain. When Winston Churchill famously told the House of Commons on 20 August that "never in the field of human conflict was so much owed by so many to so few," he disguised the reality of a rising graph of British aircraft and pilot supply.

At the beginning of September, there came a sudden change in German tactics. The attack on the RAF was much

ABOVE Interior of the Sector "G" Operations Room at the RAF base at Duxford, Cambridgeshire, September 1940. The callsigns of the sqadrons operating out of Duxford are visible on the wall behind the operator third from left. On the extreme right are the radio operators in direct contact with the aircraft.

reduced and German bomber fleets, escorted by large numbers of Messerschmitt Me109 fighters, were directed to attack London and other urban centres. Although the switch is often attributed to Hitler's desire to get revenge for RAF attacks on Berlin on the night of 25/26 August, it had already been planned on the assumption that Fighter Command had been destroyed. On 2 September, Göring ordered phase two of the attack, to destroy Britain's military and economic capability and demoralize the population prior to invasion. Hitler's speech on 4 September promising revenge was a propaganda stunt designed to make it look as if Britain had started the bombing. The switch in emphasis suited Fighter Command. It was now possible to attack the bombers as they approached London in large numbers and on their return, while German fighters were tied to protecting the slower and more vulnerable bombers and so less free to combat British fighters. In the first week of attacks, the German air force lost 298 aircraft, with 60 losses on 15 September, the day that has been celebrated ever since as Battle of Britain Day. Thanks to the survival of the radar chain, there was always advance warning of attack. British tactics were designed to maximize the damage to the attacking force and by the end of September it was clear to German commanders that they could not maintain the levels of attrition they were suffering. At the cost of only 443 pilots, Fighter Command inflicted losses of 1,733 aircraft on the German air force for the loss of 915 of their own. The conflict has gone down in British history alongside the defeat of the Spanish Armada in 1588 as one of the legendary moments in Britain's military past.

THE EAST AFRICAN CAMPAIGNS

When Italy declared war on Britain on 10 June 1940, Mussolini hoped to be able to use the opportunity presented by Britain's preoccupation in Europe to mop up British territory in North and East Africa and create an enlarged Italian empire. There were 326,000 Italian troops in Abyssinia in June 1940, 200,000 of them colonial troops (*askari*), supported by 244 mostly obsolete aircraft and 866 artillery pieces. They confronted a diffuse British Empire force, composed mainly of African recruits, numbering 40,000 supported by 100 mainly antique aeroplanes. In the first days of the British–Italian war, Italian forces occupied a number of towns on the border with Sudan and Kenya, and a force of 25,000 entered British Somaliland, compelling an evacuation of British Empire troops by 19 August to the British territory of Aden, on the Arabian coastline.

At this point, the Italian armies halted, giving the British commanders time to build up reinforcements from India, Nigeria, the Gold Coast (Ghana) and South Africa, including an invaluable squadron of South African Hurricane fighters, the most modern aircraft in the theatre. By the end of the year, there were 9,000 troops in Sudan, but in Kenya, which was to be the base for an invasion of Italian East Africa, General Alan Cunningham had 77,000 men, including 6,000 Europeans, supported by six South African air force squadrons. By November 1940, the British had cracked the Italians' codes and could read their plans and deployments almost immediately. In October, a force under the command of Brigadier William Slim began the campaigns with attacks on the Sudanese towns of Kassala and Gallabat, capturing the latter on 6 November. The full offensive was launched on 19 January by Lieutenant General William Platt, Commander-in-Chief Sudan, against northern Abyssinia, supported by two Indian divisions and a special unit known as Gideon Force made up of Abyssinian resistance fighters

ABOVE Bombs exploding among hangars and buildings of the Italian base at Asmara during a raid by five RAF Vickers Wellesley bombers, 20 July 1940.

LEFT Soldiers of the King's African Rifles during the British advance into Italian Somaliland, 13 February 1941. African troops from British Empire territories in both East and West Africa were mobilized for the campaign.

BELOW Italian Arab cavalry during the Italian capture of British Somaliland shortly before the withdrawal of British Commonwealth forces to Aden, 9 August 1940.

led by Major Orde Wingate, who, like Slim, was to become a famous name in the later campaign in Burma. After the heaviest fighting of the campaign in the mountainous region around Keren – where Italian forces held out for 53 days – Platt's army broke through, reaching the Eritrean coast at Massawa by 8 April.

THE DUKE OF AOSTA (1898–1942)

A cousin of the King of Italy, Victor Emmanuel III, Prince Amedeo Umberto of Savoy, the Third Duke of Aosta, was Governor-General and Commander-in-Chief of Italian East Africa from 1937 until its conquest by British Empire forces in 1941. A product of Eton and Oxford who enjoyed fox-hunting and spoke English with an impeccable upper-class accent, Prince Amedeo became an artillery officer during the First World War. In the 1920s, he joined the Italian air force and took part in the pacification of the Senussi tribesmen in the Italian colony of Libya. He assumed the title of Duke of Aosta in 1931 on the death of his father, a famous First World War general, and in 1937 took over Italy's new Ethiopian empire. He commanded all Italian forces in the war in East Africa, but recognized the limitations of what could be done. He withdrew with some of his troops to a mountain fortress at Amba Alagi where he surrendered on 18 May 1941. He died of tuberculosis in a British POW camp in Kenya in 1942.

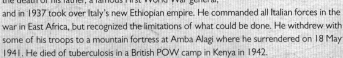

GENERAL ALAN CUNNINGHAM (1887–1983)

General Cunningham was Commander-in-Chief of Empire Forces in the East African colony of Kenya when war broke out with Italy. The younger brother of the British fleet commander Admiral Andrew Cunningham, he became briefly famous for leading his troops on a remarkable 2,300-km (1,700-mile) trek into Somaliland and Abyssinia in less than eight weeks of successful campaigning, during which he took 50,000 prisoners and suffered only 500 casualties. He was posted to North Africa in August 1941 to command the newly formed Eighth Army, but following the tough battles in Operation Crusader in November 1941, and suffering from ill health, he was sacked and spent the rest of the war in home commands. He was the Commander-in-Chief in Palestine during the three years before the creation of Israel in 1948.

LEFT Heavily armed with captured Italian weapons, Ethiopians gather in Addis Ababa to hear the proclamation announcing the return of the Emperor Haile Selassie, who entered his capital again on 5 May 1941.

BELOW Men of the King's African Rifles at the Wolchefit pass collecting surrendered arms from Italian soldiers after the end of one pocket of remaining Italian resistance in Ethiopia, 28 September 1941. Small groups of Italian soldiers continued fighting until November.

In the south, General Cunningham launched a two-pronged attack from Kenya. The frontier town of Moyale was recaptured on 18 February by a small force designed to stimulate an Abyssinian revolt. The bulk of British Empire forces attacked on 11 February along the African coastline into Italian Somaliland. Although greatly outnumbered, the attack was a remarkable success. Mogadishu was captured on 25 February by the 23rd (Nigerian) Brigade, and the possession of the port allowed the 11th (East African) Division to link up with the move northwards into Abyssinia, amalgamating units from very different parts of Britain's African empire into a single fighting force. The inland city of Harar was captured in late March and Cunningham's force, joined by a seaborne invasion force from Aden which had landed on the coast on 25 February, reached the capital Addis Ababa on 6 April; there, following his triumphal entry on 5 May, the Emperor Haile Selassie was restored to the throne he had lost five years before. There remained large pockets of Italian forces in the mountainous regions of the country and these were gradually forced to capitulate by November 1941. The Italian commander, the Duke of Aosta,

retreated to the region around the northern mountain city of Amba Alagi, where, short of weapons and supplies and with no hope of reinforcement, he surrendered on 19 May.

The British Empire victory was emphatic. For some 3,100 casualties killed and wounded, Allied forces captured 420,000 enemy troops and killed an estimated 12,000. Italian forces had suffered many disadvantages, for not only were their secret intelligence codes broken, but British naval power made it impossible to send supplies or reinforcements. Italian equipment was old-fashioned or ineffective: many artillery shells were left over from 1918 and failed to detonate. For an area almost as large as Western Europe, the Italians had only 6,200 vehicles, little fuel and 50,000 mules and horses. Above all, Italian forces were fighting for a cause for which they had little stomach against an enemy with higher mobility, more effective supply routes and complete dominance at sea and in the air. For British commanders, this was a vital area to secure for it prevented any threat to the Suez Canal area from the south and ensured that the long route to the Far East would not be threatened by any enemy presence in eastern Africa.

RIGHT Aircrew of No.47 Squadron RAF change into flying suits outside their huts in Kassala, Sudan, in spring 1941 during the attack on Italian-held Ethiopia.

OPERATION "SEALION"

27 JUNE 1940
German air force proposes landing in England.

16 JULY 1940
Hitler issues "Sealion" directive.

9 AUGUST 1940
British garrison pulled out of Shanghai for use on other fronts.

13 SEPTEMBER 1940
Italian army enters Egypt.

7 OCTOBER 1940
German forces occupy Romania to protect oil interests.

12 OCTOBER 1940
Hitler postpones "Sealion" indefinitely.

The defeat of France and the expulsion of British forces from mainland Europe presented Hitler with a quite unexpected opportunity. German leaders assumed that Britain would see sense and find a way to end a conflict that could no longer be won. "We are very close to the end of the war," Joseph Goebbels, Hitler's Propaganda Minister, told his staff on 23 June. Hitler preferred a political solution and thought the idea of an invasion of Britain "very hazardous", but he decided in early July to explore both possibilities. On 7 July, the armed forces were instructed to begin preliminary planning for a possible invasion and on 16 July Hitler finally approved War Directive 16 for Operation "Sealion", the invasion of the south-eastern coast of England. This was to be a last resort if a political solution could not be found. On 19 July, Hitler made a peace offer in the German Reichstag. The speech was a celebration of German victory and Hitler made it clear that he would discuss terms "as a conqueror", but he also assured the British that he had no desire to destroy the British Empire. If war continued it would, Hitler concluded, be Britain's choice.

In Britain there had been talk since late May in some political circles of reaching a compromise peace but Churchill was irrevocably committed to fighting on and that became the official position. Hitler's speech was almost disregarded, evoking a brief rebuttal by Lord Halifax, the Foreign Secretary, on 22 July. German leaders found the British position hard to understand, but on 23 July the German press were officially informed by the government that the war would continue. At Hitler's headquarters, Operation "Sealion" now became a serious option, though it soon became clear that there were many barriers to its operational feasibility. The German navy, whose commander-in-chief, Grand Admiral Raeder, had been

BELOW Civil defence forces digging tank traps on a golf course in 1940.

ABOVE A fighting column from the South Wales Borderers in a training exercise in Bootle, Liverpool, 16 August 1940. All over the country soldiers prepared for the threatened German invasion.

LEFT The English novelist Virginia Woolf and her husband Leonard planned to commit suicide with their car exhaust if the Germans landed. Virginia killed herself on 28 March 1941 during an attack of depression.

FIELD-MARSHAL EDMUND IRONSIDE (1880–1959)

William Edmund Ironside was a soldier of the old school who served in every conflict in which British forces fought from the Boer War onwards, including the ill-fated British intervention in the Russian Civil War at Archangel in 1918–19. Close to retirement by the 1930s, he was chosen at the outbreak of the Second World War to succeed Gort as Chief of the Imperial General Staff, a role in which he tried to pressure the government to begin military action. He misjudged Polish strength in 1939 and German strength in 1940 and was replaced at the height of the Battle of France on 27 May. He was appointed to command the Home Forces for the expected invasion of England but he had a poor professional relationship with Churchill and was finally retired for good in the midst of making extensive preparations to reform the home army and to repel the expected invasion.

LEFT Royal Artillery gun crews run to man a 9.2inch- (23.5cm) gun during a practice shoot at Culver Point Battery, Isle of White, 24 August 1940.

among the first to suggest invasion to Hitler in June, remained hesitant over recommending a hazardous cross-Channel operation against British air power and the Royal Navy. The destruction of the RAF was a priority without which invasion was regarded as too risky.

The tentative date set for a landing was 15 September. The invasion plan was for six divisions from the 9th and 16th armies to invade on a broad front from Hythe in Kent to Newhaven and Rottingdean on the Sussex coast. The armies would then move rapidly inland, supported by the German air force, to reach a preliminary line running from Gravesend to Portsmouth, and after capturing London to a second line between the Essex coast and the Severn Estuary. Barges and small boats were gathered from all over occupied Europe to ports along the French, Belgian and Dutch coasts and intensive training in beach assault undertaken over the summer. Bomber Command kept up a relentless attack on the invasion ports which added to the many difficulties of organizing a large-scale maritime invasion, something that the German armed forces had done only against light resistance in Norway, and then at great cost in shipping losses. On 30 August, with no clear sign that the Royal Air Force had been defeated, the invasion date was switched to 20 September. In Britain expectation of invasion marked the whole of September. On 7 September, the codeword "Cromwell" was issued to all units to be on full alert. The weekend of 14–15 September was widely regarded as the most likely date and as troops moved into position along the coast they were ordered to sleep with their boots on.

When nothing happened, the full alert was dropped, to be reinstated on 22 September. Only in late October was the signal "invasion improbable" sent out to units.

On the German side, there were mixed feelings about the risk of invasion. Defeat would not have been disastrous but would have been politically unfortunate. At a meeting on 14 September, with British forces at full alert and the RAF undefeated, Hitler announced that although preparations were complete, the invasion of Britain was too risky. He proposed a review two days later for possible landings on 27 September or 8 October, but the situation had not improved. On 19 September, the preparations were ordered to be scaled down and the invasion shipping was dispersed from the vulnerable North Sea ports. On 12 October, Hitler finally ordered "Sealion" to be dismantled. Fear of the Royal Navy and the failure to dent British air power rendered invasion impossible. Hitler ordered a sustained air attack on British cities in case the British government could be terrorized into surrender.

THE ROYAL NAVY AT SCAPA FLOW

The Royal Navy's major base in the bleak anchorage at Scapa Flow in the Orkney Islands, off the north Scottish coast, was a permanent threat to any German invasion plans. The base was attacked on 14 October 1939 by a German submarine that managed to evade the defences. The battleship HMS *Royal Oak* was sunk with the loss of 833 lives. After this efforts were made to make the base more secure and the attacks were not repeated. Scapa Flow was out of effective range of German bomber and dive-bomber aircraft, which made it an ideal area to concentrate the main units of the fleet. During the invasion crisis the Royal Navy was prepared for large-scale intervention, a fact that encouraged Admiral Raeder to tell Hitler on 14 September 1940 that the risk was too great to undertake "Sealion".

BELOW LEFT German infantry and marines preparing for Operation "Sealion" at the French port of St Malo, September 1940.

BELOW Sappers of 211 Field Park Company, Royal Engineers, make "Molotov cocktails" from beer bottles at a base in Yorkshire, to be used for the expected German invasion.

ABOVE General Field Marshal Gerd von Rundstedt was Commander-in-Chief West for the planned invasion of England. He commanded army groups in the invasion of Poland and France and later opposed the Allied landings in Normandy.

THE GERMAN BLITZ ON BRITAIN

22/23 AUGUST 1940
First bombs fall of central London.

28 AUGUST 1940
Liverpool suffers serious attack.

7 SEPTEMBER 1940
First major raid on London.

21 SEPTEMBER 1940
Permission given for Londoners to shelter in the Underground system.

16 NOVEMBER 1940
RAF bombers attack the German city of Hamburg.

29/30 DECEMBER 1940
Bombers destroy large part of the City of London.

6 FEBRUARY 1941
Hitler orders attacks on ports.

20 FEBRUARY 1941
British and German forces clash for the first time in desert war.

10/11 MAY 1941
1,400 killed in final large raid on London.

The heavy bombing of British cities began with an attack on London on 7 September 1940. Bombing had been conducted intermittently against ports and other military and economic installations since June. In July, 258 civilians had been killed; in August 1,075. The first attacks on the London area began on 18/19 August and on central London on the night of 22/23 August. A heavy attack took place on Liverpool on 28/29 August. The attack on 7 September, however, was the first to be carried out in response to Hitler's orders issued on 5 September to destroy the industrial, military and supply systems of the capital. The 350 German bombers who attacked the docks in east London two days later initiated what became known in Britain as "the Blitz".

The German plan was to degrade Britain's capacity to wage war and to undermine the war-willingness of the population, but once the invasion plans were suspended in mid-September, the attacks assumed a more directly political purpose. German leaders hoped that the attacks on cities would force Britain to negotiate and make invasion unnecessary, and on 16 September Göring ordered the new phase of city bombings to begin in earnest. Up to 5 October, there were 35 major air assaults, 18 of them against London, and all conducted in daylight. Unsupportable loss rates forced the German air force to switch to night bombing, and from early October until 16 May 1941, German aircraft attacked a wide range of major cities on

ABOVE The London Fire Brigade at Eastcheap in the City of London. By the end of 1940 around 20,000 incendiary bombs had been dropped on the capital.

GENERAL HANS JESCHONNEK (1899–1943)

Hans Jeschonnek was appointed Chief of the Air Force Staff by Hermann Göring on 1 February 1939 after a meteoric rise through the fledgling German air force. He had joined the German army aged 15 at the outbreak of the First World War and rose to be a lieutenant by 1917, when he joined the air service. He then returned to army duties and joined the German air force in September 1933 when it was still secret. He became Operations Chief in February 1938 and a year later Chief of Staff. He favoured tactical air power in support of the army, but argued for terror attacks against British cities in September 1940 following failure in the Battle of Britain. Struggling to keep the bombers at bay and subject to growing criticism, Jeschonnek finally committed suicide on 18 August 1943 at Hitler's headquarters in East Prussia after the heavy bombing raid on the rocket research station at Peenemünde.

BELOW Londoners shelter in Aldwych underground station, 8 October 1940, one of 79 stations used as deep shelters. Several were hit during the Blitz causing heavy casualties.

Glasgow 1329
Belfast 440
Newcastle 152
Manchester 578
Hull 593
Liverpool 1957
Sheffield 355
Nottingham 137
Birmingham 1852
Coventry 818
Cardiff 115
Bristol 919
Southampton 647
Portsmouth 687
London 18,000 (71 major raids)
Plymouth 1228

UNITED KINGDOM
IRELAND
North Sea
Hamburg
Bremen
Amsterdam
Soesterberg
Nijmegen
Gilze-Rijen
Eindhoven
Antwerp
Calais
St. Omer
BELGIUM
Wissant
Brussels
Berck-sur-Mer
Lille
Arques
Cologne
Tramecourt
Arras
Abbeville
Crécy-en-Ponthieu
Cambrai
Cherbourg
Rosières-en-Santerre
Montdidier
LUX.
Rouen
Beauvais
Clermont
Laon
Caen
Evereux
FRANCE
Dinard
St Malo
St. Andre-de-l'Eure
Paris
Villacoublay
Dreux
Orly

Atlantic Ocean
English Channel
Thames
Weser
Rhine
Frankfurt
GERMANY

Legend	
1–5 major air raids	more than 10 major air raids
6–10 major air raids	647 bomb tonnage dropped per city
	Luftwaffe bomber base

nights when the weather conditions permitted. The air units were instructed to attack specific targets and they were helped in this by a system of radio navigation beams known as *Knickebein* which worked effectively until British scientists found ways to jam the German beams during November and December 1940. During the campaign German aircraft also used navigation systems known as *X-Gerät* and *Y-Gerät* but these too became subject to increasingly effective jamming.

The Blitz was concentrated on London, which was attacked for 57 days in a row between 7 September and 2 November and then regularly until 10 May. The most famous day of the Blitz was the night of 29 December when a large part of the City of London was destroyed by 136 German bombers. It was on that night that the symbolic photograph was taken of St Paul's Cathedral rising above the flames and smoke. The Blitz was also directed at most British ports and industrial centres, from Belfast in Northern Ireland, to Glasgow in Scotland and, to Plymouth (which was heavily bombed between 21 and 23 April 1941), Southampton and Portsmouth in the south. The raid that provoked the widest publicity was that on Coventry on the night of 14/15 November 1940 which killed 554 people. In the major raids on London, 18,800 tons of bombs were dropped; in major

ABOVE A panorama of the city of Liverpool after heavy bombing raids in 1940. The River Mersey is visible to the left of the photograph, the Liver Building in the centre.

BELOW A wrecked bus standing in the ruins of Coventry, heavily bombed on the night of 14/15 November 1940. The city became a symbol for the horror of the Blitz and later established close links with the German city of Dresden, destroyed in February 1945.

attacks against other cities the total was 11,800 tons. The bombing killed 43,000 people and destroyed or damaged one million houses, but did little serious or long-term damage to the British economy or military effort.

The British response focused on both active and passive defence. By May 1941, there were 16 squadrons of night fighters which became more effective as the battle wore on but found it difficult to locate the bombers without sophisticated detection devices. There were 1,785 heavy and light anti-aircraft guns in the summer of 1940, and over 4,500 searchlights, though these too were of limited effectiveness. A high proportion of German losses during the Blitz came from accidents to crews flying long distances in poor weather conditions. The passive defences were organized country-wide by more than two million volunteers of the Air Raid Precautions organization, including evacuation and the distribution of gas masks.

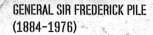

GENERAL SIR FREDERICK PILE (1884–1976)

A career artillery officer who rose to the rank of major in the First World War, Frederick Pile was a gifted organizer and a keen modernizer. He played an important part at the War Office between 1928 and 1932 in planning the mechanization of the armed forces. After a brief period in Egypt, he returned in 1937 to command the London 1st Anti-Aircraft Division. On 28 July 1939, he was appointed commander of the Anti-Aircraft Command, a post that he filled throughout the war, the only senior commander to do so in the British army. He reorganized Britain's anti-aircraft defences, expanded the supply of guns and shells and when labour shortages took men away, he recruited 74,000 women into the anti-aircraft ranks. After the war he took up a business career.

RIGHT General Sir Frederick Pile (right) watches the firing of Britain's "rocket gun" on the South West Coast, 1944.

By 1940, around 2.5 million cheap Anderson bomb shelters – named after Sir John Anderson, responsible for Civil Defence measures – had been produced for householders and in every city deep concrete bunkers were constructed or cellars and underground facilities converted. Nevertheless, civilian casualties were high and in many of the most heavily attacked cities there was an exodus from the threatened area and evidence of demoralization and rising crime levels. The government made many concessions, which included the use of parts of the London Underground network as improvised air-raid shelters, and domestic morale stiffened as the Blitz continued. When it finally ended in May 1941, Britain was more, rather than less, determined to continue to fight.

THE TRIPARTITE PACT

23 NOVEMBER 1936
Romania signs the Tripartite Pact.

22 SEPTEMBER 1940
Japanese forces begin occupation of northern Indo-China.

25 SEPTEMBER 1940
American intelligence cracks the Japanese "Purple" diplomatic code.

29 SEPTEMBER 1940
Luxembourg is incorporated into the Greater German Reich.

5 NOVEMBER 1940
Roosevelt elected for an unprecedented third term as US President.

25 NOVEMBER 1940
Japan and Germany sign the Anti-Comintern Pact.

7 JANUARY 1941
Japanese plan Operation "Z" for an attack on Britian and the United States.

1 MARCH 1941
Bulgaria joins the Tripartite Pact.

15 JUNE 1941
Croatia accedes to the Tripartite Pact.

ADMIRAL MIKLÓS HORTHY DE NAGYBÁNA (1868–1957)

An admiral in the Austro-Hungarian navy during the First World War, Horthy led the Hungarian and Romanian forces in 1919 that toppled the brief Communist regime in Hungary of Bela Kun. Horthy had himself declared "Regent" of Hungary in January 1920 in place of the exiled Habsburgs and imposed an authoritarian rule on the country which ended only on 17 October 1944, when he was deposed by the intervention of the German army and imprisoned in Germany. Never a real enthusiast for close links with Hitler, he chose the German alliance in 1940 out of his fear of communism.

Before the outbreak of war in 1939, Germany, Japan and Italy were united by the Anti-Comintern Pact, signed between Japan and Germany in November 1936, and joined a year later by Italy. They shared not only common hostility to communism but also a mutual commitment to revising the existing international system in their favour. The German–Soviet Pact of August 1939 placed a severe strain on relations between the three states, but a year later, following Italy's declaration of war on the Allies on 10 June 1940, an agreement was negotiated between the three states which cemented the "Axis" and linked all three in a common cause. The treaty was negotiated in Tokyo but signed in

ABOVE An informal discussion during the ceremonies surrounding the signing of the Tripartite Pact. Seated left to right are the Japanese Ambassador, Saburo Kurusu, the Italian foreign minister Count Galeazzo Ciano, Joachim von Ribbentrop and the soon to be Spanish foreign minister, Serrano Suner.

BELOW LEFT Japanese, German and Italian diplomats toast the signing of the Pact on 27 September 1940 at a reception in Tokyo. In the centre is the army minister General Hideki Tojo who was a strong advocate of the Pact.

BELOW The formal signing of the Pact in Berlin, 27 September 1940 with Adolf Hitler, Count Ciano and Saburo Kurusu all seated. The Pact sealed the creation of the later wartime Axis.

Berlin on 27 September 1940. The Tripartite Pact, as it was called, confirmed that Europe was the sphere for a New Order created by Germany and Italy, while Japan was free to construct a New Order in eastern Asia. All three pledged to come to the aid of the others if they were attacked by a third party not already at war. This clause was inserted as a threat to the United States and was not intended to apply to relations with the Soviet Union. Japan hoped to be able

to use the Pact as a bargaining counter with America, but it only served to confirm the Western view that the three states were intent on a dangerous transformation of the world order.

The Pact was supposed to lead to closer collaboration and some effort was made to send scarce raw materials from Asia to Europe and military equipment and industrial goods back to Japan. This proved a difficult trade and the so-called "Yanagi missions" which carried the military goods between Japan and Europe involved dangerous and lengthy voyages. Japan hoped to get advanced German scientific secrets but some of the most important, such as the process for turning coal into fuel oil, were sent only in the last months of the war. There was almost no military or strategic collaboration and no high-level staff committees like the Western Combined Chiefs of Staff. Hitler was content to allow Mussolini to expand in the Mediterranean and Africa and for Japan to tie down the British and Americans in the Far East, but on most major strategic or military decisions the three states acted independently.

The Pact was extended over the following months to include German allies in Europe. Hungary joined on 20 November 1940 and Romania and Slovakia, already closely tied to Germany by trade and military agreements, signed on 23 and 24 November respectively. German negotiators held out the possibility to the Soviet Union of joining the Pact as one of Europe's revisionist states and when Molotov visited Berlin on 12 November 1940, there were half-hearted discussions about what price the Soviet Union wanted for continued collaboration. When Molotov indicated that the Soviet side sought control of the Turkish Straits and of bases in Bulgaria, and a possible free hand in Iran, the

German side was non-committal. Molotov returned to Moscow and shortly afterwards Hitler confirmed his plans, already well-advanced, for an invasion of the Soviet Union in the late spring of 1941. Hitler realized that there was no way that the Soviet Union could easily be accommodated in the three-way division of the world. Worried by the Soviet threat, Bulgaria joined the Pact on 1 March 1941. Yugoslavia, tied like Romania to German trade agreements, finally signed on 25 March the same year, but two days later the regime of Regent Prince Paul was overthrown by the army, and the young King Peter was installed on the throne.

The effort to build the European and Asian New Orders began in earnest in 1941 with the invasion of the Soviet Union by Germany and its allies in June and the Japanese decision to fight the United States in December. Although Japan attacked America and was not the victim of aggression, both Germany and Italy followed the Japanese attack with declarations of war against the United States. The three states gambled that they would win: Japan would keep America away from Europe; and Germany would keep the Soviet Union away from Japan while they all carved out new imperial regions and remodelled the political map of the world.

BELOW Romanian "Iron Guard" fascists parade through Bucharest on 6 October 1940 past the Romanian premier General Ion Antonescu. On 23 November Romania signed the Tripartite Pact and later fought with Germany against the USSR.

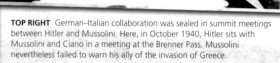

ABOVE Japanese forces advance through the Indo-Chinese port of Haiphong, 24 November 1940. The Vichy French authorities were forced to accept the stationing of Japanese troops in the French colony along the Yunnan–Haiphong railway which had been used to supply Chinese forces in their war with Japan.

TOP RIGHT German–Italian collaboration was sealed in summit meetings between Hitler and Mussolini. Here, in October 1940, Hitler sits with Mussolini and Ciano in a meeting at the Brenner Pass. Mussolini nevertheless failed to warn his ally of the invasion of Greece.

LIEUTENANT GENERAL HIROSHI OSHIMA (1886–1975)

A Japanese army officer who became a diplomat with close links to Germany. He helped to negotiate the Anti-Comintern Pact in 1936, and was Japanese ambassador in Berlin from 1938–39 and again from 1941–45. He also played an important part in arranging the Tripartite Pact in 1940. His diplomatic messages sent back to Tokyo were intercepted by Allied intelligence and became a very useful source of information on German policy. After the war he was tried in the Far East war crimes trials and sentenced to life imprisonment, but was released in 1955.

NAVAL WAR IN THE MEDITERRANEAN

9 JULY 1940
HMS *Warspite* damages Italian
battleship *Giulio Cesare*.

13 SEPTEMBER 1940
Italian forces invade Egypt.

28 OCTOBER 1940
Italian army begins invasion of
Greece from Albania.

11 NOVEMBER 1940
British aircraft destroy Italian
warships at Taranto.

20 NOVEMBER 1940
Hitler offers Mussolini German
air support in Mediterranean.

30 MARCH 1941
Cunningham's fleet returns to
Alexandria without loss after the
Battle of Matapan.

When the war opened in the Mediterranean in June 1940 the balance of forces between the *Marina Italiana* and the Royal Navy was strongly in Italy's favour. Italy needed to be able to control the sea in order to ship supplies and military resources to its North African empire, which was to be the take-off point for an attack towards the Suez Canal. The Royal Navy needed to be able to interrupt Italian supply lines while at the same time keeping open its own routes from Gibraltar in the west, via Malta and Cyprus to the naval base at Alexandria and the Suez Canal in the east.

The effectiveness of surface vessels was compromised by the use of submarines and aircraft, both of which took a heavy toll of naval and merchant shipping during the war. In the Mediterranean the traditional heavy battle fleet was exposed to permanent danger unless it could be protected by effective air cover. This lesson was driven home by two operations conducted by the British fleet in November 1940 and March 1941 which effectively neutralized any threat posed by the large Italian surface fleet. The first operation, codenamed "Judgement", was an attack by naval aircraft on the major Italian naval base at Taranto, on the southern coast of the Italian peninsula. It was the brainchild of the Mediterranean fleet carriers' commander, Rear-Admiral Lumley Lyster, who arrived in September 1940 at Alexandria aboard the carrier HMS *Illustrious*. He had already prepared a contingency plan for just such an attack when he had been a captain in the Mediterranean in 1938 and the Fleet Commander, Admiral Andrew Cunningham, responded to the revived plan enthusiastically. Originally scheduled for Trafalgar Day, 21 October, it was postponed until 11 November because of a fire on board the carrier. In the interval Mussolini launched a war against Greece, which gave a British attack a greater sense of urgency.

LEFT The most powerful Italian battleship, *Vittorio Veneto*, played a central role in the Battle of Cape Matapan.

ABOVE An aerial reconnaissance photograph of the damaged warships at Taranto on the morning after the attack by the Fleet Air Arm on the base, 12 November 1940.

ABOVE LEFT Admiral Sir Andrew Cunningham, Commander-in-Chief of the Royal Navy's Mediterranean Fleet. He was an acting Admiral until his rank was confirmed following Taranto.

ABOVE The Short Sunderland Mk 1 flying boat which spotted the Italian fleet on a flight from Scaramanga in Greece on 27–28 March 1941 and made possible the Battle of Matapan.

Of the two carriers available only *Illustrious* took part since HMS *Eagle* had been damaged by bombing. The attack was undertaken by Fairey Swordfish torpedo bombers, old bi-planes with open cockpits, but very effective in the absence of air defence. Two waves of 12 and nine aircraft were launched, two of each wave instructed to drop flares to illuminate the area and then attack the port installations. Good reconnaissance had given warning of barrage balloons and protective netting, and both were avoided. The two waves seriously damaged three battleships for the loss of two aircraft. The Italian navy immediately ordered all units to withdraw to safer harbours on the more distant

MERS-EL-KEBIR

After the French defeat in June 1940 the fate of the powerful French fleet was a source of anxiety for the British, who did not want German or Italian control of French ships. Under the terms of the Franco–German armistice the French fleet was to be immobilized under their supervision, although some French naval units were in British territory. Britain acted to pre-empt any prospect of Vichy France handing over its vessels to the Axis. On 3 July 1940 all French ships in British ports were seized, and a Royal Navy group, Force "H", under the command of Admiral James Somerville, was sent to the French naval base at Mers-el-Kébir to negotiate with the French commander for the destruction, handing over or immobilization of the French naval forces stationed there. When British requests were refused Somerville opened fire, destroying the battleship *Bretagne* and damaging a number of other ships. Vichy France broke off diplomatic relations and made a brief attack on Gibraltar in retaliation, but the threat of the French fleet was effectively removed.

western coast. The major new battleship *Vittorio Veneto* was unscathed but she was damaged in a second operation against the Italian fleet mounted four months later, in March 1941.

The second engagement, the Battle of Cape Matapan, was a direct result of the war in Greece. German pressure on Italian forces to interrupt the flow of British supplies and reinforcements brought a reluctant Italian naval high command to plan an operation around the battleship *Vittorio Veneto* to surprise and destroy an escorted British convoy to Greece. The Royal Navy could break Italian codes and were warned in advance of the Italian move. Convoys were suspended and a mixed force of carriers and battleships converged on the Italian force. The battle again highlighted the importance of air power at sea. The Italian battleship was hit by a torpedo in the second wave of attack by Albacore torpedo bombers, but was able to limp away to safety. Confused intelligence combined with Admiral Cunningham's reluctance to mix his battleships with the air pursuit of the Italian fleet resulted in losses less severe than they might have been. Nevertheless the cruiser *Pola* and a number of smaller Italian ships were sunk and the operation to interrupt British convoys defeated. The Italian fleet never again sought a fleet encounter, and the war against the Royal Navy was now conducted by aircraft and submarines. This was a lesson not lost on the Japanese navy. Taranto was a rehearsal for the later devastating attack on Pearl Harbor.

BELOW Fairey Swordfish Mk 1 torpedo bombers on a training exercise from Crail in Scotland. The slow bi-planes proved very effective against targets where there was no effective air cover.

BELOW AND LEFT The Royal Navy aircraft carrier HMS *Illustrious* in the Mediterranean. The inset photograph shows the ship under attack from the German air force. The stationing of the German aircraft in the Mediterranean in 1941 led to a sharp increase in shipping losses.

OPERATION "COMPASS": DEFEAT OF ITALY IN NORTH AFRICA

With the outbreak of war between Italy and Britain on 10 June 1940, it seemed certain that the large Italian forces concentrated in the colony of Libya – more than 236,000 – would be used to threaten the British position in Egypt where, under the terms of the 1936 Anglo-Egyptian treaty, Britain had stationed air, naval and land forces. Control of the Suez Canal was the Italians' final objective, which, if achieved, would open up supply routes to their beleaguered forces in East Africa. Not until 13 September did Mussolini order the Italian army forward. The five divisions of the Italian 10th Army, led by General Mario Berti, greatly outnumbered the two poorly equipped mobile divisions available for the defence of Egypt under the command of Major General Richard O'Connor. Italian forces advanced 95km (60 miles) into Egyptian territory, and then dug in along a defensive line from Sidi Barrani on the coast.

The Italian failure to press forward into Egypt gave British Empire forces time to consolidate and to absorb the new supplies of Matilda tanks and other equipment arriving

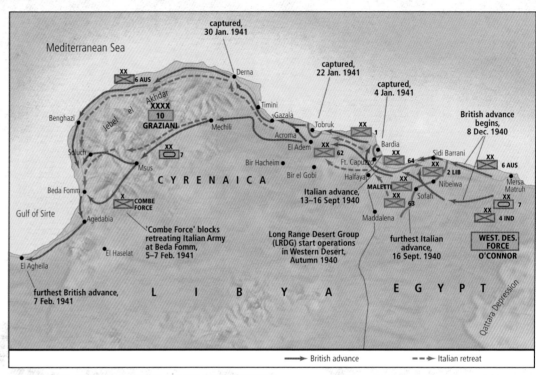

FAR LEFT General Sir Archibald Wavell (right), Commander-in-Chief Middle East, in discussion with the Commander Western Desert Forces, Lt. General Richard O'Conner, during the assault on Bardia, 4 January 1941.

LEFT Australian troops of the 7th Australian Division march towards Bardia on 6 January 1941 during the rapid advance along the Libyan coast.

BELOW Gloster Gladiator fighters of the Royal Australian Air Force flying over the mobile operations room on a landing ground near Sollum in Egypt used during Operation "Compass".

LONG RANGE DESERT GROUP (LRDG)

The Long Range Desert Group was formed in June 1940 by Captain Ralph Bagnold at the start of the North African campaign against Italy. Driving in specially converted trucks, the group penetrated behind Axis lines, provided intelligence and carried out acts of sabotage against enemy supplies and airfields. The group consisted at first of New Zealanders, but they were later joined by British and Rhodesian volunteers. They were part of a broader movement encouraged by Churchill from the summer of 1940 to set up battalion-size units of special forces – which came to be known as Commandos – to work behind enemy lines. In addition to the LRDG, there were three Commandos raised in the Middle East, as well as the Special Boat Section, all of which engaged in forms of unconventional and covert warfare. The LRDG was transferred to fight in the Dodecanese Islands in September 1943, where it suffered heavy losses before being transferred to the Italian campaign.

from Britain. With the permission of the Commander-in-Chief Middle East, General Archibald Wavell, O'Connor undertook a risky large-scale raid – codenamed Operation "Compass" – to try to push the Italian front back. On 8 December, the Indian 4th Division infiltrated the loosely-held Italian defensive line while the 7th Armoured Division skirted round the Italian line and attacked it from the rear. The Italians broke and over 38,000 prisoners were taken. The rapid success of the raid encouraged O'Connor to move on to invade the eastern Libyan province of Cyrenaica, the Australian 6th Division pursuing Italian forces along the coastline, while the 7th Armoured again pursued a wide sweep towards the port of Tobruk. After stiff fighting, the Libyan port of Bardia fell on 4 January, and on 22 January Tobruk was captured, denying the enemy an important supply base.

The Italian army under Marshal Graziani was pulled back to the defence of Tripolitania, the western province of Libya, where the first German reinforcements arrived to shore up Italian resistance. British Empire forces pushed on rapidly,

BELOW A column of Italian prisoners-of-war captured during the attack on Bardia marching to an army base on 6 January 1941. Over 40,000 became prisoners during the operation.

MARSHAL RODOLFO GRAZIANI (1882–1955)

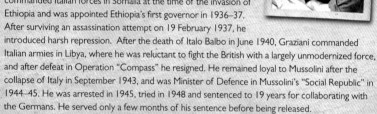

Rodolfo Graziani began his military career serving in the Italian East African colony of Eritrea. He fought as a young officer in the Italian-Turkish war of 1912 and in the First World War was wounded a number of times, decorated for valour and became in 1918 the youngest colonel in the Italian army. In the 1920s, he commanded Italian forces during the pacification of Libya, where thousands of Senussi prisoners died in Italian concentration camps. He commanded Italian forces in Somalia at the time of the invasion of Ethiopia and was appointed Ethiopia's first governor in 1936–37. After surviving an assassination attempt on 19 February 1937, he introduced harsh repression. After the death of Italo Balbo in June 1940, Graziani commanded Italian armies in Libya, where he was reluctant to fight the British with a largely unmodernized force, and after defeat in Operation "Compass" he resigned. He remained loyal to Mussolini after the collapse of Italy in September 1943, and was Minister of Defence in Mussolini's "Social Republic" in 1944–45. He was arrested in 1945, tried in 1948 and sentenced to 19 years for collaborating with the Germans. He served only a few months of his sentence before being released.

until by early February almost all of Cyrenaica was in their hands. A long trek across the desert by 7th Armoured, who arrived on 5 February at Beda Fomm near the coast of the Gulf of Sirte just half an hour before the retreating Italians, succeeded in cutting off their line of escape. After a brief conflict the Italian army surrendered on 7 February, while British Empire forces pressed on to El Agheila, where their attack came to a halt. Reinforcements had to be transferred to the Balkan campaign in an effort to stem the Axis assault on Greece, which left behind only a light force in North Africa. However, for some 2,000 British Empire casualties, around 30,000 Allied troops had routed an army eight times their size. Over 130,000 Italians were taken prisoner, and those who returned to Tripolitania needed extensive re-equipping. In six months the Italian empire in Africa had suffered defeats from which the Italian war effort never effectively recovered.

RIGHT British Commonwealth troops arrive in the Libyan town of Benghazi, 29 December 1940 under the curious gaze of the inhabitants.

BELOW Port installations burning in Tobruk, 24 January 1941, two days after British and Commonwealth troops had captured the town. Italian tanks are in the foreground with a white kangaroo symbol to show they have been captured by Australian forces.

GERMAN INVASION OF YUGOSLAVIA AND GREECE

ABOVE Badge of the Greek Sacred Squadron, part of the SAS, formed in 1942 to carry out raids on German occupied Greece.

The Balkans played very little part in the early stages of the Second World War but the growing interest of the Soviet Union in extending its influence at the expense of Romania and Bulgaria forced Hitler to increase German political authority and military presence in the region. German forces were stationed in Romania from September 1940 to safeguard German supplies of oil from the Ploesti oilfields, while Hungary and Romania joined the Tripartite Pact in November 1940.

Strong diplomatic pressure was maintained on Bulgaria and Yugoslavia to retain them in the Axis sphere of influence. At the height of this initiative, Mussolini decided to present his fellow dictator with an Italian triumph by invading Greece. He told none of his Axis partners of his intention and the attack was completely unprovoked. On 28 October, Italian forces attacked across the Albanian-Greek frontier, pitching six Italian against four Greek divisions. The Greek army resisted and with British air support drove back the Italian forces 80km (50 miles) into Albania in December 1940. By early January, most of southern Albania was in Greek hands.

For Hitler, preparing to invade the Soviet Union in late spring the next year, the Italian crisis was an unwelcome diversion. On 4 November 1940, he ordered the armed

LEFT Major General Bernard Freyberg, commander of the New Zealand Expeditionary Force in the Middle East, led W Force in Greece. Known affectionately as "Tiny" because of his bulky body, he had a reputation for fearlessness under fire.

ABOVE Italian forces in action against the Greek army, 1941. Despite plans for a quick victory, Italian troops proved a poor match for the determined Greek resistance.

FIELD MARSHAL WILHELM LIST (1880–1971)

Wilhelm List was one of the most successful of the commanders in Hitler's new German army. He commanded German troops in Austria after the Anschluss and was appointed a general in April 1939. He led the German 14th Army during the Polish campaign and the 12th army in the invasion of France, and was promoted field marshal in July 1940 as a reward. His 12th Army successfully seized Yugoslavia and Greece in April 1941, and he became Commander-in-Chief South East until October 1941. During this period he approved an order for killing 100 hostages for every German soldier killed. He was transferred to the Eastern Front, where he commanded the assault on the Caucasus in summer 1942. His failure there led to his dismissal in September 1942 and he retired from military life. He was tried as a war criminal in 1948 for atrocities committed in the Balkans under his command, but served only four years of a life sentence.

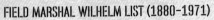

RIGHT Hitler welcomes the Yugoslav prime minister, Zwetkowitsch, to Berchtesgaden for talks in February 1941. The German leader hoped to get support from Yugoslavia for German military action in the Balkans and the Yugoslav signature of the Tripartite Pact.

GENERAL IOANNIS METAXAS (1871–1941)

In April 1936, General Metaxas was chosen as prime minister by the Greek king, George II, who had returned only recently from exile after a long period of republican rule. Metaxas was a successful staff officer from the First World War who turned to politics in the 1920s, leading a small Greek nationalist party which was hostile to parliamentary rule. When a general strike was threatened in the late summer of 1936, Metaxas declared martial law, suspended parliament and inaugurated a dictatorship of the "Third Hellenic Civilization" on 4 August. Despite his imitation of aspects of fascism, he was determined to retain Greek neutrality after the outbreak of war and was sympathetic to the British cause. When Mussolini presented an ultimatum on 28 October 1940, Metaxas rejected it. After the war the date was declared a national holiday as *Okhi* ("No") Day. Metaxas died in January 1941 but lived long enough to see Greek forces humiliate the Italian army.

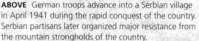

ABOVE German troops advance into a Serbian village in April 1941 during the rapid conquest of the country. Serbian partisans later organized major resistance from the mountain strongholds of the country.

BELOW German soldiers executing 18 Yugoslavs in Pancevo after the death of two Germans. The murder of civilians in Serbia paved the way for atrocities in the USSR later in the year.

forces to prepare Operation "Marita", a German invasion of Greece. Bulgaria agreed to allow the passage of German troops, while pressure on Yugoslavia eventually produced agreement on 25 March 1941 to join the Tripartite Pact. In Greece, an accord was reached on 23 February for a British Empire expeditionary force to help the Greeks resist the Italians. W Force, composed mainly of British Empire forces from Australia and New Zealand, arrived in Greece on 7 March, though British forces had been based on the islands of Crete and Lemnos since October 1940. A fresh Italian offensive on 9 March with 28 divisions was again halted with British assistance. Secret ULTRA decrypts of German messages sent using the Enigma machine alerted the British to the new threat from Germany, but the Greeks failed to pull back their forces on the northern frontier with Bulgaria to a better defensive position as the British commanders wanted. Just as German forces moved forward to begin the assault on Greece, a coup in Belgrade resulted in the new Yugoslav government repudiating the Tripartite agreement with Germany. Hitler ordered an extended campaign against both Yugoslavia and Greece, and on 6 April launched a devastating air attack on Belgrade, killing 17,000 people, while Field Marshal List's 12th Army assaulted Greece and southern Yugoslavia.

The Yugoslav campaign was improvised in a remarkably short time, but its impact was overwhelming. On 8 and 10 April, German, Hungarian and Italian armies attacked northern and central Yugoslavia, reaching Belgrade by 12 April. On 18 April, Yugoslavia capitulated following the mutiny of the Croatian units, its army of over one million men having inflicted just 151 dead on the German forces. The rapid defeat of Yugoslavia doomed Greece, as German forces poured down from southern Yugoslavia and across the "Metaxas" line on the Greek-Bulgarian border. Despite stiff resistance, the Greek and British Empire forces became divided. Although the RAF sent substantial forces to Greece,

ABOVE A detachment in Banya Luka of the newly formed Croat militia recruited from the fascist Ustaša movement. On 19 April Hitler agreed that Croatia could be independent under Ustaša rule.

they were overwhelmed by the German air force, losing 209 aircraft from the Middle East Command's limited reserves. On 23 April, General Tsolakoglu signed the Greek surrender, while 50,000 British Empire and Greek troops were evacuated from the south coast of Greece by a Royal Navy force, some to the island of Crete, some to Egypt. This was the second time in less than a year that British forces had been compelled to abandon mainland Europe by the German army. For Hitler, the diversion had secured his right flank for the invasion of the Soviet Union, protected Romanian oil supplies and inflicted a humiliation on both his Italian ally and his British enemy.

THE GERMAN CONQUEST OF CRETE

With the expulsion of British forces from mainland Greece, Hitler was anxious to complete the campaign by capturing the island of Crete which would otherwise remain a potential base for air attacks on the German flank or against oil targets in Romania. He ordered the rapid capture of Crete. Operation Mercury was prepared at great speed and was based around the deployment of Germany's elite paratroop force, XI *Fliegerkorps*, heavily protected by the German air force. The campaign was launched on 20 May, just three weeks after the expulsion of British Empire forces from southern Greece.

The defenders of Crete were a mixed force of British, Australian, New Zealand and Greek troops which numbered around 35,000, substantially more than the attacking force. They were commanded by Lt General Bernard

ABOVE German paratroopers and Ju52 aircraft over Crete, May 1941. The German force took very heavy casualties and was never used in an invasion role again.

RIGHT The commander of the British Commonwealth forces on Crete, Lt General Bernard Freyberg, watches the German advance from his dugout. He was retired from the army in 1937 on gorunds of poor health, but was brought back in 1939 and commanded the New Zealand Expeditionary Force in the Mediterranean theatre.

LEFT German paratroopers of the 5th *Gebirgs* (Mountain) Division, boarding a Junkers Ju52 transport plane at a Greek airfield before flying to Crete on 20 May 1941. On that morning 3,000 soldiers landed at Malme, Rethymno, Chania and Heraklion.

ABOVE German Parachutist Badge.

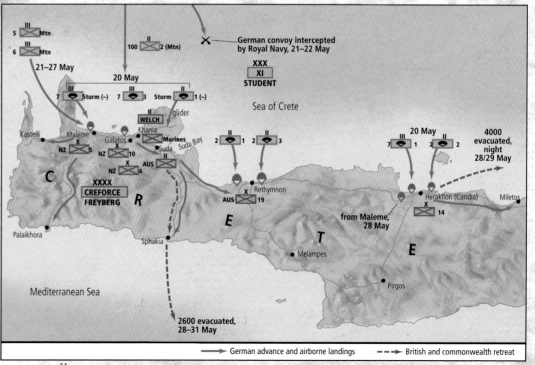

German advance and airborne landings — — — British and commonwealth retreat

GENERAL KURT STUDENT (1890-1978)

Kurt Student is usually regarded as the founder of modern paratroop forces. An airman in the First World War, he developed an interest in gliding during the 1920s which he used when developing Germany's first airborne unit, *Fliegerdivision* 7, in 1938. He was promoted to Inspector of Airborne Forces later in 1938, and in 1940 his men played a key role in the invasions of Norway and Belgium. His plan for the invasion of Crete backfired with heavy losses and Hitler refused to let Student use mass airborne assaults again. His forces were largely confined to ground operations and Student ended the war as Commander Army Group Vistula in May 1945. After the war, he was tried by the British in May 1947 for war crimes and though found guilty on three counts the verdict was not upheld. Britain denied a Greek application for his extradition to stand trial for atrocities against Greek civilians, which Student had ordered as reprisals against partisan attack. Student was freed on medical grounds but lived on to the age of 88.

Freyberg, a British-born New Zealander with a reputation for fearlessness. Though large in numbers, the force lacked adequate artillery, tanks or communications equipment. The one advantage Freyberg enjoyed was ULTRA intelligence information. He was the first field commander to be given this secret intelligence, which indicated the precise date of the German attack. He disposed his forces around the three key airfields on the north coast at Maleme, Retimo and Heraklion, but the force was spread very thin. When General Kurt Student's paratroopers descended on 20 May, they faced fierce resistance and suffered heavy casualties, but after a parachute battalion under Colonel Bernard Ramcke landed on either side of the airfield on the morning of 21 May, Maleme fell to a determined German assault, allowing German transport aircraft to bring in General Julius Ringel's 5th *Gebirgs* (Mountain) Division. Hitler was disillusioned at the high level of losses during the initial paratroop assault and Student was forced to give way to Ringel for the conquest of the rest of Crete.

The battle hung in the balance for several days. On 21–22 May, a German convoy bringing reinforcements

from Milos was mauled by a Royal Navy force with the loss of around 5,000 men. But German air superiority was gradually achieved and the Royal Navy lost three cruisers and six destroyers, with damage to 17 other vessels, almost all from air attack. By 23 May, German forces deployed on Crete had increased from 9,500 on the opening day of the operation to 17,500, and Freyberg's forces were pushed back to the south of the island, with small pockets holding out in Retimo and Heraklion, aided by Cretan guerrillas whose attacks provoked a savage series of reprisals against the civilian population. By 26 May, Freyberg reported that he could no longer hold the island and over the next four days the Royal Navy evacuated most of the garrison, the last ship leaving in the early hours of 31 May. Around 5,000 men were left behind, most of whom went into German captivity; a small number escaped into the hills with the Cretan partisans or found small ships to take them to Egypt after the main force had left. The ships plying back and forth between Alexandria and Crete were subjected to regular bomb attack; of the 3,700 British Empire dead, 2,000 were from the Royal Navy.

LEFT A series of three photographs taken by a German airman of the sinking of HMS *Gloucester* off Crete, 22 May 1941. British ships took heavy losses from German aircraft stationed in Greece.

BELOW Wounded soldiers disembark at an Egyptian port after evacuation from Crete, 31 May 1941. This was Britain's fourth major evacuation in a year of fighting.

ABOVE Two British ships burning in Suda Bay in Crete, May 1941, after an attack by German bombers of XI *Fliegerkorps* stationed in Greece.

For the German forces the conquest of Crete was a pyrrhic victory. The German dead numbered 3,352, of whom 1,653 alone were from Student's XI *Fliegerkorps*. Total casualties were 6,698, which exceeded losses for the whole of the Balkan campaign in April. Almost 200 transport aircraft were destroyed during the operation, denying valuable resources to the imminent invasion of the Soviet Union. General Freyberg was not given an independent command after Crete, but he did lead the New Zealand Corps in Italy, and later became Governor-General of New Zealand; but Kurt Student was never again trusted by Hitler, even though Crete had been a significant victory completing German domination of Europe.

SINKING THE *BISMARCK*

15 APRIL 1940
British intelligence crack part of the Enigma Code.

10/11 MAY 1941
London hit by heaviest air raid of the war leaving 1,500 dead.

15 MAY 1941
US takes over Vichy French ships in American ports.

18 MAY 1941
Bismarck and *Prinz Eugen* sail for the Atlantic.

27 MAY 1941
Bismarck sunk by Royal Naval destroyers.

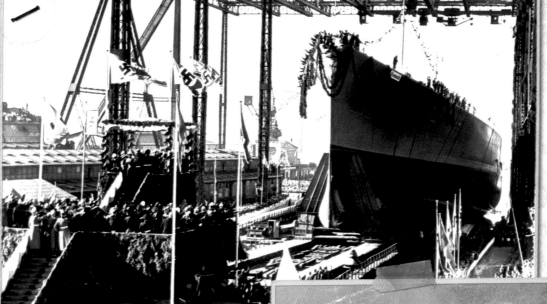

BELOW The break-out into the Atlantic, 19–23 May. Here the *Bismarck* is photographed from the deck of the heavy cruiser *Prinz Eugen*.

LEFT Adolf Hitler attends the launch of the Bismarck on 14 February 1939 at the Blohm & Voss shipyards in Hamburg. She was named after Prince Otto von Bismarck, the architect of German unification in 1871.

LEFT The end of the British battlecruiser HMS *Hood* on 24 May 1941. After accurate fire from *Bismarck*, which had been intercepted by the Royal Navy in the Denmark Strait, the ammunition stored on *Hood* exploded and the ship sank at once.

All the evidence from the first 18 months of the war showed that the traditional role of naval vessels had been subverted by the arrival of air power. The German navy, however, persisted with plans for a large battle fleet and failed to build the aircraft carriers which were now essential to give surface ships effective protection. The most up-to-date and largest German battleship was the 41,000-ton *Bismarck*, launched on 14 February 1939 and commissioned on 24 August 1940. The ship was intended

as a convoy raider in the Atlantic, and her design reflected this, with a broad beam to cope with heavy seas and large fuel tanks. The break-out into the Atlantic, codenamed Operation "Rhine Exercise", was planned to include the battlecruisers *Gneisenau* and *Scharnhorst* and the new battleship *Tirpitz*, but the first two were damaged or under repair and the *Tirpitz* was still engaged in trials before full commissioning. The original force would have been a formidable fleet, but in the end *Bismarck* left on 18 May 1941 accompanied only by the heavy cruiser *Prinz Eugen*.

The commander of the operation, Vice Admiral Lütjens, had reservations about its feasibility but he obeyed commands to the letter, anxious not to be sacked like his predecessor, Vice Admiral Wilhelm Marschall, for

VICE-ADMIRAL GÜNTHER LÜTJENS (1889–1941)

After joining the Imperial German Navy in 1907, Günther Lütjens became the young commander of torpedo boats on the Flemish coast in the First World War, raiding Allied shipping around Dunkirk. He worked for a shipping firm after the war before rejoining the slimmed-down German navy in 1921, where he again commanded torpedo boats. In 1933, he was given command of the light cruiser *Karlsruhe*, and in 1937 was promoted to Rear Admiral and Commander of Torpedo Boats. In June 1940, he was promoted to Fleet Commander of German battlecruisers and led Gneisenau and Scharnhorst on the Atlantic shipping raid in early 1941 which sank 115,000 tons of Allied shipping. He commanded the small Bismarck force in May 1941 and was killed on board the battleship on 27 May. He was not an enthusiast for Hitler, and was never seen to give the Hitler salute or to wear swastika insignia. He was one of three senior officers to protest against the Kristallnacht pogrom in November 1938.

ABOVE Able Seaman Alfred Newall aboard the cruiser HMS *Suffolk*. He was the first to sight the *Bismarck* as she emerged into the Denmark Strait.

disebeying orders. The British were forewarned of the break-out through ULTRA intelligence and from Swedish and Norwegian sources. The ship was spotted by a Spitfire reconnaissance aircraft near Bergen, but contact was not made until 23 May, when the German units entered the Denmark Strait between Iceland and Greenland and a radar-equipped heavy cruiser, HMS *Norfolk,* detected them. The force was shadowed until heavier British ships became available. Early in the morning of 24 May 1941, the new British battleship *Prince of Wales* arrived, accompanied by the battlecruiser *Hood* commanded by Vice Admiral Lancelot Holland. Within minutes, *Hood* had been hit by accurate German gunfire, and at 6.00 a.m. blew up and then sank in three minutes with the loss of all but three of the 1,418 crew. Captain Lindemann aboard *Bismarck* wanted to pursue and destroy the *Prince of Wales*, which had also sustained serious damage, but Lütjens obeyed his instructions not to engage heavy enemy units and insisted on moving on. *Bismarck* had also been damaged: the forward radar was not operational and the fuel tanks were leaking, forcing her to reduce speed to 20 knots. *Prinz Eugen* made off into the Atlantic while *Bismarck* made for the French coast at St Nazaire for essential repairs.

The British shadowed the battleship, but a sudden turn by *Bismarck* confused the pursuers and contact was lost. Only Lütjens's insistence

– against Lindemann's advice – on sending a half-hour radio message, which was duly intercepted by the British, gave a clue to the ship's whereabouts, but the pursuing battleship *King George V* miscalculated the position and the German ship drew closer to air cover and destroyer assistance from France. But on 26 May, a Catalina flying-boat of Coastal Command spotted *Bismarck* and at 9.00 p.m. that evening a Swordfish torpedo-bomber from the carrier *Ark Royal* succeeded in scoring a hit that jammed the rudder and steering equipment. On the morning of 27 May, the British battleships *Rodney* and *King George V* moved in for the kill, bombarding a slow and listing target and, just after 9.00 a.m., destroying the bridge and eliminating the ship's command. The final sinking is usually attributed to the torpedoes of the destroyer HMS *Dorsetshire* which fired three at the *Bismarck* shortly before the ship sank, at 10.39 a.m., with the loss of all but 100 of more than 2,000 crewmen. Recent research of the wreckage and the testimony of survivors have suggested that the German battleship was scuttled rather than sunk by the enemy. The end of *Bismarck* epitomized Grand Admiral Raeder's gloomy hope, expressed when war broke out, that his men would understand "how to die gallantly" in what he always viewed as an unequal struggle with the Royal Navy. In reality, it was one aircraft that succeeded in slowing down and disabling *Bismarck*, further testimony that the days of traditional fleet engagements were now in the past.

BELOW The *Bismarck* on fire on 27 May 1941, photographed from one of the Royal Navy vessels shadowing her last hours.

ABOVE An aerial reconnaissance image of *Bismarck* and *Prinz Eugen* in a Norwegian fjord before their breakout into the Atlantic.

RIGHT A Fairey Swordfish returns to the aircraft carrier HMS *Ark Royal* after making a torpedo attack on the *Bismarck*. The attack damaged the rudder and steering and sealed *Bismarck's* fate.

HMS ARK ROYAL

This was the third ship to bear the name *Ark Royal* and the second aircraft carrier. Launched in April 1937, the 22,000-ton ship was the first of Britain's carriers to have an integral flight deck. *Ark Royal* saw combat off Norway, at the sinking of the French fleet at Mers-el-Kébir and during the naval war against Italy in 1940. She was serving in the Mediterranean as part of Force "H" in May 1941 when she was alerted to the presence of *Bismarck* and went in pursuit. Planes from the *Ark Royal* crippled the enemy battleship. For the rest of 1941 the carrier protected Mediterranean convoys to Malta until she was damaged by a German submarine, U-81, on 13 November 1941 and sank the following day while being towed to Gibraltar.

HITLER TURNS EAST

9 DECEMBER 1940
First British offensive in the
Western Desert begins.

29 DECEMBER 1940
Roosevelt pledges that the US
will be "the great arsenal of
democracy".

30 JANUARY 1941
Germany threatens to attack
all neutral shipping supplying
Britain.

27 MARCH 1941
Coup in Belgrade – Yugoslavia
– renounces the Tripartite Pact.

10 MAY 1941
Rudolf Hess, Hitler's deputy,
flies to Britain to broker peace.

27 MAY 1941
Roosevelt declares unlimited
national emergency.

14 JUNE 1941
German and Italian assets
frozen in the US.

Hitler had since the 1920s thought that a natural area for German imperial expansion lay in the agriculturally and raw-material rich territories of the western Soviet Union. This was the area designated as "living space" (*Lebensraum*) for the German master race. "Russia", Hitler once remarked, "will be our India." He also displayed a visceral hatred of "Jewish Bolshevism" which he thought menaced European civilization and threatened the degeneration of the German race. These ideas formed the background of his decision to settle accounts with the Soviet Union once and for all, an ambition laid down in War Directive 21 for Operation "Barbarossa" signed on 18 December 1940.

The more immediate roots of the German-Soviet conflict lay in Hitler's view of the international situation in 1940. Unable to defeat the British Empire and anxious about the nascent threat of the United States, on 31 July 1940 Hitler called his military leaders together and announced that he wanted to launch an annihilating attack on the Soviet Union the following spring "to smash the state heavily in one blow". Such a move would remove Britain's last potential ally, Hitler argued, and make it impossible for the United States to intervene in Europe. Planning was undertaken over the autumn months, led by the same General Paulus who later surrendered at Stalingrad.

The Soviet Union had taken advantage of Hitler's war in the west to extend its influence in eastern Europe, first occupying the Baltic States in June 1940, then compelling Romania to hand over the territory of Bessarabia and northern Bukovina. In November 1940, Molotov was invited to Berlin to try to gauge the extent of Soviet ambitions. Molotov's desire for Soviet bases in Bulgaria and Turkey confirmed Hitler's view that the Soviet Union posed an immediate strategic and military threat, and he ordered active preparations for invasion to begin. On 5 December, he approved the military plans for a massive three-pronged invasion of the whole Soviet western frontier and timetabled the attack for May 1941. Hitler thought German forces were well prepared – "visibly at their zenith" – while the Red Army was at "an unmistakable nadir". All the military planners assumed the war could be won in a matter of weeks.

ABOVE Hitler in conference with senior army leaders in July 1940. Franz Halder, the army chief of staff, stands on Hitler's right, his headquarters chief, Field Marshal Wilhelm Keitel, behind him. Hitler played a central role in planning and preparing operations.

BELOW LEFT German tanks approaching the Soviet border in Poland in the weeks before the launch of Operation "Barbarossa" on 22 June 1941. The four Panzer groups of the German army played a decisive role in the early victories.

ABOVE German Infantry Assault badge in silver. Instituted on 20 December 1939, it was awarded to infantry troops for all manner of combat including hand-to-hand combat in an assault position.

JOSEPH STALIN (1878–1953)

Joseph Dzhugashvili was born in the small Georgian town of Gori, the son of a cobbler. Academically successful, he earned a place in a local seminary, where he first came into contact with underground Marxist organizations. He joined the Russian Social Democrats, and in 1904 sided with Lenin and his "Bolshevik" faction. In 1912, he adopted the political pseudonym Stalin, or "steel". He was in exile in Siberia when the Russian Revolution broke out and returned to play a part in Leningrad before the Bolshevik coup in October 1917. He became Commissar for Nationalities and in April 1922 was appointed General Secretary of the Central Committee of the Communist Party. By the 1930s, he had used his power base to assume an informal dictatorship over the party. Only in 1941 did Stalin become Chairman of the Council of Commissars (premier). After the German invasion, he headed the State Defence Committee and dominated the Soviet war effort. He died of a cerebral haemorrhage in 1953.

armoured divisions supported strongly by aircraft.

Stalin did think that Germany might risk war at a later date, but wanted time to complete defensive preparations and modernize Soviet forces. Despite strict instructions from Hitler to keep all preparations secret and to pretend that the invasion of Britain was still a priority, the Soviet leadership was given regular intelligence warnings of German intentions in the months leading up to invasion, including the original plan to invade in May and the modified decision to postpone until 22 June. Stalin dismissed it as attempts at provocation by the British to get the Soviet Union to do their fighting for them. Only in May did the new army chief of staff, General Georgii Zhukov, order a stealthy mobilization, but out of 33 divisions planned for redeployment to the western areas, only four or five were ready by the time of invasion. Only on 19 June did the order go out to begin camouflaging airfields and most were unconcealed by the time German aircraft attacked.

During the preparations for "Barbarossa" Hitler succeeded in recruiting Finland, Hungary, Romania and Slovakia as co-belligerents in the campaign. The initial date for a May attack was changed to 22 June to allow for final preparations after the intervention in the Balkans. On the eve of the "Barbarossa" campaign, there were 153 Axis divisions, including an estimated 3.3 million Germans and 650,000 allied troops, the largest invasion force ever assembled. Opposed were 186 Soviet divisions with 3 million men. On paper Soviet aircraft and tanks outnumbered the Axis – 11,000 tanks against 4,000, and 9,100 aircraft against 4,400 – but they were parcelled out among all the army units and were poorly organized to oppose a concentrated assault. When Axis forces in the early morning of 22 June smashed across the Soviet frontier, surprise was almost complete and the effect devastating.

The Soviet leadership was divided on the threat posed by Germany, but because Stalin insisted, right up to the day of invasion, that Hitler was too involved in the war in the west to risk a two-front conflict, inadequate preparations were made to meet the German onslaught. A new set of frontier defences, the Stalin Line, built along the new frontier in Poland and the Baltic States, was unfinished by 1941. Soviet strategic planning was based on the idea that if an enemy did attack, light frontier forces would hold the invaders up for several weeks while the bulk of the Red Army mobilized in the rear and then prepared for a hammer-blow to drive the enemy back on to his own territory. Little account was taken of the lessons of 1939 and 1940 about the power of fast mobile

A talented staff officer during the First World War, Franz Halder was appointed Chief of the Army General Staff in September 1938. He was part of a group of senior officers who explored the idea of overthrowing Hitler in 1938–9, but the difficulty of reconciling his duty as an officer and his hostility to Hitler produced a nervous collapse in the autumn of 1939. He remained in his post through the invasion of France, the Balkans and the Soviet Union, but often disagreed with Hitler's strategic judgments. He was sacked by Hitler in September 1942 and retired from army life. Arrested in July 1944 after the attempted assassination of Hitler, he ended the war in Dachau concentration camp. After the war he worked for the US Army Historical Division on their studies of the German war effort.

BELOW LEFT The Russian-born German journalist Richard Sorge. A committed Communist, Sorge supplied high-level intelligence to Moscow about the impending German attack from his base in Tokyo, but his warnings were ignored.

BELOW A gas-mask drill in the Ukrainian city of Kiev. Training against chemical-weapons attack was routine in the Soviet Union where more than 13 million belonged to the Osaviakhim civil defence association.

OPERATION "BARBAROSSA"

The attack by Axis armies on 22 June 1941 along the whole length of the Soviet western frontier was an overwhelming success. The Soviet plan to hold the attacker at the frontier was torn apart in hours and the Red Army was given no time to mobilize a large force to push the enemy back across the frontier, as Soviet military doctrine dictated. The Soviet forces fought with often suicidal determination but from the outset the German plan completely unhinged Soviet military preparations and exposed the Red Army to a looming catastrophe.

The German forces were organized in three main army groups, North, Centre and South. Each attacked on a different axis, using four armoured (Panzer) groups to force a way through the Soviet line while the vast infantry armies followed behind at their own pace. In the far north, Finnish armies supported the assault; in the south large Romanian forces, directed by a German overall commander, moved towards Odessa and the Crimea. The armour ploughed forward at a rapid pace, sometimes covering 30 kilometres (19 miles) a day. By the end of June, Army Group North was across Lithuania and deep into Latvia, whose capital fell on 1 July. By 19 August, General Hoeppner's 4th Panzer Group had reached the outskirts of Leningrad and a few weeks later the city was surrounded and under siege. Progress was slower in the south, but by 5 August Odessa too was under siege by Romanian armies, and finally captured in mid-October.

TOP A 7.92mm German Gewehr 41 (W) rifle used on the eastern front.

ABOVE German tanks prepare to attack on 21 July 1941 deep inside Soviet territory. Though outnumbered by Soviet armour, German tanks proved much more effective because they carried radios and had close air support.

LEFT The bodies of Soviet soldiers killed in the determined defence of the frontier fortress at Brest-Litovsk in June and July 1941. The 3,500 men of the garrison fought almost literally to the last man, long after German forces had moved on hundreds of miles into the Soviet Union.

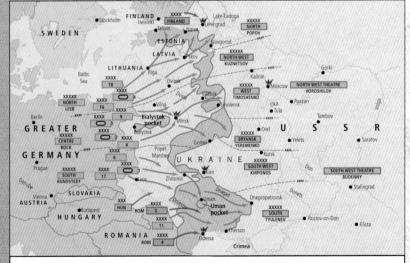

heavily bombed cities · occupied by Germans, mid-July · occupied by Germans, 25 Aug.

FIELD MARSHAL FEDOR VON BOCK (1880–1945)

Descended from a famous Prussian military family, von Bock was a battalion commander in the First World War and rose rapidly in the inter-war years to achieve the rank of general in March 1938, a few days before he commanded the forces that occupied Austria. He led Army Group North in the Polish campaign, and Army Group B in the Battle of France. For the invasion of the Soviet Union, he was given command of Army Group Centre, which came within a few kilometres of the centre of Moscow in December 1941. He then commanded Army Group South for the invasion of southern Russia in 1942, but after failing to do what Hitler wanted was replaced in July and never served in command again. He was almost a caricature of a Prussian general, stiff, hard-working and arrogant, though he was no supporter of National Socialism. He was killed in his car by a British aircraft on 4 May 1945.

MARSHAL SEMYON TIMOSHENKO (1895–1970)

An NCO in the Tsarist cavalry, Timoshenko became a commander in the First Cavalry Army under Stalin's leadership during the Russian Civil War. The Red Army purges led to his rapid promotion, and by 1939 he was commander of the Ukrainian Front Army that occupied eastern Poland. He was appointed to command armies in the Finnish war after the early disastrous Soviet defeats and in March 1940 forced an armistice on the Finns. In May 1940, he became a Marshal of the Soviet Union and Commissar for Defence. When the Germans invaded he was sent to organize the western front and held the Germans around Smolensk. Although regarded as one of the best Soviet commanders, he failed in the spring offensive of 1942 against Kharkov and was not given a major command again until August 1944 when he led the First, Second and Third Ukrainian army groups in the long march to Budapest and Vienna. Stalin favoured the officers who had fought with him in the First Cavalry Army and Timoshenko survived his mistakes when other officers did not.

BELOW LEFT Burning houses in the Ukrainian capital of Kiev, captured by German forces in early September 1941. Most of Kiev's large Jewish population was murdered in the Babi-Yar massacre on 29–30 September.

BELOW A German soldier mounts guard over some of the 650,000 Red Army prisoners captured in the Kiev pocket between 10 and 16 September 1941. Most of the prisoners died of disease and starvation over the winter of 1941–2.

The most spectacular advances were made by Army Group Centre under Field Marshal von Bock. By 28 June, 2nd and 3rd Panzer Groups had encircled the Belorussian capital, Minsk, and trapped 280,000 Soviet soldiers. The fast-moving German armour cut two pincers through the Soviet front and then closed them, forming one pocket after another. Although Soviet forces fought bravely and held up the German advance in small local battles, the speed and destructiveness of the German attack, which had almost destroyed Soviet air power in a matter of days, led to widespread demoralization and the collapse of Soviet communications and supply. By the autumn, around 90 per cent of existing tank strength had been destroyed, and Soviet losses of manpower approached 5 million killed, wounded or captured. The sheer scale and brutality of the conflict also took a heavy toll of the attackers. By the end of September, around 550,000 German casualties were reported, dwarfing anything the German army had so far experienced.

Despite heavy losses and fierce Soviet resistance, Hitler remained confident that the Soviet Union could be broken. In early September, a Soviet counter-attack at Smolensk was finally beaten off by Army Group Centre, exposing Moscow to the German army. Hitler instead insisted that von Bock's forces support the attack on Leningrad and help the embattled Army Group South against General Kirponos's South West Front. The siege of Leningrad was completed and in the south a spectacular victory was achieved when 1st and 2nd Panzer groups encircled the Ukrainian capital, Kiev, on 15 September and with it 650,000 Soviet soldiers.

ABOVE Soviet soldiers wait to be evacuated from the port of Odessa by the Soviet Black Sea Fleet in early October 1941. Around 80,000 troops and 15,000 civilians were rescued before Romanian forces captured the city.

Around 150,000 others managed to fight their way out but the defeat opened the way to German conquest of the rest of the rich industrial region to the south. On 6 September 1941, Hitler's War Directive 35 finally gave Army Group Centre the opportunity to advance on Moscow.

On the Soviet side the Axis campaign seemed unstoppable. New divisions were mobilized and sent to the front and as quickly disappeared. Stalin made himself Supreme Commander of the Armed Forces on 10 July and Commissar for Defence on 19 July. He ordered harsh treatment for anyone who did not fight to the death. In August, Order 270 was published which condemned any soldier who surrendered as a traitor to the motherland. Senior soldiers were arrested and shot for failing to halt the German onslaught. Timoshenko and

ABOVE A woman in Odessa, the Ukrainian port captured by the Romanian army on 16 October 1941. Following its capture an estimated 50,000 Jews were murdered.

Zhukov succeeded in holding up the German advance at Smolensk, and on 6 September the city of Yelna was briefly recaptured from German forces, but the collapse of Soviet resistance was impossible to disguise. By the end of September, most of the huge forces that had opposed the attack were destroyed or captured. Eyewitnesses recall a sense of euphoria at Hitler's headquarters.

THE SIEGE OF LENINGRAD

30 AUGUST 1941
Last rail link to Leningrad cut by German forces.

19 SEPTEMBER 1941
Kiev captured by the Germans.

29 SEPTEMBER 1941
Hitler orders Leningrad to be razed to the ground.

19 OCTOBER 1941
State of siege declared in Moscow.

11 DECEMBER 1941
Germany and Italy declare war on the United States.

12 AUGUST 1942
Churchill meets Stalin in Moscow to discuss course of war.

6 NOVEMBER 1943
Soviet forces capture Kiev.

The city of Leningrad (the old capital of Russia, now St Petersburg) was the main objective in the "Barbarossa" campaign for Field Marshal von Leeb's Army Group North. In August 1941, German armies from the south and Finnish armies to the north began the progressive encirclement and isolation of the city. Hitler decided that it should be put under siege rather than stormed to avoid the high casualties already experienced elsewhere in fighting through city streets. One after another, the defensive lines established around the city were captured. The last rail link for the city was cut on 30 August at Mga. By early September, the German armies were only 11 kilometres (seven miles) from the centre of the city. The first shell fell on the central zones on 4 September, the first bombs two days later. On 8 September, the last land link was severed and Leningrad was blockaded. Stalin sent General Zhukov to the city to organize its final defence, and he succeeded in holding up the advance. On 25 September, the German forces dug in and the siege began.

During August some 636,000 – many of them women and children – were evacuated by the remaining slim land routes, but when the siege was imposed, 3.3 million remained trapped in the city and the pocket of land to the north and east. The Soviet Baltic Fleet was also caught in the trap and offered additional firepower to the embattled defenders. Hitler's object was to starve and bombard

Leningrad into defeat. Food supplies were limited to a few weeks, and by 1 November only a meagre ration for a further seven days was left. Between August and October, Soviet armies to the east launched a rescue campaign, Operation "Sinyavino", but they failed to break the ring. Only the opening of a long and difficult route across the ice of Lake Ladoga saved the city's population. A trickle of food supplies came in, not enough to prevent widespread deaths from malnutrition and disease, but sufficient to keep much of the population alive. In an effort to sever the remaining thin supply line, the German army pushed eastwards to capture the Russian railhead at Tikhvin on 9 November, but the Red Army won the town back on 9 December and Leningrad continued to receive supplies.

ABOVE Soviet women digging tank traps in the approaches to Leningrad in the late summer of 1941. Labour duty was compulsory for all able-bodied citizens, male and female.

RIGHT Russian infantry cap badge.

BELOW Finnish troops in a trench north of Lake Ladoga in September 1943. Warfare in this northern sector came to resemble the war on the Western Front in 1914–18 with static lines and heavy artillery bombardment.

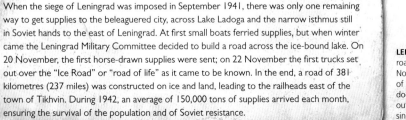

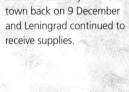

THE ICE ROAD

When the siege of Leningrad was imposed in September 1941, there was only one remaining way to get supplies to the beleaguered city, across Lake Ladoga and the narrow isthmus still in Soviet hands to the east of Leningrad. At first small boats ferried supplies, but when winter came the Leningrad Military Committee decided to build a road across the ice-bound lake. On 20 November, the first horse-drawn supplies were sent; on 22 November the first trucks set out over the "Ice Road" or "road of life" as it came to be known. In the end, a road of 381 kilometres (237 miles) was constructed on ice and land, leading to the railheads east of the town of Tikhvin. During 1942, an average of 150,000 tons of supplies arrived each month, ensuring the survival of the population and of Soviet resistance.

LEFT A Soviet lorry on the "ice-road" built across Lake Ladoga in November 1941 to give the people of Leningrad a lifeline. The open door allowed the driver to jump out quickly if the lorry began to sink through the shallow ice.

LEFT Wooden houses damaged during the German bombardment of the city are torn down and used for fuel. By the end of the first winter of the siege almost anything that could burn had been used by the population, whose resistance to freezing temperatures was lowered by the shortage of food.

BELOW LEFT A familiar image in Leningrad under siege. A Soviet couple pull a body on a sled to the municipal cemetery. In the cold winter months bodies were piled on the ground because the earth was too hard to dig.

RIGHT A Soviet poster by V P Serov,s 1942. The caption reads "We Defended Leningrad! We Will Restore It!" Women made up a large proportion of the construction workforce because of the loss of men during the war.

The German forces began a regular shelling and bombing of the city, firing a total of 150,000 artillery shells during the course of the siege. For the city's inhabitants, life was primitive in the extreme: wooden houses were demolished for firewood; electricity supply was cut off except for the most urgent production needs; medical services collapsed; and the production of war equipment was maintained only with the greatest difficulty. During 1942, the Red Army made several attempts to break the siege: in Operation "Lubyan", from January to April 1942; and another Operation "Sinyavino" from 19 August to 10 October 1942. The second attack upset German plans to storm the city but failed to dislodge the enemy. On 18 January 1943, the blockade was finally lifted when a Soviet force succeeded in opening an eight-kilometre-(five-mile-) wide corridor south of Lake Ladoga (Operation "Iskra"). A road and rail link was established and, although under constant fire, this was able to supply the city. The siege was only lifted a year later, when on 27 January 1944 the Soviet Volkhov Front pushed Army Group North back from the city as part of a general Soviet offensive against the northern sectors of the front.

The death toll in the siege of Leningrad has never been known with any certainty because of the large number of refugees from the German attack housed in the city. The official Soviet death toll records 632,253 civilian dead, but the figure may well have been over one million. Some 77,000 Soviet soldiers were lost in the final campaign to liberate Leningrad, which had endured 900 days of siege.

SHOSTAKOVICH AND THE LENINGRAD SYMPHONY

The young Soviet composer Dmitri Shostakovich (1906–75) was in Leningrad when it was besieged. He worked on the score of his Seventh Symphony in the threatened city and was photographed in a fire-warden's uniform for propaganda purposes (right). In October, he and his family were taken out of the city to Kuibyshev where the symphony was completed. Shostakovich dedicated it to Leningrad and it has been known by that name ever since. It was first performed in March 1942 and both in Russia and abroad came to symbolize Soviet resistance.

OPERATION "TYPHOON"

On 6 September 1941, Hitler finally decided that Moscow had to be captured to complete the defeat of the Red Army that year. Operation "Typhoon" called for two massive armoured thrusts north and south of the capital which would close in and encircle remaining Soviet resistance. Preparations took much of September but on the last day of the month German Army Group Centre began its attack. By 17 October, large Soviet forces were encircled and destroyed at Briansk and Vyazma and over 700,000 prisoners taken. German commanders considered that the Red Army had few reserves left and pressed on. But by mid-October, the autumn rains brought the annual *rasputitsa*, the "time without roads" and the German advance slowed. Nevertheless, by 18 October German forces had taken Kalinin to the north of Moscow and Kaluga to the south, remorselessly closing the vice around Stalin's capital.

For the Red Army the situation once again threatened a catastrophe. By early October, there were only 90,000 troops left out of the 800,000 that had held the front in September. Stalin summoned Zhukov back from the Leningrad front to try to save Moscow. The last line of defence, the Mozhaisk Line, was strengthened with six weakened Soviet armies while Zhukov improvised a final defensive line 16 kilometres (10 miles) from the centre of the capital. The capital became gripped with panic and by mid-October much of the government machine had been evacuated to Kuibyshev. On 19 October, Stalin made the historic decision that he would stay in his threatened capital and declared a state of siege. Looters and panicmongers were shot and the population mobilized to dig anti-tank ditches and rough barricades. Zhukov had 240,000 men to hold the front and around 500

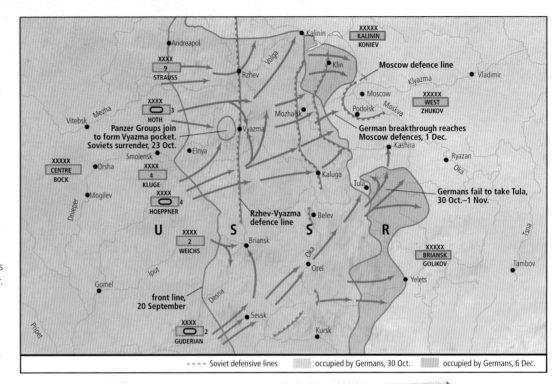

----- Soviet defensive lines   ▓ occupied by Germans, 30 Oct.   ▓ occupied by Germans, 6 Dec.

BELOW German tanks and infantry on the outskirts of Moscow during the winter battle for the city. By 28 November German forces were only a few miles from the centre of the Soviet capital but lacked the resources to complete its capture.

LEFT Battle-weary German soldiers pause in the Soviet city of Vitebsk on the path towards Moscow. The city was left in flames by retreating Soviet forces who had orders to leave nothing behind that the enemy could use.

ABOVE Luftwaffe Ground Assault Badge.

RIGHT A salvo of the famous *Katyusha* rockets during the battles around Moscow in the winter of 1941–2. Fired from the back of a lorry, the rockets, primed with four tons of explosives, spread out over a wide area. The Soviet name was derived from a popular song, but German forces called it "Stalin's Organ".

LEFT Soviet troops dressed in their winter camouflage suits attack German positions during the battle for Moscow. German forces were short of all kinds of winter equipment for a campaign that was supposed to have finished by October.

RIGHT Adolf Hitler addresses a gathering in Berlin on 4 October 1941 in the Sportpalast assembled for the annual ceremony for the Winter Relief Work. He announced that the Soviet Union was defeated "and would never rise again".

tanks. He ordered them to die where they stood or face a firing squad. When the frosts came in late October and the armies could move forward again, the German commanders assumed they would now seize the city. On 28 November, the 3rd and 4th Panzer armies reached the Moscow–Volga canal only 19 kilometres (12 miles) from the centre of Moscow, but in the south the 2nd Panzer army was held up at Tula and the German advance slowed.

The Soviet High Command planned a counter-offensive using forces brought from the Soviet Far East. Stalin had intelligence information that Japan was preparing to move south against the United States, and so he could run the risk of weakening his eastern front. The reserves were held back while the German attack was absorbed. German forces became weakened by long supply lines and the bitter weather, which produced 133,000 cases of frostbite alongside other losses that reduced the army to 75 per cent of its strength at the start of the campaign in June. Although the forward German units could see Moscow in the distance, determined Soviet resistance prevented its capture. The reserve armies were moved into place in

early December and, while they were detected by German intelligence, the German High Command dismissed the idea that the Red Army was capable of mounting a serious offensive. On the morning of 5 December, the counter-offensive began, driving the two German pincers back to where they had been in November. By the end of the month Kalinin was recaptured, the siege of Tula lifted and Kaluga retaken.

In bitter sub-zero temperatures the German front gave way but did not collapse entirely. The Soviet counter-offensive saved Moscow, where the official news of Soviet victories was announced on 13 December, but the Red Army was still too weakened by months of losses to inflict a decisive defeat. Though Stalin urged his armies forward, the German defence exacted another 444,000 deaths from the Soviet side in the campaign around Moscow. On 19 December, frustrated at German retreats, Hitler sacked Field Marshal von Brauchitsch and assumed command of the German army himself, determined to "educate it to be National Socialist". By the spring of 1942, the two sides had reached a stalemate.

MARSHAL GEORGI ZHUKOV (1896–1974)

The son of a shoemaker from a village outside Moscow, Zhukov rose to become the most famous of the cluster of marshals who led the Red Army to victory in 1945. He became an NCO in a cavalry regiment during the First World War, fought for the Reds during the Civil War after 1917 and became a keen Bolshevik. He went to Spain as a Soviet observer of the Spanish Civil War, and successfully defeated Japanese forces in a small conflict at Khalkhin-Gol in 1939. In January 1941, he became Chief of the General Staff, was sacked in July for arguing with Stalin, and was sent to stabilize one front after another, first Leningrad, then Moscow, and then Stalingrad. On 27 August 1942, Stalin named him Deputy Supreme Commander, and in January 1943 he became the first wartime Marshal. He was a tough, courageous, loud-mouthed officer with a natural flair for battlefield command. He ended the war commanding the First Belorussian Front in the attack on Berlin, and on 1 August 1945 as military governor of the Soviet zone of Berlin, he became a member of the Allied Control Council for Germany. In 1946 he was demoted by a jealous Stalin, rehabilitated in 1953 but finally retired from public life in 1957.

BELOW German soldiers struggle with the muddy conditions in the retreat before Moscow. The German army came to rely on more than 750,000 horses, which were more suited to the harsh Russian terrain.

DEFEAT IN NORTH AFRICA

On 12 February 1941, General Rommel arrived in the Libyan port of Tripoli to command a German expeditionary force, the Afrika Korps, which had been sent by Hitler to shore up the collapsing Italian position in North Africa. Although ordered to behave cautiously, he immediately took advantage of the weakening of British Commonwealth strength caused by the diversion of resources to the Greek campaign. On 24 March, he launched an attack together with the Italian *Ariete* and *Brescia* divisions against the weakly held line at El Agheila, and by 31 March was ready to advance across Cyrenaica in defiance of orders from Berlin. He organized mobile Axis units into three lines of attack: the Italian armour advanced along the coast towards Benghazi, while two German columns moved across the desert to cut off the Allied position.

The campaign was an exceptional success. The British abandoned the defensive line in central Cyrenaica on 6 April, and their two commanders, General Neame and General O'Connor, were captured by an Axis patrol on 7 April. By 8 April, Italian and German forces met at the coast and pressed on to Tobruk, where the Australian 9th Division had retreated. Tobruk was under siege by 11 April, but all attacks were repelled and the city remained besieged until December, reinforced by convoy to prevent its surrender. By this time the German High Command was anxious that Rommel not over-commit his forces and General Paulus was sent to order him in person to hold a defensive line west of Tobruk at Gazala. This order was transmitted to Berlin and intercepted and deciphered by British intelligence. Churchill was keen to use this information to launch a counter-attack and ordered General Wavell to use new supplies of tanks and aircraft, delivered by the "Tiger" convoy, to carry the battle back to Rommel. By this time, in defiance of Paulus, the Afrika Korps had reached Bardia and Sollum, close to the Egyptian border.

ABOVE A gun of the Royal Horse Artillery firing at German forces on the perimeter of the Libyan port of Tobruk during the campaign for the city in 1941.

RIGHT Australian soldiers from the 9th Infantry Division guard German and Italian soldiers in Tobruk. These were among the first Germans taken prisoner in the North African campaign.

ABOVE Insignia for the 7th (top) and 9th Australian divisions which formed part of the British, Commonwealth and Empire forces in North Africa.

FIELD MARSHAL ERWIN ROMMEL (1891–1944)

Rommel was the most famous of Hitler's generals. A dedicated and effective commander, he was a soldier's soldier, daring and tough and willing to share the dangers of his men. A career soldier who fought with distinction in the First World War on the Western and Italian fronts, he was a champion of fast, mobile warfare and commanded a Panzer division in the campaign in France. He was made a General in January 1941 and sent to command the Afrika Korps, a formation set up to support Italian forces in the Western Desert. In June 1942, he was made Germany's youngest Field Marshal, but his force was defeated in North Africa in May 1943. He helped organize the German defence of northern France but was wounded in an aircraft attack on 17 July 1944. Implicated in the bomb plot against Hitler three days later, he chose suicide rather than face a trial for treason.

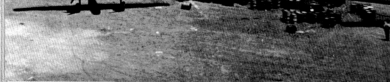

ABOVE Afrika Korps armband.

LIEUTENANT COLONEL "JOCK" CAMPBELL (1894–1942)

An artillery officer in the First World War, Lieutenant Colonel Campbell commanded the Royal Horse Artillery in North Africa in 1940–1 in the campaigns against Axis forces. He was best known for commanding a mobile unit for harassing the Italian army. So successful was his leadership of these combined-arms forces for rapid incursions across desert terrain against the enemy that they were nicknamed "Jock" columns. In 1941–2 he commanded the 7th Support Group and was promoted Major General in early 1942. He died in an accident on 26 February 1942 when his jeep overturned.

ABOVE A German 88mm Flak 36 gun in action in the desert war against British tanks. The anti-aircraft gun doubled up as a very effective "tank-buster" add was used in this role on all German fronts.

LEFT German air-force base in Cyrenaica during the campaign in 1941. Junkers Ju 52 transport aircraft (on the ground and in the air) were the backbone of Rommel's airborne supply system. In the foreground are Me110 twin-engined fighter bombers.

BELOW The Special Air Service was set up in August 1941 as a result of the need to create small, hard-hitting units to infiltrate and sabotage Axis installations. Here men of the SAS are in training for parachute jumping. They co-operated closely with the Long-Range Desert Group which operated throughout 1941.

The British Commonwealth counter-attack, Operation "Brevity", began on 15 May against German forces at Sollum. The campaign made little headway, and by 27 May German forces had recaptured the ground temporarily lost. Wavell was under pressure to act and on 15 June launched a second counter-attack, Operation "Battleaxe", which was even less successful in penetrating the Axis line at Bardia. The Afrika Korps used the 88mm anti-aircraft gun as anti-tank artillery to devastating effect. Having blunted the Allied attack, Rommel's forces pushed on towards Egyptian territory to end the threat from a demoralized enemy. On 17 June, British forces withdrew into Egypt to defend the Suez Canal. Rommel's forces dug in to a defensive line at Sollum, having recaptured almost all of Cyrenaica in a lightning two-month campaign.

Wavell was relieved by Churchill on 1 July and replaced with General Claude Auchinleck as Commander-in-Chief Middle East. By this time the British Commonwealth forces and support troops in the Middle Eastern theatre numbered over one million men, and represented the largest combat theatre command in existence, with an airforce of 49 squadrons and over 700 aircraft. Auchinleck resisted Churchill's efforts to go over to an early offensive, preferring to build up substantial reserves and equipment before running the risk that a premature assault like "Brevity" and "Battleaxe" would bring a third defeat. Throughout the desert campaigns Egypt was virtually taken over by the British: large transit and training centres were set up, oil pipelines constructed, water pipes laid from the Nile into the desert, and new roads and air bases constructed, most of it using Egyptian labour. The British presence was accepted reluctantly by many Egyptians, and British commanders knew that they faced not only a formidable military foe, but the possibility of political instability in the rear.

THE ALLIED INVASION OF IRAQ & SYRIA

2 MAY 1941
British troops occupy Basra and the oilfields of southern Iraq.

10 MAY 1941
London experiences the heaviest air raid of the Blitz.

20 MAY 1941
German paratroops begin the invasion of the island of Crete.

3 JUNE 1941
Anti-Jewish rioters in Baghdad murder Jews and destroy Jewish shops.

11 JUNE 1941
Roosevelt agrees to station US troops in Iceland to replace a British garrison.

12 JULY 1941
Britain and the Soviet Union sign a mutual aid treaty in Moscow.

ABOVE Cap badge for The King's Own (Royal Lancaster) Regiment.

ABOVE Formation badge for the 6th Infantry Division. The division was moved to Syria in June 1941 and took part in the battle for Damascus against Vichy French forces.

With German forces in the Balkans and pressing forward in the Western Desert, British leaders became anxious that the position of British interests in the Middle East, particularly oil, which was vital for the whole war effort in the Mediterranean, might be threatened by a combination of Axis military success and pro-Axis sympathy among the Muslim populations of the Middle East. Plans were discussed as early as March 1940 for possible action in Iraq where anti-British nationalism was a threat to the Mosul oilfields; Operation "Sabine" was prepared for the possible transfer of troops from India to Basra. When Iraq's regency was overthrown by a military coup in early April 1941, the British ambassador, Sir Kinahan Cornwallis, who arrived in Baghdad in the midst of the coup, urgently requested British military intervention before the anticipated arrival of German aircraft and troops.

On 17 April the first Indian troops arrived in Basra and two days later 400 men of the 1st King's Own Royal Regiment flew in to reinforce the Habbaniya air base near Baghdad. The rebel leader, Rashid Ali, decided to destroy the British military presence and on 1 May the Iraqi army began to dig in around the air base to prepare to capture it, hoping that their action would bring German support. The British commander of the base, Air Vice-Marshal Smart, decided to fight and on 2 May, before Iraqi forces were ready, launched a heavy air attack against them. The Iraqi air force of 56 largely obsolete aircraft was soon halved in strength and relentless bombing forced retreat from the perimeter of

ABOVE An Australian-manned Vickers Light Tank Mk VI during the advance of Commonwealth forces into Syria, 11 June 1941.

ABOVE LEFT Arab legionaries guard a landing ground beside the Iraq Petroleum Pipeline in Trans-Jordan where a group of Gloster Gladiator fighters are refuelling. The aircraft were on their way from Egypt to help the besieged airfield at Habbaniya in Iraq.

LEFT Following the defeat of the Iraqi army, which surrendered on 30 May 1941, British forces occupied Baghdad. They can be seen here gazing at the city across the Tigris River.

ABOVE Armed tribal warriors gather in an Iraqi village in May 1941 as part of the revolt against the presence of British bases in the country.

THE IRAQ REBELLION

Iraq had been a British Mandate under the League of Nations but was granted independence in 1932. The Anglo-Iraqi Treaty of 1930 gave the British economic and military concessions, including the right to station troops and two permanent air bases at Basra and Habbaniya. A group of anti-British army officers in Iraq, known as the Golden Square, led by the military commander and former prime minister Rashid Ali al-Gaylani (1892–1965) launched a coup against the pro-British Regent Emir Abdullah in early April 1941. Rashid Ali became prime minister on 3 April and the Regent retreated to Basra. Following the defeat of the Iraqi army in May 1941, Rashid fled to Iran and finally to Germany where he remained in exile until 1958.

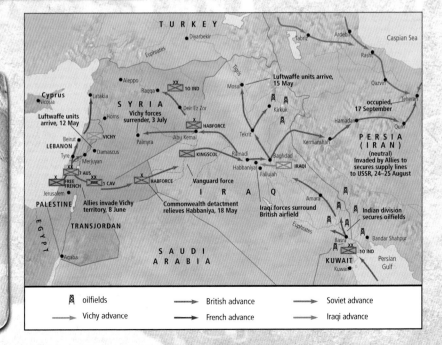

🛢 oilfields	⟶ British advance	⟶ Soviet advance
⟶ Vichy advance	⟶ French advance	⟶ Iraqi advance

ABOVE A six-inch howitzer firing at Vichy French forces in Beirut in the battle for the Lebanese capital during 6–10 July 1941. The 7th Australian Division reached the outskirts of the city but was faced with stiff resistance by the French Commander, General Dentz.

FREE FRENCH FORCES

Free French forces, under the overall command of Charles de Gaulle but operationally subordinate to British officers, played a part in the Middle East campaigns but their presence produced problems for British plans for the region. De Gaulle wanted Syria and Lebanon to be administered by the Free French and to be able to recruit soldiers from the Vichy garrison for the Free French cause. De Gaulle lost the first argument, and had to agree to the principle of Syrian and Lebanese independence; but he won the second, and 6,000 new recruits joined his forces.

RIGHT A Free French fighter from the French colony of Chad mans a machine-gun in a city street during the Allied advance into Syria and Lebanon, June 1941.

ABOVE British soldiers on 12 July 1941 comb the ruins of the Temple of Ball, near Palmyra in Syria, for Arab snipers employed by the Vichy French regime to obstruct the British advance.

the base. A relief force was organized from Trans-Jordan codenamed "Habforce", under the command of Major General John Clark. Out of almost 6,000 troops, a rapid-movement column of 2,000 was created to reach the air base quickly. By this time around 25 German aircraft were available from Iraqi and Syrian airfields to help the rebels. The advance column was attacked by German bombers, but reached Habbaniya on 18 May.

By this time Iraqi resistance was crumbling. The forces available at the air base moved out to Fallujah on 19 May, captured the town and moved on Baghdad. German air forces were outnumbered and 21 aircraft destroyed. On 30 May, Iraq's five-division army abandoned the fight and an armistice was signed. The Regent returned to power in October and on 17 January 1943 Iraq declared war on the Axis. The help given to Rashid Ali from bases in Syria, a French mandate loyal to Vichy France, prompted Churchill to authorize a further operation to secure the Middle East for

the Allies. On 23 June, an operation under the command of Lieutenant General Maitland Wilson was launched against the Vichy French in Lebanon and Syria from Palestine in the south and Iraq in the east, using "Habforce" and the 10th Indian Division, which had been landed at Basra during May, as well as the Australian 7th Division. Slow progress was made against the French garrisons, but by 6 July the 7th Australian Division began the battle for Beirut, which followed the occupation of Damascus on 21 June. The commander of Beirut capitulated on 10 July and the Vichy authorities signed an armistice (the Acre Convention) on 14 July. Some 32,300 French troops were repatriated and Syria was placed under British military control until its independence in 1946. Wilson remained in the area, commanding what was now called Ninth Army against the risk of a German thrust from the north through the Soviet Caucasus. The two campaigns secured a vital area that combined Britain's war effort in Europe and Asia and frustrated further Axis advance.

BELOW French cavalry on the march near the frontier between Syria and Palestine during the brief war with British Commonwealth forces in June and July 1941. The Syrian garrison remained loyal to Vichy France and found itself fighting against Free French soldiers on the Allied side.

THE ATLANTIC CHARTER

2 AUGUST 1941
Roosevelt extends US aid programme to include the Soviet Union.

10 AUGUST 1941
Plots to stage pro-German coups are uncovered in Argentina, Cuba and Chile.

10 AUGUST 1941
Britain and the USSR pledge their support to Turkey in the event of an attack by an Axis power.

12 AUGUST 1941
Hitler issues orders to halt the move on Moscow in order to capture Leningrad in the north and the Ukraine in the south.

12 AUGUST 1941
Pétain suspends independent political activity and bans all political meetings creating a quasi-fascist authoritarian state in Vichy France.

13 AUGUST 1941
Japanese bombers destroy much of Chungking, the Chinese wartime capital.

From 9 to 12 August 1941 the first major summit meeting of the war took place between President Franklin D Roosevelt and Britain's Prime Minister, Winston Churchill. The site chosen was in Newfoundland, off the coast of Canada. Churchill arrived by battleship, Roosevelt arrived aboard the US cruiser *Augusta*, and it was here that most of the meetings took place. At Placentia Bay the two men came face-to-face for the first time in the war to discuss the future of the conflict and the extent of American assistance, short of war, that Roosevelt could offer. It was an emotional moment for both men, but for Churchill the meeting had a special importance. Without American assistance, Britain's war effort was simply insufficient to defeat the Axis enemy. Churchill set out to seal what soon became known as "the special relationship".

On the very first day Roosevelt told Churchill that he wanted them jointly to make a statement of long-term political aims which could be announced publicly. That same evening Churchill retired to the ship that had brought him to Newfoundland and drafted a five-point statement which became the core of a document that came to be called the "Atlantic Charter". Over the next two days the two delegations argued about

RIGHT Vivien Leigh as Lady Hamilton in the 1941 film *That Hamilton Woman*. It was Churchill's favourite film and he is said to have watched it repeatedly whilst on route to his meeting with Roosevelt at Placentia Bay, just off the coast of Newfoundland, Canada.

THE RE-ELECTION OF ROOSEVELT

In November 1940 President Franklin D Roosevelt was re-elected for an unprecedented third term of office. For the British, Roosevelt was seen as a vital ally in their efforts to win greater support for their war effort from the United States. Yet Roosevelt was forced to campaign on the slogan that no American boys were going to be killed in any foreign war to avert popular suspicion that he wanted the United States to join the war against Hitler. His defeat of the Republican candidate Wendell Wilkie was much narrower than his victory in 1936, but it paved the way for a more active policy of intervention in 1941.

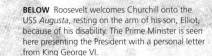

BELOW Roosevelt welcomes Churchill onto the USS *Augusta*, resting on the arm of his son, Elliot, because of his disability. The Prime Minister is seen here presenting the President with a personal letter from King George VI.

ABOVE and LEFT Churchill and Roosevelt, back on their home soils, days after signing the historic agreement of cooperation between the USA and Great Britain.

LEFT Hitler and Himmler in conference, 1941. Hitler saw the Atlantic Charter as a declaration of war by world Jewry against the German peoples. A few days after it was published he ordered Himmler to begin a more active campaign of persecution against Jews in the Soviet Union.

RIGHT A pile of human bones discovered at Majdanek death camp in the outskirts of Lublin, Poland, by the Russian troops liberating the camp in 1944. Some claim that Hitler's outrage at the Atlantic Charter hastened the move to extermination of the Jews.

ABOVE Prisoners at Buchenwald concentration camp, 1945. The Atlantic Charter, and later the Charter of the United Nations, sought to create a new democratic order in which such horrors would not recur.

BELOW Representatives of the "Big Five" of the US, UK, France, China and the USSR meet on 29 May 1945 to continue the discussions which would lead to the signing of the Charter of the United Nations, 26 June 1945. The Atlantic Charter of 1941 paved the way for the creation of the UN some four years later.

the wording and about what was missing from Churchill's statement. The Americans wanted a greater commitment to an open post-war economy; Churchill did not want to compromise the future of Empire trade. So irritated did he become at the thought that Roosevelt might damage British imperial interests that at one point he angrily waved a finger under Roosevelt's nose and accused him of trying to destroy the British Empire.

In general the two sides agreed and on the final day an eight-point charter was finally signed committing both states to a post-war world in which self-determination of peoples and freely-elected governments would be the central principles. There was a vague commitment to giving open access to the world's raw-material supplies and maintaining freedom of the seas, and a final clause that suggested abandoning force as a means to settle disputes and reducing the level of armaments. The principles were loosely worded and bound neither party to anything definite. The Atlantic Charter was announced on 14 August and its terms soon became known worldwide. In September the major Allies all signed the pact in London, and on 1 January 1942 26 nations, who signed the United Nations Declaration which launched what became the UN some three years later, also signed the Atlantic Charter. Though it had not been Roosevelt's original intention, since the United States had not been at war, the Charter became a consolidated statement of Allied war aims. As such its principles underlay all the later efforts to construct a durable post-war settlement in terms of international justice.

The Charter was viewed differently in Berlin and Moscow. Stalin did not like the idea of the Soviet Union being bound to respect the sovereignty of other peoples

PRINCE OF WALES BATTLESHIP

The battleship that conveyed Winston Churchill to the conference in Placentia Bay, HMS *Prince of Wales*, was one of Britain's newest additions to the fleet, with 10 massive 14-inch guns. It had seen action in the sinking of the German battleship *Bismarck* and completed its refit in time for the transatlantic trip. There was some degree of risk in crossing seas infested with submarines, but the battleship made the five-day crossing without incident. A few months later, in December 1941, the *Prince of Wales* was sent to south east Asia to protect the British Empire from Japanese attack. Confident that battleships could defend themselves against air attack, the ship was caught in the open sea by Japanese aircraft and sunk on 9 December. "In all the war," wrote Churchill, "I never received a more direct shock."

nor the commitment to freely-elected governments. The Soviet Union associated itself with the Charter but never subscribed to it fully. After the war no effort was made to protect the smaller states under Soviet control and freely-elected governments had to wait until 1990. In Berlin the Charter was viewed in a more menacing way. Hitler took the statement as an indication that the United States intended at some point to fight Germany and counted America now firmly among Germany's enemies. He saw the Charter as the work of American and British Jews and a day after the Charter was published he ordered Himmler to begin a more active campaign of persecution in Germany and the occupied areas. In Hitler's warped world view, the Atlantic Charter was tantamount to a declaration of war by world Jewry against the German people.

OPERATION "CRUSADER"

The failure to dislodge Rommel's Afrika Korps from the Egyptian frontier in the summer of 1941 led to one of the few periods of static warfare in the Desert War. Rommel and his Italian allies created a defensive line around the towns of Sollum and Bardia, while the newly-appointed General Auchinleck refused to bend to pressure to attack the Axis until he could be certain of a preponderance of force. While the army built up its strength, the RAF Western Desert Air Force, under the overall command of Air Chief Marshal Arthur Tedder, kept up a relentless bombing of German positions, including 100 attacks on the port of Benghazi and 70 attacks on Tripoli. Tedder organized new tactics of close support for the army with standing fighter patrols linked by radio to army liaison units to permit quick battlefield response, a lesson learned from German practice. The army's Western Desert Force (renamed the 8th Army on 18 September 1941) was strengthened, so that by November 1941 it numbered 118,000 men, drawn from British, New Zealand, South African and Indian forces. The Axis were outnumbered in tanks (680 to 390) and even more in aircraft (1,000 to 320). Auchinleck planned a major campaign, Operation "Crusader", to win

BELOW Officers of the Royal Horse Artillery in Tobruk at the unit's command post, 1 November 1941. One officer is watching where the shells land while the other is shouting fire orders through a loudhailer. The siege of Tobruk was lifted by 10 December.

ABOVE In a scene more reminiscent of the London Blitz, British searchlights and anti-aircraft fire light up the night sky above the Egyptian port and British naval base of Alexandria. Bomb bursts from Axis aircraft attack can be seen in the background.

BELOW An Axis petrol-tanker and trailer on fire on the road between Homs and Misurata in Libya following an attack by RAF Bristol Blenheim light bombers during Operation "Crusader".

BELOW An American-built Martin Maryland of the South African Air Force flies over vehicles of the 15th and 21st German Panzer Divisions which have just been bombed during their attempt to push through British positions east of Sidi Rezegh.

LEFT A British Matilda tank and truck in the desert at the start of Operation "Crusader". British Empire and Commonwealth forces had a superiority of two to one in tanks by the time the battle started.

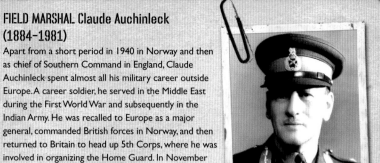

FIELD MARSHAL Claude Auchinleck (1884-1981)

Apart from a short period in 1940 in Norway and then as chief of Southern Command in England, Claude Auchinleck spent almost all his military career outside Europe. A career soldier, he served in the Middle East during the First World War and subsequently in the Indian Army. He was recalled to Europe as a major general, commanded British forces in Norway, and then returned to Britain to head up 5th Corps, where he was involved in organizing the Home Guard. In November 1940, he was appointed Commander-in-Chief in India, and then on 5 July 1941 Commander-in-Chief Middle East, by which time he was a full general. His mixed performance against Rommel in 1941–42 led Churchill to remove him from office in August 1942. He returned to India in June 1943 as Commander-in-Chief, a post he held until 1947. He was promoted field marshal in 1946.

back Cyrenaica and to lift the siege of Tobruk. When the moment came to attack, German forces were in the process of preparing yet again to attack Tobruk and remove the threat to the long Axis flank.

"Crusader" began with mixed fortunes: Allied forces moved forward on 18 November, meeting stiff resistance. The attempt by the Tobruk garrison to break out and meet the XXX Corps as it advanced west across the desert was broken by Rommel, who had begun to retreat back towards Tobruk once he realized the scale of Auchinleck's plan. The Italian forces were abandoned at Bardia and Sollum, where they surrendered only after fierce resistance on 2 and 12 January respectively. German counter-attacks south of Tobruk around Sidi Rezegh produced a chaotic battlefield, and at one point Rommel ordered his remaining tanks to drive for the Nile Delta, thinking that enemy armour was all but annihilated. The commander of the Allied force, Lieutenant General Sir Alan Cunnigham, the victor in East Africa, uncertain about his position, requested permission to retreat. Auchinleck replaced him with his deputy chief of staff, Acting Major-General Neil Ritchie, who stabilized the operation. The XXX Corps linked up with the Tobruk garrison, threatening to cut off Axis forces. Rommel instead retreated westwards in good order on 8 December, while Allied forces entered Tobruk on 10 December, lifting at last the 240-day siege. By this time the town was no longer defended by the Australian troops who had occupied it in the spring, but by a mixture of British, Indian, South African and Polish forces, including the Polish Carpathian Brigade.

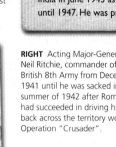

LEFT Badge of the 3rd Carpathian (Polish) Division which formed part of the British Eighth Army in North Africa.

Rommel was pursued across the territory won earlier in the year. Gazala, Benghazi and Mersa Brega all fell again to Allied forces, who by the end of 1941 had travelled 475 kilometres (300 miles) and recaptured the whole of Cyrenaica. After Soviet defeats and the onset of quick victories for Japan in the Pacific, the advance in Libya was an important morale boost for the embattled Allies. The victory, however, proved to be a hollow one. Rommel retreated with his undefeated Afrika Korps back to El Agheila, where he could regroup and exploit the fresh supplies which were landed at Tripoli in January. Once these reached the front line he prepared to push back the British Commonwealth forces, by now overstretched and short of supplies. Auchinleck failed to appreciate his enemy's true position and planned a new campaign, Operation "Acrobat", to seize the western Libyan area of Tripolitania. On January 21, Rommel pre-empted him by launching what was to prove a devastating riposte to the apparent success of "Crusader".

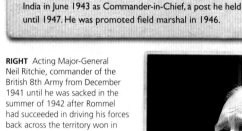

RIGHT Acting Major-General Neil Ritchie, commander of the British 8th Army from December 1941 until he was sacked in the summer of 1942 after Rommel had succeeded in driving his forces back across the territory won in Operation "Crusader".

BELOW German forces advance in the area between Tobruk and Sidi Omar. The battles during Operation "Crusader" flowed back and forth across the desert until Rommel's decision to withdraw on 8 December once it was clear he was outnumbered.

PEARL HARBOR

BELOW Purple heart awarded posthumously to Private Jack H Feldman who died in the Japanese attack on Pearl Harbor at the age of only 19.

In the early morning of 7 December – 8 December in Japan – waves of Japanese naval aircraft with bombs and torpedoes attacked the major United States naval base at Pearl Harbor on Oahu in the Hawaiian Islands. They attacked without warning or a declaration of war and unleashed four years of conflict in the Pacific basin which would end with the final destruction of the Japanese Empire.

The assault on Pearl Harbor came at the end of a long deterioration in relations between Japan and the United States. The American government favoured the Chinese side in the Sino-Japanese war, but would do nothing to provoke war with Japan. The United States assumed that Japan would never risk all-out war and hoped to arrive eventually at a diplomatic solution. In July 1940, when the first Japanese forces were allowed to enter northern Indo-China, Roosevelt authorized restrictions of scrap steel and oil exports to Japan. Japanese naval planners, anxious about the threat of a total oil embargo, began to argue in favour of a pre-emptive "Southward Advance" against America and the British Empire, seizing the oil-rich region of the Dutch East Indies and establishing an unassailable perimeter in the Pacific.

The German invasion of the Soviet Union created confusion in Japan. The powerful Japanese army argued for the opportunity to settle accounts with Russia by joining forces with Germany in the destruction of the Soviet Union. The navy continued to press for a southern strategy on the grounds that the Soviet-German war reduced any risk in the north, while seizing the rich resources of the south would

ABOVE A Japanese navy Mitsubishi "Zero" fighter takes off from the flight-deck of the Japanese carrier *Akagi* on the way to attack the US naval base at Pearl Harbor on the morning of 7 December 1941. The Japanese navy had a corps of around 600 elite pilots who trained for long over-sea flights prior to the attack.

create conditions for the final triumph against China and the Soviet Union. On 26 July 1941, following further Japanese incursion in Indo-China, the United States froze all Japanese assets and tightened the oil embargo. The navy in early September 1941 proposed a showdown with the United States if diplomatic efforts to reverse American policy were not successful. A deadline was set for 30 November, after which war would be launched. The American government could read Japanese codes and knew that Japanese plans for aggression were hardening. On 26 November, Cordell Hull, Roosevelt's Secretary of State, presented new conditions to Japan for the withdrawal of their forces from Indo-China

GENERAL HIDEKI TOJO (1884–1948)

General Tojo, the son of a Japanese army general, was appointed Army Minister in 1940 and then Prime Minister on 16 October 1941. He had little campaign experience, but was a hard-working, strict and effective administrator and military politician.

He was a committed nationalist and was at the forefront of those arguing for a tough military policy in China and against compromise with the Western powers. He faced growing criticism in 1944 over Japanese military reverses and was forced to resign in July 1944. He tried and failed to commit suicide when American military police arrived to arrest him in 1945, and was hanged as a war criminal in December 1948.

BELOW A Japanese aerial photograph of Ford Island in the Hawaii group after the Japanese attack on 7 December 1941. Two aircraft are visible pressing home further attacks on the US fleet.

JAPANESE-AMERICANS

In 1942 around 110,000 Japanese-Americans, many of them American citizens, were "relocated" from their homes, mainly on the West Coast, to ten camps further inland. The move followed President Roosevelt's Executive Order 9066, signed on 19 February 1942, which gave the Secretary of War the right to designate prescribed military areas from which people could be legally and forcibly expelled. Most of the Japanese-Americans were held in the camps for up to three years even though not a single case of spying or sabotage was ever discovered. The same rules were not applied to American citizens of German or Italian descent, but only to German and Italian aliens. Around 22,500 young Japanese-American men volunteered for combat, 18,000 of whom served in segregated units.

RIGHT A group of Japanese interned in the US-controlled Panama Canal Zone on 10 December 1941. Following the Japanese attack on Hawaii, Japanese, German and Italian citizens in the Zone were forced into an internment camp like those set up throughout the continental United States.

ABOVE Blazing oil from fractured fuel tanks in the aftermath of the Japanese bombing of the port installations at Pearl Harbor. A damaged battleship is visible behind the screen of smoke.

FAR RIGHT USS *Shaw* explodes during the Japanese attack on Pearl Harbor. She was hit three times during the Japanese bombardment. She was not ready for action again until June 1942.

RIGHT US President Franklin D Roosevelt signs the document declaring war on Japan, 8 December 1941.

BELOW A naval launch approaches the US battleship *West Virginia*, hit by six torpedoes during the attack by Japanese aircraft on the base at Pearl Harbor. Altogether 2,403 civilians and servicemen were killed in the attacks.

and China. The Japanese government rejected the idea out of hand, and on 1 December, Emperor Hirohito approved the onset of war.

In early December, a large force made up of all five of Japan's fleet carriers, with 460 aircraft, sailed in complete radio silence for the seas north of Hawaii. Although intelligence did eventually reach the listening station on the islands, it was lost among a mass of detailed radio traffic. An intercepted message to the Japanese Embassy in Washington from Tokyo on 6 December was incompletely decoded so that the instructions to sever diplomatic relations, indicating war, failed to be noticed. At 7.49 a.m. on 7 December the first wave of 183 Japanese bombers, dive-bombers and fighters struck Pearl Harbor and the US air bases. A second wave hit at 8.50 a.m. Of the 394 US aircraft on the island, 347 were destroyed or damaged for

the loss of only 29 Japanese planes. Surprise was total and the impact devastating. A corps of highly trained naval pilots succeeded in sinking or damaging 18 vessels, including eight battleships. Some 76 ships were undamaged, among them the submarines, while US aircraft carriers were by chance not in port. Despite the outrage provoked in the United States at the attack, the damage was not as severe as Japanese planners had hoped and Pearl Harbor remained a central base for subsequent American operations.

In Congress the following day Roosevelt condemned "a date which will live in infamy" and war was formally declared against the Japanese Empire. Japanese politicians had hoped that Pearl Harbor would demoralize American opinion and limit their war effort. As it turned out nothing could have prompted greater outrage and a stronger American urge to fight the war with Japan to the finish.

BLITZKRIEG IN ASIA

12 DECEMBER 1941
Romania declares war on the United States, followed by Bulgaria the next day.

1 JANUARY 1942
United Nations Declaration signed by Britain, the United States, China and the Soviet Union and 22 other states.

13 JANUARY 1942
German submarines begin Operation "Drumbeat" against shipping along the US Atlantic coastline.

14 FEBRUARY 1942
Directive to RAF Bomber Command allows onset of area bombing of cities.

4 APRIL 1942
Hitler orders retaliatory air raids on British cities.

5 MAY 1942
Allied forces land in northern Madagascar to prevent Japanese occupation.

The Japanese attack on Pearl Harbor was planned to coincide with a number of complex and daring combined operations to seize Southeast Asia, the East Indies and a string of small islands in the western Pacific to secure supplies of oil, rubber, tin and other minerals, and to discourage the British and American governments from attempting the difficult and expensive task of recapturing the new southern zone of the Japanese Empire. Within four months the vast area of the European powers' empires in the Far East was under Japanese rule.

On 7 December, a Japanese seaborne striking force under General Tomoyuki Yamashita assembled in the Gulf of Siam destined the following day to occupy the Kra Isthmus in southern Thailand and to assault the British airfields in northern Malaya. Other strike forces prepared to seize Hong Kong, assault the Philippines, and then conquer the British and Dutch possessions in the East Indies. The campaign was an extraordinary success. In Malaya Yamashita commanded around 60,000 men, but defeated a British Empire force more than twice as large. The attempt by the Allied army to hold up the Japanese advance was half-hearted at best. By 9 January, the Japanese were almost at the Malayan capital of Kuala Lumpur. Adept at jungle warfare and tactics of infiltration, the Japanese army proved an irresistible force against a poorly prepared enemy with limited air power. By 31 January, Malaya had been abandoned and the British forces were withdrawn to the island of Singapore.

Japanese progress in the Philippines was less spectacular. The northernmost island of Batan was occupied on 8 December and the main island of Luzon assaulted by seaborne forces two days later. Further out in the Pacific,

LEFT Japanese forces were among the first to master effective combined operations. Here Japanese soldiers haul an artillery piece onto the shore from the landing boats during one of many similar operations in the early weeks of 1942.

BELOW Burning oil stocks after a Japanese air attack on Dutch bases in the Dutch East Indies during the three-month campaign for the archipelago. The oil of the region was one of the chief factors encouraging the Japanese attack.

ABOVE Badge of the 11th Indian Infantry Division, which eventually surrendered to the Japanese when Singapore fell on 15 February 1942.

BELOW Japanese soldiers of General Yamashita's force storm a British-held village during the rapid conquest of Malaya. In seven weeks a larger British Empire and Commonwealth force was relentlessly driven back by an army whose soldiers were regarded in the West as racially inferior.

GENERAL DOUGLAS MACARTHUR (1880–1964)

MacArthur was born into an upper-class American family, the son of a soldier. He was an outstanding officer cadet, scoring the highest marks ever achieved at the military academy at West Point. At the end of the First World War, he was already a brigadier general. In 1930, he served as Army Chief of Staff, and in 1935 went as military adviser to the Philippines, where he retired from the American army to become a Philippines field marshal. In July 1941, Roosevelt made him commander of US forces in the Far East, and he organized the defence of the Philippines against Japanese assault. He was appointed Commander-in-Chief South West Pacific Area in April 1942, and despite his reputation for flamboyance and self-promotion, became an inspirational leader of men. After recapturing the Philippines in 1945, he was made commander-in-chief of all US army forces in the Pacific. He became Supreme Commander Allied Powers in the post-war administration of Japan and played a key part in Japan's democratic reconstruction. He was finally relieved of command in April 1951 following arguments with President Truman over policy on the Korean War.

VICE ADMIRAL CHUICHI NAGUMO (1887–1944)

The leader of the operation at Pearl Harbor, Nagumo was regarded as a particularly aggressive and effective fleet commander, with a reputation for speaking his mind. He rose to prominence in the 1930s as a torpedo expert, and was among the circle of senior Japanese naval officers who favoured a confrontation with the United States. He followed up the Pearl Harbor attack with command of the raids on northern Australia, India and Ceylon (Sri Lanka) and at the Battle of Midway. The disaster at Midway showed the limits of his grasp of naval air power, and he was relieved of command, posted back to Japan and then, in 1944, to the Marianas. He committed suicide in July 1944 during the American invasion of Saipan.

small islands were seized to prevent any threat from the central ocean area. The US base at Guam was occupied on 10 December. The garrison on Wake Island resisted the first Japanese attack on 11 December, but succumbed to a larger air and sea assault 12 days later. The attack on the East Indies, defended by Dutch, British, Australian and colonial troops, began a week later on 15 December with landings on the island of Borneo. In a daring series of combined operations the Japanese army swarmed out over the archipelago, targeting airfields and oil installations. One branch of the assault moved southeast to capture the British Solomon Islands. Admiral Takahashi's task force concentrated on driving through the central zone, taking Bali on 19 February and Timor the next day. The capital of the Dutch East Indies, Batavia (Jakarta), was captured on 5 March. Japanese warships and aircraft hunted down surviving Allied shipping and destroyed it, although some of the Allied force was evacuated to Australia from Java, harried by Japanese aircraft. On 19 February, to drive home the Japanese success, bomber aircraft destroyed a large part of the northern Australian port of Darwin. The Dutch surrendered on 9 March, the rest of the Allies three days later.

Japanese plans worked almost like clockwork. There was no intention of creating a larger campaign area than their limited forces could protect and Australia was safe for the present. In the Indian Ocean the British naval presence, weakened by the sinking of HMS *Prince of Wales* and HMS *Repulse* on 10 December, was challenged by a daring raid led by Vice Admiral Nagumo, whose task force attacked Colombo in Ceylon on 5 April 1942, then the naval base at Trincomalee, sinking four warships, including the carrier *Hermes*, the first to be sunk by carrier aircraft. There was no intention yet of extending the Japanese Empire into the Indian Ocean area, but simply the aim to undermine the delicate British political position in southern Asia and to warn Britain to stay at arm's length from the new Japanese Empire which had been established across thousands of miles in the space of little more than four months.

ABOVE RAF American-made Brewster Buffalo fighters flying over Malaya.

BELOW LEFT On 18 April 1942 US naval and air forces launched a reprisal raid on Tokyo and other Japanese cities with 16 B 25 bombers launched from the US carrier *Hornet*. The bombers, seen here leaving the carrier, inflicted little physical damage but gave the American public a psychological boost.

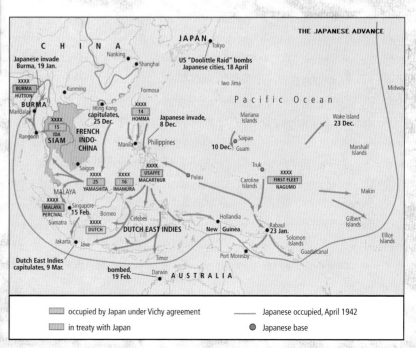

THE JAPANESE ADVANCE

Japanese invade Burma, 19 Jan.

US "Doolittle Raid" bombs Japanese cities, 18 April

Hong Kong capitulates, 25 Dec.

Japanese invade, 8 Dec.

Wake Island 23 Dec.

10 Dec. Guam

Dutch East Indies capitulates, 9 Mar.

Singapore 15 Feb.

bombed, 19 Feb. Darwin

Rabaul 23 Jan.

occupied by Japan under Vichy agreement

in treaty with Japan

Japanese occupied, April 1942

Japanese base

LEND-LEASE

On 29 December 1940, President Roosevelt announced in a national radio broadcast his determination that the United States should become "the great arsenal of democracy". Three weeks before, Winston Churchill had sent him an urgent appeal for economic and financial aid to fight the war in 1941. Roosevelt knew that there were powerful voices in the United States hostile to the idea of helping Britain, but on 2 January he asked the Treasury Department to draft a bill that would allow the President to sell, transfer, exchange, lease or lend war supplies to those states whose fight protected American security. This was the origin of what became known as the Lend-Lease scheme under whose terms the United States gave vast economic assistance to almost all states fighting the Axis.

Roosevelt introduced the scheme in Congress in January, provoking a storm of protest. He persisted in his view that America's interests could best be served by giving resources to end the German threat and on 11 March Congress approved the bill. Churchill described it as the most "unsordid act" and without question the supply of generous Lend-Lease aid allowed the British people to continue their war effort. But the transfer of resources was never one-way. Under the Reciprocal Aid Agreements signed in September 1942 the British undertook to help US forces stationed in Europe. One-third of US supplies for D-Day came from British mutual aid, including 16 million boxes of matches and 37 million cakes of soap. When the Soviet Union entered the war in June 1941, Britain and the United States both promised aid on a large scale to help the new combatant. By 1943, the United States was supplying goods to 35 states.

2 MAY 1942
Lend-Lease aid to Iraq and Iran authorised.

11 JUNE 1942
New Lend-Lease aggreement signed with the Soviet Union.

5 JULY 1942
British aid on the perilous Arctic Convoy route suspended following heavy losses.

12 AUGUST 1942
Churchill visits Stalin in Moscow and promises more aid.

1 MARCH 1943
Convoy conference in Washington to co-ordinate the effort to keep the sea lanes open in the Atlantic.

ABOVE Dried eggs imported from the United States described on the packet as "one of the United Nations". Such products became staples of the British wartime diet.

MAXIM LITVINOV (1876–1951)

Born into a wealthy Jewish family in Russian Poland, Litvinov joined Lenin's Bolsheviks and became a leading diplomat for the new Soviet state after 1917. He was appointed Foreign Affairs Commissar in 1930, and helped to bring the Soviet Union back into the international arena. He was sacked in May 1939, but brought back as Deputy Commissar for Foreign Affairs in 1941 and then from 1941 to 1943 ambassador in Washington where he played an important part in securing American aid and arguing the Soviet case for high levels of economic and military assistance.

ABOVE Not all Americans welcomed the Lend-Lease bill. Here representatives of the Massachusetts Women's Political Clubs, led by Father Christmas, picket the Department of the Treasury building in Washington, 26 February 1941.

LEFT A British dock worker unloads cheese from the United States, 14 October 1941. Food totalled 12.1 per cent of all Lend-Lease aid to the allies.

TOP American aid began even before the outbreak of war in Europe. Here Chinese soldiers and workers in January 1939 are carrying the parts of a US vehicle for reassembly on the Burma Road, the main supply route to aid the Chinese in their struggle against Japan.

ABOVE Pistol provided to the British forces under the Lend-Lease scheme. It is inscribed "United States Property":

ABOVE Soviet and American technicians examine a Douglas A-20 Havoc, part of a delivery supplied under the American-Soviet agreements in August 1941. These aircraft were shipped via Persia (Iran), part of the 14,203 planes supplied over the period of the war.

HARRY HOPKINS (1890–1946)

Hopkins was one of President Roosevelt's closest advisers. He began his career working for welfare organizations in New York where he came to the attention of Roosevelt, who was then the state governor. In 1933, Hopkins was recruited to administer the New Deal federal aid programme. During the war he became Roosevelt's unofficial emissary to Churchill and Stalin, with rooms in the White House. He was a major influence on the idea of creating Lend-Lease in 1940–41 and then in extending aid to the Soviet Union in the summer of 1941. Though in poor health, Hopkins continued to act as Roosevelt's confidant down to the conference at Yalta in February 1945. He died the following year after a long battle with illness.

The bulk of American assistance was sent to Britain in the form of weapons, raw materials, oil and food, including the famous tins of compressed meat known as Spam. Aid for the Soviet Union was more problematic because of deep distrust of Communism. On 2 August 1941, Roosevelt announced that the USSR would not formally qualify for Lend-Lease but would be given resources up to the limit that the United States could afford. Two weeks later the Soviet Embassy in Washington presented a 29-page list of everything the Soviet Union wanted. Churchill had been less wary and had pledged aid for the USSR as soon as the German-Soviet war began. Supplies were sent by the dangerous northern sea route around northern Scandinavia to Murmansk and Archangel, involving a total during the war of 739 merchant ships, escorted by the Royal Navy, of which 677 arrived safely. A second route was set up in Persia (modern Iran) which necessitated a British-Soviet occupation of Teheran on 17 September 1941 to secure the road, but the following year administration was taken over by the United States. A third line of supply was established through the eastern port of Vladivostok and thence to the Trans-Siberian railway.

The supplies were slow to arrive and not until late 1942 did they begin to make a significant impact in the Soviet Union. The quantity of finished weapons was a small proportion of the whole and the most valuable assistance came in the form of food, raw materials, railroad supplies and, above, all telecommunications equipment, including 380,000 field telephones, 5,899 radio stations and over one million miles of telephone wire. Although the Soviet side made endless complaints about the quality or insufficiency of supplies, Stalin privately admitted that without the aid the Soviet Union "would not have been able to cope". American aid to the British was much more substantial, a total of $29.9 billion over five years. Most of the supplies were in the form of munitions, aircraft and vehicles, a total of 70 per cent of all supplies in 1943 and 68 per cent in 1944. As the threat from Axis submarines receded in 1943, so the number of successful sailings across the Atlantic increased.

Lend-Lease turned out in the end to be something of a misnomer, as Roosevelt had always recognized. Almost none of the aid could be returned and little of it was directly paid for, except by reciprocal aid. Around 17 per cent of the American war effort was devoted to the aid programme and its impact in sustaining the fighting power of Britain and the Soviet Union was without question of fundamental importance in securing ultimate Allied victory.

ABOVE LEFT Children in an English school in Staffordshire in the autumn of 1941 eating eggs supplied under the Lend-Lease agreements. Food supplied to the Soviet Union was said to be enough to feed every Red Army soldier each day of the war.

BELOW Edward R Stettinius Jr (left), who ran the Lend-Lease organization before later becoming Roosevelt's Secretary of State, demonstrates on a world map the destination of US goods.

THE WANNSEE CONFERENCE

3 OCTOBER 1940
Jews in Nazi-occupied Warsaw are ordered into the ghetto.

19 MAY 1941
Hitler issues guidelines for troops in Russia giving permission to murder Communist Jews.

31 JULY 1941
Hermann Göring authorizes Reinhard Heydrich to find a "final solution" to the Jewish question.

18 AUGUST 1941
Hitler orders Berlin's remaining Jews to be deported eastwards.

13 MARCH 1942
The Belzec death camp is opened for the mass murder of Jews.

BELOW A group of emaciated children in the Warsaw ghetto, January 1942. The Ghetto was sealed up by the German authorities on 16 November 1940 and an estimated 100,000 died of disease and hunger before the population was deported to the death camps.

On 20 January 1942, 14 German officials and police leaders met with Reinhard Heydrich in a large villa on the shores of Lake Wannsee in a respectable suburb of Berlin. Heydrich was chief of the Reich Main Security Office (RSHA) responsible for most issues of security and surveillance in the Third Reich and in this role had been formally given the task by Hermann Göring, on 31 July 1941, of implementing a "final solution" to the Jewish question. In mid-July 1941 this meant evacuation of Jews to the newly conquered areas in the east of Europe, but by the time Heydrich met officials at Wannsee the term "evacuation" now signified destruction.

At the 20 January meeting, Heydrich presented figures on the Jewish population in Europe, over 11 million, a total which had been calculated by his assistant, the Gestapo official Adolf Eichmann. Heydrich had been authorized to organize the mass deportation of all Europe's Jews by his immediate superior Heinrich Himmler, head of the elite SS organization. Himmler was almost certainly acting on Hitler's authority, but the exact point at which Hitler ordered the mass murder of the Jews of Europe is not clear. Most historians date the decision to November or early December 1941, but the murder of certain categories of Jews in the conquered areas of the Soviet Union had already begun in June 1941. In August 1941, Hitler approved the murder of Jewish women and children in Russia; in September 1941, the male Jews of Serbia were slaughtered and Jews in the former Polish areas of Warthegau and Galicia were exterminated; and on 15 October 1941 the first mass deportation of

German Jews to the east began. The decision to exterminate Jews was thus taken piecemeal across the second half of 1941. The Wannsee Conference was the opportunity for Heydrich to bring all these strands together into a single comprehensive programme of genocide.

To carry out the new policy a number of purpose-built extermination camps were set up on occupied Polish territory at Chelmno, Sobibor, Belzec, Treblinka, Maidanek and Auschwitz-Birkenau. Construction had begun in 1941 of camps that included gas chambers where large numbers of victims could be killed at once using either carbon-monoxide poisoning or – as at Auschwitz – the delousing agent Zyklon-B. The first camp with purpose-built gas chambers began operation in March 1942, but

ABOVE The villa on the shores of the Wannsee in Berlin used as an SS guest house during the war. It was here that the notorious Wannsee Conference took place on 20 January 1942 which sealed the fate of Europe's Jews.

ABOVE LEFT The Corporate Jewish Shoemakers parade through the Greek city of Salonika (Thessaloniki) before the war. Salonika had one of the oldest and culturally rich Jewish communities in Europe but its Jewish population was destroyed during the genocide of 1942–4.

LEFT A yellow Star of David worn by Rosa Dalberg, a Dutch Jew who subsequently went into hiding in the Netherlands with false papers. The Star was compulsory for all Jews in occupied Europe and in Germany, and failure to wear it was a criminal offence. The Star isolated the Jews made them an easy target for victimisation.

ADOLF EICHMANN (1906–62)

From his position as head of the Gestapo office for "Jewish Affairs", Adolf Eichmann played a central role in the task of registering, collecting and deporting the Jewish population of Europe to the death camps in Poland. He was born in Germany but brought up in Austria, where he did a number of salesman's jobs in the 1920s. In 1932 he joined the Austrian National Socialist party and the SS, but a year later moved to Germany and joined the German SS and the security police. He was made responsible for Jewish affairs in Austria after the Anschluss, and in 1939 was promoted to head office IV B 4 (Jewish affairs) in the Reich Main Security Office, which controlled the Gestapo. In this position he oversaw the "final solution of the Jewish question", first organizing emigration and deportation, then supervising the transfer of Jews to the east. In 1950 he fled to Argentina, from where he was snatched by Israeli security men in May 1960, taken to Israel, put on trial and executed in 1962.

before that an estimated 1.4 million Jews had already been killed, most of them in the campaign in the Soviet Union where the Einsatzgruppen, following in the wake of the army, murdered Jews as a potential threat to the German war effort. Himmler was anxious that these so-called "wild killings" made too great a demand on the SS men who did the shootings and favoured the shift to factory-based killing in the extermination camps. From March 1942 until the gassings finished in October 1944, an estimated 3.7 million Jews were murdered in the camps, most of them from Poland, the Baltic states and Czechoslovakia.

JEWISH RESISTANCE IN THE HOLOCAUST

In Eastern Europe under German occupation thousands of Jews in Poland, Belorussia and Ukraine escaped into the forests and marshlands where they fought as partisans against the occupiers or set up villages and camps where Jews fleeing from the ghettos could be protected. Jewish partisans faced hostility from Ukrainian nationalists and Russian partisan groups, where anti-Semitism remained a strong prejudice. Life for Jewish partisans was harsh. Babies born to women partisans had to be abandoned or killed in case their cries alerted the enemy. Capture meant certain death, and wounded companions were often shot by their own side.

LEFT A group of Jewish partisans pose for the camera sometime in 1942 or 1943 in the Naliboki forest, near Novogrudok, Poland.

ABOVE A Jewish family in the Dutch city of Amsterdam on their way to a transit camp and ultimately to their deaths in the extermination centres in Nazi-occupied Poland. An estimated 106,000 Dutch Jews, among them the young diary-writer Anne Frank, died during the war.

LEFT The destination for over a million of the Jewish deportees was the combined labour and extermination camp of Auschwitz-Birkenau. In this picture, taken in 1944, prisoner-labourers can be seen in the foreground, helping to organize the arrivals before the majority were marched to their deaths.

BELOW LEFT An image that became all too familiar across German-occupied Europe. German officers walk through a crowd of Jews clutching the possessions they were allowed to bring with them on the crowded and unsanitary trains that shipped them across Europe.

The genocide of the European Jews was organized from Berlin on directives from the German leadership but the programme was carried out with the help of many non-German perpetrators. In Romania there was a long tradition of anti-Semitism and the war against the Soviet Union was used as an excuse to deport or murder large numbers of Romanian Jews. In southern Ukraine, the invading Romanian Army perpetrated its own genocide of the Jewish populations in its path. In the Baltic states and Ukraine, the German invaders found enthusiastic local militia and police willing to hunt out or murder Jews. Elsewhere in occupied Europe, local collaborators or fascists helped German officials to identify, assemble and deport Jewish populations. Only in Denmark were almost all Jews saved, by shipping them secretly to Sweden. The Hungarian regime resisted demands for deportation until 1944 when German forces occupied the country. Half of Hungary's Jews perished in Auschwitz-Birkenau in the final months of killing in 1944. The genocide was both a German and a European crime.

THE FALL OF SINGAPORE

The loss of Singapore was the largest and most humiliating defeat suffered by British Empire forces throughout the Second World War. The island of Singapore was the major British naval base in the Far East and the hub of the defence of British possessions in the Pacific. It had been reinforced during the interwar years by the addition of heavy guns pointing seaward to ward off any possible invasion by a naval force. The rapid invasion of the Malay Peninsula in December 1941 and January 1942 by Lieutenant General Yamashita's 25th Army upset all the plans for the defence of Singapore. On 31 January, the evacuation from Malaya to Singapore across the Strait of Johore was completed. The British commander, Lieutenant General Percival had to face an attack from the north against a coastline which had not been effectively prepared for major defensive action.

Percival had under his command around 70,000 troops, mainly Indian and Australian. A British formation, the 18th Division, arrived just before the Japanese attacked but played only a small part in the subsequent battle. Yamashita could muster around 35,000 troops supported by substantial numbers of aircraft. To meet the expected assault, Percival deployed his forces in a broad but light covering line along the coast, too weak to hold a sustained assault and lacking any mobile reserve force to help repel a landing. On the night of 8/9 February, Japanese forces landed in strength, soon broke the defensive line and drove in two waves towards the city of Singapore. After the long retreat through Malaya the British Empire forces had exaggerated respect for the Japanese enemy and a growing sense of hopelessness about the battle.

LEFT Badge of "Dalforce" – the Singapore Overseas Chinese Anti Japanese Volunteer Army – set up in December 1941 and named after its founder, John Dalley. The force took part in the Battle for Singapore and later some of the volunteers fought a guerilla campaign against the Japanese occupiers.

ABOVE A stream of British army vehicles fleeing from the Japanese invasion of Malaya on their way to the island of Singapore across the bridge over the Straits of Johore which linked the island with the mainland.

RIGHT The island base of Singapore, completed in the late 1930s, was protected by huge 15-inch (38-centimetre) coastal guns. Here one can be seen elevated for firing in a training session in December 1941. In the end the Japanese invaded on the opposite side from the coastal defences.

BELOW The city of Singapore under Japanese air attack on 10 February 1942. Japanese forces, though fewer in number than the British Empire garrison, were helped by overwhelming superiority in the air.

LIEUTENANT GENERAL ARTHUR PERCIVAL (1887–1966)

Arthur Percival was a volunteer for the army in 1914, and after that became a successful career officer with a great deal of experience in staff work. He was posted to Malaya for the first time in 1936, returning to Britain two years later. As a Major General in April 1940, he was briefly an assistant to the Chief of the Imperial General Staff. In March 1941, he was promoted to Lieutenant General and posted to Malaya in May as Commander-in-Chief, Malaya Command. He was an effective administrator but not, by general opinion, a very inspiring personality. He was taken into captivity in February 1942, sent to a camp for senior officers, and was freed in 1945 at the end of the war. He became president of the Far East POWs' Association after the war.

LEFT Lieutenant General Percival (far right) leads the British surrender party to meet Japanese negotiators on 15 February 1942. This was the largest military force to surrender in British history and it astonished the Japanese, who had expected greater resistance.

BELOW LEFT The surrender negotiations at the headquarters of Lieutenant General Yamashita (seated, centre) in the Ford Works Building in Singapore. The Japanese commander insisted on immediate and complete surrender.

BELOW RIGHT Singapore civilians being herded together by Japanese soldiers after the fall of the city in February 1942. The Japanese military and security police selected thousands of the town's inhabitants for murder because of their political beliefs or race.

LIEUTENANT GENERAL TOMOYUKI YAMASHITA (1885–1946)

A career soldier, generally regarded as one of Japan's best operational commanders, Yamashita had a chequered career because of his association with an attempted coup in 1936 in Tokyo and his rivalry with General Tojo. He was made a Lieutenant General in 1937 but served much of his time in Manchukuo (Manchuria) to keep him away from the centre of military power. In November 1941, he was appointed to command the 25th Army for the capture of Malaya. He became a national hero after the campaign but Tojo posted him again to Manchukuo. He later commanded the defence of the Philippines from October 1944. After his surrender he was tried as a war criminal for the "rape of Manila", for which he had little responsibility, and was hanged on 23 February 1946.

By 12 February, the Japanese had reached the city itself, around which Percival had thrown up a primitive defensive screen. Retreating soldiers began to panic and a stream of deserters and refugees added to the confusion in the attempt to defend the central districts.

Fighting for the city proved more determined nonetheless. Yet after three days of resistance, with Yamashita's supply lines under growing pressure, Percival bowed to his fellow officers' view that further resistance was a pointless waste of lives. On the afternoon of 15 February Percival surrendered along with an estimated 100,000 British Empire troops and officials, some of whom had arrived only to experience almost immediate imprisonment. Many of the 45,000 Indian troops were invited to join the Indian National Army inspired by the radical nationalist Subhash Chandra Bose. By August 1942, only around 15,000 had refused to join. The 50,000 European and Australian prisoners were taken to Changi camp in the north-east of Singapore Island and thousands of them later died in the work projects on mainland Asia.

Their mistreatment arose partly from the Japanese military ethic which deplored surrender; Yamashita and his officers were astonished that 70,000 men could surrender against a much smaller force without showing greater determination to fight. Japanese casualties from the campaign amounted to only 1,714 killed.

For the civilian inhabitants of Singapore there followed several years of victimization and mass murder. An estimated 30–50,000 were killed, including not only many from among the Chinese population but also ethnic Malays suspected of criminal activities, anti-Japanese sentiment or communist sympathies. The term used by Chinese to describe these activities by the Japanese military and secret police was *sook ching* or "purification by elimination". Singapore then became one of the major centres of the Japanese southern empire. It was renamed Shonan ("Light of the South") and became the headquarters of the Southern Army. When Yamashita surrendered to the Americans in Manila in 1945, Percival, recently freed, was invited to witness the signing.

COMMANDO RAIDS: NORWAY TO ST NAZAIRE

17 NOVEMBER 1941
Abortive Commando raid on Rommel's headquarters in North Africa.

1 FEBRUARY 1942
Vidkun Quisling appointed Minister President in Norway.

14 APRIL 1942
Pierre Laval becomes premier in Vichy France.

18 APRIL 1942
Doolittle air raid on Tokyo and other Japanese cities.

4 OCTOBER 1942
Commandos raid the Channel Island of Sark.

11–12 DECEMBER 1942
Commando raid against Axis shipping in the Gironde river in western France.

In the summer of 1940, Churchill ordered the creation of a number of small units for raiding the enemy coast in Europe. The initial 11 battalion-size groups were known as Commandos; each comprised 500 men who were highly trained for the dangerous task of breaching the German-held coastline and inflicting local damage or securing vital intelligence. No. 2 Commando would later become the Parachute Regiment. A Royal Marines officer, Lieutenant General Alan Bourne, was appointed Commander of Raiding Operations, charged with using the commando units for organized raids, but he was replaced almost at once by Admiral Roger Keyes. The first operations were minor raids in June and July 1940, but by 1941 the force was sufficiently prepared to begin more ambitious projects.

The most successful operations were mounted against the northern Norwegian Lofoten Islands on 4 March and 26 December 1941. The first of these netted valuable information to help crack the German navy's "Enigma" codes. The second was designed as a diversionary attack while another raid took place against the Vaagsö Islands in central Norway, on 27 December, where a small force, supported by naval gunfire, destroyed military installations and communications and captured 100 Germans for the loss of 19 commandos.

BELOW LEFT British commando troops on the quayside watch an oil installation burning during their raid on the Norwegian island of Vaagso on 27 December 1941.

ABOVE A commando of the Newfoundland Heavy Artillery Regiment on a training exercise in Britain in 1942. Commandos were given a tougher regime of preparation than the normal soldier and were all volunteers.

Larger and more significant raids were planned for the French coast at Bruneval and St Nazaire. Both were carried out under the new adviser on Combined Operations, Lord Louis Mountbatten. The first landing, on the night of 27/28 February, was designed to seize material from the new German Würzburg radar which was used to control night fighters against British bombing attacks. The raid at Bruneval, near the French port of Le Havre, was mounted by a paratroop unit, which overcame the local German garrison, took parts of the radar and returned to Britain successfully across the Channel. The second attack, against the French port of St Nazaire, was a larger and more dangerous operation designed as part of the Battle of the Atlantic which was reaching its height in the summer of 1942.

St Nazaire, on the French Atlantic coast, had the only dry dock large enough for the German battleship *Tirpitz*, which it was feared would use the base to raid Allied merchant shipping. An American-built destroyer, *Campbeltown*, made available to the British under the September 1940 destroyers-for-bases deal, was packed with explosives in its bow, and on the night of 27/28 March was sailed into

BELOW Badges for the Combined Operations forces created in the Second World War to carry out raids on enemy territory.

ADMIRAL LORD LOUIS MOUNTBATTEN (1900–79)

A great-grandson of Queen Victoria, Louis Mountbatten joined the Royal Navy in the Great War, and had risen to the rank of captain by 1937. He was an ambitious, charming and flamboyant personality though an ineffective naval commander. In October 1941, Churchill appointed him as adviser on Combined Operations. In April 1942, he was promoted to vice-admiral and chief of Combined Operations with orders to undertake raids on the enemy coast, and he organized the raids on Bruneval, St Nazaire and later Dieppe. In October 1943, he became Supreme Commander, South-East Asia Command where he organized the defence of Imphal against the Japanese. After the war he became the last Viceroy of India. He was assassinated by the IRA while on a fishing trip in 1979.

the French harbour under the range of German guns. The destroyer avoided detection and rammed the dock's outer wall. A force of 268 commandos stormed the dock and destroyed equipment. The following day, five tons of explosive blew up the dock wall, killing the Germans who had gone on board the destroyer and two captured Commando officers (who had revealed nothing about the impending explosion). The raid took a heavy toll on the force – 611 took part, of whom 397 were caualties, including 144 killed – but the damage done was severe enough to justify the attack.

The success of the commando operations was mixed, but they became a regular feature of British warfare, a useful source of intelligence and a growing irritation to the German High Command. Following a raid on the Channel Islands on 3 October 1942, in which a number of bound German soldiers were killed, Hitler ordered that British and Canadian prisoners should be placed in shackles. On 18 October he issued a decree that any British commandos or special forces caught on raids were no longer to be treated as regular prisoners-of-war but were to be handed over to the German security forces for interrogation and punishment. The shackles were removed after the British had responded in kind on German prisoners, but Hitler's Commando Order stayed in place.

ABOVE An aerial reconnaissance photograph taken on 5 December 1941 of the Würzburg radar installation at Bruneval on the French Channel coast which helped in the planning of the raid on 27/28 February when vital parts of the radar were captured and taken back to Britain.

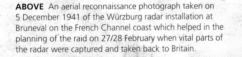

BELOW The destroyer HMS *Campbeltown* crashed into the sluice gate in St. Nazaire harbour on the night of 27/28 March 1942. It was loaded with explosives which blew up shortly after this photograph was taken, destroying the sluice-gate.

ABLE SEAMAN WILLIAM SAVAGE VC

Able Seaman William Alfred Savage was awarded the Victoria Cross for his part in the St Nazaire Raid. He was aboard a motor gun boat (MGB) in charge of a pom-pom gun and during the attack on the port engaged enemy shore-fire and shipping even though his position was completely exposed to enemy fire. He was killed at his gun and was one of three naval personnel to be awarded the decoration as a result of the raid.

THE SIEGE OF MALTA

11 DECEMBER 1941
Germany and Italy declare war on the United States.

20 APRIL 1942
The German air force destroys 20 spitfires on Malta.

5 MAY 1942
Allied forces begin invasion of the island of Madagascar.

21 JUNE 1942
Axis forces capture the port of Tobruk after a brief siege.

23 OCTOBER 1942
Second battle of El Alamein starts in Egypt.

8 NOVEMBER 1942
Alllied forces invade Morocco and Algeria in Operation "Torch".

The island of Malta, some 95 kilometres (60 miles) from the coast of Sicily, was home to a medium-size British naval base midway between Gibraltar and the Suez Canal. The island had a small but vociferous Italian community which had campaigned during the 1930s for the island to become part of the new Italian empire, and it was a prize that Mussolini coveted when he declared war on Britain on 10 June 1940. The following day Italian aircraft bombed the island, beginning an ordeal of aerial siege that was to last over two years.

Although the Italian navy had developed plans for the seizure of Malta as early as 1935, a frontal assault was regarded as costly, despite the fact that in June 1940 there were only three obsolescent Gloster Gladiator biplanes to defend the whole island. Nicknamed "Faith", "Hope" and "Charity", they were sent up to engage the Italian bombers. Of the trio, "Faith" succeeded in surviving the entire siege. Malta remained a thorn in the Axis side, but not until January 1941, when the Italian air force was reinforced with a German Fliegerkorps X based on Sicily, did intensive bombing begin the systematic destruction of much of the above-ground targets in Malta. In July 1941, an Italian naval flotilla attempted an unsuccessful attack on the harbour at Valetta, Malta's capital. During the course of the year, it proved possible to keep Malta supplied and a flow of munitions, aircraft, food and medicine made its way on the dangerous convoy routes into the island.

In December 1941, heavy bombing began again, in support of Axis operations in North Africa, with continuous attacks by German and Italian aircraft. Between 1 January and 24 July 1942, there was only a single day on which bombs did not fall. This was a period of exceptional hardship for the island population, which was forced to live a subterranean existence for much of the time, short of food and medical supplies. The first half of 1942 was a difficult time for the British war effort in the Mediterranean. A combination of Axis air power, minefields and submarines threatened to end the British presence in the region, while

ABOVE Royal Navy vessels escorting a convoy from Alexandria to Malta on 22 March 1942 engage Italian vessels. HMS *Cleopatra* creates a smokescreen for the convoy while HMS *Eurylas* prepares to fire.

LEFT British warships burning in the waters off Malta after attack by Italian bombers at some point during the siege of the island in 1941–2. Italian aircraft kept up regular attacks for three years on an island that Mussolini wanted to incorporate in the new Italian empire.

ABOVE Badge of the Maltese Light Anti-Aircraft Brigade.

ABOVE Badge of the 231st Infantry Brigade stationed on Malta throughout the siege.

LIEUTENANT GENERAL WILLIAM DOBBIE (1879–1964)

A career soldier who served in the Boer War, by the end of the First World War Dobbie was serving on the staff of Field Marshal Haig. It was in this capacity that he signed and sent out the order for British forces to cease firing on 11 November 1918. He was a devout Christian and an inspirational leader. He was Commander-in-Chief Malaya from 1935 to 1939. Although retired, Dobbie was sent out to Malta as Governor-General and Commander-in-Chief in April 1940. He organized the defences of the island, helped to develop effective bomb shelters in the island's network of caves, and succeeded in taking a heavy toll of attacking Axis bombers with the small RAF forces at his disposal. He was retired in May 1942.

ABOVE Soldiers and civilians clear up the damage in Kingsway, the principal street in the Maltese capital of Valetta, after air attack in April 1942. During the siege a large part of the city and its surroundings was destroyed.

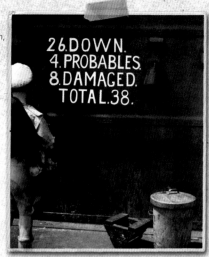

by June 1942 Rommel had succeeded in pushing the British Commonwealth forces back into Egypt. The decision to hold on to Malta made increasingly less sense as its capacity to strike back by sea or air was progressively undermined. In May 1942, the German Commander-in-Chief, Field Marshal Kesselring, announced that Malta was now neutralized, but by July, now under the command of Lord Gort, Malta once more had operational Spitfire fighters and operational submarines.

The month before, the island had been awarded the George Cross by the British king, the highest decoration for civilian bravery in recognition of the suffering it had endured; over the course of the siege there were 5,257 civilian casualties, including 1,540 deaths. By now, the siege was almost complete: in March 1942, just three merchant ships arrived at Malta out of a convoy of only four, shielded by 28 Royal Naval vessels. Two convoys sent from Gibraltar and Alexandria to relieve the island in June 1942 were able to bring only two merchant ships through, for the loss of six naval vessels and six merchantmen. Close to starvation, the population was saved by the arrival of the "Pedestal" convoy in August which lost nine out the convoy of 14 but brought five into Valetta harbour. Allied victory at El Alamein and the conquest of Axis air bases in North Africa brought the siege effectively to an end by November, despite Kesselring's decision to inflict a further round of heavy bombing on the battered island in October. A few weeks later, in Operation "Torch", American and British forces landed in Algeria and Morocco, and the Mediterranean became a major theatre of war.

FIELD MARSHAL ALBERT KESSELRING (1885–1960)

Field Marshal Kesselring was one of Germany's most successful commanders during the Second World War. A Bavarian by birth, he became a staff officer in the First World War, and an effective administrator and co-ordinator. His organizational skills brought him promotion as one of a number of army officers transferred to the newly formed German air force in 1935. He commanded the First Air Fleet in Poland, and the Second Air Fleet in the Battle of France and the Battle of Britain. In November 1941, he was sent as commander-in-chief of Axis forces in the Mediterranean theatre. His most notable achievement was the long defensive retreat through Italy from July 1943. Injured in a driving accident in October 1944, he returned briefly to his post in Italy and ended up as commander-in-chief, Western Europe at the end of the war. He was tried for his role in ordering the killing of hostages in Italy and condemned to death but the sentence was commuted and he was released in 1952.

LEFT In recognition of the courage and endurance of the Maltese people under intense bombardment, King George VI presented the island with the George Cross, the highest civilian honour. Here Lord Gort, governor of the island, presents the medal to Sir George Borg, Malta's Chief Justice, in September 1942.

CORREGIDOR: FALL OF THE PHILIPPINES

5–7 MAY 1942
Battle of Coral Sea prevents Japanese conquest of southern New Guinea.

5 MAY 1942
Chinese mount attacks on Japanese-occupied cities.

5 MAY 1942
British Empire forces land on Madagascar.

15 MAY 1942
Japanese drive British Empire and Chinese troops out of Burma.

22 MAY 1942
Mexico declares war on the Axis Powers.

ABOVE Badge of the US Philippines Division.

The only major United States presence in the western Pacific was in the Philippines, an island group south of Formosa (Taiwan) which had been taken over by the United States after the Spanish-American war of 1898, but which by 1941 enjoyed a semi-autonomous status under American supervision. The island group lay directly in the path of the Japanese assault on the oil and raw-material riches of Malaya and the East Indies. The Japanese planned to capture it within 50 days of the sustained air attacks on 8 December which signalled the start of their campaign. The forces opposed to the Japanese 14th Army under Lieutenant General Homma were a mixture of recently arrived American soldiers, some 30,000 strong, and five divisions of the poorly resourced Filipino army, numbering 110,000 men. The garrisons were scattered around the many islands of the archipelago, with the largest concentration on the island of Luzon. General MacArthur, the senior US commander, had tried to strengthen the air component of the Philippines defence, including the addition of 35 of the new B17 "Flying Fortress" bombers, but the reinforcement of the region was not a high priority in Washington.

The surprise Japanese attack on 8 December was made from air bases in Formosa by specially trained pilots in aircraft modified to cope with the long cross-sea flight. The US aircraft on Luzon were almost all on the ground and undispersed. Half were destroyed in the first wave of attack, and more in the next two days. The battle for the Philippines was waged on the Allied side with no effective air power. Japanese air superiority also compelled the commander of the US Asiatic Fleet, Admiral Thomas Hart, to withdraw US naval shipping from the defence of Luzon. Small units

LEFT The besieged garrison in the fortress of Corregidor in the Malinta Tunnel. The room here houses the Signal Corps and the Finance Office. The fortress eventually held 11,000 men who were forced to surrender on 6 May.

RIGHT Manuel Quezon was the first elected president of the independent Commonwealth of the Philippines in 1935. He left the islands with MacArthur in March 1942, and led the Philippines government-in-exile in Washington where he died in 1944.

BELOW Japanese soldiers assault an American-held pillbox with flame-throwers in the bitter fighting in May 1942 on the Bataan peninsula on Luzon, largest of the Philippine islands.

RIGHT A group of soldiers from the Filipino army surrender to the Japanese during the assault on the Philippines in the first months of 1942. The Filipino army comprised only a few divisions and although it fought back against the Japanese invaders alongside the American garrison, it was an unequal struggle.

LIEUTENANT GENERAL MASAHARU HOMMA (1888–1946)

A successful career officer, Lieutenant General Homma had more understanding of the West than most Japanese commanders. He was a military attaché in London for a total of eight years and was briefly attached to British forces on the Western Front in 1918. He participated in the Japanese-Chinese war as a major general, and, despite his outspoken fears of the risks run by Japan, was chosen to command the Japanese 14th Army for the invasion of the Philippines. By May, the conquest was complete but the long delay in clearing the islands and Homma's liberal reputation disappointed the army leadership in Tokyo and he held no further operational commands for the remainder of the war. He was tried and executed in 1946 for the many atrocities committed by the troops under his command.

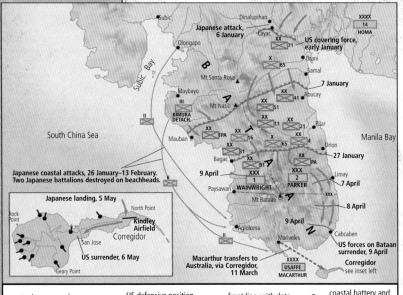

Map labels: Subic · Dinalupihan · Olongapo · Subic Bay · **Japanese attack, 6 January** · Layac · XXXX 14 HOMMA · Orani · Samal · **US covering force, early January** · Mt Santa Rosa · Maybayo · Mt Natib · Abucay · **7 January** · Pilar · KIMURA DETACH. · Mauban · Orion · Bagac · Manila Bay · **27 January** · **9 April** · Limay · WAINWRIGHT · PARKER · **7 April** · Paysawan · Mt Bataan · **8 April** · **9 April** · Agloloma · Cabcaben · Mariveles · **US forces on Bataan surrender, 9 April** · **Corregidor see inset left** · South China Sea

Japanese coastal attacks, 26 January–13 February. Two Japanese battalions destroyed on beachheads.

Macarthur transfers to Australia, via Corregidor, 11 March · XXXX USAFFE MACARTHUR

Inset map: **Japanese landing, 5 May** · North Point · Rock Point · Kindley Airfield · San Jose · Corregidor · **US surrender, 6 May** · Geary Point

Legend: → Japanese advances · ---- US defensive position with date · — front line, with date · ◆ coastal battery and rail supply link

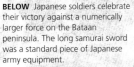

BELOW Japanese soldiers celebrate their victory against a numerically larger force on the Bataan peninsula. The long samurai sword was a standard piece of Japanese army equipment.

LIEUTENANT GENERAL JONATHAN WAINWRIGHT (1883-1953)

Trained as a cavalryman, Lieutenant General Wainwright served in the First World War and in the interwar years commanded cavalry units during the period of their transition to armoured warfare. In September 1940, he was made a major general and sent to command the Philippines Division, which he led at the start of the Japanese invasion. He was promoted to head the 1st Philippine Corps before being made overall commander-in-chief of forces in the Philippines after General MacArthur had left for Australia on 11 March 1942. He surrendered after the final struggle for the fortress of Corregidor and was imprisoned in Manchukuo, the Japanese puppet-state in Manchuria, where he was liberated by the Red Army in August 1945. He returned to a ticker-tape welcome in New York on 13 September 1945.

LEFT US troops surrender to the Japanese army on the Bataan peninsula in April 1942. Around 78,000 American and Filipino soldiers went into captivity, where thousands died from overwork, disease and violent mistreatment.

of Japanese troops were landed over the following week, including a force on Mindanao, the main southern island in the group, where the air base at Davao was captured. On 22 December, the main body of Homma's force landed on either side of Luzon island in an attempt to encircle the enemy's forces around the capital, Manila. Bowing to reality, MacArthur ordered his forces to retreat to the Bataan peninsula on the southern flank of Manila Bay, and moved his headquarters to the island fortress of Corregidor at the seaward end of Bataan.

Although they were short of military supplies and food, the army units on Bataan greatly outnumbered Homma's force – which had totalled 43,000 at the start of the campaign – and they held up the conquest of the island for almost three months. High Japanese casualties and the withdrawal of a division to help in the conquest of the Netherlands East Indies forced Homma to halt and wear down the Filipino and American defenders by siege. By March, when MacArthur was ordered to leave the Philippines, it was evident to the defenders that there would be no aid or reinforcement. Lieutenant General Wainwright, who was given overall command by MacArthur following his own withdrawal to the safety of Australia, kept up a spirited defence, but when Homma attacked with fresh troops on 3 April the front collapsed, and on 9 April Major General Edward King, commanding the forces on Bataan, surrendered. Some 78,000 Filipino and American soldiers and civilians were taken captive and forced to walk 100 kilometres (65 miles) across the peninsula. The Bataan Death March, as it came to be known, saw atrocities routinely committed against prisoners already debilitated by hunger and disease.

Around 2,000 soldiers had escaped to join the garrison in Corregidor and here Wainwright made his last stand with a total of 11,000 men. The system of deep tunnels under the fortress housed extensive stores and offered protection to the defenders. But relentless Japanese aerial and artillery bombardment destroyed almost

ABOVE A burial party at Camp O'Donnell, the destination for US POWs who were forced to walk there from Bataan on the notorious "Death March". Men died of hunger, dehydration and disease.

everything on the surface, including most of the heavy guns, and on 5 May Homma's 4th Division landed on the fortress island itself. On 6 May, Wainwright surrendered to avoid further losses, and the following day announced the surrender of all forces throughout the Philippines. Fighting nonetheless continued as Japanese forces occupied all the outer islands. Some Filipinos escaped into the mountains to become guerrilla fighters. Forces on Negros only surrendered on 3 June and on Samar by 9 June, bringing the conquest of the islands to an end. By this time, almost the whole southern region was in Japanese hands.

BELOW A Filipino guerrilla fighter, Amicedo Farola, June 1944. Some Filipino soldiers retreated to the mountains in 1942 where they kept up a limited resistance against the Japanese occupiers as members of the People's Anti-Japanese Army.

JAPAN CONQUERS BURMA

BELOW V Force badge. V Force was set up to gather intelligence on the Japanese in Burma and made up of British officers of the Indian army and locally employed guerrilla agents.

The conquest of most of Burma by Lieutenant General Shojiro Iida's Japanese 15th Army in the first five months of 1942 represented the furthest limit of Japanese westward expansion. Burma became important to Japanese planners as a means to interrupt the flow of resources along the "Burma Road" to the Chinese armies they were fighting and to the area already conquered in Southeast Asia with its rich material resources. Burma also possessed oil and significant supplies of the rare metal tungsten. Later, it was to be a possible stepping stone for the invasion of India.

Burma's sudden strategic significance was understood far too late by the British authorities who controlled the country in conjunction with a Burmese native administration established under the Burma Act of 1935. Many leading Burmese politicians were anti-British and pro-Japanese, and the nationalist Burma Independence Army, an organization of Burmese dissidents, waited in the wings. In late 1941, there were around 27,000 British and Empire troops in Burma, 15,000 of whom were Burmese, organized into frontier forces and the 1st Burma Division formed in July 1941. The great bulk of remaining forces were Indian troops, officered by the British. There was little artillery, and only 32 aircraft. When General Iida's 15th Army attacked with two under-strength divisions on 19 January 1942, Japanese

ABOVE A military truck carries boiler equipment for China along the "Burma Road" supply line through a decorated archway on the Burma-China border, January 1942. The road was the principal means of supplying the Chinese war effort.

RIGHT British Commonwealth troops face the Japanese in a hastily dug trench on a river in Burma during the Japanese invasion. Most of the forces under British command were Burmese or Indian.

ABOVE A brick blast-proof bomb shelter under construction in the Burmese capital of Rangoon as protection against Japanese bombing. Heavy air attack began in January 1942, rendering the port almost unusable.

LEFT Indian army troops and vehicles outside the Burmese town of Pyinmana, which was bombed by Japanese aircraft in an incendiary attack in April 1942, shortly before the British decision to abandon Burma.

ABOVE During the invasion of Burma a Japanese carrier task force sailed into the Indian Ocean to attack British naval units and bases. Here the aircraft carrier HMS *Hermes* is sinking after an attack by 90 Japanese carrier aircraft on 9 April 1942.

FIELD MARSHAL WILLIAM SLIM (1891–1970)

Most of Field Marshal William Slim's soldiering was conducted in India and the Middle East following service at Gallipoli (where he was severely wounded) during the First World War. A brigadier in the Indian Army by 1939, he commanded an Indian army brigade in the conquest of Italian East Africa and then led the Indian 10th Division in the capture of Syria in June 1941. His powerful presence and popularity with his troops led to his appointment in March 1942 as commander of the Burmese Corps to try to stem the tide of Japanese advance through Burma. He orchestrated a successful retreat and later, in command of the 14th Army, he drove the Japanese back again across Burma in 1944. He was made a full general in 1945 and field marshal in 1949 while serving as Chief of the Imperial General Staff. He later served as Governor of Australia from 1953 to 1960, and ended his career as Governor of Windsor Castle.

aircraft, operating from airfields captured in December, had already inflicted heavy damage on the capital Rangoon and other military targets. Resistance was limited and when the Indian 17th Division, defending Rangoon, was isolated on the wrong side of the Sittang River after the bridge was blown up prematurely, the Allied front collapsed. Some 3,300 Indian soldiers succeeded in crossing the river, but all their equipment was abandoned. The British 7th Armoured Brigade, newly arrived at the port, had to disembark and move almost at once into combat. Further reinforcement proved impossible and over the following two weeks Japanese forces converged on Rangoon from the north and captured the city on 8 March.

British Empire forces were fortunate not to suffer a similar fate to the defenders of Malaya. Extricating themselves from almost certain Japanese encirclement before Rangoon was captured, the Burma Corps, created on 19 March and placed under the command of Lieutenant General Slim, retreated in fighting order much of the length of the Irrawaddy river valley running through central Burma, reaching the Indian town of Imphal in late May after a hazardous trek through jungle, plain and mountain. Japanese forces, supported by units of the Thai army and members of the Burma Independence Army, moved rapidly east and north, cutting

off communications with the Chinese army, whose 38th Division fought alongside Burmese and Indian troops in an effort to keep the Japanese away from the north of the country. On 25 April, the decision was taken by the British authorities to abandon Burma, and Chinese forces in the north retreated back into Yunnan province. The Japanese army reached the Chinese border by 17 June and captured the airfield at Akyab, on the Bay of Bengal, on 4 May. Over the following months, Japan consolidated control of the region but, with British Empire forces entrenched at Imphal, and after a gruelling six-month campaign, no effort was made to push on further into India.

The Japanese occupiers allowed the Burma Independence Army to rule parts of the country after the expulsion of the British, and Burma was nominally granted "independence" in August 1943, when the Burmese premier, Ba Maw, declared war on the Allies, the last state to do so. Japan nevertheless controlled the economy of the region and in reality acted as an occupying power with a significant garrison to guard the outer reaches of the new Japanese empire.

BELOW Japanese tanks and infantry cross a bridge somewhere in Burma in June 1942 after completing the defeat of British Empire and Chinese forces. The Japanese tanks were poorly armed and armoured compared with European tanks, but there were no Allied tanks to defend Burma in 1942.

BELOW LEFT A Chinese soldier in camouflage runs through the Burmese jungle during the campaign against the Japanese in 1942. The Chinese army sent units to help the British because it was essential to keep open the Burma Road supply route.

THE BATTLE OF CORAL SEA

28 APRIL 1942
Nimitz has intelligence that Japan will strike south towards Port Moresby.

1 MAY 1942
Japanese capture Mandalay in Burma.

4 MAY 1942
Fletcher attacks Japanese naval forces at Tulagi in the southern Solomons.

8 MAY 1942
Von Manstein launches attack on the Crimean Kerch Peninsula.

13 MAY 1942
Opening of the Battle of Kharkov which results in Soviet defeat by 29 May and loss of c.200,000 men.

By early May 1942, Japan had almost accomplished the seizure of the southern region which had been planned for in 1941. The outer perimeter of the new imperial area was to be completed by the capture of the remaining southern part of the island of New Guinea, the islands of Malaita and Guadalcanal in the southern Solomons, and the outlying Nauru and Ocean Island. The decision to take these last outposts was made to ensure that Japanese naval and air forces could cut the supply line between the United States and Australia and end any remaining threat from the south. Admiral Yamamoto organized a task force in April under the command of Vice Admiral Shigeyoshi Inoue consisting of four separate elements – a force to seize Port Moresby and southeast New Guinea, a second to capture the Solomon Islands, where air bases were to be established, a third covering force and a carrier group around *Shokaku* and *Zuikaku* designed to engage and destroy any American naval units sent to the area. The plan was to be completed between 3 and 7 May.

Intelligence information warned Admiral Nimitz, who had recently taken over as commander of the Pacific Fleet, that a major Japanese force was moving south. He sent the US carriers *Lexington* and *Yorktown*, both unscathed from the Pearl Harbor attack, to rendezvous with an assortment of smaller Allied ships to form a task force to oppose the Japanese. The Allied force, commanded by Rear Admiral Frank Fletcher, arrived in the Coral Sea, bordered by the Great Barrier Reef, just as the Japanese began their assault on Tulagi. On 4 May aircraft from the *Yorktown* attacked but failed to repel the Japanese landing. Poor weather and visibility made it difficult for the two sides to find each other. Fletcher mistook the light force converging on Port Moresby

ABOVE Vice-Adimral Frank Fletcher who commanded the task force for the Coral Sea battle. Nicknamed "Black Jack", he had a reputation for excessive caution and was posted to the North Pacific in October 1942, away from the main action of the campaign.

RIGHT The USS carrier *Yorktown* nears the Coral Sea, April 1942, photographed from a TBD-1 Torpedo plane that has just been launched from the carrier. A heavy cruiser, oiler and destroyer can be seen in the background.

BELOW American navy torpedo aircraft attack the Japanese light carrier *Shoho* on 7 May 1942 during the Battle of the Coral Sea. The ship was the first Japanese carrier to be sunk and its loss forced the Japanese to abandon their attack on southern New Guinea.

FLEET ADMIRAL CHESTER NIMITZ (1885-1966)

Born of German-American parents, Nimitz joined the US Navy in 1901 and rose to distinction in the interwar years as an expert on the new submarine arm. In 1938, he was promoted to vice admiral and the following year became Chief of the Bureau of Navigation. On 17 December 1941, he was chosen as commander-in-chief of the US Pacific Fleet with the rank of admiral, and he set out to reverse the disaster suffered at Pearl Harbor. He was made overall commander-in-chief of Allied forces in the Pacific Ocean Area in March 1942 and was responsible as fleet commander for the victories at Coral Sea and Midway. His strategy of "island-hopping" led to the isolation and defeat of Japanese garrisons in the central Pacific area for which he was rewarded with the title of Fleet Admiral in December 1944. After the war he became Chief of Naval Operations but retired from active duty in December 1947.

ABOVE LEFT A Japanese Type 93 Long Lance torpedo. Japanese torpedoes were an advanced design and played an important part in securing Japanese domination of the western Pacific area.

LEFT The USS carrier *Lexington* on fire after attack by Japanese carrier aircraft from *Shokaku* and *Zuikaku* on 8 May 1942. The carrier had to be sunk later that evening by a US navy destroyer.

LEFT A destroyed Japanese Nakajima B5N5 Type 97 "Kate" bomber from the carrier *Shokaku*. Poor weather forced many Japanese aircraft to land in the sea when they were unable to find their home carrier and ran out of fuel.

for the main Japanese carrier units and sent his aircraft to intercept. They pounded and sank the light carrier *Shoho* on 7 May, after which the New Guinea task force turned back, anxious about the loss of air cover. The Japanese carrier units, under the command of Rear Admiral Takeo Takagi, dispatched their aircraft despite poor conditions, but they failed to find the US fleet, sinking a tanker and a destroyer which they found stranded on their own. Some of the Japanese planes, at the end of their fuel supply, were attacked by American fighters, and some tried to land on *Yorktown*, which they finally located but mistook for their own. Only a fifth of the aircraft returned safely to their home carriers.

The following day both fleets found the other's carriers. Fletcher's naval aviators attacked *Shokaku*, and with just three bombs disabled the engine-repair shops and the flight deck, but failed to inflict any damage on *Zuikaku*. The two American carriers were both badly hit by the experienced Japanese crews, *Lexington* so severely that it had to be sunk by a US destroyer later that evening, but Takagi decided to withdraw after the loss of so many pilots and the battle came to an inconclusive end. The Battle of the Coral Sea, as it came to be known, was a confused engagement in which poor intelligence made it difficult for either side to fight to full effect. Nevertheless, the Allied fleet succeeded in turning back the invasion of New Guinea and held the Japanese advance at the southern Solomons. Both Japanese carriers were forced to abandon the next part of Yamamoto's strategy to cut the trans-Pacific route at Midway Island and in the process to meet and destroy the US Pacific Fleet. The battle was above all a welcome relief for the Allies after months of remorseless Japanese advance.

ADMIRAL ISOROKU YAMAMOTO (1884–1943)

Born Isoroku Takano, Yamamoto was adopted by a Japanese samurai family in 1916 and took their name. He joined the navy in 1901, fought at the Battle of Tsushima against the Russian navy (1905), and was a captain by 1924. He studied at Harvard and was naval attaché in Washington on two occasions. He was unhappy about Japan's imperial expansion and the prospect of conflict with America, and as a result became the target of repeated death threats. He nevertheless did what he was supposed to do as commander-in-chief of the Japanese Combined Fleet, a post he took up in 1939. He was a pioneer of naval aviation and his ideas on carrier action played an important part in the early Japanese victories. He was shot down by US fighter aircraft on 18 April 1943 over the Solomon Islands after US intelligence intercepted messages about his flight plans.

OPERATION "IRONCLAD"

ABOVE Royal Welch Fusiliers cap badge.

With Japanese expansion in Southeast Asia and naval forays towards India, the British and South African governments feared that Japan might move into the western Indian Ocean to occupy the Vichy French island of Madagascar. The natural bay at the northern tip of the island, Diégo Suarez, was large enough to hold an entire Japanese fleet. In February, Churchill informed Roosevelt that the occupation of the island was something the British intended to effect when they could, but interception of a MAGIC intelligence message in March 1942 from the Japanese ambassador in Berlin to Tokyo revealed German pressure on the Japanese to capture the island and interrupt the British supply route round the Cape. Jan Smuts, the South African Prime Minister, and a close confidant of Churchill, urged a full takeover of Madagascar as soon as possible. In April, the British Chiefs of Staff finally sanctioned an operation at first called "Bonus" but finally titled "Ironclad".

A convoy sailed from Britain to the South African port of Durban in mid-April carrying British troops destined for the combined operation against Madagascar. A fleet was assembled under Rear Admiral Neville Syfret, made up of Force H from Gibraltar and some naval units from the Indian Ocean. The eventual invasion fleet contained the battleship *Ramillies*, the carriers *Indomitable* and *Illustrious*, two cruisers and nine destroyers. Two brigades of British troops, No. 5 Commando and a brigade of South African forces, all under the command of a Royal Marine officer, Major General Robert Sturges, were opposed by

ABOVE Men of No. 5 Commando crowded on a motor launch during the invasion of northern Madagascar on the morning of 5 May 1942. This was one of the first successful combined operations undertaken by British forces.

ABOVE RIGHT Motorcycle troops of the 7th South African Brigade used for communication during the campaign on Madagascar which lasted exactly six months.

BELOW RIGHT As the French garrison on Madagascar retreated southwards on the island it became necessary to launch other landings at strategic ports on the east and west coasts. Here British Empire forces storm a beach at Tamatave on 4 November 1942.

FIELD MARSHAL JAN SMUTS (1870–1950)

A South African soldier of Dutch ancestry, Smuts fought the British in the Boer War of 1899–1902, but then became a Lieutenant General in the British Army during the First World War. He helped to found the Royal Air Force in 1917–18, and played a part in the founding of the League of Nations. He became prime minister of South Africa during 1919–24 and again in 1939, after he had persuaded parliament to join the British war effort. He was made an honorary Field Marshal in 1941, and played an important part as an adviser to Churchill. He was overall commander-in-chief of South African forces which fought in all the African campaigns, including Madagascar. He was defeated at the election in 1948 by Daniel Malan, a harsh critic of South African belligerency and one of the architects of the apartheid system.

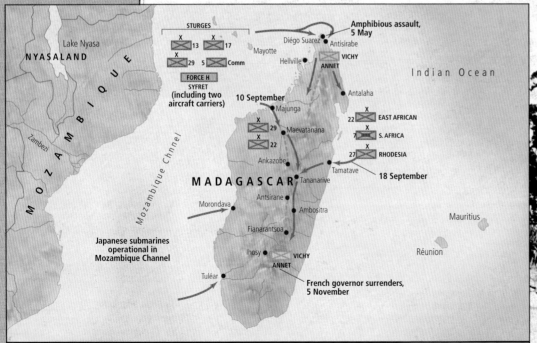

Map of Madagascar campaign

- Lake Nyasa
- NYASALAND
- MOZAMBIQUE
- Zambezi
- Mozambique Channel
- MADAGASCAR
- STURGES — X 13, X 17, X 29, X 5 Comm
- FORCE H — SYFRET (including two aircraft carriers)
- Mayotte
- Diégo Suarez
- Antisirabe
- Amphibious assault, 5 May
- VICHY — ANNET
- Hellville
- Indian Ocean
- Antalaha
- 10 September
- Majunga
- X 29 Maevatanana
- X 22
- 22 X EAST AFRICAN
- 7 X S. AFRICA
- 27 X RHODESIA
- 18 September
- Ankazobe
- Tamatave
- Tananarive
- Antsirane
- Ambositra
- Morondava
- Fianarantsoa
- Mauritius
- Réunion
- Ihosy — VICHY — ANNET
- Tuléar
- French governor surrenders, 5 November
- Japanese submarines operational in Mozambique Channel

→ British and Commonwealth advance   - - -▶ Vichy forces retreat

ABOVE LEFT The destroyer HMS *Anthony* in harbour in March 1943. The ship became famous in May 1942 for breaching the port defences at Diégo Suarez under fire and bringing about the rapid French capitulation.

LEFT A South African soldier with a "pet" snake on Madagascar. The British Commonwealth forces were compelled to spend a whole summer and autumn trying to force French surrender in difficult sub-tropical conditions. There was little actual fighting in what was, for both sides, an increasingly pointless conflict.

RIGHT Air power played a limited part in the conquest of Madagascar. Here four Westland Lysander communications aircraft, based on the island at Ivato, are in flight. Most of the aircraft came from the South African air force.

ABOVE Badge of the 29th Infantry Brigade who took part in the invasion of Madagascar.

around 8,000 French and Malagasy troops, five submarines and 30 aircraft. The convoy and fleet left Durban between 25 and 28 April and assembled on 4 May for the final approach. The last 145 kilometres (90 miles) were covered in complete darkness and radio silence, while minesweepers cleared a path to the northwestern coast, where the assault landings were to take place. Despite the explosion of two mines, the landings went undetected, and British forces stormed the beach and headed for the port. Here the Vichy French garrison, under heavy attack from Fleet Air Arm carrier aircraft, made a firm stand. Only when the destroyer *Anthony*, with 50 marines on board, sailed under fire directly into the port to attack from the rear did French resistance

crumble. The garrison surrendered early in the morning of 7 May. Two French submarines were sunk, for the loss of one British corvette.

This was the start of a long and fruitless campaign. The Vichy governor of the island refused to surrender the rest of his territory and retreated southwards, destroying bridges and roads and laying mines and tank traps. The British troops left for Ceylon in June and the pacification campaign was waged by troops from East Africa, Northern Rhodesia and South Africa. Diégo Suarez, where two Japanese midget submarines damaged the battleship *Ramillies* on 29 May, was guarded by a battalion of the Mauritius Regiment, which later mutinied and had to be disbanded. Conditions for

the forces on Madagascar were poor, and high winds, which whipped up a persistent red dust, combined with tropical disease, led to a degree of demoralization. In September, landings were made to capture the ports on the southern coastlines, and on 5 November, exactly six months after the attack in the north, the French governor surrendered, entitled (with his troops) to extra pay and awards for sustaining six months of combat. The northern naval base remained under British control during the war, while the rest of the island was administered by a Free French administration. Although the invasion was a small-scale affair, conducted against the French rather than the Axis enemy, it was, Churchill later wrote, "for long months the only sign of good and efficient war direction".

THE FIRST THOUSAND-BOMBER RAID

ABOVE Badge of the headquarters of the US Eighth Air Force which joined RAF Bomber Command on later raids.

The bombing of German cities began in May 1940 and continued, when weather permitted and the forces were available, through to almost the last days of the war. The early attacks were made with low performance twin-engined bombers with small bomb loads flying at night, many of which found it difficult to locate even the town they were supposed to attack. The arrival of the Vickers Wellington medium bomber in larger numbers in 1941 and 1942 made it possible to mount more significant raids, but the problem of scale and accuracy persisted. When Arthur Harris was appointed as Commander-in-Chief Bomber Command in February 1942, support for the bombing campaign was growing thin. A report based on investigation of photo-reconnaissance in the autumn of 1941, known as the Butt report after the civil servant who drew it up, showed that only 20 per cent of aircraft actually attacked the 195 square kilometres (75 square miles) surrounding a designated target.

Harris set out to reinvigorate the bombing campaign and to show the politicians in Britain and the United States that bombing was a worthwhile strategy. His campaign was based on a directive issued by the Air Ministry on 14 February, before he took command, which detailed a list of German industrial cities as targets for what came to be known as "area bombing". Harris searched for an operation that would attract maximum publicity and in May decided on mounting a "thousand-bomber raid" against the western German city of Cologne. The operation was to bring together all available bomber aircraft, including those from the training schools, since there were only 400 operational bombers in frontline units. Instead of a cluster of bombers, Harris planned to use a bomber stream (in which all bombers flew at a single speed on a common route to the target, so overwhelming the defences), which

RIGHT RAF ground crew preparing to arm a Vickers Wellington bomber with a 4,000lb bomb on 27 May 1942 at the bomber base at Mildenhall, Suffolk. Poor weather postponed the planned attack on Cologne for four days but crews had to remain on standby.

ABOVE Exeter cathedral stands above the ruins of the medieval city following a heavy raid on 4 May 1942 which killed 156 people. Exeter was one of the cultural centres chosen for the so-called Baedeker raids in retaliation for the burning down of Germany's medieval port cities.

RIGHT A vertical aerial reconnaissance photograph taken of the centre of the German city of Cologne before the thousand-bomber raid at the end of May 1942. The cathedral can be seen at the bottom left of the picture.

AIR MARSHAL ARTHUR HARRIS (1892–1984)

Arthur Harris became the best-known of Britain's RAF commanders during the war as a result of his prosecution of the bombing campaign against Germany between 1942 and 1945. He was the son of an Indian Civil Servant who chose in 1908 to go out to Rhodesia to make his mark. He joined the 1st Rhodesian Regiment in 1914, but in 1915 came to Britain to join the Royal Flying Corps. He served in the interwar RAF in Iraq, India and Palestine, and in September 1939 was appointed commander of No. 5 Bomber Group. In 1941, he became an Air Marshal and on 21 February 1942 commander-in-chief of Bomber Command. He conducted a ruthless campaign of bombing against German industrial cities. His conviction that this was the efficient key to victory made him a difficult collaborator when bombers were needed for other tasks. He was made a Marshal of the Royal Air Force in 1945, and fought a long conflict with the critics of bombing in the years that followed.

ABOVE The Operations Room of RAF Bomber Command in a bunker near High Wycombe in Buckinghamshire in August 1941.

RIGHT A vertical aerial photograph taken during Operation "Millennium", the attack on Cologne, on 31 May 1942. The sky is illuminated by searchlights and tracer fire from anti-aircraft batteries, while the first bombs dropped can be seen on the lower left of the picture.

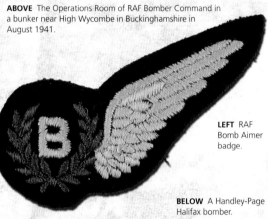

LEFT RAF Bomb Aimer badge.

BELOW A Handley-Page Halifax bomber.

was made possible by the introduction of a new navigation device, first used in a minor attack against Cologne on 13 March, known as Gee (Ground electronics engineering). Leading aircraft guided by the radio beam dropped flares and incendiaries to illuminate the target, while the bombers that followed dropped their bombs on the burning area one after the other. The result was a much larger concentration of more accurate bombing.

The attack was planned for 27 May but had to be postponed because of poor weather. Finally, after four days of waiting on alert, the crews were ordered to fly off on 30 May. The Gee-guided bombers found and illuminated the target and of the 1,050 aircraft assembled some 868 bombed the city. The attack resulted in the death of almost 500 people and the destruction of 12,000 dwellings, but did not seriously affect the industrial activity of the city. In all, 41 aircraft were lost to anti-aircraft fire and accident. Two days later, 956 bombers attacked the Ruhr city of Essen, and on 25 June 1,006 were assembled for an attack on the port of Bremen, but neither attack created serious levels of damage. In retaliation for earlier heavy raids on Lübeck and Rostock, the German air force launched the so-called Baedeker raids (an official in Berlin announced that British cities with three stars in the Baedeker tourist guide would be targeted) at the same time, killing 1,637 people in raids on Exeter, Norwich, Bath, York and Canterbury.

Harris achieved part of his purpose and bombing remained a central element in Britain's war effort, but the thousand-bomber raids were considered an extravagant use of scarce aircraft and more modest operations were planned thereafter, with increased bomb-load made possible by the introduction of the heavy Avro Lancaster, Short Stirling and Handley-Page Halifax bombers during the course of 1941 and 1942. In 1942, however, Bomber Command, joined by the bombers of the US 8th Air Force, dropped only 2.7 per cent of the total weight of bombs dropped throughout the whole war in Europe.

BELOW The stark ruins of the city of Cologne at the end of the war in 1945. Although badly hit during Operation "Millennium" most of the damage to the city was sustained in more than 200 raids experienced between 1942 and 1945.

OIL: THE VITAL RESOURCE

4 DECEMBER 1940
German-Romanian credit agreement gives Germany increased access to oil.

23 JUNE 1941
Soviet bombers attack the Romanian Ploesti oilfields.

26 JULY 1941
Roosevelt embargoes supplies for Japan, including oil products.

9 MARCH 1942
Dutch East Indies surrendered to Japan.

AUGUST 1944
Undersea pipelines laid across the English Channel in Operation "Pluto" to supply oil to Allied forces in France. By VE Day the pipelines had pumped 781 million litres of fuel.

No other raw material was as important for the conduct of modern warfare as oil. It was used to fuel the new mobile armoured warfare, the vast new air fleets and the huge ocean-going navies and merchant fleets operating in the Pacific and the Atlantic. So important was oil as a resource that the German invasion of the Soviet Union and Japanese invasion of Southeast Asia were both based on the hope that the large oil supplies of the invaded regions would fall into Axis hands.

In 1939 the future Allied states controlled 94 per cent of the world's output of oil. Germany and Japan could supply only 10 per cent of their own oil needs from domestic resources, Italy only 1 per cent. This situation placed great pressure on the aggressor states because their aggression was only possible with enhanced oil supplies. Germany had access to Romanian supplies after 1940 once the British and French had been defeated on the Continent; supplies also came from the USSR under the terms of the German-Soviet trade agreements signed in August 1939. But the only way in which Hitler could guarantee a secure oil basis was the

ABOVE German motorized units leave behind the burning oil wells of Maikop after failing to control the flames, August 1942. Stalin's "scorched earth" policy of retreat meant that most of the oil fields in the Caucasus region were destroyed before the Germans got to them.

RIGHT An oil tanker burns five miles off the Atlantic Coast of the United States after being torpedoed, 1942.

ABOVE An early (1939) example of a German car converted to run on gas as opposed to oil-based liquid fuels. By the end of the war sights like this, or vehicles with gasbags on their roofs, were common in both Germany and Italy.

seizure of oil in the Caucasus and the Middle East. In 1942 German forces struck at the Caucasus region to try to seize the Soviet oil fields around Maikop, Baku and Grosny. They got as far as Maikop, but the Red Army had destroyed as much as possible and in the end the Germans extracted only 70 barrels a day. After that Germany was forced to live on its reserves and a growing supply of synthetic oil.

The Japanese were more fortunate. The decision taken in June 1941 by the United States to embargo the supply of oil accelerated the Japanese decision to invade the Pacific and Southeast Asia. Within weeks the rich oilfields of the Dutch East Indies, Borneo and Burma were in Japanese hands and production rapidly resumed. Most of the oil was used by the navy and armies in the field and far too little reached mainland Japan. American air and submarine attack reduced the flow of oil even more and by 1944 only 1.6 million barrels were imported against 22 million barrels in 1940. Despite substantial stockpiles that had been set up, the Japanese economy and armed forces were down to a few weeks' stock by the summer of 1945.

Although the Allies had abundant oil, the wartime situation brought its own problems. The Soviet Union's production sank from 33 million tonnes in 1941 to 18 million tonnes by 1944 because of wartime disruption. For much of the war American supplies of high-quality aviation fuel were needed to keep the Soviet air force

LIGNITE (BROWN COAL)

The soft coal lignite, also known as "brown coal", was the core material for the German invention of "oil from coal". Unlike the harder black coals, lignite could be transformed into a high-quality oil by the industrial "hydrogenation" process, perfected by the German chemical giant I. G. Farben in the 1930s. In 1936 a massive programme was launched to produce synthetic oil, but not until the German occupation of the Sudetenland after the Munich Agreement were there adequate supplies of lignite. Synthetic fuel played an important part in the German war effort but the production plants were easy targets for the bombers once the Combined Bomber Offensive was under way.

THE BIG INCH

The United States was one of the world's largest oil producers in the 1930s but the coming of war placed great pressure on the capacity of the oil industry to supply what the war economy needed. To move oil quickly to the northern and eastern industrial regions a huge engineering programme was set up to lay pipelines from Texas direct to where the oil was needed. The so-called Big Inch pipe, a 60-centimetre (24-inch) pipeline from Longview, Texas to Norris City, Illinois was started in June 1942 and completed six months later. It was then extended 720 miles eastwards to Phoenixville, Pennsylvania. Capable of delivering 300,000 barrels of oil a day, it was the longest pipeline of its kind in the world.

ABOVE Invented by the Germans on Hitler's order before 1939, the design of this fuel container was soon adopted by the British – hence the name "jerrycan". Three handles meant there were numerous options for carrying and they even floated on water due to a design feature which meant an air pocket was always retained even when full.

BELOW A US Army Air Force B-24 Liberator bomber over a burning oil refinery in Ploesti, Romania, August 1943. Operation "Tidal Wave" was launched from North Africa on 1 August in an attempt to destroy German oil production there. It was thought to be so essential that the Allies went ahead despite a predicted loss rate of 50 per cent of the 178 bombers which took part. The attack was largely unsuccessful and production was back to pre-raid levels within weeks.

flying. Britain relied on imports of oil which were badly hit by the submarine campaign but by 1943, with the U-boats defeated, oil supplies increased to 80 per cent above the pre-war levels. The United States found that increasing oil supply was a problem after years of the Depression, and oil rationing had to be introduced for motorists. But large new pipelines and facilities saw American oil output increase from 200 million barrels in 1940 to 366 million in 1944. The United States provided 80 per cent of the oil requirements of the Allied powers throughout the war.

The shortages of oil led to all kinds of innovations. German and Italian vehicles were converted to use gas or wood. Cars and trucks carried large gas bags on top, like miniature Zeppelins. Efforts were made to find natural oil supplies and German scientists produced an effective lubricating oil from the European acorn crop. But there was no real substitute for mineral oil. By the autumn of 1944 the German air force was supplied with just 5 per cent of its requirements. Not for nothing did the vice-chairman of the American War Production Board claim that the responsibility resting on the oil industry "is nothing less than the responsibility for victory".

BELOW Petrol (or gas as it is known in the US) was rationed on both sides of the Atlantic during the Second World War. The British had to endure nearly 11 years "on the ration" while in the US it lasted from just December 1942 to 15 August 1945.

OPERATION "BLUE"

ABOVE Luftwaffe Flak badge.

The German retreat in front of Moscow in December 1941 was followed by Soviet offensives along much of the German line. Both sides were exhausted by the long conflict in 1941 and, though Stalin drove his armies on, the gains they made were localized and at great cost. The spring thaw turned the countryside to mud and not until May did serious conflict start again. On 12 May, four Soviet armies opened an operation to regain the city of Kharkov on the southern front. They made slow progress, but opened up a wide salient south of the city. The German front launched a counter-attack, Operation "Fredericus", and cut the salient from the rear. Over 200,000 soldiers and 1,200 armoured vehicles were captured. The defeat of the Soviet offensive opened the way for a plan that Hitler had already been preparing for seizing the whole area of the southern Soviet Union as a prelude to the final defeat of the Red Army.

On 5 April, after much argument about the merits of capturing the Soviet capital, Hitler issued Directive No. 41 for an operation first called "Siegfried", and then changed to "Blue". The objective was to seize the southern steppe area, cut the Volga supply line and capture the oil of the Caucasus region. This would at a stroke remove much of the food and oil supply for the Soviet population and armed forces, and open the way to control of the Middle East if Axis forces could meet up with Rommel's drive through North Africa. The plan was revealed to Stalin by British intelligence but he refused to believe it; a German aircraft carrying the battle plan crashed behind Soviet lines on 19 June, but Stalin again assumed that this was a ruse to divert attention from a German plan to capture Moscow. On 28 June, Operation "Blue" was launched against a weak and unprepared front by a combined force of German, Romanian, Hungarian and recently arrived Italian forces under the overall command of Field Marshal Fedor von Bock. The initial thrust was

ABOVE Marshal Andrei Yeremenko, seen here in discussion with his staff, was one of the most successful Soviet battlefield commanders. He commanded the southeast front facing Operation "Blue" and later the Stalingrad front during the battle for the city.

BELOW Soviet infantry and tanks storm a village during a rare counter-attack against the remorseless German advance across the Don steppe in August 1942.

ABOVE German Panzer III tanks destroyed in June 1942 during the early stages of Operation "Blue", which involved two tank armies, 1st and 4th Panzer.

FIELD MARSHAL ERICH VON MANSTEIN (1887–1973)

Generally regarded as one of Germany's finest operational commanders during the Second World War, Field Marshal von Manstein (left) was born Erich von Lewinski, son of a Prussian general, but was adopted by another Prussian military family and adopted their name. He served in France and Poland during the First World War, and remained in the small 100,000-man army after the war. He became Head of Army Operations in 1935, and a Deputy Chief of Staff in October 1936. He fought with distinction in Poland in 1939, and in 1940 the plan adopted to defeat France was his inspiration. He commanded a Panzer Corps in the invasion of the Soviet Union, and occupied the Crimea and besieged Sevastopol late in 1941. In the prelude to Operation "Blue" he cleared the Crimean peninsula of remaining Soviet forces and, by 4 July 1942, captured Sevastopol. He was sent to Leningrad to try to capture that city, and returned to the southern operation in November 1942. He was dismissed by Hitler in March 1944 for arguing with his strategy. He was tried after the war for war crimes, sentenced to 18 years, but served less than four.

ABOVE A German JU87B dive-bomber over the Volga city of Stalingrad in September 1942. Hitler had not intended this to be a major target of Operation "Blue", but rapid German success tempted him to speed up the conquest of the whole region.

overwhelming: between 6 July and 23 July the whole area from Voronezh, north of Kharkov, to Rostov-on-Don on the Sea of Azov was captured. Rostov failed to emulate Sevastopol and was abandoned by panicking Soviet soldiers. On 23 July, confident of victory in the south, Hitler divided his forces into two army groups, the first, Army Group A, under Field Marshal Wilhelm List, drove on into the Caucasus while Army Group B, commanded first by von Bock then by General Maximilian von Weichs, crossed the Don river and advanced on the Volga city of Stalingrad.

The Soviet forces in the south melted away, either captured or retreating in disorder across the steppe. On 28 July Stalin issued Order 227 "Not a Step Back" which ordered Soviet soldiers to defend every metre of Soviet soil to the death. The order was relayed to the troops and had, according to veterans of the conflict, a sober impact on the soldiers that read it. Behind them stood special "blocking units" of security troops who were ordered to use the harshest methods to ensure that retreat did not turn into rout. Nevertheless, it proved impossible to halt the Axis advance. The city was subjected to heavy air attack, and on 19 August General Friedrich Paulus, in command of the German 6th Army, ordered his forces to take it. The Don was crossed in strength by the 6th Army, and on 23 August the first German forces created an eight-kilometre-(five-mile)-wide salient on the banks of the Volga north of Stalingrad. Paulus and the German high command expected to capture it and to cut the Volga within a matter of days. In front of the German army were two Soviet armies under the command of General Gordov, the 62nd and the 64th, both heavily battered in the fight across the Don steppe. They were to bear the brunt of the furious fighting that followed for the capture of the city.

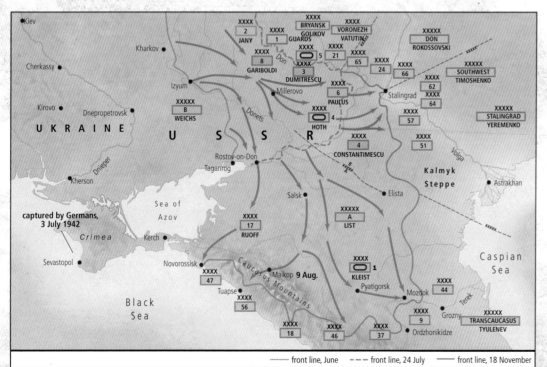

ABOVE German troops look across the desolate steppe country to the distant city of Stalingrad. German forces reached the Volga on 15 August and expected to capture the city in a matter of days as they had captured Rostov-on-Don a few weeks before.

------ front line, June   - - - front line, 24 July   —— front line, 18 November

THE BATTLE OF MIDWAY

25 MAY 1942
Small Japanese fleet leaves Hokkaido island bound for the Aleutians off the coast of Alaska.

27 MAY 1942
USS *Yorktown* returns to Pearl Harbor for repairs following Coral Sea battle.

5 JUNE 1942
United States formally declares war on Hungary, Bulgaria and Romania.

7 JUNE 1942
German army begins its final assault on the Crimean port of Sevastopol.

11 JUNE 1942
German submarines begin a minelaying programme in US coastal waters.

12 JUNE 1942
Anglo-Soviet agreement on creating a "Second Front" published.

ABOVE Shoulder title of a Warrant Officer in the Japanese navy.

The Japanese failure at the Battle of the Coral Sea confirmed the navy commander-in-chief, Admiral Isoroku Yamamoto, in his conviction that a decisive action should be taken against the United States Pacific Fleet to prevent further American activity in the western Pacific area. The tiny island of Midway, lying between Hawaii and Japan, was chosen as the target, not because it was important in itself, but as the lure to obtain the decisive fleet engagement which would eradicate the American threat. Preparations for Operation "MI" began in early May, just before the Battle of the Coral Sea.

Midway was claimed by the United States in 1859, occupied in 1903 and finally turned into a small naval and flying-boat base in 1940. The naval force sent across the Pacific from Japan was vast for the invasion of a small island, but that was not its principal purpose. The Japanese fleet was divided into

BELOW US navy Dauntless dive-bombers attacking units of the Japanese fleet during the Battle of Midway. In the centre of the picture can be seen a burning Japanese cruiser, *Mikuma*, which had collided with another Japanese ship. The dive-bombers were responsible for the devastating damage suffered during the battle by the four Japanese carriers.

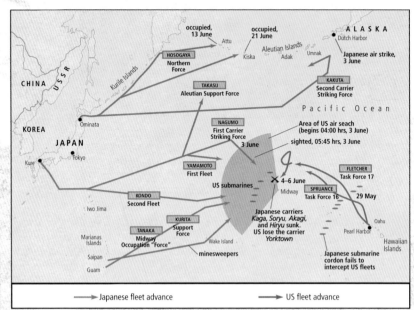

Japanese fleet advance → US fleet advance →

LEFT The aftermath of a Japanese diversionary attack on Dutch Harbor in the Aleutian Islands off Alaska on 3 June 1942. It was hoped that US naval vessels would be tempted north, leaving the way clear for the attack on Midway.

BELOW Blazing oil tanks on Midway Island during the Japanese operation on 4 June. Despite Japanese air attacks, torpedo-bombers from the USS carrier *Hornet* were able to land and refuel on the island during the battle.

ADMIRAL RAYMOND A SPRUANCE (1886–1969)

Admiral Spruance became a career naval officer before the First World War and by 1940 was commander of the Caribbean Sea Frontier. After the attack on Pearl Harbor he commanded Cruiser Squadron Five in the Pacific under command of Admiral William Halsey. Spruance – nicknamed "electric brain" – had a reputation for a sharp mind and cool temperament. When Halsey fell ill in May 1942, he recommended Spruance should control his carrier task force for the Battle of Midway. After the engagement he became Nimitz's chief-of-staff and in mid-1943 was appointed to command the Central Pacific Force which captured Iwo Jima and Okinawa. He succeeded Nimitz as commander of the Pacific Fleet in late 1945, and then became President of the Naval War College until his retirement in 1948. Between 1952 and 1955 he was US ambassador in the Philippines.

five attacking groups: a carrier strike force, the heart of the operation, under the command of Vice Admiral Nagumo; an occupation force for Midway; the main battle fleet of seven battleships, including Yamamoto's huge flagship, the 72,000-ton *Yamato*, designed to eliminate the American fleet; a diversionary force to capture two of the Aleutian Islands in the north; and finally a forward screen of submarines. The date for the attack on Midway was set for 5 June Japanese time, 4 June in the United States. Japanese intelligence on the United States carrier force was scanty, but it was assumed that the two remaining carriers after the Battle of the Coral Sea were far away to the south, protecting Australia.

This was the first of the Japanese miscalculations. Nimitz had two carriers, *Hornet* and *Enterprise*, and thanks to an extraordinary technical feat of repair, the damaged *Yorktown* was also available by 31 May. The force was placed under the overall command of Admiral Fletcher, and the carriers placed under Rear Admiral Raymond Spruance. Against the Japanese four carriers, seven battleships, 12 cruisers and 44 destroyers, the Americans could muster only three carriers, eight cruisers and 15 destroyers. The one solid advantage enjoyed by the American side was intelligence, and without it the battle could not have been fought and won. The Fleet Radio Unit Pacific at Pearl Harbor could decode and decipher the Japanese main code, JN-25, and knew by 21 May that Operation "MI" meant Midway. A few days later, the exact time for the attack on Midway and the Aleutians was also known. The American strategy was to sail the small carrier force northeast of Midway, out of range of Japanese search aircraft and submarines. Once the Japanese units had been identified by aircraft from Midway, the plan was to assault them with waves of torpedo- and dive-bombers but at all costs to avoid the big fleet engagement sought by Yamamoto.

The battle represented a great risk for the American side, heavily outnumbered in ships and aircraft, but the failure of Japanese reconnaissance to detect Spruance's force until well after the attack on Midway had begun left the Japanese carriers exposed to a dangerous counter-attack as their

aircraft were refuelled and rearmed on deck. The American torpedo-bombers were too slow and the force was decimated, but around 50 Dauntless dive-bombers, undetected by the Japanese, dropped enough bombs onto the carriers' crowded decks to create havoc. By early next morning all four Japanese fleet carriers, *Hiryu*, *Kaga*, *Soryu* and Nagumo's flagship, *Akagi*, were sunk. Yamamoto ordered his battleships forward to destroy the enemy but in thick fog they could not be found, and without air cover the ships faced a great risk. *Yorktown* was damaged by aircraft, and sunk by a submarine three days later, but the great fleet engagement eluded the Japanese. The American victory was decisive, and it was achieved in a battle conducted and won by aircraft from two carrier forces that never even sighted each other. Senior Japanese commanders later admitted that this was the turning point in Japan's war effort. In 1943 and 1944, Japanese shipyards turned out another seven aircraft carriers, the United States built 90. The death and injury of 70 per cent of Japan's highly trained naval pilots was never satisfactorily made good.

CAPTAIN JOSEPH ROCHEFORT (1898–1976)

Captain Rochefort was one of the leading American experts on cryptanalysis. He joined the US navy in 1918, was trained in code-breaking and learned fluent Japanese. His wide intelligence experience led to his appointment early in 1941 to head the radio intercept office at Pearl Harbor. Here he assembled a large team of cryptanalysts and linguists who made it their task to break the Japanese naval code JN-25. During the early part of 1942 they succeeded in breaking the complicated cipher mechanism and could read some of the messages, although dates proved difficult. This intelligence information – known, like its European counterpart, as ULTRA – was vital for the Battle of Midway. The dating system was finally broken in May and Rochefort's unit provided the vital intelligence needed for the coming battle. From 1942 to 1946 he was in Washington as head of the Pacific Strategic Intelligence Group, and he retired in 1946.

ABOVE LEFT A Japanese torpedo-bomber takes off from the deck of a Japanese carrier. Although Japanese pilots were highly trained, during the Battle of Midway almost three-quarters of carrier pilots were killed or injured.

BELOW A damaged F4F US fighter on the island base of Midway after the Japanese attack in the early hours of the morning of 4 June 1942. Midway Island was regarded by the Japanese as a stepping stone to further attacks against Hawaii.

BELOW The Japanese cruiser *Mikuma* on fire after attack by aircraft from the USS carrier *Enterprise* on 6 June 1942. Despite continued American attacks, the cruiser was the only major casualty apart from the four Japanese carriers.

ABOVE The US carrier *Yorktown* was hit by Japanese torpedo-bombers in two attacks on 4 June 1942. Listing badly, the carrier eventually had to be abandoned.

CRISIS IN EGYPT: GAZALA AND TOBRUK

ABOVE Afrika Korps breast emblem.

ABOVE Formation badges of the 1st (top) and 8th Armoured Divisions serving in North Africa.

The results of Operation "Crusader", which had pushed Axis forces back across the Western Desert to El Agheila by December 1941, were reversed almost as soon as they were achieved. Rommel, helped by the arrival of substantial supplies and reinforcements across the short Mediterranean supply route, launched a surprise counter-attack on 21 January 1942 which drove the tired British Empire forces more than halfway back to Egypt. The front stabilized at Gazala, where a line of strongpoints and minefields had been constructed stretching across the desert to the Free French garrison at Bir Hakeim. Neither side was in a position to take the initiative after months of combat in difficult conditions, and so the front stood firm at Gazala as both sides brought in reinforcements and fresh supplies of fuel and ammunition.

On 26 May, Rommel launched a renewed offensive. He had 560 tanks, almost half of them Italian, against a British Empire force of 700, recently reinforced with US-built Grant tanks. The Italian 10th and 21st Army Corps attacked the Allied front at Gazala in the north, while the bulk of Rommel's armoured forces swung south towards Bir Hakeim to try to encircle Ritchie's 8th Army. Although neither attack worked as Rommel had planned, the battle that followed showed how effective German armour could be in the

ABOVE A picture of Rommel in characteristic pose, directing his armoured forces near the front line. He proved adept at using his forces in the confused desert conditions and was held back chiefly by the supply difficulties across the Mediterranean.

ABOVE German tanks in desert camouflage make their way on 1 May 1942 towards the jumping-off point for the Axis attack launched against the British 8th Army on 26 May.

LEFT British POWs after the fall of Tobruk on 21 June walk past a German tank. The city fell after only a few days having survived a prolonged siege during 1941.

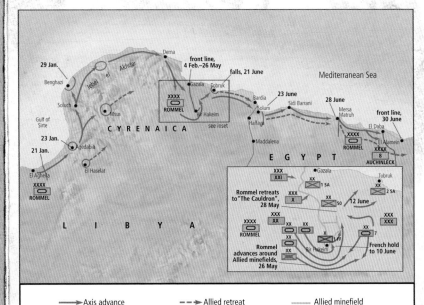

front line, 4 Feb.–26 May   falls, 21 June

Mediterranean Sea

29 Jan.

Derna

Benghazi   Jebel el Akhdar

Soluch

Gulf of Sirte

Msus

XXXX ROMMEL   Gazala   Tobruk

Bir Hakeim   see inset

Bardia   Solum   23 June

Sidi Barrani   28 June

Mersa Matruh

front line, 30 June

Halfaya

C Y R E N A I C A

23 Jan.

Agedabia

El Daba

XXXX ROMMEL

El Alamein

XXXX 8 AUCHINLECK

21 Jan.

Maddalena

E G Y P T

El Agheila   El Haselat

XXXX ROMMEL

L I B Y A

Inset map:

XXX XXI   Gazala

XX 1 SA

XX 2 SA

Tobruk

Rommel retreats to "The Cauldron", 28 May

XXX X

XX 50   12 June

XXXX ROMMEL

XXX XXX

XXXX XX ROMMEL

XX

X It

French hold to 10 June

Rommel advances around Allied minefields, 26 May

Bir Hakeim

→ Axis advance   - - → Allied retreat   —— Allied minefield

COUNT LÁSZLÓ ALMÁSY (1895–1951)

The Hungarian aviator and explorer László Almásy became a counter-intelligence officer for Rommel's Afrika Korps in 1941. He fought as an airman in the Austro-Hungarian armed forces during the First World War, and made several attempts to restore the Habsburg dynasty to the throne after the collapse of the monarchy in 1918. He went to Egypt, where he became well-known as an explorer and map-maker of the desert regions of southern Libya. The Bedouin tribesmen named him "Father of the Sands"; he has become better-known as the model for the fictional "English Patient". When war broke out, he returned to Hungary, and was recruited by the German *Abwehr* (counter-intelligence) and posted to join Rommel in the desert war. He guided two German spies into Cairo in 1942 in Operation "Salaam", including Johannes Eppler, who set up the Condor spy-ring. In 1943, he fled to Turkey, where he continued to work for the *Abwehr*, but also for the British. He was tried for treason by the Hungarian Communist regime after the war, acquitted, and died in Vienna in 1951.

ABOVE British artillery fire at Axis positions during the battle for Gazala on the night of 2 June 1942. As Axis forces broke through the Allied line further to the south, the British front at Gazala rapidly withdrew back towards Tobruk.

KING FAROUK I (1920–1965)

King Farouk, a descendant of Muhammad Ali, the founder of modern Egypt, came to the throne of Egypt and Sudan in 1936. He was critical of the British presence in his country and tried to avoid any Egyptian commitment to the Allied cause. He refused to declare war on Germany and Italy and, as Egypt was technically a neutral country, Axis residents could continue to live there without fear of internment. Only at the end of the war, under strong British pressure, did he agree to declare war. In 1952, he was overthrown in a military coup led by Muhammad Naguib and Gamal Abdel Nasser and went into exile in Italy and Monaco. He died prematurely in Rome, aged 45.

ABOVE An aerial photograph of German and Italian air attacks on the port of Tobruk in June 1942. The port, which changed hands a number of times during the Desert War, was captured after only a few days of siege, giving Rommel a valuable harbour to discharge further supplies.

hands of an imaginative commander. In the north, the Italian assault was held, while at Bir Hakeim, Free French forces offered stubborn resistance. Rommel was forced by 28 May to withdraw his forces, two German and two Italian armoured divisions, back into a defensive circle or "cauldron" (Kessel). Here he cleared minefields and with the help of "tank-busting" 88-milimetre (3.5-inch) anti-aircraft guns, repelled poorly co-ordinated attacks by British Empire forces from a zone codenamed "Knightsbridge" to the east of the "cauldron". By 1 June, Rommel was in a position to strike east in force and the Allied front crumbled. By 12 June, German armour and the Italian *Ariete* Division drove the enemy from Knightsbridge, while the Trieste Division was sent to help clear the French from Bir Hakeim, which finally succumbed on 10 June.

Unable to plug the gaps in the line, Ritchie ordered a retreat towards Tobruk, which was garrisoned by 35,000 troops, most of them South Africans. The 8th Army was unable to defend the port as it retreated in some disorder towards the Egyptian frontier, pursued by Rommel's armour. Tobruk was once again besieged but this time the defence was poorly organized and by 21 June, after an assault of only three days, the fortress was taken and with it 32,000 British Empire forces and their equipment and – from

Rommel's point of view – vital supplies of fuel. The overall commander of British Empire forces in the Middle East, General Auchinleck, sacked Ritchie and took command himself. In order to avert complete disaster, which might have meant Axis control of the Suez Canal and access to the oil of the Middle East, Auchinleck abandoned the next defensive line further along the coast at Mersa Matruh, which was briefly contested between 27 and 29 June, for a more secure front at El Alamein and Alam Halfa, only 240 kilometres (150 miles) from Cairo. Though the scale was not the same as the struggle on the Russian steppe towards Stalingrad, there was a sense at Allied headquarters that the struggle for North Africa had reached its most critical stage. Axis armies here and in the Soviet Union seemed poised for victories that might turn the tide of war.

As Rommel's forces fast approached, the mood in Cairo worsened. Relations between the Egyptian population and the British Empire occupiers became increasingly strained, with food shortages and the sometimes disorderly behaviour of white troops. In February 1942, the British Resident Minister in Cairo had surrounded the royal palace with tanks and forced King Farouk to appoint a pro-British regime led by the Wafd Party. The King complied, but there remained important elements in the Egyptian military and political elite that waited expectantly for an Axis victory.

RIGHT A German Focke-Wulf 190 fighter attacked and destroyed a British tank on the Via Balbia on 20 June 1942 during the British retreat across Libya.

ABOVE Winston Churchill and Franklin Roosevelt confer at the White House in Washington on 25 June 1942 over the world situation. News of the fall of Tobruk was a severe blow to Churchill, already anxious about the deteriorating anti-submarine war.

THE BATTLE OF THE ATLANTIC

12 JANUARY 1942
First ship sunk off the US East
Coast by a German submarine.

5 JULY 1942
First German submarine sunk
by aircraft using Leigh Light.

30 MAY 1942
Doenitz reports to Hitler that
Atlantic battle is lost for the
moment.

O n 6 March 1941, stung by the high losses of merchant ships to German submarines during the winter months, Winston Churchill announced that Britain was now fighting "the Battle of the Atlantic". The situation for the country was critical because so much of the raw material, oil and food the British war effort relied on, as well as the American aid promised through Lend Lease, had to be shipped across the Atlantic to British ports. In 1938, Britain imported 68 million tons of supplies, but in 1941 only 26 million. German submarines sank 1,299 ships in 1941 and the losses could not all be made good. By the spring of 1942, German naval commanders were convinced that Britain could be strangled into submission. So began a duel of the Royal Navy and the RAF against a force of around 300 German submarines under the command of Admiral Karl Dönitz, whose outcome was, as Churchill recognized, vital to the continued conduct of the war.

In the early months of 1942, following the entry of the United States into the war, German submarines, organized in packs with predatory codenames ("Leopard", "Panther" and "Puma") were sent to intercept American shipping. Unprepared for war, American ships were poorly equipped for anti-submarine warfare and could still be found sailing singly rather than in regular convoy. In the first four months of the year, 1.2 million tons of shipping was sunk off the American coast alone. Submarine losses were small, three in January,

BELOW Royal Navy
clasp knife.

BELOW The original cavity
magnetron developed by John
Turton Randall and Harry Boot
at the Nuffield laboratory in
Birmingham University. The
device, first operated on 21
February 1940, enabled Britain,
with American assistance, to
develop new centimetric radar
to help detect submarines at sea.

ABOVE A flotilla of German submarines in port on the Atlantic coast of France. Over the course of the war around 1,000 German submarines were commissioned for the campaign against Allied merchant shipping.

RIGHT The aerial view of an Atlantic convoy taken in May 1942. Thanks to careful intelligence work, well over half of all convoys crossed the ocean without loss. Submarines preyed particularly on stragglers and slower ships.

only two in February. The situation worsened over the year because the German B-Dienst intelligence unit had broken the British Naval Ciphers 2 and 3, directing convoy traffic across the Atlantic, while the British lost the knowledge they had gained from ULTRA when the German navy introduced the new Triton cipher in February. The Allies extended air patrols, forcing submarines into the so-called "Atlantic Gap" in mid-ocean, which aircraft could not reach, but here the submarines preyed on weakly escorted convoys or convoy stragglers. During 1942, 7 million tons of shipping was lost in all areas, and by January 1943 the Royal Navy was down to just two months' supply of fuel.

The situation might well have deteriorated further without the work of the British Admiralty's Tracking Room and Trade Plot Room, both located in London, which used a variety of intelligence sources to assess the submarine threat and to route convoys safely. In the year between May 1942 and May 1943, 105 out of 174 convoys sailed without loss. During 1942, the Allies introduced new technology and tactics to try to blunt the submarine threat.

LEFT A signalman aboard HMS *Viscount* uses a signal light to send a message to the commodore of a convoy somewhere in the Atlantic in October 1942.

ADMIRAL MAX HORTON
(1883–1951)

Horton joined the Royal Navy in 1898 and had risen by the First World War to the rank of Lieutenant Commander in command of a submarine. He remained a submariner for the rest of the war, but in the interwar years served on a number of battleships and reached the rank of Vice Admiral by 1939. In 1940, he was put in command of all home-based submarines. His experience made him an ideal choice to contest the German submarine arm, and on 17 November 1942 he was appointed Commander-in-Chief Western Approaches, responsible for the Battle of the Atlantic. His tactical innovations, particularly his use of free-ranging support groups to hunt down submarines on the edge of Allied convoys, played a critical part in turning the tide of the sea war. He was an avid golfer and was said to have played a round of golf almost every day of the war. He retired in August 1945.

LEFT Crew on board the US Coast Guard cutter *Spencer* watch as a depth charge blows a German submarine to the surface. The convoy they are protecting can be seen in the background.

RIGHT A German submarine under attack on the surface in June 1943 by aircraft from the USS *Bogue*. By the summer of 1943 most German submarines had been withdrawn to avoid catastrophic levels of loss.

BELOW RIGHT Seamen aboard the US oil tanker *Pennsylvania Sun* fight a fire caused by a torpedo attack in July 1942 on the Atlantic run. During 1942 the Allies lost 5.4 million tons of shipping to submarine attack in the Atlantic.

Better explosive charges, improved Air-to-Surface-Vessel (ASV) radar and the introduction of powerful searchlights, known as "Leigh lights" after their inventor, all increased the kill chances against submarines. The accumulation of anti-submarine experience led to a sharp increase in sinkings during 1942 and forced the German submarines to operate in defined ocean areas.

In November 1942, with the appointment of Admiral Max Horton as Commander-in-Chief of the Western Approaches, which covered the main area of the submarine battle, greater efforts were devoted to organizing well-trained and powerful escort groups to hunt out the submarines rather than simply protect the convoys. But in the absence of detailed intelligence, and without aircraft cover, it proved difficult to reform the battle quickly. During February and March 1943, in

exceptionally poor weather, the submarine war reached a crescendo with the sinking of 21 ships in mid-Atlantic for the loss of just one submarine. Over the following few weeks, the battle suddenly turned abruptly in favour of the Allies. New escort carriers and Very Long Range Liberator aircraft were introduced to bridge the "Gap"; the Triton cipher was finally broken; and all aircraft were fitted with the new ASV Mark III radar and Leigh lights. In April, 19 submarines were sunk, in May a further 41. German forces had no answer to the technical improvements, and on 24 May, Dönitz ordered submarines to retreat to their European bases, from which they continued to be attacked every time they ventured out to sea. In June 1943, not a single ship was lost in convoy and not a single attack reported.

Although the submarine was not eliminated, the Battle of the Atlantic was effectively over.

LEFT Three German submariners rescued from their boat during the Battle of the Atlantic. Once submarine losses rose, survival chances were slight. Out of 39,000 crew, 28,000 were killed during the course of the war.

THE VERY-LONG-RANGE AIRCRAFT

The American heavy bomber the Consolidated B-24 Liberator played a critical role in the Battle of the Atlantic in helping to bridge the "Atlantic Gap" where it had been impossible to provide adequate air cover to track submarines. The aircraft only became available in March 1943, but with extra fuel tanks in the bomb bays and reduced armour it was possible for them to reach far out into the ocean from bases in Britain, Canada and Iceland. Armed with centimetric radar and Leigh lights to illuminate submarines at night, Liberators were attributed 72 submarine "kills" during the course of the war.

RIGHT A Very Long Range (VLR) PB4Y-1 Liberator bomber flying over the Bay of Biscay during 1943 in the hunt for submarines.

INTO THE CAUCASUS

19 AUGUST 1942
Start of "Sinyavino" offensive against German blockade of Leningrad.

10 SEPTEMBER 1942
British troops sent to India to quell political unrest.

14 SEPTEMBER 1942
US troops win the Battle of Bloody Ridge on the island of Guadalcanal in the Solomons.

24 SEPTEMBER 1942
General Franz Halder, German Chief of Staff, is sacked by Hitler and replaced by General Kurt Zeitzler.

23 OCTOBER 1942
Start of the second Battle of El Alamein in Egypt which rolls back the Axis threat.

5 NOVEMBER 1942
General Eisenhower sets up headquarters for the invasion of North Africa in the British colony of Gibraltar.

The extraordinary success of Operation "Blue" in the first week of July 1942 against the weaker southern Soviet front tempted Hitler to use his forces to achieve a double blow against the enemy. On 9 July, the units were divided into Army Group A under Field Marshal List and Army Group B under von Weichs. On 23 July, a new war directive from Hitler ordered Army Group A to seize the Caucasus area and its rich oil supplies, while Army Group B was to advance on Stalingrad to cut the Volga. Army Group A was based around the 1st Panzer Army and 17th Army, but was joined briefly by the 4th Panzer Army until Hitler decided to move it back to the Stalingrad front, a decision that meant the loss of several weeks' combat for a unit that might have tilted the balance on either wing of the assault.

The seizure of the Caucasus, codenamed Operation "Edelweiss", was an important gamble with the potential to be decisive. If the area was conquered quickly, it would mean cutting the Soviet armed forces off from most of their sources of oil, while at the same time ending Germany's permanent fuel crisis. This opened up the prospect of a drive into the Middle East through Iraq and Iran to meet up with

ABOVE German mountain troops salute the German flag on top of Mount Elbruz, the tallest mountain in the Caucasus range, on 21 August 1942.

Rommel's forces driving from the west, which were then poised only a short distance from the Suez Canal. There was a hope that Turkey, which had hitherto maintained a careful neutrality, might be persuaded by German success to join the Axis and so destroy the Allies' entire strategic position in the Mediterranean.

"Edelweiss" was launched on 25 July and at first fitted the pattern of all earlier summer campaigning. German armies moved forward at 50 kilometres (30 miles) a day,

ABOVE German armour from the 1st Panzer Army at the foot of the Caucasus mountains in August 1942. There are Panzer II tanks visible in the foreground. The terrain proved difficult for rapid movement, and progress in mountain country was reduced to a mile or two a day.

MARSHAL SEMYON BUDYENNY (1883–1973)

The son of a poor peasant family, Budyenny rose to become one of the most colourful and best-known of Soviet marshals. He joined the Tsarist cavalry and served in the Caucasus during the latter part of the First World War. He sided with the Bolshevik regime in 1917 and helped to organize the Soviet 1st Cavalry Army which played a key role in the Russian Civil War. He was made a Marshal of the Soviet Union in 1935 and survived the military purges. Budyenny understood little about modern warfare, and regretted the decline of the horse. He led an army in the Soviet-Finnish war and was commander-in-chief of the southwestern district facing the German invasion. His forces were destroyed around Kiev and he was demoted to command the North Caucasus Front in 1942, where he suffered further disasters before being relieved of command in August. He ended up as commander of Soviet Cavalry.

RIGHT German mountain troops relax at the top of the Caucasus mountains in September 1942. Soon after this, deteriorating weather and supply difficulties brought the German advance to a halt.

ABOVE Oil wells blazing in the Soviet city of Maikop, destroyed by the retreating Red Army with orders to let nothing fall into German hands. The wells could produce two million tons of oil a year, nearby Grozny some seven million tons.

THE SOVIET BLACK SEA FLEET

Soviet naval power was the poor relation of the Soviet armed forces. The Black Sea Fleet, commanded until May 1943 by Vice Admiral Oktyabrsky, had few modern warships and relied on small motor torpedo boats and minesweepers to support the movement of troops and supplies. The main fleet of one battleship, six cruisers and 21 destroyers was hardly used at all. Its greatest success was in shipping 40,000 troops to the Crimean peninsula in December 1941. During the Caucasus campaign, small vessels supplied equipment and men to the armies defending the mountain range. In February 1943, the fleet supported landings near the port of Novorossisk in an attempt to cut the German armies off from retreat once the Caucasus operation had been abandoned.

ABOVE Units of the Soviet Black Sea Fleet in 1943 near the Kerch peninsula in the Crimea.

ABOVE MIDDLE A group of Romanian soldiers from the Third Romanian Army attached to List's Army Group A use spades as improvised oars to cross a river under Soviet artillery fire in October 1942.

LEFT Soviet soldiers of the North Caucasus Front in October 1942 loading an anti-tank battery. Although short of supplies and reinforcements, the Caucasus front held the German attack and protected the oil supplies of Grozny and Baku.

BELOW A young German guard from the Reich Labour Service watches Soviet prisoners of war by the Terek river in the Caucasus in October 1942. German forces captured far fewer prisoners in 1942 as the Red Army learned to anticipate German tactics and avoid encirclement.

RIGHT German Eastern Front medal.

covering 300–500 kilometres (200–300 miles) by early August against a weakly armed Soviet North Caucasus Army Group under the veteran cavalry commander Marshal Semyon Budyenny, who had fought on the southern front during the Russian Civil War. As the 1st Panzer Army forged towards the oil centres of Maikop and Grozny, Budyenny's front was dissolved and a new Transcaucasus Army Group created under General Tiulenev. The progress of German forces gradually slowed, due partly to the terrain, with its mixture of steppe, mountain and desert, as well as deteriorating weather conditions and the long and taut supply lines from the west. By 9 August, Maikop was in German hands, and by 24 August, the 17th Army's German and Romanian alpine troops had reached the Caucasus mountain chain. Here progress ground to a halt as the Red Army held on to the passes high in the mountains and the strip of Black Sea coast beyond them where Soviet supplies could be brought in across the sea.

To the east, the 1st Panzer Army continued to drive across the steppe towards Grozny and the Caspian Sea oil centre at Baku. The Soviet North Caucasus Front under General Petrov, with four infantry armies, made a stand along the Terek river in front of Grozny and this proved to be the furthest extent of German penetration, achieved by 9 November. In September, von List was sacked by Hitler for failing to capture the area fast enough, and Army Group A was directed from Hitler's Supreme Headquarters until late November, when Field Marshal von Kleist, commander of the 1st Panzer Army, was given overall control of the whole front. While the great drama unfolded to the northeast in Stalingrad, the two exhausted sides in the Caucasus dug in to await its outcome. Eighteen months later, in February 1944, the small nationalities of the region, the Chechens, Ingush, Karachai, Kalmyks and Meshkhetians, were accused by the Soviet regime of collaboration with the German enemy during the battles in the Caucasus and were rounded up and deported en masse to labour camps and settlements in central and northern Russia. The man who organized the deportation, Stalin's Commissar for Internal Affairs, Lavrenti Beria, had represented him on the Transcaucasus front during the German attack.

BATTLE FOR THE SOLOMONS

22 JULY 1942
Japanese land at Gona and Buna on the southern peninsula of New Guinea.

12 AUGUST 1942
Japanese army begins major operation in Shantung province of China.

22 AUGUST 1942
Brazil declares war on Italy and Germany.

31 AUGUST 1942
Start of Battle of Alam Halfa in Egypt sees Rommel try to break Allied line.

5 SEPTEMBER 1942
Australian forces compel Japanese to abandon attack on Milne Bay in southern New Guinea.

3 OCTOBER 1942
First successful test launch of the German A4 rocket.

BELOW Badge of the Marine Corps Ship Detachment known as the "Sea Marines".

After the Battle of Midway the Japanese continued with their plan to interrupt communications between the United States and the South Pacific by taking over a string of island bases east of New Guinea. At the southern end of the Solomon Islands group, on Guadalcanal, they landed a small force to construct an airfield, while they planned to use the nearby island of Tulagi as a small southern naval base. Allied intelligence on Japanese moves encouraged the decision to launch a pre-emptive attack on Tulagi and Guadalcanal with the object of neutralizing the Japanese threat to supply lines and breaching the perimeter of the southern area of their advance. Vice Admiral Frank Fletcher commanded the US naval force which arrived on 7 August, transporting 19,000 men of the 1st Marine Division under Major General Alexander Vandegrift. The landings on Guadalcanal resulted in the rapid seizure of the Japanese airfield at Lunga, while after two days of hard fighting the

BELOW Marine troops on Guadalcanal employ a 75mm howitzer artillery piece to bombard a Japanese position on the island.

ABOVE A group of US Marines landing in the Solomons during the assault on Guadalcanal leap from their boat and head for the shelter of the jungle rim. Beach assaults were the only way to gain a foothold in the long haul to drive the Japanese from their island fortresses.

port of Tulagi was captured. The Japanese command, based further to the north in the New Britain port of Rabaul, reacted at once and Guadalcanal, a small tropical island, covered with inhospitable jungle, became, like Midway, a battle over the limit of Japanese advance.

On the night of 8–9 August, a Japanese naval task force of seven cruisers arrived off Savo Island, in the strait between Lunga and Tulagi, where it sank four cruisers and damaged two more. Fletcher withdrew his carrier force, and over the next two weeks Japanese troops of the 17th Army under Lieutenant General Haruyoshi Hyakutake began to land on Guadalcanal. Although short of supplies and air support, the

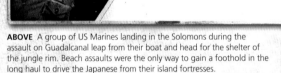

ABOVE In the Battle of Santa Cruz off the southernmost Solomon Islands, a Japanese aircraft bombs a US carrier. During the battle, the USS carrier *Hornet* was sunk along with a destroyer; the Japanese fleet suffered heavy losses of aircraft and damage to two battleships and two carriers.

RIGHT Commander of US carriers Admiral William F. Halsey was made commander-in-chief South Pacific Area in October 1942 at the height of the Guadalcanal campaign. He drove his men aggressively under the slogan "Kill Japs! Kill more Japs!".

GENERAL ALEXANDER VANDEGRIFT (1887–1973)

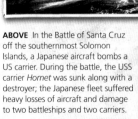

General Vandegrift joined the US Marine Corps in 1909, and after service in the Caribbean, became a Marine Corps Assistant Chief-of-Staff, and by 1940, assistant to the US Marine Corps Commandant with the rank of Brigadier General. Shortly before Pearl Harbor he was sent to command the 1st Marine Division, and in May 1942 took the division to the south Pacific where he led it in the first full-scale invasion of Japanese-held territory in the Solomons. The capture of the island of Guadalcanal earned him the Medal of Honor and promotion to command of a Marine Corps. On 1 January 1944, he was promoted to Lieutenant General and became Commandant of the Marine Corps in Washington. In April 1945, he became the first Marine Corps officer to reach the rank of four-star General.

LIEUTENANT GENERAL HARUYOSHI HYAKUTAKE (1888–1947)

A graduate from the Japanese Army Academy in 1909, whose fellow classmates included the future Chinese leader Chiang Kaishek, Hyakutake was sent in 1928 to the Kwantung Army in northern China, ending up on the general staff by 1935. After a number of field commands and training assignments he was chosen in May 1942 to command the Japanese 17th Army based at Rabaul in the south Pacific, and from here he orchestrated unsuccessful efforts to dislodge the American occupation of Guadalcanal. In the campaign in 1943 for the island of Bougainville he and his men were trapped in the interior and forced to live out the rest of the war there, hiding in jungle caves. After a serious stroke, Lieutenant General Hyakutake was relieved of duties in February 1945, but could not be evacuated to Japan until after the war was over.

LEFT A group of US soldiers look at a map on a news board set up on the island of Guadalcanal. The fighting lasted from August 1942 to February 1943, during which time there was little respite from the combat.

RIGHT Dead Japanese sailors in the campaign on Guadalcanal in the winter of 1942–3. Japanese forces lost 20,000 men in the unsuccessful attempt to hold on to the island.

Marine force at what had been renamed by the Americans Henderson Field was able to repel the first Japanese attack by 21 August in the Battle of the Tenaru River. Japanese tactics were crude and the frontal assaults against men dug in with artillery and machine guns were suicidal. Almost all the 900 men in the first attack were killed for the loss of around 40 Americans. On 24 August, a second major Japanese naval force was sent south, but this time the naval battle that followed in the Eastern Solomons was more even. The Japanese carrier *Ryujo* was sunk by US carrier aircraft and although the US carrier *Enterprise* was damaged, the Japanese force withdrew. Nevertheless, the build-up of Japanese forces continued under cover of night. They were used for further attacks on the Henderson Field enclave, but all of them were repulsed, including the battle for "Bloody Ridge" on 12 September when the Japanese troops were annihilated once again. By mid-October, both sides had approximately the same number of forces, 22,000 Japanese and 23,000 Americans, while the presence of large Japanese naval forces posed a serious threat to the American foothold on the island.

The week beginning 23 October was potentially decisive. The Japanese army began a series of heavy attacks on Henderson Field, and on 25 October a light naval force bombarded the area and sank a number of small vessels. A major fleet engagement on 26 October off the Santa Cruz Islands to the east of the Solomons led to the sinking of the US carrier *Hornet*, but also to heavy losses of Japanese carrier aircraft. The multiple attacks on Henderson Field over the period 23–26 October were once again repulsed with heavy losses in a series of hard-fought engagements, in which the two Marine divisions were joined by US army troops from the Americal Division. At the end of October, the situation was keenly balanced, but after three months of combat the US garrison had only succeeded in securing a small section of coast not much larger than the area they had first occupied in August. Over the following weeks, the duel between Vandegrift and Hyakutake reached a bloody climax.

BELOW An aerial view of Henderson airfield on Guadalcanal in the Solomons in August 1944, some two years after US Marines assaulted the island and established a preliminary base there. The Lunga landing ground, renamed Henderson Field, was captured on 8 August and brought into operation by 21 August.

THE DIEPPE RAID

When Lord Louis Mountbatten became Chief of Combined Operations in March 1942, he inherited plans for small-scale raids on German-held coastlines to test their defences and secure intelligence. Working together with the headquarters of the Home Army, Mountbatten and the Commanding Officer, South Eastern Command, Lieutenant General Bernard Montgomery, planned Operation "Rutter", a raid on the French port of Dieppe on the Channel coast. The raid was assigned to the Canadian 2nd Division, which was stationed in southern Britain, under the command of Major General John Roberts, and was to take place in July.

The purposes of the raid were not only operational. In the summer of 1942, there was strong pressure on the British War Cabinet from Moscow and Washington to show that Britain was capable of taking action against the German enemy. It was clear that no major cross-Channel invasion was possible in 1942 because of shortages of shipping and trained men, but the two men chosen to organize the raid, Mountbatten and the commander of No. 11 Group Fighter Command, Air Marshal Leigh-Mallory, were both strongly in favour of taking action against the enemy whenever possible. Leigh-Mallory had already organized what were called "Circuses", large groups of fighters with a few bombers to attack the north European coast and lure the German air force into battle. Mountbatten had already overseen the raids on St Nazaire and Bruneval.

AIR MARSHAL TRAFFORD LEIGH-MALLORY (1892–1944)
Serving first in the army, then in the Royal Flying Corps in the First World War, Leigh-Mallory was commander of No. 12 Group RAF Fighter Command with the rank of Air Vice-Marshal when the war broke out. He argued during the Battle of Britain in favour of "Big Wing" tactics, using large numbers of fighters for a concerted attack on enemy bombers, but failed to convince his fellow commanders. As commander of No. 11 Group in 1942, he was responsible for fighter cover for the Dieppe Raid. He became Commander-in-Chief of Fighter Command in November 1942 and then commander of all tactical air forces for the Normandy landings. He was killed in an air crash in November 1944 on his way to take up a new command appointment in Southeast Asia.

Operation "Rutter" was on a different scale, but when the time for the assault came the weather caused its cancellation and Montgomery assumed that the plan was finished. Mountbatten revived it under a new codename, Operation "Jubilee". He kept the operation and its planning secret even from those under his command and it remains an open question whether the raid was ever formally approved by the Chiefs of Staff or the War Cabinet. The raid involved a total of 237 ships and landing craft, the Canadian Division, No. 3 and No. 4 Commandos, Royal Marine A Commando, 50 US Rangers and a total of 74 squadrons of aircraft, most of them fighters. This considerable force crossed the Channel on

TOP A low-level aerial-reconnaissance photograph of the waterfront in the French town of Dieppe taken by Army Co-operation Command a few days before the raid in August 1942.

ABOVE Commando knife carried by Sargeant Ken Phillott of No. 4 Commando during the Dieppe Raid.

BELOW A landing craft approaching the French shore during the Dieppe Raid of 19 August 1942 under cover of a smokescreen laid by RAF aircraft. The raid proved a disastrous gamble and alerted the Allies to the need for thorough preparation before a full-scale invasion.

BELOW Badge of 101 troop – the sea-borne division of 6 Commando which used canoes or folding boats. It was disbanded in 1943.

ABOVE German soldiers inspect a destroyed British landing craft used during the raid on Dieppe. In all some 33 landing craft and one destroyer were lost during the operation out of a total of 237 ships of all kinds used for the raid.

LEFT No. 4 Special Service division shoulder title.

ABOVE Stills from an airborne camera aboard a Spitfire Mark V as it engages and shoots down a German Do 217 bomber over the English Channel while escorting a convoy home after the Dieppe raid.

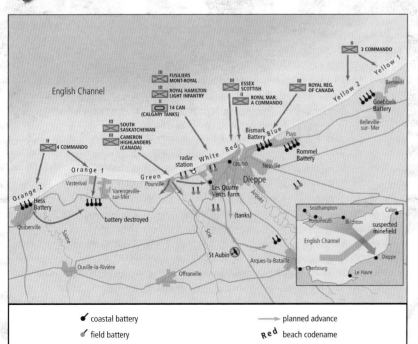

coastal battery   → planned advance

field battery   **Red** beach codename

19 August. Intelligence information was poor and the assault plan – for a frontal attack on the port – carried dangerous risks. Two flank attacks on the guns on either side of Dieppe were made by the Commando units, but the one to the east was detected by a German convoy and the coastal garrison alerted. Only the batteries to the west were captured by No. 4 Commando. Half an hour after the flank attacks, at 5.20 in the morning, the main force landed on the port beaches under cover of a smokescreen. They came under heavy fire, and losses were high. Roberts called in his reserve forces to try to strengthen the assault, but the decision only compounded what was an evident disaster. The few tanks which were successfully landed either failed to scale the sea wall or were quickly immobilized in the town. By 11.00 a.m., the troops were ordered to withdraw and the evacuation of what was left of the force was completed by early afternoon.

The losses from the raid were exceptionally high. Out of the 4,963 Canadians, 3,367 were killed, wounded or captured. The total killed from all the forces committed was 1,027. The RAF lost 106 aircraft and destroyed only 48. The outcome had many causes, but the principal failure was not to recognize how difficult a frontal assault on a heavily defended port and coastline could be without prior bombing or naval gunfire, and with poor reconnaissance preparation. The lessons of Dieppe were absorbed in the later preparations for the landings in France, but the immediate impact was to rule out any prospect in the near future of a "Second Front" to help the Soviet war effort.

MAJOR GENERAL JOHN ROBERTS (1891–1962)

John Roberts served as an artilleryman in the First World War, during which he was awarded the Military Cross. Known as "Ham" from his middle name, Hamilton, he was the commander of the Canadian 1st Field Regiment in the Battle of France in 1940 and succeeded in bringing back his artillery during the evacuation from Brest, which won him the reputation as an effective officer. He then commanded the Canadian 2nd Division in a series of field exercises in 1942 in which the division emerged as one of the top four units in the army. As a result, the division was chosen for the Dieppe operation, but failure there, and further failures in major exercises in spring 1943 in preparation for D-Day, led him to be demoted to commanding reinforcement units.

THE TIDE TURNS IN NORTH AFRICA

12 AUGUST 1942
Churchill arrives in Moscow for summit meeting with Stalin to announce that there will be no second front in 1942.

17 AUGUST 1942
US Air Force's 8th Air Force conducts its first bombing raid in Europe against the French town of Rouen.

19 AUGUST 1942
Dieppe Raid against the German-held French coast proves a disaster with high losses.

21 AUGUST 1942
German forces reach the summit of Mount Elbrus in the Caucasus Mountains.

22 AUGUST 1942
Brazil declares war on Germany and Italy.

5 SEPTEMBER 1942
The Western Allies confirm plans for Operation "Torch", the invasion of northwest Africa.

When Rommel's successful Axis offensive reached into Egypt to the Alamein Line in June 1942, he was determined to push on to capture Cairo and the Suez Canal. His success in the summer offensive had earned him the rank of field marshal. On 1 July, the Axis forces attacked the Allied defensive line but British Commonwealth forces were dug in well and the attacks were repulsed. General Auchinleck then decided on a counter-offensive, taking advantage of a substantial superiority in tanks and aircraft. The attacks, launched on 10 July, proved a costly failure. Rommel was prevented from going any further, but Allied tank strength, which had been four times that of Rommel's forces, was severely reduced. Allied casualties from what became known as the First Battle of El Alamein were over 13,000.

Churchill, frustrated at repeated failure, removed Auchinleck and replaced him as commander-in-chief Middle East with General Harold Alexander. Command of the 8th Army was given to Lieutenant General William Gott, but he died on 7 August, when the transport plane in which he was travelling was shot down. His replacement, Lieutenant General Bernard Montgomery, was to forge a remarkable alliance with Alexander which led Allied armies across North Africa and on into Sicily and Italy. Montgomery was reluctant to commit to a further offensive until he had substantial additional forces; instead the defensive line was strengthened in anticipation of a further German assault, whose details had been revealed by ULTRA decrypts.

Rommel's plan was to mount a diversionary attack towards the Australian and South African forces on the coast around El Alamein, while taking the bulk of his armour and that of his Italian ally in a wide southern sweep to outflank the Allied line and encircle Montgomery's forces.

ABOVE Italian Fascism continued to pretend that Italy was a powerful military state despite defeats in Africa. Here a wartime military parade in front of visiting German dignitaries in the Piazza Venezia in Rome is supposed to display the might of the new Italy.

FIELD MARSHAL HAROLD ALEXANDER (1891–1969)

Harold Alexander was one of Britain's most successful wartime commanders. After a distinguished combat career in the First World War, he became the youngest general in the army in 1937. He commanded the First Division in France in 1940 and then commanded the BEF (British Expeditionary Force) during the Dunkirk evacuation. In March 1942 he organized the British retreat from Burma, and was appointed commander-in-chief Middle East in August 1942. In early 1943 he became Eisenhower's deputy for the campaign in Tunisia, where he reorganized a poorly co-ordinated Allied front and forced Axis surrender in May. He commanded the invasion of Sicily and Italy and in November 1944 was made supreme commander in the Mediterranean. Created a field marshal in September 1944, he was governor general of Canada from 1946 to 1952.

It was an ambitious but predictable move and Montgomery prepared his forces to meet the encircling Axis on the high ridge at Alam Halfa, some 25 kilometres (15 miles) behind Allied lines. Short of fuel and with a limited number of tanks, Rommel began the attack on the night of 30/31 August with four armoured units, the German 15th and 21st Panzer, and the Italian Ariete and Littorio divisions. They made rapid progress through the series of defensive

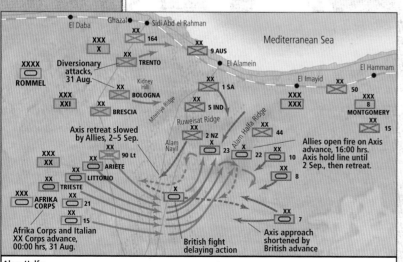

Alam Halfa
31 August–5 September 1942

Minefields

Mediterranean Sea

El Daba · Ghazal · Sidi Abd el Rahman

164
X
XX

9 AUS
TRENTO
Diversionary attacks, 31 Aug.
ROMMEL

El Alamein

El Hammam
El Imayid

Kidney Hill
BOLOGNA
1 SA
50
MONTGOMERY

BRESCIA
5 IND
8

Ruweisat Ridge
Miteirya Ridge

Axis retreat slowed by Allies, 2–5 Sep.
2 NZ
44
15

Alam Nayil
90 Lt
ARIETE
23
22
10
Allies open fire on Axis advance, 16:00 hrs. Axis hold line until 2 Sep., then retreat.

LITTORIO
8
TRIESTE

AFRIKA CORPS
21
15

Afrika Corps and Italian XX Corps advance, 00:00 hrs, 31 Aug.

British fight delaying action

Axis approach shortened by British advance

7

ABOVE A German soldier uses a "donkey's ears" periscope to observe Allied lines during the probing attacks organized by Rommel in early July 1942.

OBJECT Armband awarded to German forces who took part in the North Africa campaigns.

"boxes" on the south of the Allied line and turned on Alam Halfa ridge to complete the encirclement.

Montgomery's strategy worked just as intended. Axis forces became bogged down in extensive minefields, were attacked on the flank by the British 7th Armoured Division and hit by effective anti-tank fire from forces dug in on the ridge. After two days of fruitless fighting, Rommel ordered a retreat, leaving 50 tanks and 400 vehicles behind. This was the furthest Axis forces got in the North African campaign, and the last prospect that Rommel had of snatching a rapid victory. Over the next two months Rommel established a thick defensive line against the expected counter-offensive, with wide minefields and armoured divisions dug in behind them.

The victory at Alam Halfa has attracted none of the attention given to the eventual victory at Alamein in November, but it was an important turning point and it gave Montgomery the opportunity to display his mettle while Churchill pressed him for action. It was a victory won by substantial superiority in weapons and supplies. The Middle Eastern air force comprised 96 squadrons of more than 1,000 aircraft by October 1942, with a genuinely international flavour. Beside units staffed by British crew, there were American, South African, Australian, Greek, Canadian, French, Rhodesian and Yugoslav squadrons. Air power proved a substantial bonus for Allied forces as the German and Italian air component dwindled, hampered by regular shortages of fuel oil. These advantages were to prove decisive in the next, and most famous, of Montgomery's offensives.

ABOVE British forces depended on generous supplies from the United States for the Middle Eastern campaigns. Here the 5th Royal Tank Regiment displays its Grant tanks for the camera on 17 February 1942.

BELOW Supply was a big advantage the Allies held over the Axis in North Africa because Axis supply routes were easily interrupted by Allied submarine and air attack. Here a convoy unloads RAF parts and equipment in Port Said in Egypt in August 1942.

ABOVE Churchill flew to Cairo in August 1942 to see for himself what should be done to ensure that North Africa could be defended. Here he sits with the South African premier Jan Smuts with, behind, General Alan Brooke (right) and Air Marshal Arthur Tedder (left).

THE BATTLE FOR STALINGRAD

26 AUGUST 1942
General Zhukov appointed deputy supreme commander-in-chief under Stalin.

12 SEPTEMBER 1942
British liner *Laconia* sunk in the South Atlantic with 1,500 Italian POWs on board.

3 OCTOBER 1942
German rocket scientists successfully launch the A4 missile which was to become the V2 rocket.

18 OCTOBER 1942
Hitler orders that all British commandos who fall into German hands are executed.

4 NOVEMBER 1942
Axis forces in Egypt under Rommel are forced to retreat after defeat in the Second Battle of Alamein.

8 NOVEMBER 1942
Allied forces land in northwest Africa in Operation "Torch".

11 NOVEMBER 1942
German forces occupy Vichy France in reaction to the Allied landings in North Africa.

ABOVE German artillerymen give close support to the infantry as they edge forward through the ruins of Stalingrad. The picture is from November 1942, shortly before the encirclement of the 6th Army.

GENERAL VASILY CHUIKOV (1900–82)

Chuikov was the son of a peasant family who joined the Red Army during the Russian Civil War. He became a career officer and in 1939 commanded the Soviet 4th Army in the occupation of Poland. His poor performance in the Soviet-Finnish war led to his demotion and he was sent as adviser to Chiang Kaishek in China. He was recalled in May 1942 and posted a few weeks later to command the 64th Army trying to hold the steppe in front of Stalingrad. In September he was transferred to command of the 62nd Army in the defence of the city itself, and distinguished himself as an inspiring, brave and innovative commander. He later commanded the army that reached the centre of Berlin first, in May 1945. In 1955, he was promoted to marshal and was commander-in-chief of the Soviet army from 1960 to 1964. He was buried in Stalingrad on the hill of Mamayev Kurgan, scene of the most bitter fighting in the city.

When German and Romanian forces finally reached the outskirts of Stalingrad in mid-August and forced a small salient as far as the Volga river in the north, there was wide confidence at Hitler's headquarters that the city would be in German hands in a matter of days; weeks at the most. On 19 August, Paulus launched a major offensive against the city together with some units of the 4th Panzer Army. On 23 August, the German air force in southern Russia, commanded by General (later Field Marshal) Wolfram von Richthofen, sent 600 bombers to devastate the city. The decision to leave the population in place to avoid the disruption that would be caused by a stream of refugees resulted, according to Soviet estimates, in the death of 40,000 people. The savage bombardment from artillery and aircraft pushed the Soviet defenders back towards the river.

On 7 September, Paulus massed his forces for a concerted push to drive the Soviet defenders across the Volga. The two armies defending the area, 62nd and 64th, were split apart and block by block, factory by factory, German forces pressed forward. The commander of the 62nd, General Lopatin, thought the situation was hopeless and argued for withdrawal. He was dismissed and his place taken by a young, ebullient commander, Vasily Chuikov. He arrived the same day as the German thrust on 7 September to find a city in ruins. The Red Army survived only by using the destroyed urban landscape as a natural defence. In cellars and warehouses small groups of soldiers hid themselves, sniping at German infiltrators, using the cover of night to retake buildings that had been abandoned to heavier German daytime firepower. During September and October, the German army pushed the 62nd back into a handful of factory complexes – the Red October factory, the Barricades factory – right on the edge of the river.

BELOW Under "rolling cover" from storm artillery forces, German infantry enter the suburbs of Stalingrad, 12 November 1942.

ABOVE German soldiers storm part of the Red October plant near the edge of the Volga River in the heart of Stalingrad. Each building was fought for room by room.

ABOVE Soviet troops stage a counter-attack on German forces in the vicinity of the Red October plant, 26 November 1942.

Neither Paulus nor Chuikov fought a campaign entirely isolated from the rest of the Axis and Soviet forces. A stream of supplies and reinforcements crossed the Volga from the far bank; artillery and rocket fire was directed at German strongholds from the same area. On either flank of the city were much larger Soviet armies: to the south General Yeremenko's Stalingrad Army Group, to the north the Don Army Group of General Rokossovsky. They provided what assistance they could by attacking the exposed flanks of the German armies, while overhead large numbers of Soviet aircraft, directed in a co-ordinated way by radio (the earliest example of this), began to contest local air superiority for almost the first time in the campaign. German forces were stretched out across the Don Steppe, with the vulnerable corridor into Stalingrad guarded by Hungarian, Italian and Romanian allies. The German 4th Air Fleet was pressed heavily by the battle, but continued to provide assistance to the ground war as well as challenging Soviet air power.

The determination of the 62nd Army to hold the city at all costs has sometimes been attributed to fear of Soviet security forces in the rear who would shoot deserters or defeatists, or send them off to penal battalions. A figure of 13,500 has been estimated for those shot by their own side. But Soviet records show only 203 arrests for "panic" from November 1942 to February 1943 among all the Soviet armies defending Stalingrad. The evidence from eye-witnesses suggests instead that the Soviet defenders had at last found a cause they could

LEFT Almost all of Stalingrad was destroyed during the bombing and shelling of the city. Residents continued to eke out a living where they could in cellars and ruins, but at least 40,000 civilians died in the battle.

ABOVE Propaganda played an important part in keeping the Red Army fighting at Stalingrad. Vladimir Serov's 1942 poster reads "Let's Defend the Volga!".

OBJECT Medal awarded to Soviet troops for "success in combat".

identify with and a military challenge that made sense. The Russian novelist Viktor Nekrasov, who served as a junior officer at Stalingrad, found that the battle produced "wonderfully hardened soldiers". German soldiers also fought with great tenacity and desperation. The urban battlefield became a small, enclosed, violent microcosm of the larger battle that surrounded it.

On 9 November, German forces finally succeeded in punching a 500-metre (550-yard) hole in Chuikov's front, reaching the Volga. Soviet troops could not dislodge them, but German exhaustion brought a lull on 12 November. Six days later, Chuikov received a cryptic message from front headquarters that he should stand by for special orders. On the morning of 19 November, Chuikov was told that a massive Soviet counter-offensive had just been launched whose purpose was to cut off and encircle Paulus's 6th Army.

SECOND ALAMEIN

13 AUGUST 1942
Montgomery takes over as
commander of the 8th Army.

14 OCTOBER 1942
German forces begin major
assault on Stalingrad defences
to drive Red Army into the
Volga.

31 OCTOBER 1942
Heavy German bombing raid
on the English cathedral city of
Canterbury.

ABOVE Formation badge for the British 7th Armoured Division, known as the "Desert Rats".

ABOVE Badge of the 51st Highland Infantry Division.

The Second Battle of El Alamein was the first major victory of British Commonwealth forces against the German enemy and it opened the way to the destruction of Axis forces throughout North Africa. Although the battle was dwarfed by the campaigns on the Eastern Front, it was nonetheless a decisive turning point in Allied fortunes, making the Middle East secure and opening the way for a campaign to liberate the Mediterranean from the Axis.

Rommel knew after the failure at Alam Halfa that he lacked the depth of resources needed to penetrate further into Egypt. Instead, he established a thick defensive line, providing German troops and tanks to strengthen the Italian divisions; the greatest concentration of Axis forces was in the north, protecting communications along the coast. Rommel had four German and a maximum of eight Italian divisions at his disposal (a balance reflected in the decision to rename Panzer Army Africa the German-Italian

LEFT British infantry advance through the dust and smoke of combat during the Second Battle of Alamein, October 1942.

ABOVE Italian soldiers on the Egyptian front at El Alamein in action against Allied forces. Some 60 per cent of the Axis troops at Alamein were Italian.

Panzer Army). The Axis fielded around 500 tanks, of which fewer than half were German, and had support from 350 aircraft. All Axis forces were short of fuel and spare parts. Montgomery, on the other hand, saw his forces grow steadily during September and October. The armoured divisions could call on 1,030 tanks, 300 of which were new American Grants, and there were over 1,500 aircraft in the Middle East and Malta. He refused to act until he was confident that his forces had a decisive superiority and the army understood the nature of his plan.

After years of rapid mobile warfare, the Second Alamein battle was a set-piece operation. Montgomery planned to attack where Rommel was strongest in the north, around Kidney Hill, but to disguise the weight of his assault by diversionary attacks in the south. His object, in what was codenamed Operation "Lightfoot", was to send forward the infantry divisions to open up a pathway through the minefields, and then to pour the tanks of the 10th Armoured Corps through the gap. With a salient secured, a second operation, "Supercharge", would push through large

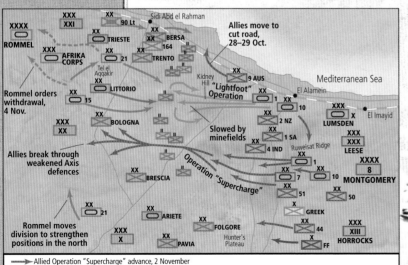

BELOW German soldiers man the tank-busting 88-millimetre (3.5-inch) anti-aircraft gun during the Battle of Alamein. It was found that the gun could be used against tanks as well as aircraft and was very effective against Allied tanks throughout the war.

Map labels:
XXXX ROMMEL
XXX AFRIKA CORPS
Sidi Abd el Rahman
90 Lt
TRIESTE
BERSA
164
TRENTO
21
Tel el Aqqakir
LITTORIO
15
Allies move to cut road, 28–29 Oct.
Kidney Hill
"Lightfoot" Operation
9 AUS
Mediterranean Sea
El Alamein
El Imayid
Rommel orders withdrawal, 4 Nov.
10
1
BOLOGNA
2 NZ
LUMSDEN
Slowed by minefields
1 SA
Ruweisat Ridge
4 IND
LEESE
Allies break through weakened Axis defences
BRESCIA
Operation "Supercharge"
7
10
51
8 MONTGOMERY
50
Rommel moves division to strengthen positions in the north
21
ARIETE
GREEK
FOLGORE
44
XIII
Hunter's Plateau
PAVIA
HORROCKS
FF

→ Allied Operation "Supercharge" advance, 2 November
→ Allied Operation "Lightfoot" advance, 26 October
ⁿ Minefields

FIELD MARSHAL BERNARD MONTGOMERY (1887–1976)

The son of an Anglo-Irish clergyman, Montgomery joined the army in 1908 and saw service in the early battles of the First World War before a bullet in the lung almost killed him. He returned to duty as a staff officer, and served between the wars in Ireland, India, Egypt and Palestine, where he was responsible for suppressing a revolt in 1938. He made his reputation as an excellent trainer of men and a master of meticulous preparation. In the Battle of France he commanded the 3rd Division, which he successfully withdrew at Dunkirk with relatively low casualties. In December 1941 he was appointed commander-in-chief Southeastern Command, where he insisted on intensive training for his men. Appointed to command the 8th Army in August 1942, he transformed its morale in a matter of weeks. El Alamein was his most famous victory, and subsequent campaigns in Sicily, Italy and northwest Europe made him a household name. He was a difficult personality – acerbic, intolerant, boastful, egotistical – and this soured his strategic performance. He collaborated poorly with others; tact was entirely foreign to him. He was ground commander for the Normandy invasion, then commander of the 21st Army Group. After the war, he was appointed chief of the Imperial General Staff and created Viscount Montgomery of Alamein.

armoured forces for the final blow. The start was set for 23 October, when fortuitously Rommel was away on sick leave.

Operation "Lightfoot" began with a massive artillery barrage in the evening of 23 October. Rommel's replacement, Lieutenant General Stumme, died during the Allied air attacks, leaving Axis forces in some confusion until Rommel's return on 25 October. Nevertheless, resistance was fierce, and only by the second day was progress made along the coast road and around Kidney Hill. Rommel ordered his tanks north to dislodge the enemy, but exposed the Italian divisions to Allied attacks, which were pressed forward during fierce armoured fighting on 27 and 28 October. Montgomery then withdrew the diversionary forces in the south and concentrated a heavy armoured force to carry out "Supercharge". When the fresh armour poured through on 2 November, supported by strong air attacks, Rommel realized he was defeated; Axis forces were down to only 35 fully serviceable tanks. Hitler refused permission to withdraw, but two days later he had to accept reality, and Rommel began a rapid westwards retreat along the coast road. Some Italian divisions continued to fight after the German forces had abandoned the battle, but the Axis

position was hopeless. Rommel left over 400 destroyed tanks; the Allies lost around 250. Allied casualties were 13,500, but Montgomery's forces netted over 30,000 Axis prisoners.

The 8th Army raced in pursuit of the retreating Rommel and by 13 November had retaken Tobruk. Axis forces made brief defensive attacks at Benghazi on 20 November and El Agheila between 23 November and 13 December, but the pressure was relentless. Tripoli was occupied on 23 January and Rommel raced for the last defensive line in Tunisia, the Mareth Line, where Axis forces finally halted and turned. Victory at Alamein was complete and permission was given for church bells in Britain to ring out in celebration for the first time since May 1940.

ABOVE Sherman tanks of the Allied armoured forces in North Africa move swiftly along desert routes in pursuit of the retreating German and Italian forces after the victory at El Alamein in November 1942.

RIGHT A British Daimler-Benz armoured car opens fire at the start of the attack on German-held Tripoli, 18 January 1943. The port fell to the Allies five days later.

RIGHT A British Bofors mobile anti-aircraft gun being moved forward in November 1942 to the Libyan frontier, past a dead German soldier, left unburied during the rapid Axis retreat.

MARSHAL UGO CAVALLERO (1880–1943)

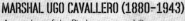

A member of the Piedmontese nobility, Cavallero joined the Italian army in 1898 and rose rapidly on account of his organizational and tactical skills. He fought in the Italo-Turkish war of September 1911–October 1912, and during the First World War joined the Italian Supreme Command where he rose to be chief of operations responsible for organizing the Italian victory at Vittorio Veneto. He was a keen Fascist and served as undersecretary of war during 1925–28. He left the army but was recalled in 1937 and took command of Italian forces in East Africa the following year. In December 1940, he succeeded Badoglio as chief of the Italian Supreme Command, and took personal control of the Italian forces in Greece, where he stabilized the front line. He was nominally Rommel's superior for the Axis campaigns in North Africa, but found it difficult to overrule his German allies. He opposed Rommel's invasion of Egypt, and when Libya was lost following Alamein, he was sacked. He committed suicide in September 1943 after refusing Hitler's request to lead those Italian forces still committed to fighting the Allies.

OPERATION "TORCH"

In the summer of 1942 the British and American chiefs-of-staff discussed the possibility of opening a "second front" in France in 1942. A frontal assault was rejected as too risky with unproven American forces and shortages of shipping, and on 22 July it was agreed to launch a smaller combined-arms assault on French North Africa. The object was to help the British in the east to clear the Axis out of Libya and to give American forces an opportunity to gain combat experience. The operation, codenamed "Torch", was to be largely an American affair and it was placed under the command of the recently arrived Lieutenant General Eisenhower.

The plan was to land substantial forces in French Morocco, and at Oran and Algiers in Algeria. It was hoped that the large French garrisons could be persuaded not to oppose the landings, and on 22 October Eisenhower's deputy, Major General Mark Clark, landed secretly in Algeria to make contact with the local commander of French forces, but a guarantee could not be secured that there would be

no resistance. The task force sailed in two large formations. The men and equipment for the Moroccan landings under Major General George Patton sailed directly across the Atlantic. A vast armada of 650 warships took the forces for the central and eastern sectors from British ports. The total assault force of 65,000 men was roughly half the size of the French garrison, but was strongly supported by naval vessels and by two large air forces, one for the western landings, one for the east.

The landings on 8 November achieved complete surprise since the fleet was disguised as a convoy bound for Malta. There was strong resistance in Morocco and also in Oran, but in Algiers the situation was confused by a coup launched by 400 French resistance fighters on the day of the

GENERAL DWIGHT D EISENHOWER (1890–1969)

The son of a poor Texas family, Eisenhower succeeded in entering the West Point Military Academy and embarked on a military career that made him one of the United States' most famous generals. He failed to see active service in the First World War – he was recruited to create America's first tank corps – and between the wars held various staff appointments before being posted to the Philippines to serve with MacArthur. In September 1939, he returned to the United States and by September 1941 was a brigadier general and chief-of-staff of the 3rd Army. After Pearl Harbor, General Marshall made him head of the new Operations Division. He was chosen to command the American European Theater of Operations in June 1942, and was supreme commander for the "Torch" landings, having never yet heard a shot fired in anger. He became supreme commander of the invasion of northwest Europe, for which his diplomatic and organizational skills and amiable disposition made him an ideal candidate. After the war, he became United States Army chief-of-staff until 1948, and was president of the United States from 1953 to 1961.

ABOVE LEFT Grumman Wildcat fighters and Supermarine Seafires, the naval version of the Spitfire, wait to take off from the flightdeck of HMS *Formidable* in support of the landings in Operation "Torch", November 1942.

LEFT American troops of the Centre Task Force aboard a landing craft on their way towards the beaches near the Algerian port of Oran.

BELOW Troops landing on the beach at Arzeu near Oran on the morning of 8 November 1942, prelude to two days of fighting before the city surrendered.

LEFT The "white ensign" hoisted by a Britsh naval signal party after landing west of Algiers in the early hours of 8 November 1942 as part of Operation "Torch".

ABOVE A US officer talking to Algerians shortly after the "Torch" landings.

BELOW RIGHT The German occupation of Vichy France on 11 November 1942 followed the successful "Torch" landings. Here German tanks enter Toulouse in southwestern France.

RIGHT A Moroccan sergeant major of the French North African Army pictured on the cover of *Picture Post*, 28 November 1942. Moroccan and Algerian units joined the Free French at once and were used in the subsequent invasion of Italy.

PICTURE **POST**

A NEW ARMY FOR THE ALLIES
A Sergeant-Major of the French
North-African Army.
See pages 13 to 17.

HULTON'S NATIONAL WEEKLY

In this issue:
ITALY'S CHOICE by TOM WINTRINGHAM

4^D

NOVEMBER 28, 1942 — Vol. 17. No. 9

landings which immobilized some of the troops and brought the occupation of most government buildings. Vichy forces fought back and tried to resist the Allied landing, but Admiral Darlan, overall commander-in-chief of Vichy French forces, who happened to be in Algiers, finally agreed to a ceasefire, but then promptly tried to withdraw it when the Vichy government refused to endorse his decision. Arrested by the American authorities, he agreed on 10 November to order a ceasefire in Oran, and the following day gave orders for an end to hostilities in Morocco.

The response to the Allied landings was immediate: on 10 November, Hitler ordered the German occupation of Vichy-controlled France; Italian forces occupied Corsica; and Vichy was compelled to agree to the transfer of Axis forces in large numbers to the as yet unoccupied French territory of Tunisia. Darlan tried to persuade the French fleet to sail to North Africa and join the Allies, but the naval command refused and on 27 November the fleet was scuttled at Toulon. When Darlan was murdered on 24 December, his place was taken by the pro-Allied General Giraud and French forces willing to fight with the Allies were placed under the field command of General Juin.

The landings were supposed to clear the way to link up with Montgomery's now advancing 8th Army in Libya, but in the race to reach Tunisia the German and Italian forces acted faster, bringing 17,000 troops and substantial numbers of aircraft into the area around Tunis by the end of November.

In the south, Rommel reached the defensive Mareth Line and almost the whole of Tunisia was in Axis hands. A combined British and American 1st Army tried to reach Tunis and came within 20 kilometres (32 miles) of their target, but the newly created 5th Panzer Army under General von Arnim succeeded in preventing the breakthrough and the 1st Army ground to a halt in poor weather and deep mud. During January 1943, the Axis forces succeeded in a number of small operations in pushing back French and British forces and stabilizing a defensive line in the Dorsale Mountains. By early February, with Rommel's forces arrived in Tunisia, a formidable garrison had been formed. An operation that had promised a quick end to the Axis presence in North Africa had instead provoked a final stand.

ADMIRAL FRANÇOIS DARLAN (1881–1942)

Darlan was a successful and ambitious French naval officer, who joined the navy in 1902 and rose by 1936 to the rank of admiral and naval chief-of-staff. In 1939, he was given the unique title of "admiral of the fleet" and put in supreme command of French naval forces. He was a firm supporter of Pétain and in February 1941 became Pétain's deputy and effective head of the government. He collaborated with the German occupiers, and in May 1941 agreed the Paris Protocols that gave substantial concessions to the Germans in French Africa and the Middle East. In April 1942, the Germans, uncertain of Darlan's reliability, pressured Pétain to replace him with Laval. Darlan remained commander-in-chief of French forces. On 7 November he arrived in Algiers to visit his sick son and was caught up in the "Torch" invasions. He changed sides, agreed to a French ceasefire, and was declared high commissioner for French North Africa, but on 24 December he was assassinated by a French royalist resistance fighter, Fernand de la Chapelle, who was executed two days later.

GUADALCANAL

LEFT A Japanese ship in the major base at Rabaul is hit by a bomb from the US 5th Army Air Force during an attack. Air attack on the base neutralized it as a threat throughout the conquest of the Solomons and the other southwest Pacific islands.

BELOW LEFT A group of American servicemen celebrate Christmas midnight mass at an improvised service on Guadalcanal, 23 December 1942.

The battle for Guadalcanal reached a critical point by November 1942. Though on a scale very much smaller than the battles in the North African desert or around Stalingrad, the struggle for the island came to be regarded by both sides as a vital testing ground for American resolve on the one hand and Japan's capacity to protect her new-won empire on the other.

Japanese forces on the island were strengthened after the failure of the October assault on the American-held Henderson airfield by men shipped in Japanese naval vessels on the "Tokyo Express" supply route through the central Solomons. By 12 November the forces at the disposal of Lieutenant General Hyakutake exceeded American numbers for the first time – 23,000 against 22,000. But that same day a United States task force delivered reinforcements to Guadalcanal supported by air cover from aircraft carriers in the Coral Sea and heavy bombers on the island of Espiritu Santo. By early December the balance was once again in American favour, 40,000 troops against 25,000.

This situation might well have been reversed had it not been for a series of destructive naval battles off the northern coast of Guadalcanal between 12 and 15 November in which a United States task force tried to prevent further reinforcement. A large convoy of Japanese troops, heavily supported by naval vessels, arrived off Guadalcanal in Ironbottom Sound on the night of 12/13 November. A fierce ship-to-ship engagement followed which left six American ships sunk and cost the Japanese three, including a battleship. The following day American aircraft attacked the Japanese landing fleet, sinking a cruiser and seven transport ships. During the night of 14/15 November a second major naval engagement took place in which the Japanese

REAR ADMIRAL RAIZO TANAKA (1892–1969)

A career officer in the Japanese navy, Tanaka became an expert on torpedoes in the 1920s and taught at the navy's torpedo school. In September 1941 he was appointed to command Destroyer Squadron 2 and in October promoted to rear admiral. He fought in the invasion of the Philippines and the Dutch East Indies. During the Solomons campaign Tanaka's destroyer force supplied Japanese forces on Guadalcanal along the "Slot" between the islands of the Solomons group. The Japanese called the supply runs "rat transportation", but the Allies nicknamed them the "Tokyo Express". Tanaka became critical of Japanese strategy and was redeployed to shore duties in Burma, where he remained for the rest of the war.

RIGHT A tired US soldier on his way back to Base Operations camp on Guadalcanal, February 1943, after 21 days of continuous combat. The fighting conditions for both sides were exceptionally tough throughout the island campaign.

was replaced as commander by Major General Alexander Patch, commander of the Americal Division (a contraction of "American New Caledonian"). With more than 50,000 men under his command, he began a series of offensives against the poorly supplied Japanese. By this stage the Japanese navy command had decided that Guadalcanal would have to be abandoned and the Japanese Imperial Headquarters confirmed this decision on 31 December. The isolated Japanese forces fought with suicidal determination but were pressed back to the north of the island. Unknown to the Americans, Japanese destroyers off the coast successfully evacuated 10,650 troops, including Hyakutake, between 2 and 8 February, leaving Guadalcanal in American hands.

Japanese losses for the island struggle were high. Over 20,000 troops were lost, 860 aircraft and 15 warships. The United States Navy also lost heavily, but the ground troops suffered only 6,111 casualties, including 1,752 killed. This remarkable disparity in losses was to be repeated in the island battles across the Pacific. If the Battle of Midway had determined the limit of Japanese naval expansion, the failure at Guadalcanal decisively halted the onward march of the Japanese army.

ABOVE Two American soldiers of the US 32nd Division fire into a dugout near the port of Buna in New Guinea in the drive to expel the Japanese from southern Papua at the same time as the operations on Guadalcanal.

BATTLE FOR NEW GUINEA

While the struggle was continuing in Guadalcanal, a second battle was taking place in eastern New Guinea where the Japanese had landed on 22 July 1942 to try to seize Port Moresby and expel Allied forces from the island. They landed at Gona and Buna and marched inland to seize Kokoda, and by September were 40 kilometres (25 miles) from the port. Stiff Australian and American resistance and the crisis in Guadalcanal forced a Japanese retreat and on 15 November Kokoda was recaptured. On 9 December the Japanese lodgement at Gona was eliminated by the Australian army and on 1 January 1943 Buna was captured as well. Japanese failure in New Guinea was further evidence that the outer perimeter of the southern zone could not be made secure.

battleship *Kirishima* and a destroyer were sunk for the loss of three US destroyers. In the end only 2,000 troops could be landed, with virtually no military supplies. The battles of Ironbottom Sound marked the end of Japanese efforts to save the position on Guadalcanal. One further attempt was made when Rear Admiral Tanaka personally commanded his destroyer squadron on 30 November in a run to Guadalcanal. His eight destroyers were surprised by a larger American force of five cruisers and four destroyers in Ironbottom Sound, but Tanaka's skilful handling of his ships produced a salvo of torpedoes that sank one cruiser and crippled the remaining three, before Tanaka retreated back up the Slot. The Battle of Tassafaronga, as it was known, was a tactical victory, but no supplies reached the embattled Japanese garrison.

In December 1942 the 1st Marine Division was replaced on the island by the 25th US Infantry Division and Vandegrift

ABOVE (BOX) An Australian mortar crew fire on the Japanese defenders of their stronghold of Buna, New Guinea, 8 February 1943. The Australians took the objective, one of the last held by the enemy in the area of the island.

RIGHT Japanese prisoners, sick and hungry, are taken down to the beach by American troops after the capture of a Japanese stronghold on Guadalcanal, 22 February 1943. Most Japanese troops had been evacuated to safety by this time.

OPERATION "URANUS"

12 NOVEMBER 1942
British Commonwealth forces retake Tobruk as they pursue Rommel in North Africa.

25 NOVEMBER 1942
Launch of Operation "Mars" against German Army Group Centre results in heavy Soviet losses.

30 NOVEMBER 1942
Battle of Tassafaronga when an inferior Japanese naval force inflicts heavy losses on the US Navy in the Guadalcanal campaign.

11 DECEMBER 1942
Hitler insists that the surrounded 6th Army must remain where it is in Stalingrad.

ABOVE Soviet order of the Red Star.

The view from Moscow in the autumn of 1942, as German forces pressed into Stalingrad and across the Caucasus region, threatening to cut the Volga and seize Soviet oil, looked increasingly desperate. Stalin and many of his senior commanders still assumed that German forces were planning a third operation to take the Soviet capital, and kept the largest part of the Red Army and air force along the front defending Moscow. On 27 August, Stalin finally summoned Zhukov, who had saved Leningrad and Moscow, and appointed him deputy supreme commander with the task of saving Stalingrad.

Zhukov visited the besieged city and returned to Moscow in mid-September. In conference with Stalin, Zhukov and the army chief-of-staff, Alexander Vasilevsky, hinted at a radical solution for saving the city. Stalin sent them away with instructions to bring back a definite plan. They returned with the outline for what became known as Operation "Uranus" – the first time the Soviet command had given a name to an operation. The object was to create a large reserve force north and south of Stalingrad and then to attack and sever the long, extended German flank, encircling Paulus in the city. Stalin approved, and during October and early November the Red Army, utilizing an elaborate plan of deception and camouflage, built up a force of over one million men, 14,000 heavy guns, 979 tanks and 1,350 aircraft. The German commanders, although anxious that the long line of communications stretching across the steppe to Stalingrad was vulnerable, particularly as it was mainly

ABOVE Soviet soldiers armed with hand grenades attack an enemy position on the outskirts of the Stalingrad pocket. The "Uranus" campaign required Soviet forces to secure a front line on either side of the corridor carved through the Axis lines, facing west towards the Don river and east towards Stalingrad.

ABOVE Artillery and rocket fire from Red Army units in the attack on Romanian forces at the start of Operation "Uranus", 19 November 1942.

protected by Romanian, Hungarian and Italian troops of Germany's Axis allies, believed that the Red Army had no reserves available to mount any kind of extensive operation.

The date set for Operation "Uranus" was 19 November, but it was not the only element in the Soviet plan. A second operation, codenamed "Mars", was planned for the central front to attack the German Army Group Centre, still only 160 kilometres (100 miles) from Moscow, and drive it back from the key salient around Rzhev-Vyazma. This operation, originally intended for October, was launched on 25 November, six days after "Uranus". Zhukov took charge of it while the encirclement of Stalingrad was entrusted to Vasilevsky. "Mars" was a costly failure, with over 70,000 casualties for an operation that was unable to push the German army back and eliminate the threat to Moscow. It succeeded only to the extent that it prevented the redeployment of German forces southwards to help to stem the disaster that swept over the southern front.

On 19 November, Operation "Uranus" began when forces from General Vatutin's Southwest Front and Rokossovsky's Don Front surprised and swept aside the

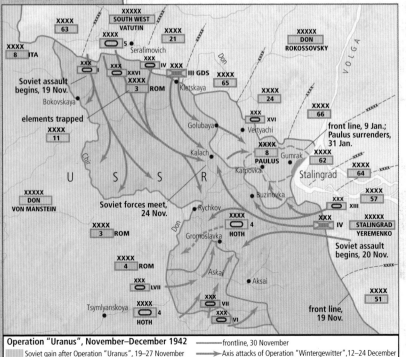

Operation "Uranus", November–December 1942
frontline, 30 November
Soviet gain after Operation "Uranus", 19–27 November
Axis attacks of Operation "Wintergewitter", 12–24 December

Map labels: XXXX 63; XXXXX SOUTH WEST VATUTIN; XXXX 21; XXXX 8 ITA; Serafimovich; XXXXX DON ROKOSSOVSKY; Don; VOLGA; **Soviet assault begins, 19 Nov.**; Bokovskaya; III GDS; XXXX 65; ROM; Kletskaya; XXXX 24; **elements trapped** XXXX 11; XVI; XXXX 66; Golubaya; Vertyachi; **front line, 9 Jan.; Paulus surrenders, 31 Jan.**; Kalach; 8 PAULUS; Gumrak; XXXX 62; XXXX 64; U S S R; Karpovka; Stalingrad; XXXXX DON VON MANSTEIN; Buzinovka; XXXX 57; **Soviet forces meet, 24 Nov.**; Rychkov; XIII; XXXX 3 ROM; Gromoslavka; HOTH; IV; XXXXX STALINGRAD YEREMENKO; **Soviet assault begins, 20 Nov.**; XXXX 4 ROM; Askai; LVII; Tsymlyanskaya; HOTH; VII; VI; Aksai; **front line, 19 Nov.**; XXXX 51; Chir

COLONEL GENERAL KURT ZEITZLER (1895–1963)

Zeitzler was chief of the army General Staff during the battle of Stalingrad. He joined the army in 1914 and was promoted to officer rank for bravery in the field. He became a career officer after 1919 and served as a staff officer, rising by 1939 to the rank of colonel and a position in the army High Command. He became chief-of-staff to von Kleist's Panzer Group A, and served under him in France, the Balkans and the Soviet Union. He became chief-of-staff of the 1st Panzer Army in October 1941, and was promoted on 24 September 1942 to chief of the army General Staff, jumping ranks to become a full general. He was appointed by Hitler as someone who would not be as critical as the more senior generals, but during the Stalingrad battle Zeitzler argued that Paulus should be allowed to break out of his encirclement against Hitler's orders. He was a reluctant chief-of-staff, and in July 1944 finally persuaded Hitler to let him retire on grounds of ill health. He retired from the army in January 1945. He was arrested after the war and held in British hands until his release in 1947.

MARSHAL ALEXANDER VASILEVSKY (1895–1977)

Vasilevsky was one of the architects of Soviet victory in the Second World War as chief of the Soviet General Staff from 1942 to 1949. The son of a priest, he worked as a teacher before joining the army in the First World War. He took up teaching again in 1918, but was drafted into the new Red Army and remained there. As a junior officer, he benefited from the Red Army purges of 1937. He was promoted to the General Staff in October that year, and two years later was deputy of the Operations Directorate, responsible for planning the war with Finland. He played a key role in the defence of Moscow, by which time he was commander of operations, and in April 1942 became acting chief of the General Staff, confirmed in June. He was instrumental in shaping the Red Army's defence at Stalingrad and in February 1943 was created marshal of the Soviet Union. He was liked by Stalin and suffered none of the problems after the war that other successful commanders faced, but his close links with the dictator led to his demotion in 1953 on Stalin's death and he never held another senior post.

ABOVE A Soviet Cossack unit on horseback during Operation "Uranus". Cavalry remained an important element in the Red Army, allowing troops to move at speed over difficult countryside.

Romanian 3rd Army, which surrendered two days later. On 20 November the southern wing, Yeremenko's Stalingrad Front, moved forward against the Romanian 4th Army, which disintegrated with the same speed. Stiffer resistance was met as the Red Army encountered German reserve forces, but the scale and surprise of the attack gave it a powerful momentum. By 24 November, the two prongs of the attack met at a village near the town of Kalach and the encirclement was complete. Soviet forces quickly established an outer and inner defensive ring so that a heavily armed corridor more than 160 kilometres (100 miles) wide separated Paulus's 6th Army from remaining Axis forces.

At this stage it was possible that Paulus might have successfully broken out of the trap and retreated towards the rest of the German forces further west. Hitler ordered him to hold fast, while the German air force commander, Hermann Göring, promised to supply Stalingrad by air with 500 tons of equipment and food a day. Field Marshal von Manstein was ordered to mount a rescue operation, codenamed "Wintergewitter" (Winter Thunderstorm),

which began on 12 December from the southwest of Stalingrad. Von Manstein, Paulus's front commander, ordered him to break out to meet him, but still bound by Hitler's instructions, Paulus failed to do so. In poor weather, von Manstein's force battled 65 kilometres (40 miles) towards Stalingrad but was then threatened with encirclement by a Soviet armoured attack and had to withdraw by 24 December. Operation "Uranus" had been a complete success. Stalingrad was surrounded while the Red Army began a second campaign, "Little Saturn", to push German forces in the south back across the Don steppe. By January, Paulus was more than 325 kilometres (200 miles) from friendly forces.

ABOVE Romanian POWs captured during Operation "Uranus" when the German 6th Army was encircled in Stalingrad. The Red Army calculated rightly that the Romanians would fight with less determination than the Germans.

BELOW Soviet soldiers in December 1942 on the outskirts of Stalingrad after the German forces in the city had been encircled. While some laid siege to the city, other forces moved westwards towards Kharkov.

DEFEAT AT STALINGRAD

10 NOVEMBER 1942
Admiral Darlan agrees to a general ceasefire in North Africa following "Torch" invasion.

2 JANUARY 1943
Allied forces capture the New Guinea port of Buna.

13 JANUARY 1943
Hitler issues his so-called "Total War" decree, calling for the highest sacrifices from the German people.

ABOVE One of the shoulder boards worn by Stalin after his appointment as Marshal of the Soviet Union in 1943.

The success of the Soviet Operation "Uranus" sealed the fate of an estimated 200–250,000 Axis troops in the Stalingrad pocket, including the 6th Army, most of the 4th Panzer Army and some units from Germany's Axis allies. Though there were stocks of ammunition and food in the city and three working airfields, supply to the trapped force failed to materialize on the scale promised. The airlift averaged less than 100 tons a day and the German air force lost 488 transport aircraft in the process. By January, food rations were down to 55 grams (two ounces) of bread a day and 28 grams (an ounce) of sugar. It was possible to fly out around 30,000 wounded men, but thousands of others suffering from frostbite and dysentery fought on from fear of what might happen to them or in the hope that rescue might be possible.

The Soviet High Command believed that the city contained only 80,000 of the enemy and that their exposed position would lead them to surrender. A force of 47 Soviet divisions was drawn up around the Stalingrad area, with 300 aircraft and 179 tanks to fulfil what was codenamed Operation "Kol'tso" (Ring). The attack was scheduled for 10 January, but Paulus was given the opportunity to surrender two days before, which he refused out of hand. Soviet planners expected the operation to last only a few days, but their miscalculation of the size of the trapped force resulted in a campaign of three weeks before the battle was over.

Operation "Kol'tso" began with the largest artillery barrage the Red Army had yet mounted. Paulus's forces

TOP Red Army motorized forces prepare for the final Stalingrad offensive late in 1942. After surrounding Stalingrad, Operation "Kol'tso" was mounted to destroy German resistance.

ABOVE The Soviet commander of the Don Army Group, Colonel General Rokossovsky, pictured in January 1943 shortly before the German surrender. Rokossovsky had been purged in 1937; allowed back into the army in 1940, he became one of the Red Army's most successful commanders.

RIGHT German soldiers unloading a plane inside the Stalingrad "cauldron". The only way they could be supplied was by air and by late January there was just one working airfield left, bringing in supplies and taking out the wounded and the mail.

VICTORY STATUE, VOLGOGRAD

In 1967 the remarkable statue "The Motherland Calls" was officially dedicated in a ceremony on the Mamayev Kurgan hill in the centre of Volgograd (formerly Stalingrad). Sometimes known as "Mother Motherland" or "The Motherland", the colossal statue was the tallest sculpture in the world, 85 metres (279 feet) high, with a vast sword some 33 metres (108 feet) long, and weighing 7,900 tons. From the foot of the hill 200 steps lead up to the monument, one for each day of the siege of Stalingrad. The principal sculptor was Yevgeny Vuchetich and the chief engineer was Nikolai Nikitin. The model for the statue was a native of Stalingrad, Valentina Izotova. The site was a symbolic recognition of the historic turning point in the war with Germany represented by the Battle of Stalingrad.

ABOVE German prisoners wearing rags and blankets to keep out the cold are marched through the streets of Stalingrad on their way to camps. A total of 91,000 prisoners were taken but many failed to survive the journey.

MARSHAL ALEXANDER NOVIKOV (1902–76)

A career infantry officer from 1919, Novikov switched to the air force in 1933 as a very young chief of operations, but fell foul of the purges in 1937, when he was expelled from the armed forces. Reinstated, by 1939 he was chief-of-staff of the air force in the Leningrad Military District and a year later promoted to major general. A talented and creative military thinker, in April 1942 he was appointed commander-in-chief of the Soviet air force. He reorganized air forces into independent air divisions and corps and greatly improved air–ground co-ordination. His forces played an important part in eliminating the Stalingrad pocket, destroying around 1,200 German aircraft. After the war, he began to plan the postwar Soviet air force, but in April 1946 he was arrested, stripped of his rank, tortured into confessing absurd crimes and sent to a Gulag camp for 15 years. He was released in 1953 on Stalin's death and reinstated. He retired in 1956 to head the Civil Aviation School.

were stretched out in open country around Stalingrad as well as in the ruins of the city. The steppe was quickly cleared, reducing the pocket to half its original size within a week. But the Soviet forces found fighting amidst the urban ruins as difficult as the Germans' experience of it. In the heart of the city General Chuikov's 62nd Army was still fighting its own battle, turned now from defender into attacker by the success of the encirclement. His army pushed German troops back from the riverfront block by block. On 22 January, Soviet armies grouped for a final push into the city. Isolating each quarter at a time, they eliminated remaining resistance. German soldiers began to surrender in large numbers. On 26 January, contact was finally made between Chuikov's army and the vanguard of the attacking force near the Barricades Factory. By 31 January, Heroes of the Revolution Square, in the centre of the city, was finally reached.

Interrogators discovered that Paulus was sheltering in the Univermag department store on one side of the square. A young Soviet officer, Lieutenant Fyodor Yelchenko, was led into the basement of the building, where he found an unkempt and miserable commander. Paulus agreed to surrender and was taken away by car to Rokossovsky's

headquarters. In the north of the city, the remnants of the 4th Panzer Army fought a fierce final action, but were finally forced to surrender on 2 February. The defeat was the worst ever suffered by the German army. Some 91,000 went into captivity, but an estimated 147,000 had died in combat, or of frostbite, disease and hunger during the course of the battle. Soviet losses for the operations to encircle and destroy the Stalingrad pocket numbered 485,000, including 155,000 dead or captured.

Stalingrad was a signal that the tide had finally turned in the German-Soviet war. Most of the German army was still deep in the Soviet Union, stretched out along a 2,400-kilometre (1,500-mile front), but the contest between the two sides was no longer one-way. The victory reversed the long period of demoralization and uncertainty among Soviet leaders and the wider public. Stalin got himself appointed Marshal of the Soviet Union, his first military title. In Germany the defeat was greeted with disbelief and anxiety. Hitler, who had promoted Paulus to field marshal the day before the capitulation, was outraged that Paulus had not committed suicide. The day following German surrender, the radio repeatedly played "Siegfried's Funeral March" from Wagner's *Twilight of the Gods*.

BELOW The wreckage of a German unit in the battle for Stalingrad. The dead lay where they had fallen, left rigid by the extreme cold.

LEFT General Friedrich Paulus arrives at the Soviet headquarters to surrender formally on 31 January 1943.

THE CASABLANCA CONFERENCE

Between 14 and 24 January 1943, President Roosevelt and Prime Minister Churchill met in a hotel in a suburb of the French Moroccan city of Casablanca to discuss with the combined chiefs-of-staff (American and British) the future direction of western strategy once Africa was in Allied hands. Stalin was invited to the discussion but declined on the grounds that he was needed in Moscow to oversee the struggle in Stalingrad. Though this was true, Stalin also had a strong dislike of flying and obsessive concern with security.

The choice of Casablanca was Roosevelt's. Churchill had travelled extensively during the course of the war, but this was the President's first flight since assuming office in 1933 and he was keen to make a long overseas trip. He travelled by Pan-Am Clipper from Florida to The Gambia in

ABOVE Roosevelt and Churchill pose for the camera with General Henri Giraud (left) and General Charles de Gaulle (second from right). The Americans wanted Giraud to become the leader of Free French forces in North Africa, but de Gaulle refused to be subordinated to a general with close links to Vichy.

LEFT A Moroccan newspaper vendor sells photographs of President Roosevelt during the Casablanca Conference in January 1943.

BELOW War correspondents at the Casablanca Conference in a press conference with Roosevelt and Churchill, the two figures who dominated the discussions.

West Africa, and thence in a converted transport aircraft to Casablanca. He arrived with a large security detachment and travelled in a limousine with blacked-out windows. Churchill, in contrast, flew to Morocco in a noisy, cold converted bomber, which almost caught fire on the way. The two leaders arrived in an area that had only recently been liberated from Vichy French control; the conflict to eliminate the Axis presence enitrely in North Africa was reaching a climax at some distance along the Mediterranean coast in Tunisia.

During the course of 1942, high-level talks between the United States and Britain had revealed substantial differences in strategic perception. Roosevelt and his army chief-of-staff, George Marshall, were keen to see American troops in combat as soon as possible in Europe, but faced strong pressure to divert resources to the Pacific theatre. The two allies had agreed to undertake a cross-Channel invasion in 1943, codenamed Operation "Roundup", but this had not satisfied the president or Stalin, who hoped for a second front in 1942. Operation "Torch" was a compromise to allow US troops to see action in 1942, but the campaign made it unlikely that "Roundup" would be possible in 1943, and it committed Americans to a Mediterranean strategy which Marshall was generally opposed to.

CASABLANCA – THE FILM

The Hollywood film *Casablanca* was first screened in New York on 26 November 1942, two weeks after American forces entered Casablanca as part of the "Torch" landings in North Africa, and went on general release during the period of the Casablanca Conference. Directed by Michael Curtiz and starring Humphrey Bogart and Ingrid Bergman, the film became a propaganda vehicle for exposing the harsh realities of occupied and war-torn Europe. Most of the actors were European, many of them refugees themselves from Hitler's Germany or Austria, including Conrad Veidt who played National Socialist (Nazi) villains in this and other films. There were plans to change the film's now-famous ending by showing Bogart and a detachment of Free French soldiers on their way to invade North Africa but the idea was abandoned. Efforts to screen the film for troops in North Africa were prevented by the US Office of War Information in case it offended former Vichy officials.

GENERAL GEORGE C MARSHALL (1880–1959)

George Marshall was chief-of-staff of the United States Army and the senior military commander from 1939 to 1945. He provided a continuity of leadership found among none of the other combatant powers, and although his role was in an office rather than on the battlefield, his contribution to Allied victory was exceptional. Marshall was a born organizer whose value was observed in the First World War as chief of operations for the US 1st Infantry Division. He reached the rank of brigadier general by 1938 and became chief of the War Plans Division in Washington. The following year he was chosen by Roosevelt, above more senior candidates, as chief of the army staff. He spent the years before Pearl Harbor building up the American army and creating a framework for rapid mobilization. Favouring a "Germany first" strategy, he was instrumental in forcing through the idea of an invasion of northwest Europe. He became a five-star general in 1944 and retired from his post in November 1945. He was President Truman's secretary of state in 1947–49, during which time he launched the plan for the economic reconstruction of Europe that bore his name.

ABOVE A painting of German Propaganda Minister Joseph Goebbels addressing an audience at the Berlin Sportpalast, 30 January 1943, to mark the 10th anniversary of the Hitler regime. Responding to the Allies' demand for unconditional surrender, Goebbels made it into a propaganda tool to keep the German people fighting from fear of what might happen if they were defeated.

LEFT President Roosevelt (front left) talking to his close confidant Harry Hopkins on the return flight from the Casablanca Conference. The flight out had been Roosevelt's first trip in an aeroplane since becoming president in 1933.

RIGHT Winston Churchill sits in the sun in Marrakesh in Morocco convalescing after a bout of pneumonia in December 1943. Marrakesh was one of Churchill's favourite places, where he did much of his painting.

At Casablanca these differences were vigorously aired between the two leaders and the army chiefs-of-staff. Churchill and his chief-of-staff, General Alan Brooke, argued in favour of a Mediterranean strategy to attack Italy, which would compel the diversion of German forces and probably knock Italy out of the war. The campaign, they believed, would also weaken resistance in northern France and make an invasion there in 1943 or 1944 more likely to succeed. After a good deal of bitter argument, the American side accepted an invasion of Sicily, and reluctantly conceded that a major operation into France would have to be postponed until 1944.

These were not the only issues aired at Casablanca. Senior air force commanders also attended in the hope that they could persuade Roosevelt and Churchill to step up the bombing war as a substitute for a second front. Both men needed to be convinced, but the US commander-in-chief of the army air forces, Henry Arnold, together with Ira Eaker, commander of the US 8th Air Force in Britain, succeeded in presenting a compelling case. The Combined Bomber Offensive was agreed at Casablanca and a preliminary directive issued on 21 January for a campaign of round-the-clock bombing, the American air forces attacking by day, the RAF by night.

The most important outcome of Casablanca was the announcement at the final press conference of the principle of "unconditional surrender". Roosevelt used the phrase in his final remarks, but it was not repeated in the official communiqué from the conference. The issue had been discussed beforehand in Washington and in London, and Churchill was almost certainly unhappy about it since it tied British hands in their attempt to woo Italy away from the German alliance. Nevertheless, it became an immediate catchphrase and it bound the Allies to a policy of complete military victory, with no room for negotiation or armistice. Unconditional surrender has sometimes been criticized as too absolute a requirement but in the middle years of the war against powerful and implacable enemies it gave a clear statement of the minimum that the Allied powers expected from victory.

OPERATION "LONGCLOTH": CHINDITS IN BURMA

When combat came to an end in Burma (Myanmar) in 1942, a stalemate followed. The Japanese were too overstretched to attempt to penetrate any further, but British Indian forces in Assam needed to regroup, retrain and prepare thoroughly for warfare in the inhospitable conditions of Burma. An ill-prepared attack on the port of Akyab on the Burmese coast in autumn and winter 1942–43 ended in disaster, with no ground gained and 5,000 casualties.

The commander-in-chief in India, General Archibald Wavell, had invited Lieutenant Colonel Orde Wingate to India in March 1942 to prepare special forces for action behind Japanese lines. Wingate had served under Wavell in Palestine before the war and in East Africa in 1940–41. His force was officially designated the 77th Indian Infantry Brigade, but it was always known by the nickname "Chindits", derived from the Burmese word *chinthé*, a mythical winged lion, whose carved image was common on temples in Burma. Wingate developed the idea of long-range penetration operations using small units of specially

ABOVE Major General Orde Wingate (centre, with hat) briefing men of the 77th Indian Infantry Brigade at an airfield at Sylhet in Assam before an operation. The forces that Wingate led into Burma had to be supplied entirely from the air.

BELOW Chindit soldiers with mules trekking through the Burmese jungle. They had to carry with them everything they needed, but food was always scarce.

trained men to infiltrate Japanese-held territory, cutting vital communication links and harassing the enemy. Although Wavell approved the tactic in principle, he was reluctant to endorse the idea of a risky adventure, but Wingate finally persuaded him to allow an experimental operation. Codenamed "Longcloth", it was planned for February 1943.

The Chindit force was organized into seven columns, each with between 400 and 500 men. The plan was to supply them from the air so that they could move with little equipment, and independent of any supply line. On the night of 14/15 February 1943, they crossed the Chindwin River into Burma, those columns commanded by Wingate moving north, and two columns heading southeast towards the Irrawaddy river. They succeeded in crossing large areas of the country and destroyed railway lines and bridges, but they also encountered Japanese forces, fighting at least nine engagements. Air supply was difficult to organize, and the Chindits found themselves short of food and supplies and crippled by disease. Instead of moving to the planned area of operation for the period up to May around the town of Pago, they were ordered to make their way back to India in late March.

Out of the original 3,000 men, some 818 were dead or prisoners-of-war, and many of the rest too ill to continue. The operation achieved little in strategic terms, but it did act to boost morale in the Indian army, by showing that Japanese troops were not invincible. Wingate also won Churchill's admiration and the small guerrilla force became

MAJOR GENERAL ORDE WINGATE (1903–44)

Orde Wingate was one of the most unorthodox officers in the British army. A regular officer who served in Palestine in the 1930s, where he became a Zionist, he joined SOE (Special Operations Executive) and in the East African campaign in early 1941 formed "Gideon Force", an irregular guerrilla unit which fought in Ethiopia with the exiled emperor, Haile Selassie. He was virtually dismissed for insubordination after the campaign, and attempted suicide. In 1942, he was summoned by General Wavell to India to organize guerrilla combat against the Japanese in Burma. His "Chindit" force fought in 1943 and again in 1944, but he was killed in an air crash on 24 March 1944 before the second campaign had got very far. He had a mixed reputation. Rude, opinionated and irreverent, he also inspired loyalty among his men and the strong support of Winston Churchill, who liked his unconventional view of warfare.

MERRILL'S MARAUDERS

After the first Chindit campaign, an American force was raised to fight the Japanese in Burma using the same methods. The 3,000-strong force was codenamed "Galahad"; its official title was 5307 Composite Unit, but it was known as "Merrill's Marauders" after the group's commander, Brigadier General Frank Merrill. It trained with the Chindits, and was then assigned to work with the American General Joseph Stilwell and his Chinese forces in an operation against Japanese forces in northern Burma between February and August 1944. Despite early successes, the unit, like the Chindits in 1943, suffered from heavy losses, particularly due to disease and the arduous conditions in which they had to fight. In the end the force was decimated and at the end of the campaign was disbanded, its surviving members absorbed into the regular US army.

ABOVE Merrill's Marauders in action in the Pacific jungle, December 1943.

temporary heroes. Wingate was invited to attend the Quebec Conference in August 1943, where generous funds and equipment were put at his disposal. The operation also prompted the Japanese military to accept the need for a pre-emptive campaign of their own, which they launched in March 1944 against the towns of Imphal and Kohima in Indian Assam.

A second Chindit operation, codenamed "Thursday", was organized in February 1944 with some 20,000 special forces, designed to impede the Japanese assault on India. But Wingate's death in an air crash in March led to the abandonment of his irregular, deep-penetration tactics and the force fought in conventional formation alongside the forces of General Stilwell and elements of the Chinese army. This campaign also proved costly, with 3,628 casualties among the original Chindit force. The force was wound up in February 1945. Although their military achievements were modest, the Chindit campaigns were a model of heroism and endurance.

ABOVE A Chindit column crossing a river somewhere in Burma. They were organized into small self-contained groups to operate behind the lines. They all marched at least 1,000 miles during Operation "Longcloth".

LEFT Formation badge of the 3rd Infantry Division – the Chindits.

BELOW Chindit forces prepare to blow a railway line far behind Japanese lines in Burma. They cut the main Mandalay–Lashio link before returning to India in March 1943.

THE END OF THE AXIS IN AFRICA: TUNISIA

6 MARCH 1943
Stalin is named marshal of the Soviet Union and aquires a handsome new uniform.

13 APRIL 1943
Germans reveal the Katyn massacres of Polish officers by the Soviet security service, carried out in 1940.

18 APRIL 1943
Japanese Admiral Yamamoto, commander of the Japanese navy, is shot down and killed by US fighter aircraft on a flight over the Solomons.

23 APRIL 1943
Allies set up a planning centre in London under General Morgan to prepare the invasion of Europe in 1944.

ABOVE Badge of the British 78th Infantry Division.

After the success of the Second Battle of Alamein and the "Torch" landings in North Africa, the Allies had hoped to complete the elimination of enemy resistance within weeks. Instead Rommel successfully brought his battered Afrika Korps back to southern Tunisia by the end of January 1943, while in the north the 5th Panzer Army and the remnants of the Italian 1st Army, despite shortages of equipment, oil and ammunition, established a new Axis front line running the whole length of Tunisia.

The Allied plan was to try to divide the northern force under General von Arnim from Rommel's forces in the south with a drive by the US 1st Armored Division to the coastal port of Sfax (Operation "Satin"). But shortages of supply led to the cancellation of "Satin", and instead von Arnim and then Rommel took the initiative in attacking the US 2nd Corps from the eastern Dorsale Mountains in central Tunisia. On 14 February, the American force was driven back to the Kasserine Pass, and there, on 20 February Rommel, some of whose forces had moved up from the southern Mareth Line, inflicted a heavy defeat on the retreating American army. German units pushed on beyond the pass, but by 22 February they were halted by British and American counter-attacks. Rommel moved back through the mountains, and moved south to defend against an anticipated attack by Montgomery's 8th Army.

The baptism of fire for American forces against experienced German and Italian troops was a harsh one. Relations between the American, British and French forces

ABOVE Local inhabitants in Tunis leave the city during the spring of 1943 to avoid the final showdown between Allied and Axis forces which reached its peak in May.

LEFT Following an Allied air attack on Tunis, a French auxiliary policeman carries a wounded child to a first aid station. The civilian population was caught in the middle of a conflict they had not expected.

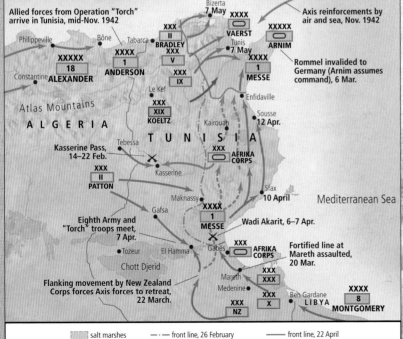

Allied forces from Operation "Torch" arrive in Tunisia, mid-Nov. 1942

Axis reinforcements by air and sea, Nov. 1942

Rommel invalided to Germany (Arnim assumes command), 6 Mar.

Kasserine Pass, 14–22 Feb.

Eighth Army and "Torch" troops meet, 7 Apr.

Wadi Akarit, 6–7 Apr.

Fortified line at Mareth assaulted, 20 Mar.

Flanking movement by New Zealand Corps forces Axis forces to retreat, 22 March.

Philippeville · Bône · Tabarca · Bizerta 7 May · VAERST · ARNIM

XXX II BRADLEY · XXXXX 18 ALEXANDER · XXXX 1 ANDERSON · V · IX · XXXX 1 MESSE

Constantine · Le Kef · Tunis 7 May

Atlas Mountains · ALGERIA · XXX XIX KOELTZ · Enfidaville · Sousse 12 Apr. · Kairouan

TUNISIA

Tebessa · Kasserine · XXX AFRIKA CORPS

XXX II PATTON · Maknassy · Sfax 10 April · Mediterranean Sea

Gafsa · XXXX 1 MESSE

Tozeur · El Hamma · Gabes · XXX AFRIKA CORPS

Chott Djerid · Mareth · XXX · Medenine · XXX NZ · XXX X · Ben Gardane · LIBYA · XXXX 8 MONTGOMERY

salt marshes · — · — front line, 26 February · —— front line, 22 April

COLONEL GENERAL HANS-JÜRGEN VON ARNIM (1883–1962)

The son of a Prussian general, von Arnim joined the German army in 1907, fought in the First World War on the Western and Eastern fronts, and in the 1920s became commander of the elite 68th Infantry Regiment. He commanded divisions in Poland and France, and commanded the 17th Panzer Division for the invasion of the Soviet Union. He was seriously wounded a few days into the campaign, but by November 1942 had risen to command a Panzer corps. He was sent to North Africa to command the 5th Panzer Army and promoted to colonel general. When Rommel was invalided in March, he took over command of the Afrika Korps. He was captured by Indian troops in May 1943 and asked to be taken to Eisenhower. The Allied commander refused to meet any senior German officer until final surrender. Von Arnim was released in 1947.

MARSHAL GIOVANNI MESSE (1883–1968)

Marshal Messe was generally regarded as one of the most successful of Italian commanders in the Second World War. He joined the army in 1901, served in the Italo-Turkish war in 1911–12, and fought in the First World War, during which he was decorated for exceptional bravery and promoted to lieutenant colonel. He saw service in the Ethiopian war as a deputy divisional commander and in 1936 was promoted to general in command of the 3rd Mobile Division. He saw service in Albania in 1939 and in the Italian-Greek war in 1940–41. In July 1941, he was appointed commander of the Italian expeditionary force for the Eastern Front and fought in the battles on the Don towards Stalingrad, but was sent back to Italy in November 1942 for questioning Italian strategy. In February, he was sent to command Italian forces in Tunisia. He was promoted to Marshal of Italy on 12 May, and surrendered the following day. After the Italian surrender in September 1943, Messe was freed and returned to Italy to become chief of the Italian General Staff on the Allied side.

were strained and supplies were difficult to bring across the long North African routes in poor weather and mud. Eisenhower appointed General Alexander to restore order to the Allied front and complete the destruction of the Axis pocket. Much depended on Montgomery breaching the Mareth Line, but in early March Rommel launched his own offensive. On 6 March, three Panzer divisions moved forward, but Montgomery, warned in advance by decrypted German messages, had prepared a trap. Rommel's tanks ran into a wall of withering anti-tank fire and were forced to retreat. On 9 March, Rommel flew to see Hitler to demand more assistance, but instead he was ordered on sick leave, his command taken by von Arnim.

On 20–21 March, Montgomery attacked with the bulk of the 8th Army against the Mareth defences, while the New Zealand Division was sent in a wide outflanking movement through hilly country to capture El Hamma in the Axis rear. Poor weather made progress slow in the frontal assault, and further armour was sent on the flanking attack. To the north, Alexander ordered the US 2nd Corps to drive for the coast and cut off the Axis retreat. The assault proved too difficult, and when Axis forces were compelled in late March to abandon the Mareth Line, they moved northwards, pursued by the 8th Army until they met up with the remaining German and Italian

forces in the north of the country. On 7 April, 8th Army troops met up with American forces coming from the northwest.

Von Arnim and the Italian commander, Marshal Messe, organized a final stand in the northeast corner of the country around Bizerta and Tunis. They judged their position to be hopeless, but after a meeting between Hitler and Mussolini in Salzburg on 8 April, they were ordered to hold fast at all costs. Supply was down to a fraction of what was needed. In three weeks in April, Allied fighter aircraft destroyed 432 Axis planes for the loss of just 35, including half the entire German air transport fleet. Axis forces had just 150 tanks, against more than 1,500 on the Allied side. Alexander ordered the American 2nd Corps to the north opposite the port of Bizerta; the British 1st Army under Lieutenant General Kenneth Anderson stood opposite Tunis; while the 8th Army occupied the southern section of the Allied noose. On 6 May, a general offensive was launched. Bombarded from the air and artillery, short of almost all essential supplies, Axis resistance collapsed. Bizerta and Tunis fell on 7 May, and five days later von Arnim, who had retreated to the very furthest tip of Tunisia on Cape Bon, surrendered. Marshal Messe, further south, surrendered to Montgomery a day later with the scattered remnants of his 1st Italian Army. Some 240,000 prisoners were taken, a defeat that ranked in numbers with Stalingrad three months before.

BELOW An American M3 Grant tank patrolling the streets of the Tunisian port of Bizerta, 8 May 1943. The city had fallen to the US II Corps the day before.

LEFT A wounded British soldier shares a cigarette with a captured German soldier during the battles for the Mareth Line in southern Tunisia in March 1943. In the end 125,000 Germans were captured in Tunisia.

BELOW General von Arnim, the German commander in Tunisia after Rommel's departure to Germany on health grounds, shortly after the Axis surrender on 12 May 1943.

THE DAMBUSTERS RAID

11 MAY 1943
US and Canadian forces land on the Aleutian Islands to recapture Attu and Kiska from the Japanese.

11–25 MAY 1943
Allied Trident Conference to decide details of the invasion of Italy.

13 MAY 1943
Axis forces surrender in Tunisia after six-month campaign.

15 MAY 1943
French National Council of the resistance movement formed at the instigation of Jean Moulin.

19–20 MAY 1943
Heavy Allied bombing raids on Sicily and Sardinia as a prelude to invasion in July.

24 MAY 1943
Admiral Dönitz decides to withdraw U-boats from the Atlantic battle.

The decision to attack the major dams in the German Ruhr valley originated with the development of a "bouncing bomb" by the British engineer Barnes Wallis, who was convinced that attacking Germany's water supply would have a crippling effect on production and morale. The drum-shaped bomb was designed to rotate at speed as it was dropped from no more than 28 metres (60 feet) and then bounce across the surface of the water until reaching the dam wall, when it would spin to the foot of the wall and explode. The bomb was extensively tested and found to be a viable design. There then followed efforts to persuade the Air Ministry that an operation against the dams would work.

In Bomber Command there was a prejudice against what the commander-in-chief Arthur Harris called "panacea targets". The strategy pursued during 1942 and 1943 was to attack major industrial cities in order to reduce German economic capability, rather than attack a particular industrial or utility target. Harris finally agreed and aircraft were released to form what was called at first "Squadron X", but became designated 617 Squadron. The plan to bomb

ABOVE The production of shells in a factory in the Ruhr industrial region in 1942. The attack on the dams was supposed to undermine armaments production but it had very little direct effect.

LEFT An aerial reconnaissance photograph of the Möhne Dam taken before the Dambusters Raid. Together with the Sorpe Dam, the reservoirs supplied 75 per cent of the water needed by Ruhr industry.

RIGHT Three separate frames show an aircraft of 617 squadron practising dropping the "bouncing bomb" at the Reculver bombing range in Kent, southern England.

BARNES WALLIS (1887–1979)

A British aeronautical engineer, Barnes Wallis was responsible for developing a number of different aircraft and bomb designs during the Second World War. He joined the Vickers armaments company as a young engineer in 1913 and remained with the firm until his retirement in 1971. He designed the revolutionary geodesic airframe, first for airships, then in the Wellington bomber, an exceptionally sturdy aircraft capable of sustaining high levels of damage and still remaining airborne. He designed the bomb for the dams raid, and later the "Tallboy" and "Grand Slam" bombs for deep-penetration attacks. After 1945, he pioneered the "swing-wing" concept for fighter aircraft but saw his ideas developed first by American aircraft producers.

the dams was accepted on 26 February 1943, and there followed an intensive period of training in low-altitude flying and the use of the bouncing bomb, codenamed "Upkeep". A special aiming device was developed to ensure that the bomb was released at the right moment, and spotlights placed in the nose and tail of the Lancaster bombers used for the raid to provide a guide to altitude. By early May, the preparations were complete.

The operation, codenamed "Chastise", was undertaken on the night of 16/17 May 1943. The attacking force was organized into three groups: Formation 1 was to attack the Möhne Dam and, if there were bombs left, proceed to the Eder Dam; Formation 2 was to attack the Sorpe Dam; and a third reserve formation was to take off later and attack

WING COMMANDER GUY GIBSON (1918–44)

The commander of RAF 617 squadron was Wing Commander Guy Gibson. He joined the RAF in 1936 and on the outbreak of war was a pilot in 83rd Squadron, Bomber Command. He survived his first tour of duty and then transferred to Fighter Command where he flew night-fighters. He rejoined Bomber Command in 1942, flying the new Lancaster bombers, and was chosen in early 1943 to command the unit created to attack the German dams. He flew a remarkable 174 operations with Bomber Command, but was killed when his aircraft developed a fuel fault and crashed in the Netherlands on 19 September 1944. He had a reputation for tough professionalism and bravery and took risks other pilots might not have taken. He was awarded the Victoria Cross for his role in the destruction of the dams.

any dams that had not yet been breached. On the outward flight, the first formation lost one aircraft, while of the five aircraft in the second formation only one survived to reach the target: two were forced back and two were destroyed. The attack on the Möhne Dam was carried out successfully and the five surviving aircraft then flew to the Eder Dam, which was shrouded in fog. The final bombing run successfully breached the target. Formation 2 now consisted of one aircraft, whose bomb hit the Sorpe Dam but did not destroy it. Unlike the first two targets, the Sorpe was not made of concrete but of earth. Reserve aircraft then attacked but no further damage was caused.

The raid resulted in the loss of 11 bombers out of 19 and the loss of 53 out of 133 crewmen. The effect of the raids proved a disappointment to the planners. A huge area of flooding around 80 kilometres (50 miles) in length killed an estimated 1,650 people (including 1,026 POWs and foreign forced labourers) and inundated farmland. But Ruhr industry was hardly affected, electricity supplies were soon restored, and by 27 June there was a full water supply again. German authorities were alarmed by the prospect of a sustained attack against the Reich's water supply, but the operation was not repeated and Bomber Command returned to the strategy of area bombing. Harris remained unconvinced of the value of attacking a single target-system, and was later unenthusiastic about the transportation and oil plans developed in the summer and autumn of 1944 as the key to speeding up German collapse. 617 Squadron was kept in being for specialist operations, however, and was later used to carry Barnes Wallis's super-heavy bombs which sank the German battleship *Tirpitz* and penetrated the six-metre (20-foot) reinforced concrete roofs of the submarine pens at Brest.

The operational success of the attack on the dams was exploited for propaganda purposes. Guy Gibson, the commander of the operation, was sent on a publicity tour of the United States and the raid attracted a high level of attention in Britain in the summer of 1943. Nevertheless, its strategic worth was limited and the cost in skilled crewmen very great. There was also discussion of its moral implications, which almost certainly made further similar attacks difficult to justify. In postwar international law the deliberate attack of civilian water supplies has been prohibited.

LEFT Wing Commander Guy Gibson and his crew board their Lancaster bomber for the attack on the dams, 17 May 1943. He was one of the lucky ones to return.

LEFT Albert Speer (left), the German minister for weapons and munitions, visiting the Möhne Dam after its destruction by RAF 617 Squadron. Emergency water supplies could be found within days of the attack and the dams were repaired rapidly thereafter.

BELOW Water pours through the broken dam wall of the Möhne Dam after the successful attack. The result was a flood extending some 80 kilometres (50 miles).

RATIONING: THE WAR FOR FOOD

4 SEPTEMBER 1939
German War Economy Decree introduces comprehensive rationing scheme in Germany.

8 JANUARY 1940
Britain introduces ration books for all comsumers. Bacon, butter and sugar were the first items to be rationed.

3 JULY 1954
Meat is the last foodstuff to be de-rationed in Britain.

One of the chief lessons of the First World War was the need to supply the home population with adequate food supplies. The Russian war effort collapsed in revolution partly on account of widespread hunger in the towns; the German war effort was undermined by the harsh "turnip winter" in 1917–18 when the urban population experienced real deprivation. In the 1930s, when the prospect of war loomed once again, governments began to plan the effective rationing and distribution of food to make sure that the home front did not suffer from the consequences of war. In Germany and Italy a programme of "self-sufficiency" was introduced to make both countries less dependent on imported food.

During the war, the supply of food became a critical issue once more. Germany and the areas it had conquered were cut off from all overseas sources of supply. Food of all kinds was rationed from the outbreak of war in Germany, leaving most consumers reliant on a limited range of bread, flour and potatoes, with meat and sugar in small quantities. The ration was maintained only by the ruthless requisitioning of food from occupied Europe, where ration levels were in general below those in Germany. In Britain the problem was an excessive dependence on overseas sources of supply. During the war, British agriculture was transformed, with large increases in arable land and a sharp reduction in livestock farming. Some 2.8 million hectares (7 million acres) of grassland were ploughed up and wheat, potato and barley production doubled. The result was a reduction

ABOVE Girls from the Women's Land Army dig out a bog oak from a piece of reclaimed fenland in Cambridgeshire, England. The organization had been used in the First World War and was revived in 1939. However, most farmworkers, even by the end of the war, were men.

RIGHT Poster featuring "Dr Carrot", created by Britain's wartime Ministry for Food to encourage people to make full use of the relatively plentiful carrot.

BELOW The English town of Cheltenham set up bins for scrap food during the war to be fed to pigs. The collections produced 20 tons of pig food every week.

DOCTOR CARROT the Children's best friend

of food imports by 50 per cent. Rationing was introduced for a range of basic foodstuffs, providing a diet not very different from the German one. It was possible, nevertheless, to buy more goods off the ration in Britain than was the case in Germany. Although a black market existed for those who could afford the prices, the authorities clamped down more harshly on irregular trade than had been the case in the First World War.

In the Soviet Union and the United States, the food situation was very different. America was a food-rich economy and, while a few foods were rationed to ensure a regular supply for all consumers, the impact of rising living standards during the war meant that many Americans ate better than they had done in the 1930s. Food was exported in large quantities to both the Soviet Union and Britain.

TO SAVE YOUR BACON SAVE YOUR SC...

PIG FOOD

PIG FOOD

HERBERT BACKE (1896–1947)

Herbert Backe was the acting minister for agriculture in Hitler's government, and from 1944 minister for food. His trader father lived in Russia before 1914 and Backe was interned as an enemy alien throughout the war. During the Russian Civil War, following the Revolution, he escaped to Germany and became an agricultural specialist. He joined the National Socialist Party in 1923 and became one of the party's food experts. In October 1933, he became state secretary in the Agriculture Ministry charged with expanding German food production in case of war, making Germany more than 80 per cent self-sufficient by 1939. During the war he was made responsible for squeezing food out of the occupied Soviet Union and the so-called "Backe Plan" anticipated imposing widespread hunger on the Russian population. He was arrested after the war as a war criminal and hanged himself in his cell in Nuremberg on 6 April 1947.

The situation in the Soviet Union was disastrous. The German invasion conquered the Russian "bread basket" in the Ukraine, reducing the grain area by 40 per cent and livestock by two-thirds. Rationing was introduced in July 1941 in Moscow and by November had spread to the whole urban area (peasants were expected to make do with what they could grow on their garden plots). Food was exchanged for work and those who could not work, the elderly or infirm, relied on family help. An unknown number of non-workers perished of hunger in the first years of the war. Factory canteens were set up, feeding around 25 million workers with a hot meal. Land was distributed to workers as small allotments so that they could grow their own food and by 1944 there were 16.5 million of them. Soviet citizens also existed on a monotonous diet of bread, potatoes and occasional meat or sausage. But unlike the First World War, it proved possible to keep the population fed sufficiently not to endanger the domestic war effort.

ABOVE A customer shops in an American supermarket during the war. Food supplies were plentiful in the United States and large quantities of food were sent to America's allies.

DIGGING FOR VICTORY

During the Second World War, the British government promoted the idea of "digging for victory" by bringing gardens, parks, sports fields and unused land under cultivation. People were encouraged to run allotments and by 1944 there were 1.7 million of these, producing in 1943 an estimated one million tons of vegetables. The minister for food, Lord Woolton, set up an energetic propaganda campaign to encourage people to keep pigs, poultry and rabbits as well as grow vegetables. To make a vegetable diet more palatable, helpful recipe suggestions were published with the help of Dr Carrot and Potato Pete, two characters dreamt up by the propaganda department of Woolton's ministry. The big advantage of digging for victory was access to food off the rations.

FAR LEFT Lunch in a factory canteen in a British munitions factory. In order to encourage higher productivity, factories introduced welfare facilities, crèches for children and regular food not only in Britain but also in Germany, the United States and the Soviet Union.

LEFT A child begging for food in Calcutta during the Bengal famine, December 1943. Shortages of sea transport, needed for military operations, reduced the supply of food to the region and left an estimated 2–3 million dead.

Many of those recruited into the armed forces came from the countryside. Farm labour was not treated as a reserve occupation. Their place was taken by the elderly, by the young, and above all by women. In Britain a Women's Land Army was recruited, reaching a peak of 80,300 in December 1943, and constituted a large proportion of the 117,000 women working on British farms. But in Germany women had always made up a large part of the rural workforce on the small peasant farms, and by 1944 there were 5.7 million working in agriculture, around 38 per cent of all employed women. In the Soviet Union some 80 per cent of farm workers on the collective farms were women by the end of the war. They did all the jobs usually done by men, and did them in many cases without the help of machinery or draft animals, which had long ago disappeared to the front. To do this they had to make do with payment of one potato and 200 grams (seven ounces) of bread a day. They survived on only what they could grow around their cottages, or what they could steal.

The efforts to mobilize the home front ensured that none of the combatant powers experienced a severe crisis of food supply, except for Japan in the last months of the Pacific War when bombing dislocated the whole supply system. Famine did occur – in Bengal in 1944, in Greece in 1943–44 and in the Netherlands in the last months before liberation – as a result of the exceptional circumstances of war. Hunger was more common after the war in the chaos of occupation and reconstruction.

THE BATTLE OF KURSK

After the disaster at Stalingrad it was necessary for the German army in the Soviet Union to win back the initiative. Between 29 January and 23 March, a series of battles took place around the city of Kharkov, the Soviet Union's fourth-largest city, reducing it to rubble in the process. An overstretched Soviet offensive was driven back past Kharkov by the forces of von Manstein's Army Group South (the renamed Army Group Don) as far as the city of Belgorod. This offensive created the southern side of a large Soviet salient, 190 kilometres (120 miles) wide and 95 kilometres (60 miles) long, bulging into the German front line around the city of Kursk. It was here that von Manstein and the army High Command decided the key battle of the summer 1943 campaign should be fought. The operation was codenamed "Zitadelle" (Citadel).

The German plan followed a predictable pattern. The object was to drive two heavily armed wedges into the neck of the salient from north and south to encircle and cut off the large Soviet forces stationed there. Victory here would allow German forces to swing either south again or to move behind Moscow and turn the Soviet line. A force of 900,000 men in 50 divisions, 2,000 aircraft and 2,700 tanks was assembled, including the new heavy Panther and Tiger tanks and the Ferdinand self-propelled gun. Hitler was uncertain about the operation and refused von Manstein's request to begin in May before the Red Army was ready. In the end, he postponed the start date until early July.

The interval gave the Soviet High Command plenty of time to prepare the battlefield. Zhukov and the General Staff guessed the German plan and won support from Stalin, who had wanted an immediate offensive, to build up a heavy defensive shield around Kursk prior to delivering

a knock-out blow to the German attackers with large forces held in reserve. The Kursk salient was held by two army fronts, the central front under General Rokossovsky and the Voronezh front under General Vatutin, both of whom had led the defence of Stalingrad. They prepared six separate lines of defence and a complex wall of artillery and anti-tank fire was established. Into the defensive line were moved 1.3 million men, 3,444 tanks and 2,900 aircraft, around 40 per cent of Soviet manpower and 75 per cent of its armoured force. Both sides treated the huge set-piece battle as a test of strength; the loser risked a great deal.

The Soviet side needed to know when the blow would come, and they were supplied with a large amount of accurate intelligence, but because Hitler kept altering the date there could be no certainty. The "Lucy" spy ring in Switzerland gave the approximate date in early July, but

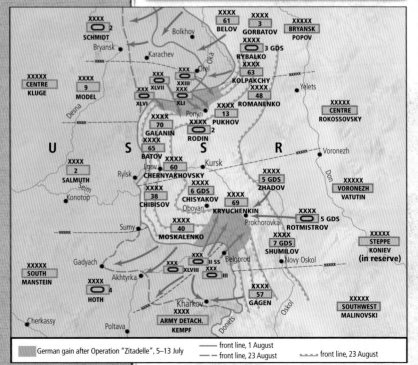

German gain after Operation "Zitadelle", 5–13 July
— front line, 1 August
--- front line, 23 August
···· front line, 23 August

COLONEL GENERAL HERMANN HOTH (1885–1971)

The son of an army officer, Hoth joined the army in 1903, fought in the First World War in a variety of roles and stayed on in the postwar 100,000-man force. He rose rapidly during the period of the Third Reich. In October 1938, he commanded the 15th Army Corps and in November that year was made a general. He fought in Poland and France and commanded the 3rd Panzer Group in November 1940, which captured Minsk in the opening weeks of the invasion of the Soviet Union. In June 1942, he took over command of the 4th Panzer army and fought in the Stalingrad campaign, unsuccessfully leading the effort to rescue Paulus in December 1942. His Panzer group fought at Kursk and later failed to prevent the Soviet reconquest of Kiev, for which he was sacked by Hitler. A ruthless officer, he endorsed harsh measures against Jews and partisans and was convicted at Nuremberg in 1948 of war crimes. He served six years of his 15-year sentence.

ABOVE Soviet partisan fighters laying explosives on a railway line behind the German front during the Battle of Kursk, July 1943.

ABOVE LEFT German infantry and armoured forces during the Battle of Kursk in July 1943. The German army deployed the large Tiger and Panther tanks at Kursk for the first time. The Tiger carried a huge 88-millimetre (3.5-inch) gun, the Panther 75-millimetre (3-inch).

GENERAL NIKOLAI VATUTIN (1901–44)

Nikolai Vatutin was one of the most successful Soviet generals of the Second World War, though he was only 39 when the USSR was attacked. He served in the Red Army in 1920–21, and then went through formal officer training and a period at the national Frunze Military Academy in 1926, where he proved to be a remarkably talented student and a natural leader. During the purges, he was one of the younger officers rapidly promoted to replace those who had been removed. He became chief-of-staff of the Kiev Special Military District, where he was responsible for organizing the Soviet invasion of eastern Poland in 1939, and in 1940 was promoted to deputy chief of the General Staff where he played a major part in prewar mobilization planning. When war broke out he was sent to Leningrad to stabilize the front and protect the city, and was involved in the defence of Moscow. He commanded the Voronezh Army Group in July 1942, and then the Southwestern Army Group which helped to carry out Operation "Uranus", followed by command of the Voronezh Army Group again for Kursk. He was shot by Ukrainian nationalist partisans on 29 February 1944 and died of his wounds.

the final date and hour, dawn on 5 July, were found out from kidnapped German soldiers. The Red Army fired a number of pre-emptive artillery barrages during the night, but the attack went ahead as planned. In the south, General Hoth's 4th Panzer Army, with nine Panzer divisions, crashed forward against the weaker of the two Soviet fronts and in two days it was 30 kilometres (20 miles) towards Kursk, fighting against frantic and stiff opposition. In the north, General Walter Model's 9th Panzer Army was held almost at once by a withering wall of fire. On 6 July, 1,000 tanks were pushed forward on a front only 10 kilometres (six miles) wide towards the town of Ponyri, but by the following day the offensive was bogged down and by 9 July the German northern thrust was halted.

BELOW Soviet infantry run past a burning T34 tank during the Battle of Kursk. Despite heavy losses, the Red Army was able to blunt the German attack and push back the German front line in a series of powerful counter-offensives.

In the south, Hoth's Panzer army moved towards the small town of Prokhorovka where it met the 5th Guards Tank Army commanded by General Pavel Rotmistrov, which had travelled for four days to reach the battlefield. What followed on 12–13 July has usually been described as the largest tank battle of the war, but recent research has suggested that most of the casualties to the Soviet side were caused by Rotmistrov's failure to recognize a Soviet tank trap into which his unfortunate armour blundered. German losses were modest, but the failure in the north and news of the Allied landings in Sicily had led Hitler to cancel the operation on 13 July. Hoth retreated back to where he had started. German commanders failed to realize what would follow because they underestimated Soviet reserves. In the north on 12 July, a massive counter-offensive was launched which liberated Orel on 5 August and Bryansk on 18 August. In the south, the attack was launched on 3 August and by 28 August Kharkov was again in Soviet hands. The way was now open for a general summer offensive to drive back the whole German front.

ABOVE LEFT German tanks make their way across the steppe during the Battle of Kursk in July 1943. The confrontation was the largest concentration of tank forces yet seen in the war.

ABOVE A destroyed Soviet column. Although a Soviet victory, the losses of the Red Army amounted to 70,000 dead or captured.

ABOVE German tanks and soldiers at the heart of the battle in July 1943. German losses were much lower than Soviet, with an estimated 15,000 dead and the loss of only 300 tanks.

OPERATION "HUSKY": INVASION OF SICILY

12 JULY 1943
Red Army begins Operation "Kutuzov" against the German-held city of Orel following the end of "Zitadelle".

17 JULY 1943
Following Allied deceptive measures, Hitler orders reinforcements to go to Greece to resist an expected Allied invasion of the region.

1 AUGUST 1943
Japan declares Burma to be an independent state, though under close Japanese supervision.

5 AUGUST 1943
US forces complete the capture of New Georgia in the Solomons.

12 AUGUST 1943
A force of over 600 RAF bombers attacks the major Italian industrial centre of Milan.

ABOVE Badge of the British 6th Airborne Divisions.

It was agreed at the Casablanca Conference that the invasion of Sicily would follow the defeat of the Axis in North Africa. Planning began in the spring for Operation "Husky", which was assigned to General Alexander's 15th Army Group, made up of Montgomery's 8th Army and Patton's 1st US Armored Corps (renamed 7th US Army for the invasion). The object was to land in force on the southern and southeastern coast and to sweep up the island quickly enough to prevent Axis forces from escaping to the mainland. The date was set for 10 July 1943.

In order to render the ambitious amphibious operation more secure – it was second in size only to the later invasion of France – a risky deception plan was mounted codenamed Operation "Mincemeat" which involved leaving a dead body dressed in the uniform of a Royal Marines major off the Spanish coast with false Allied plans concealed in a

ABOVE An aerial view of the island of Pantelleria during a heavy Allied air bombardment in June 1943. The island was on the route to Sicily and the garrison had to be eliminated before the landings on Sicily could begin.

ABOVE The British 51st Highland Division unloading supplies on a beach in southeast Sicily on 10 July 1943 as part of the invasion force. There was little opposition at first against the British sector.

briefcase. The body was handed to the British consul, but the briefcase was kept by the Spanish authorities and its contents revealed to the German consul. The fake plan described an Allied operation against Greece with Sicily as a diversion. The ruse worked perfectly and German forces were strengthened in Greece and Sardinia, but not in Sicily.

Air power was to play an important part in the invasion. In June, an Italian garrison on the island of Pantelleria, lying on the route from North Africa to Sicily, was so pulverized by bombing that the garrison surrendered without an invasion. Aircraft neutralized any threat from Axis air forces during the invasion. On 9 July, the operation began with American and British paratroop landings to secure vital bridges and communications. Strong winds produced a disaster, with 200 British paratroopers drowning in the sea. Out of 2,781 US paratroops, only 200 arrived at the objective near the Sicilian port of Licata. During the night of 9/10 July, a flotilla of 2,590 ships and landing craft approached Sicily, carrying 180,000 men. They were faced by approximately 50,000 German and 270,000 Italian troops, but it was expected that most Italians would have little stomach for the battle.

British forces landed without difficulty on the beaches at Avola and Pachino, and US forces faced serious opposition only at Gela, where the Hermann Göring Division was stationed. Within five days, Allied forces had pushed inland to a line from Agrigento to the Gulf of Catania. Progress proved slow in mountainous terrain which gave every advantage to the defender against an armoured attack. Patton was supposed to protect the flank of the 8th Army as it struck north to Messina and northwest to the central Sicilian city of Enna, but the collapse of Italian resistance against his aggressive armoured drive persuaded him that the whole of the west of the island could fall quickly

GENERAL MILES DEMPSEY (1896–1969)

Dempsey was one of Montgomery's most successful 8th Army generals. He served with the Royal Berkshire Regiment in the First World War, and continued to do so in the interwar years. He fought in France in 1940, and as a lieutenant general was sent to command the 13th Corps of the 8th Army, which he led in North Africa, Sicily and Italy. He commanded the 2nd Army in the Normandy invasion and ended the war accepting the surrender of Hamburg in 1945. He became commander-in-chief Allied Land Forces in Southeast Asia, and was commander-in-chief in the Middle East in 1946–47 during the crisis in Palestine. He retired from the army in July 1947 and was commander-in-chief of UK Land Forces Designate from 1951 to 1955.

ABOVE The population of Palermo turn out to greet units of Patton's 7th US Army on 23 July 1943 after the surrender of the city. There was widespread enthusiasm in southern Italy for the end of hostilities.

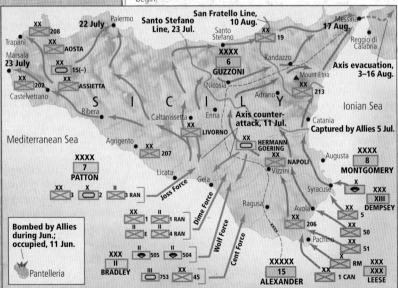

Operation "Husky", 10 July–17 August 1943

ABOVE Gunners of the British 66 Medium Regiment, Royal Artillery in action near the slopes of Mount Etna in northeast Sicily, 11 August 1943.

GENERAL GEORGE S PATTON (1885–1945)

One of the most controversial but successful of American generals during the Second World War, Patton joined the US cavalry in 1909, fought in Mexico in 1916 and in France in 1917–18, first on the staff of the US commander General Pershing, then in command of a tank brigade. In January 1942, he took command of the 1st Armored Corps. He commanded the western task force which landed at Casablanca in November 1942, and commanded the 2nd US Army Corps in Tunisia in March and April 1943, before being recalled to plan the invasion of Sicily. His public persona was flamboyant, aggressive and coarse, and he famously flaunted a pair of ivory-handled pistols, but he was also a scrupulous and hardworking commander. He made morale a high priority, but when he assaulted and abused two combat-weary soldiers in the Sicilian campaign to get them to carry on fighting, the incident almost ended his career. He was recalled to command the 3rd US Army in the Normandy invasion, and his aggression and operational awareness made him an outstanding armoured commander. He was made a four-star general in April 1945, but died in a car accident eight months later.

RIGHT A defaced portrait of Mussolini hangs on a lamppost in northern Sicily on the road from Messina to the coast, with German and Italian road signs beneath it. Mussolini fell from power on 25 July.

BELOW The 380-millimetre (15-inch) guns of the British battleship HMS *Warspite* bombarding Axis forces holding the Sicilian port of Catania in the middle of July 1943. Naval fire played an important part in securing the landings in Sicily and later on mainland Italy.

into Allied hands. This was one of many arguments that continued to sour Anglo-American co-operation. Alexander reluctantly agreed, and Patton's units reached Palermo on 22 July.

Montgomery's progress proved frustratingly slow and Catania was taken only on 5 August. By this time, Alexander had ordered Patton's forces to swing east towards Messina to assist the 1st Canadian Division as it looped west of Mount Etna, on a trajectory initially assigned to the American zone. In the midst of the final push towards Messina, the Italian dictator, Benito Mussolini, was overthrown on 25 July 1943. Hitler, who had insisted on no withdrawal, was compelled to order an evacuation across the Straits of Messina. The Italian army under General Alfredo Guzzoni saw little point in continued resistance. By the time Allied forces converged on Messina, over 100,000 Italian and German forces had successfully been removed, without any serious air or naval action by the Allies. Patton arrived in the centre of Messina two hours before the British on 17 August, but the trap had failed to be sprung and one-third of Axis forces escaped. The campaign cost the Allies 38,000 casualties, but approximately 200,000 Italian soldiers surrendered in the course of the campaign, no longer willing to fight for a cause that had collapsed.

_ur Übersetzstelle

MESSIN

THE BOMBING OF HAMBURG

In the spring of 1943, RAF Bomber Command chose Hamburg, Germany's second-largest city and a major port and manufacturing centre, for a sustained and destructive attack codenamed Operation "Gomorrah". The campaign was an opportunity to try out two tactical innovations. The first was a new navigation aid, the H2S radar scanning apparatus that provided an image of the ground, the second a device known as "Window" which would block German radar by distributing thousands of aluminium-coated foil strips to create a mass of confusing data on the radar screen. The orders for "Gomorrah" went out on 27 May and the campaign against Hamburg was scheduled to begin on 24 July.

The attack on Hamburg was planned as a series of operations to maximize destruction and dislocation and to make it difficult for the rescue and fire services to continue to operate effectively. It was a combined operation, the RAF bombing by night and the United States 8th Air Force by day against designated industrial and transport targets. The first attack came on the night of 24/25 July, when 791 bombers set out for the city, the last on the night of 2/3 August when 740 bombers were sent off from British bases. The bomber streams were led by a Pathfinder force which carried H2S equipment and whose task was to pinpoint the main bombing area with flares. During the first operation, around 2,300 tons of bombs were dropped, a mixture of incendiary and high explosive.

ABOVE American Boeing B-17 "Flying Fortress" bombers in formation on a mission over Germany. The heavily armed bomber formed the mainstay of the US 8th Air Force bomber squadrons stationed in England and was used in the raids on Hamburg on 25 and 26 July 1943.

LEFT Aerial image taken during the first raid on Hamburg. Sticks of incendiaries can be seen burning in the Altona and dock districts of the city. This first attack did not produce the terrible firestorm though it caused widespread damage.

ABOVE LEFT Door plaque for the German National Air Raid Protection League, equivalent of Britain's ARP.

BELOW German civilian dead line a Hamburg street after a bombing raid during the nine-day Operation "Gomorrah" which caused an estimated 45,000 civilian deaths.

LIEUTENANT GENERAL IRA C EAKER (1896–1987)

Ira Eaker became commander of the US 8th Air Force in 1943 and was a major architect of the United States's daylight bombing campaign over Germany. A farmer's son from Texas, Eaker joined the army in 1917 and was trained as an army pilot in 1918. He saw service in the Philippines in 1919–21 before returning to the United States where he took part in a number of endurance flights, winning the world flight endurance record in 1929. His career in the 1930s and early 1940s was with fighter aircraft, but in January 1942 he was assigned to organize the 8th Bomber Command based in England, and in February 1943 took over as commander of the 8th Air Force. He personally flew in the first US bombing mission over Rouen in August 1942. Criticism of high losses in 1943 led to his replacement in December, and he became commander-in-chief of Allied Mediterranean Air Forces. He became chief of the air staff in April 1945 and retired in 1947 as a lieutenant general. In 1985, President Reagan awarded him a retrospective general's fourth star.

The following afternoon, 123 American B-17 bombers attacked Hamburg, aiming for the main shipyards. On the night of 25/26 July a handful of British Mosquito bombers flew over Hamburg to create alarm and the following day a further American attack with 121 bombers was made against the port area.

Over the next two days further alarms sounded regularly as the Hamburg population began to leave the city to avoid the continuing threat. On the night of 27/28 July, RAF Bomber Command returned in force with 787 bombers, and it was this raid, which created the first bombing firestorm, that made the operation notorious. The firestorm, in the eastern districts of the city, was the result of the high proportion of incendiary bombs dropped and the difficulty faced by the rescue services, after three days of bombing, in tackling hundreds of fires in areas with blocked roads and disrupted water supplies. The fires gradually merged together and by 1.20 a.m. the storm began to develop,

reaching a climax at around 3.00 a.m. with temperatures of 1,800 degrees centigrade and winds of 240 kilometres (150 miles) per hour. Everything in the path of the firestorm was consumed and human bodies incinerated. In the cellars, where many people had fled, the heat literally melted their bodies. The firestorm was the most deadly bombing attack yet experienced and an estimated 40–45,000 people lost their lives in one night, the equivalent of all those killed in nine months of the Blitz against Britain.

Even though Hamburg was now a skeleton city, the RAF returned on the night of 29/30 July, creating a smaller firestorm in the northeast of the city, and once more on the night of 2/3 August, although on this occasion heavy thunderstorms scattered the force and Hamburg suffered much less. On this final raid, the bomber force suffered its highest losses, 30 aircraft in total. Over the whole campaign the RAF dropped approximately 7,800 tons of bombs on Hamburg for the loss of 87 bombers, while the two 8th Air Force raids cost 17 bombers. The damage to the city was extensive: 25 square kilometres (10 square miles) of the city were obliterated, leaving over one million people homeless. Half the city's 81,000 commercial and industrial buildings were destroyed and over 40,000 residential buildings. Losses also included 58 churches, 277 schools and 24 hospitals. Besides the 45,000 dead were 37,439 with serious injuries.

The economic impact on Hamburg was, however, much less than Harris and Bomber Command had hoped. By the end of 1943, Hamburg's industrial production had reached 82 per cent of the pre-raid level. Much of the damage had been to residential areas, but local war industries, while temporarily disrupted by the exodus of workers from the city, were quickly restored or dispersed to safer sites. Albert Speer, the German armaments minister, thought that six similar attacks would knock Germany out of the war, but Bomber Command proved unable to replicate "Gomorrah".

ABOVE LEFT An oblique aerial view of the destruction to Hamburg's residential and business buildings south of the Stadtpark. These were among the 16,000 multi-storey buildings destroyed in the firestorm on the night of 27/28 July 1943.

LEFT Child refugees after the bombing of Hamburg in July 1943. More than a million people fled from the ruined area in the first days after the attacks. Some returned only at the end of the war.

RIGHT A British Cromwell tank guards a bridge over the River Elbe in Hamburg on 3 May 1945, a few days before the German surrender. The city still functioned as a centre of production but the areas destroyed in 1943 were only rebuilt in the postwar 1940s and 1950s.

BELOW Example of the miniature wooden coffins 15 centimetres (six inches) long distributed by the Resistance to signify that a collaborator had been singled out for retributive execution.

A fter the defeat of France the reaction of the French public to occupation was divided. There was a rallying of important sections of the population to the collaborationist Vichy regime of Marshal Pétain as a way of trying to preserve a sense of French patriotism; others tried to work with the occupiers on the assumption that this was the only realistic option; a great many, perhaps the majority, while not welcoming the consequences of defeat, tried to maintain neutrality and get on with their daily lives. A small minority, however, organized clandestine resistance from the start of the occupation and the establishment of the Vichy regime.

The resistance in France was localized. Not until 1943 were attempts made to unify the various elements under an umbrella National Council of the Resistance, but diversity remained the chief characteristic of resistance down to the liberation. The first resisters printed newspapers and leaflets, challenged or threatened collaborators, but seldom engaged in violence. Attacks on collaborators in the area of Montpellier provided the embryo of what became the "Secret Army" while the Communist resistance from 1941 organized the Francs-Tireurs et Partisans which engaged in sabotage attacks. Most resistance work consisted of collecting secret intelligence or establishing networks of sympathizers or obstructing the efforts of the German administration. Thousands of French Jews were also hidden from the Germans, an act of defiance that carried risks of heavy punishment.

The resistance was divided politically as well. Some groups were sympathetic to the exiled Charles de Gaulle and collaborated with the Free French organization based in London. They were funded and supplied by the British SOE and by MI6, which flew in agents and supplies and took back large quantities of secret intelligence information. Those groups linked with Britain also helped to organize escape routes for Allied airmen and POWs on the run,

ABOVE Wrecked railway locomotives in an engine shed at the Annemasse railway depot, destroyed by members of the French resistance.

RIGHT A poster by R Louvat from 1944 shows Allied support for the French resistance.

ABOVE Armband worn by the Free French. Featuring the cross of Lorraine and the initials of the Free French Forces of the Interior.

FRENCH RESISTANCE
HELPS THROTTLE THE BOCHE

ABOVE An RAF Stirling bomber drops supplies by parachute to waiting French resistance fighters. Many of the canisters fell into the hands of the German or Vichy authorities, but it was an essential means to keep resistance in being.

JEAN MOULIN (1899–1943)

Moulin is the most famous of the many resistance leaders who emerged in France during the German occupation. He was prefect of the Eure-et-Loir department when war broke out in 1940. He was arrested in June 1940 by the Germans for refusing to sign an affidavit blaming Senegalese soldiers for atrocities, but then released. In November 1940, the Vichy regime sacked him and he then joined the resistance, using the codename "Max". In London he met de Gaulle, who authorized him to create a united resistance organization under the title National Council of the Resistance. It was during a meeting with other resistance leaders on 21 June 1943 that he was arrested. Who denounced him is not known, but he was tortured by Klaus Barbie, refused to talk and died on the train taking him to a concentration camp, probably by committing suicide, although the story persists that he was killed by Barbie.

taking them across France and seeing them safely over the Pyrenees. Other resistance movements were based on the churches, or political movements independent of de Gaulle. The French Communists established an organization called Front National in 1941, which operated across all of France because it opposed both the Germans and the authoritarian Vichy regime.

Resistance activity increased substantially in 1943 following the German occupation of the whole of France on 11 November 1942. The Maquis groups of armed resisters were set up during 1943, many of them based in the remote mountainous regions of central and southeastern France. Their growth was helped by the German requirement for compulsory labour service in the Reich. Thousands of young French men and women, known as *réfractaires*, went into hiding to avoid labour mobilization, and although not all of them became resisters, an estimated 15–20,000 did, joining the major resistance groups Combat, Franc-Tireur and Libération as well as a host of small local groups which sprang up during 1943 and 1944 as it became clear that German defeat was now a probability.

The impact of the resistance on the German war effort has been difficult to estimate. Much of its activity was directed towards Vichy rather than the Germans, or was targeted against French collaborators. The most significant effort came in the run-up to the Allied Normandy landings, when the resistance was nominally organized under the Free French to carry out specific acts of sabotage against railway lines and telecommunications, including the resistance actions that held up the arrival of the SS Das Reich division on its way across France to help repel the Allied invasion. As liberation approached, some Maquis groups decided on armed insurrection, but at Mont Mouchet in June 1944 and Vecors in July 1944 the German army ruthlessly suppressed them with heavy losses. Only in Savoy, with the arrival of Allied forces in southern France, did the resistance play an important part in liberating the region. During the course of the war an estimated 90,000 French resisters were killed or sent to camps under the notorious "Night and Fog" decree under which prisoners disappeared without trace. At the end of the war, however, surviving resisters played a grim part in punishing collaborators.

MARIE-MADELEINE FOURCADE (1909-89)

Women played an important part in the French resistance, and Marie Fourcade became perhaps the most famous of them all. She began her activity from a youth centre she ran in Vichy. She went on to run the British-funded Alliance spy network after the arrest of its leader, Georges Loustaunau-Lacau. It had 3,000 informants, 429 of whom died at the hands of the German occupiers. She was arrested on 10 November 1942, but escaped to Britain, from where she continued to run the network under her codename "Hedgehog". After the war she became a leading organizer of the postwar resistance associations and was a commander of the *Légion d'Honneur*.

RIGHT A member of the resistance French Forces of the Interior hides behind a van to shelter from a German sniper at Dreux, 19 August 1944. In the last weeks of German occupation resistance forces began their own war against the occupiers.

BELOW French resistance fighters lead away a captured German soldier. In the battles to liberate French cities in the path of the advancing Allied armies German resistance rapidly crumbled. Around 10,800 collaborators were executed by the resistance in the weeks after liberation.

FROM KHARKOV TO KIEV: THE RED ARMY BREAKS THROUGH

3 SEPTEMBER 1943
Allied forces land on the mainland in southern Italy.

13 OCTOBER 1943
Italy under Marshal Badoglio declares war on Germany.

20 NOVEMBER 1943
US forces invade Betio Island on Tarawa Atoll in the South Pacific.

26–27 DECEMBER 1943
The Battle of North Cape sees the sinking of the German battlecruiser *Scharnhorst*.

ABOVE The Soviet Order of Glory. Created in November 1943 to honour those who had performed "acts of bravery in the face of the enemy".

Following the crushing victory at Kursk, Stalin ordered a general offensive along the whole Soviet-German front. The army groups that had liberated Orel and Belgorod pressed forward across the steppe and despite hasty efforts to reinforce the German 2nd Corps at Kharkov, the speed of the Soviet advance created the danger of encirclement and General Raus withdrew his forces on 22 August, a day before the Red Army liberated a battered city.

The object was to push Axis forces back to the River Dnepr in the central Ukraine in the south, to isolate the large German forces stationed in the Crimea and to propel German Army Group Centre back from Moscow to beyond Smolensk. With no natural defensive line, von Manstein's Army Group South had to retreat at speed towards the Dnepr and cross it before the Red Army enveloped them. Over 750,000 Axis troops reached the river and crossed it by 21 September, but Soviet forces using improvised rafts and barges forced the far bank at Bukrin and Zaporozhe and established a foothold across the so-called "Panther-Wotan" defensive wall which Hitler had hoped to make his defensive rampart in the east.

The bridgehead at Zaporozhe was used as the springboard for the Soviet army groups South and Southwest, under General Tolbukhin and General Malinovsky, to launch a major assault to cut off the 650,000 troops of Field Marshal von Kleist's Army Group A who had retreated to the Crimea from the Caucasus earlier in the year. By 1 December, the Red Army had reached Kherson and had bypassed the Crimean peninsula, cutting off the German garrison and approaching the town of Odessa. General Ivan Konev's Steppe Army Group captured

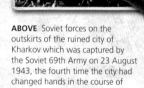

ABOVE Soviet forces on the outskirts of the ruined city of Kharkov which was captured by the Soviet 69th Army on 23 August 1943, the fourth time the city had changed hands in the course of the war.

RIGHT THE PPS43 submachine gun used by Soviet forces in the latter part of the war.

BELOW Red Army soldiers man an anti-aircraft gun in a square in Kharkov during the campaign for the city in February 1943. The German counter-offensive in March 1943 completed the destruction of Russia's fourth-largest city. When the city was liberated in August 1943 in Operation "Rumiantsev" there was little but rubble left.

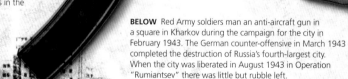

MARSHAL RODION MALINOVSKY (1898–1967)

Malinovsky was one of that remarkable cohort of senior Soviet commanders who rose from the humble rank of private in the First World War to become a marshal in the Second. The son of peasants in Odessa, he ran away to join the army in 1914 at the age of 15, was decorated for bravery and sent to France as part of the Russian Expeditionary Force. He returned to Russia in 1919 and fought for the new Red Army in the Civil War. He became a regular soldier and volunteered for service in Spain in 1936 to help the Republic. He survived Stalin's purges, unlike many of those who went to Spain, and in 1941 was commanding a rifle corps in his home town, Odessa. He fought in all the major campaigns in the south, and held off von Manstein's efforts to relieve Paulus in Stalingrad. As commander of the 3rd Ukrainian Front (and later the 2nd Ukrainian Front), he cleared the Axis from southern Russia, pushed into Hungary and captured Vienna in April 1945. He succeeded Zhukov as defence minister in 1957 and played a leading part in the Cuban missile crisis in 1962.

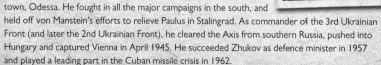

Cherkassy to the north and prepared to cross the river towards Korsun and Kirovograd. Although tank and air strength were not dissimilar, the Red Army had twice as many men in the field and four times as much artillery. Red Army soldiers had all the moral advantages of victory that German armies had possessed two years before; after Kursk there was no doubt that German forces were fighting a desperate war of defence, while Soviet soldiers were fighting to liberate their homeland.

Further to the north, two Soviet army groups attacked Army Group Centre and pushed it back beyond Smolensk, which was liberated on 25 September. The key prize was the Ukrainian capital of Kiev, which had been the scene of a humiliating encirclement for the Red Army in the late summer of 1941. Two Soviet fronts, Vatutin's Voronezh Army Group and Rokossovsky's Centre Army Group, pushed forward towards the Dnepr on either side of Kiev, establishing many small bridgeheads (a total of 40 by 25 September), which were subject to fierce German counter-attack. One small bridgehead was neglected in the swampy land around the village of Liutezh, and Vatutin, his army group now renamed 1st Ukrainian, was ordered to send men and armour into the small enclave undetected as the stepping-off point for an assault on Kiev. During late October, the 3rd Guards Tank Corps was moved into the marshland in complete secrecy.

RIGHT The German Field Marshal Erich von Manstein who organized the German retreat from Kursk in August 1943 examining operations maps with his staff. On 28 August he warned Hitler that German Army Group South could no longer hold the southern Ukraine.

RIGHT German dead from a Waffen-SS unit, the armed wing of the SS organization, which numbered around 800,000 by 1944. The SS units were, in general, better armed, and gained a reputation for greater brutality in battle.

BELOW German forces retreating in late 1943 across the last usable bridge over the Dnepr River. The remaining bridges had been blown by German engineers but Red Army soldiers improvised crossings on primitive rafts and boats.

Von Manstein expected a Soviet attack from the dry bridgeheads to the south of the city, but on 3 November two armies attacked out of the swamps to the north. By 6 November, the Red Army had entered the city and it was secured on the following day after bitter fighting. Vatutin ordered his forces to push on and by the end of December 1943 they were 160 kilometres (100 miles) beyond Kiev. Losses during the seizure of the city were remarkably low by the standards of fighting on the Eastern Front – a total of 6,491 dead or captured – but the subsequent defence of the city cost a further 26,000. In only a few months, Axis forces had been cleared from almost two-thirds of the territory they had occupied at the limit of their advance. In Moscow the capture of Kiev was celebrated with a magnificent fireworks display. At the celebration of the Revolution on 7 November, Stalin spoke of "the year of the great turning point".

ILYA EHRENBURG (1891–1967)

A Russian writer, poet and journalist, Ehrenburg is best remembered for his wartime propaganda urging Red Army soldiers to hate the Germans. He was a supporter of the Revolution when it came, but his sympathies were with the Menshevik Social Democrats rather than with Lenin's Bolsheviks. He left Russia to live in Paris but returned to Stalin's Soviet Union in 1939 where he was recruited to write poems and articles for the Red Army journals. In 1942 he wrote, "If you have killed one German, kill another. There is nothing jollier than German corpses." After the war he edited with Vasily Grossman the *Black Book of Russian Jewry*, harrowing accounts of the Holocaust in Russia, but the regime suppressed it.

ITALY: INVASION AND SURRENDER

ABOVE The forward 380-millimetre (15-inch) guns of the British battleship HMS *Warspite* bombarding the Italian coast at Reggio during the early stages of the Allied landings on the mainland of southern Italy. Naval power played an important part in supporting ground operations in the Italian campaign.

ABOVE Badge of the British 8th Army.

The decision to invade Italy after the conquest of Sicily in August 1943 was accelerated by the fall of Mussolini's regime on 25 July. The Allies hoped to be able to capitalize on the change in government to take Italy out of the war before the Germans could reinforce the peninsula adequately. Negotiations with the new regime of Marshal Badoglio were slow to produce a result. On 3 September the Italian armistice was signed at Cassibile, but by that point the Germans had succeeded in strengthening their forces in Italy from six to 18 divisions. It was essential for German strategy that the Allies should be kept as far south as possible, to avoid the establishment of airfields for the bombing of southern Germany and to make it impossible to use Italy as a military roadway into German-occupied Europe.

By the time the armistice was formally announced on 8 September, the Allies had already begun to move onto the Italian mainland. The plan was to land substantial forces in the Gulf of Salerno, south of Naples, and then to move northwards rapidly to take Naples and Rome and south to

ABOVE British troops and vehicles of the 8th Army's 46th Division unload on the beach at Salerno, 9 September 1943. After meeting light resistance at first, the bridgehead came under heavy attack.

LEFT Amphibious DUKWs, known as "ducks", enter the water at Messina in Sicily to cross the narrow straits to mainland Italy on 3 September 1943 during Operation "Baytown".

take over the Italian "heel and toe". Lieutenant General Mark Clark was put in command of the US 5th Army, consisting of the US 6th Corps and the British 10th Corps, which would land on either side of the River Sele which flowed into the gulf. Before this operation, Montgomery took part of the 8th Army across the Straits of Messina to land unopposed on the morning of 3 September, shortly before the armistice came into effect. The 8th Army then began to push up through Calabria with the eventual aim of meeting up with the forces sent ashore at Salerno.

The situation in Italy was chaotic following the declaration of the armistice; Badoglio, the king and the General Staff fled south to join the Allies, leaving no orders for the large Italian army. German forces immediately disarmed Italian soldiers, but in some cases they resisted, only to be brutally treated and shot out of hand. Some 650,000 Italian soldiers were sent as POWs to Germany, where they became forced labourers. The Italian fleet fled to Malta, but was hit by the German air force with new remote-controlled bombs and

GENERAL MARK CLARK (1896–1984)

One of the best-known American generals in the Second World War, Clark rose rapidly from the rank of major in the 1930s to become, by mid-1942, chief-of-staff of US Army Ground Forces with the strong backing of his mentor, General George Marshall. In October 1942, he was made deputy commander-in-chief of Allied forces in North Africa, and went on to lead the US 5th Army for the invasion of Italy in September 1943 as the youngest lieutenant general in the army. Though he was often criticized for his handling of operations in Italy, including the decision to bombard the historic monastery at Monte Cassino, he became commander-in-chief of all Allied ground forces in Italy in December 1944 and by the end of the war was commander of all Allied forces in Italy. In 1949, he became chief of army field forces and commanded the United Nations forces in the Korean War, signing the ceasefire with North Korea in 1953.

the battleship *Roma* was sunk. The country was divided in two, the far south governed by Badoglio together with the Allies, the north by a new Fascist Italian Social Republic, based in the town of Salò on the shores of Lake Garda, with Mussolini as its nominal leader but the German authorities under Field Marshal Kesselring the real rulers.

On 9 September, Clark's task force sailed for Salerno, already aware that the landing would be strongly resisted by the German occupiers. A fleet of 627 ships arrived off the coast and the naval vessels subjected the coastal area to a fierce bombardment. The British forces under Lieutenant General McCreery landed to the north of the Gulf of Salerno and the Americans under Major General Dawley in the south; although small bridgeheads were secured, shortages of air support and the stiff resistance of the Panzer divisions assigned to the German defence led to a dangerous situation by 12 September, as General von Vietinghoff's growing force began a powerful counter-offensive.

The Allies began to plan for evacuation, but the 82nd US Airborne Division was dropped into the danger zone, while aircraft and extra naval vessels were drafted in to bombard the enemy, and by 16 September German forces began to pull back. By 20 September, the rest of the 8th Army, making its way against much lighter opposition from Taranto and Bari, established firm contact with the Salerno beachhead. The German force pulled back to a prepared line north of Naples, and the port was occupied by Allied forces on 1 October. The scene was now set for a long and bitter campaign through difficult mountain country along the whole length of the Italian peninsula.

ABOVE Spitfire fighters with American pilots lined up on a former German airfield near Salerno on 3 October 1943. The wreckage of German aircraft and equipment was caused by heavy attacks by the Allied Mediterranean Strategic Air Forces.

COLONEL GENERAL HEINRICH VON VIETINGHOFF (1887–1952)

A career soldier from an aristocratic military family, von Vietinghoff served in the First World War as a junior officer on the General Staff, and by 1936 was a major general in command of a Panzer corps. In August 1943, he was sent to command the 10th Army in Italy, which he did until January 1945, when he was posted briefly as commander of the army group defending Courland against the Red Army. He acted as deputy for Kesselring as commander-in-chief southwest from October 1944 to January 1945, and was then made full commander-in-chief from 15 March 1945 until 29 April, when he surrendered his forces to the Allies. After the war, he was one of a group of experts recruited by Chancellor Adenauer who recommended German inclusion in a Western European defence system.

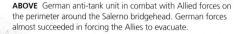

ABOVE German anti-tank unit in combat with Allied forces on the perimeter around the Salerno bridgehead. German forces almost succeeded in forcing the Allies to evacuate.

RIGHT The official signing at the Advanced Allied Headquarters, Sicily, of the Italian Armistice, on 3 September 1943. Left to right: Mr Montenari Italian Foreign Office, General W B Smith, American Chief of Staff, and General G Castellano, Chief of Staff to General Ambrosio, signing the terms of the armistice.

OPERATION "CARTWHEEL": WAR FOR NEW GUINEA

Following the defeat of the Japanese on Guadalcanal in February 1943, the Japanese naval and military leaders planned to strengthen their presence on New Guinea and to hold a defensive line from there through the northern Solomons to the Gilbert and Marshall islands. During the first three months of 1943, Lieutenant General Hatazo Adachi's 18th Army was transferred to the eastern coast of New Guinea and a large air component, the 4th Air Army, was based at Wewak, far enough from the American and Australian air forces in the southern tip of the island to avoid direct attack. The object was to move back down the island to capture Port Moresby, the target for Japanese ambitions a year before.

General MacArthur planned to consolidate the victory at Guadalcanal, which had demonstrated the growing superiority of American naval power in the southwest Pacific, by launching a major operation, codenamed "Cartwheel", against the main Japanese base at Rabaul on New Britain and the Japanese forces in northern New Guinea. On New Guinea itself an Australian army group, the New Guinea Force, with five Australian divisions and one American, was assigned to attack the Japanese based at Lae and Salamaua. The all-American Alamo Force, backed by a powerful naval and air component, was to neutralize Rabaul and attack New Britain and the Admiralty Islands, further to the north.

The Japanese attacked first in an attempt to seize the Allied airstrip at Wau but they were beaten off in bitter

ABOVE A Beaufort Bomber of No. 8 Squadron Royal Australian Air Force above the shoreline during a bombing attack on Wewak, the site of the largest Japanese airbase on mainland New Guinea.

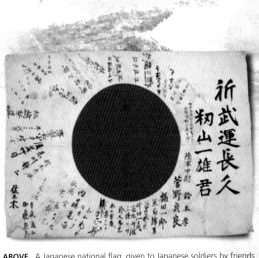

ABOVE A Japanese national flag, given to Japanese soldiers by friends and family and carried to encourage personal good luck and patriotic virtue. They were inscribed with messages of good fortune and slogans of victory and honour to the emperor.

THE BATTLE OF THE BISMARCK SEA

On 23 February 1943, 7,000 men of the Japanese 51st Division embarked in eight transport vessels at the main Japanese base at Rabaul in the northern Solomon Islands, bound for northern New Guinea. They were escorted by eight destroyers. American forces had been warned in advance of the convoy through Pacific ULTRA intelligence and on 2 March began a series of attacks by day and night as the boats crossed the Bismarck Sea. All the transport vessels were sunk and four of the destroyers, with the loss of 3,664 of the division. The Japanese commander in New Guinea, Lieutenant General Hatazo Adachi, was among the 950 survivors to reach the Japanese base at Lae.

BELOW United states troops rush ashore during the landing at Saidor on the northern coast of New Guinea, 2 January 1944. This was part of the coast-hopping operations designed to outflank the Japanese defenders during Operation Cartwheel.

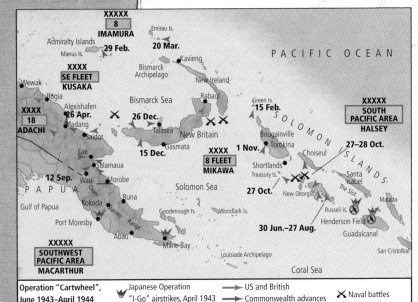

XXXXX
8
IMAMURA
29 Feb.

Admiralty Islands
Manus Is.
Emirau Is.
20 Mar.
Kavieng

PACIFIC OCEAN

XXXX
SE FLEET
KUSAKA

Wewak
Bogia

XXXX
18
ADACHI

Alexishafen 26 Apr.
Madang
Saidor
15 Dec.
Lae
Salamaua
12 Sep. Wau Morobe
PAPUA
Buna
Kokoda
Gulf of Papua
Port Moresby
Abau
Milne Bay

XXXXX
SOUTHWEST
PACIFIC AREA
MACARTHUR

Bismarck Archipelago
New Ireland
Bismarck Sea
Rabaul
26 Dec.
Talasea
New Britain
Gasmata
1 Nov.

XXXX
8 FLEET
MIKAWA

Green Is.
15 Feb.
Bougainville
Torokina
Choiseul
Shortlands
Treasury Is.
27 Oct.
New Georgia
Santa Isabel
The Slot
Russell Is.
Goodenough Is.
Woodlark Is.
30 Jun.–27 Aug.
Henderson Field
Guadalcanal
Malaita
San Cristobal

XXXXX
SOUTH
PACIFIC AREA
HALSEY
27–28 Oct.

SOLOMON ISLANDS

Solomon Sea
Louisiade Archipelago
Coral Sea

| Operation "Cartwheel", June 1943–April 1944 | Japanese Operation "I-Go" airstrikes, April 1943 | US and British | Commonwealth advances | Naval battles |

fighting. Then, on 29 June, the Allied attack began on the Japanese bases at Lae and Salamaua. To speed up the advance, Lieutenant General Kenney's US 5th Air Force built a secret airfield closer to the Japanese air base at Wewak from which he launched two devastating attacks on 17 and 18 August, leaving the Japanese with just 38 serviceable aircraft. The Japanese army defended to the death, and not until 16 September did the Australians overrun Lae and Salamaua and another three months were needed before the whole of the Huon Peninsula was in Allied hands.

While this first campaign was completed, US forces landed on western New Britain on 15 December. The previous month, strong carrier forces had neutralized any threat from the Japanese base at Rabaul, while the main concentration of the Japanese fleet, at the island of Truk in the Carolines group further north, was too weak to contest every avenue of American advance. After landings in the Admiralty Islands between 29 February and 20 March 1944, the American Fast Carrier Force commanded by Vice Admiral

Marc Mitscher swung round to mount operations on the northern coast of New Guinea far behind Adachi's retreating 18th Army, cutting off his avenue of escape. Strong forces were landed at Hollandia on 30 March and Aitape on 22 April. Adachi ordered his force to attack the US perimeter in July 1944, but was beaten back. He retreated with what was left of his force into the high mountains inland, and played no further part in the war.

Operation "Cartwheel" confirmed that the balance of power had swung firmly in favour of the Allies in the southwest Pacific. Although the Japanese had held the long frontier of their conquered Pacific empire for two years, it was only because fighting in the tough tropical conditions of the region was a slow process, while Japanese forces resisted with almost complete disregard for their losses and in spite of debilitating diseases and persistent hunger. The refusal to give up lent the fighting a brutal character which Allied forces did not encounter in the Mediterranean or Western Europe.

BELOW Australian soldiers crossing the Faria River in the Faria valley in New Guinea on their way back to base. Australian forces played a major part in the fight against the Japanese on the island.

LIEUTENANT GENERAL HATAZO ADACHI (1884–1947)

Hatazo Adachi had a reputation for leading his men from the front, even when he reached the rank of general. The son of a poor samurai family, he joined the Japanese army and began service with the 1st Imperial Guards Division. He served in Manchuria in 1933, and then as a colonel in the Sino-Japanese war, where he was wounded by mortar fire. In 1941–42 he was chief-of-staff of the North China Area Army responsible for hunting down Chinese Communists. In November 1942, he was posted to Rabaul to take command of the 18th Army for the campaign on New Guinea. In 1944, his forces were isolated on the island, and were decimated by malaria and hunger. In September 1945, he surrendered and was charged with war crimes by the Australian government. Sentenced to life imprisonment, he committed ritual suicide with a paring knife on 10 September 1947.

ABOVE An American unit on the Soputa front, near the New Guinea port of Buna, carrying wounded comrades back to headquarters after 11 days' continuous combat during the campaign to drive Japanese forces out of the southern areas of the island.

BELOW The Japanese commander on New Guinea, Lieutenant General Hatazo Adachi, arrives on 13 September 1945 at Cape Wom airbase, Wewak, for the formal surrender of his few remaining forces.

ISLAND-HOPPING IN THE PACIFIC: GILBERT AND MARSHALL ISLANDS

22–26 NOVEMBER 1943
Cairo Conference of Churchill, Roosevelt and Chiang Kaishek discusses strategy for the Far East.

28 DECEMBER 1943
Italian city of Ortona is captured after bitter fighting along the Gustav Line.

4 JANUARY 1944
Red Army crosses the pre-1939 Polish border into German-occupied Europe.

27 JANUARY 1944
The Siege of Leningrad is finally lifted after the death of an estimated one million inhabitants.

15 FEBRUARY 1944
The monastery of Monte Cassino is heavily bombed by the Allies and completely destroyed.

17 FEBRUARY 1944
Capture of "Cherkassy Pocket" by Konev's forces leaves 19,000 Germans dead or captured.

The assault on New Guinea and Rabaul in the second half of 1943 was one wing of a two-pronged campaign. A second line of attack was launched through the Solomon Islands north of Guadalcanal and on into the central Pacific against the outlying Gilbert and Marshall islands, viewed as stepping-stones to the distant Marianas, which were within striking distance of Japan for the US Army Air Force's new generation of long-range heavy bombers, the B-29 Superfortress.

LEFT An American cruiser fires at Japanese positions on Makin Atoll, 20 November 1943, during an operation in the Gilbert Islands, northeast of the Solomons.

ABOVE United States marines from the 2nd Marine Division wade through shallow water in the invasion of Makin Atoll. The US commanders had little knowledge of Japanese strength on the island, but in this case the small garrison of 800 was overcome in three days of fighting which proved less costly than on neighbouring Tarawa.

In June 1943, Admiral William Halsey's Third Fleet began the task of capturing the main islands of the southern Solomons. Rendova Island was taken on 30 June, then New Georgia was attacked and the base at Munda captured on 4–5 August. Japanese convoys sent to help the endangered garrisons were destroyed in two battles in the Kula Gulf and the Vella Gulf, and on 1 November US forces, supported by the 3rd New Zealand Division, landed on the main island of Bougainville, where air bases could be set up to bomb the Japanese base at Rabaul. Japanese reinforcements were hastily sent to the island, where the Japanese garrison

numbered around 40,000 men, but Halsey was able to call on extensive air support to contain the Japanese threat while an assault by two of his carriers on the powerful fleet of Vice Admiral Kurita at Rabaul forced a Japanese withdrawal. The Japanese were bottled up on Bougainville for the rest of the war, at the end of which 23,000 finally surrendered.

Further north, Admiral Nimitz prepared to assault the Gilbert and Marshall islands. A force of 200 ships was assembled, with 35,000 soldiers and marines and 6,000 vehicles. On 13 November, a sustained naval bombardment began against the Makin and Tarawa atolls in the Gilbert

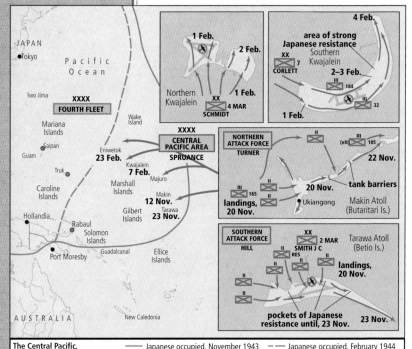

THE BATTLE FOR TARAWA

The battle for the small island of Betio on the edge of Tarawa atoll in the Gilbert Islands was one of the toughest battles of the Pacific War. Only 4,500 Japanese marines garrisoned the island, but they were well supplied and dug in to deep defensive positions, including 500 pillboxes and a network of concealed trenches. The US naval force that mounted the operation included no fewer than 17 aircraft carriers and 12 battleships and transported 35,000 US marines and soldiers. They attacked on 20 November 1943, but intense Japanese fire and difficult tidal waters pinned the invaders on the beaches. There followed three days of fierce fighting, but vastly superior manpower and supplies gradually allowed the American forces to gain the upper hand. At the end of the battle, only 17 Japanese soldiers were left alive, but a total of 990 US marines and 687 sailors lost their lives, a level of casualties that prompted strong criticism of the operation among the American public.

ABOVE US Marines clear a Japanese pillbox on the Tarawa atoll.

The Central Pacific, November 1943–February 1944 — Japanese occupied, November 1943 --- Japanese occupied, February 1944 ● Japanese base

REAR ADMIRAL MARC A MITSCHER (1887–1947)

One of the pioneers of naval aviation in the US Navy, Marc Mitscher played an important part in driving the Japanese from the central Pacific during the Second World War. He joined the navy in 1906, transferring to the Aeronautics Section in 1915. He was one of three navy pilots who flew across the Atlantic in flying boats in 1919. He was assistant chief of the Bureau of Aeronautics from 1939 to 1941, and then took command of the aircraft carrier USS *Hornet* from which the Doolittle raid was launched against Japanese cities in April 1942. His carrier saw action at Midway, and in April 1943 he became air commander in the Solomons. He was appointed to command carrier Task Force 58 (later known as the Fast Carrier Task Force) which harried the Japanese in New Guinea and the Marianas and in March 1944 was promoted to vice admiral. At the end of the war he was appointed deputy chief of naval operations responsible for aviation, and in 1946 became commander-in-chief of the Atlantic Fleet.

Islands. The attack, codenamed Operation "Galvanic", began on 20 November against Makin Atoll, which was secured by 23 November after limited but fierce fighting by a small Japanese garrison of 800 soldiers, which had no aircraft and was commanded by no one more senior than a first lieutenant. A Japanese submarine from Truk sank a US escort carrier, *Liscombe Bay*. Betio Island on Tarawa Atoll took the same time to secure, but only after bitter and costly fighting for both sides. Attention then shifted to the Marshall Islands further north, a German colony taken over as a mandate by the Japanese in 1919. The objective here was to capture the main Japanese base on Kwajalein Atoll in an operation codenamed "Flintlock". Rear Admiral Charles Pownall's Task Force 50 bombarded the Japanese positions more than a month before the assault took place, followed by heavy attacks from land-based aircraft.

On 1 February, an armada of 297 ships brought the US 7th Infantry Division to Kwajalein, while the 4th Marine Division went on to the Roi and Namur islands further to the north of the group. In total 84,000 troops were involved in

the hope of avoiding the costly battles experienced in the Gilberts. After six days of heavy fighting, all three islands were secure; on Kwajalein only 265 Japanese soldiers were taken alive out of a garrison of 4,000. Nimitz then ordered a further operation against the Engei and Eniwotek atolls, 560 kilometres (350 miles) northwest of Kwajalein. Attacks here secured the islands between 17 and 23 February. The US naval forces were now within striking distance of the Marianas, and aircraft from the Marshalls could attack the main Japanese naval base at Truk. Although there was much argument over the merits of the island-hopping campaign, where tiny atolls were secured at a high cost in casualties, Nimitz was keen to push the central Pacific avenue to Japan as a more efficient, faster and ultimately less costly strategy than MacArthur's idea of attacking through the East Indies and the Philippines against heavy Japanese force concentrations. The result was a division of resources between two different campaigns, and a growing sense of rivalry between the army and navy over who would defeat Japan first.

BELOW A US soldier uses a jeep with a billboard on the back to direct bombers to their parking places on the Eniwetok airstrip captured from the Japanese in the Marshall Islands on 23 February 1944. In the background can be seen B-24 Liberator bombers.

ABOVE A US marine prepares to throw a hand grenade during the invasion of the tiny Betio Island on the southern shore of the lagoon formed by Tarawa Atoll. The fighting for Betio was among the fiercest and most costly of the island campaign.

LEFT Dead Japanese soldiers, who shot themselves rather than surrender to the Americans, on Namur Island.

LEFT A US naval rating playing the trumpet in an informal entertainment for the troops on Tarawa Atoll on New Year's Eve 1943, five weeks after its capture.

THE BIG THREE: THE TEHERAN CONFERENCE

10 OCTOBER 1943
Foreign Ministers' Conference at Moscow prepares ground for Teheran.

18 NOVEMBER 1943
Start of major bombing campaign by RAF Bomber Command against the German capital.

28 NOVEMBER 1943
US Forces complete the conquest of Tarawa Atoll in the South Pacific.

2 DECEMBER 1943
German air force attacks the Italian port of Bari causing a massive explosion of Allied ammunition stores.

In November 1943, the three leaders of the major Allied powers met together for the first time in the Iranian capital, Teheran. The conference, codenamed "Eureka", was called to resolve major issues of Allied strategy for the last phase of the war, but Roosevelt hoped that it might lay the foundation for a close personal relationship with Stalin as the basis for a postwar political settlement.

Teheran was not the first choice for the summit venue. Roosevelt had suggested the Bering Straits, Khartoum, Cairo and Asmara in Somaliland, but Stalin insisted that he wanted to stay in touch with developments on the fighting front (Kiev was finally liberated three weeks before the conference). Roosevelt had to travel 11,250 kilometres (7,000 miles) to get to Teheran, Churchill some 6,500 kilometres (4,000 miles). On the way to Teheran, they halted at Cairo, where a preliminary conference was held with China's Nationalist leader, Chiang Kaishek, from 23 to 26 November. Stalin had been invited to this meeting, codenamed "Sextant", but he refused since the Soviet Union was not yet at war with Japan. "Sextant" was the occasion to reiterate Western Allied support for the Chinese struggle. The Cairo Declaration issued at the end of the conference committed the Allies to confiscating all Japan's imperial territories, returning Chinese territory to China and creating an independent Korea.

ABOVE Allied political and military leaders meeting in Cairo before the conference in Teheran. The first conference, codenamed "Sextant", took place from 23 to 26 November 1943 and involved Churchill, Roosevelt and the Chinese leader Chiang Kaishek (seated left).

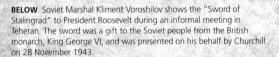

BELOW Soviet Marshal Kliment Voroshilov shows the "Sword of Stalingrad" to President Roosevelt during an informal meeting in Teheran. The sword was a gift to the Soviet people from the British monarch, King George VI, and was presented on his behalf by Churchill on 28 November 1943.

FIELD MARSHAL ALAN BROOKE (1883–1963)

Chief of the Imperial General Staff from 1941 to 1946, Alan Brooke played a central role in Britain's war effort, and acted throughout the war as a brake on Churchill's more impetuous strategic ideas. An Ulsterman by birth, he joined the Royal Artillery before 1914 and fought as an artilleryman during the First World War, rising from the rank of lieutenant to lieutenant colonel by 1918. He was an officer of outstanding talent, becoming a major general in 1935, and a lieutenant general three years later as Commander of the Anti-Aircraft Command. He led the British 2nd Corps in the Battle of France, and after his return to England was made Commander-in-Chief Home Forces. In December 1941, he was promoted to Chief of the Imperial General Staff, and became the senior advisor to the government. He was a permanent member of the combined chiefs-of-staff and negotiated firmly with his American counterparts, who respected his sharp intellect and power of speech, though he was not much liked by them. In 1944, he was created a field marshal, and in 1946 was made a viscount. After the war, he became a director of the Midland Bank and chancellor of Queen's University, Belfast.

In Teheran, formally within the British sphere in Iran, there was extravagant security, including a regiment of Indian Sikhs to protect Churchill, who stayed at the British Embassy. On the pretext that there was a risk to Roosevelt's safety, the president was persuaded to stay in a house in the grounds of the Soviet Embassy. This symbolized the pattern of the conference, in which Roosevelt sought to make common cause with Stalin and Churchill was left isolated by the two senior partners in the so-called Grand Alliance. Stalin wanted a commitment from the West for a second front in France, which Roosevelt and his military advisers were keen to promise, but Churchill wanted to use the conference as a further opportunity to press his preferred strategy of an attack from the Mediterranean on the "soft underbelly" of German-occupied Europe which had now been exposed by the surrender of Italy.

These arguments were played out in the first two days of negotiations. On the second day, Roosevelt promised a second front in May 1944 and Churchill was forced to comply even though he and his senior advisers, including the chief of the Imperial General Staff, General Alan Brooke, thought the risk of a major cross-Channel invasion very high. A diversionary attack on southern France was also promised (Operation "Anvil") and approved by Stalin, although once again Churchill was strongly sceptical of its value. The Soviet side offered to mount a powerful offensive to coincide with the invasion in the west, and Stalin also pledged the

ABOVE Sergeant Kipral Singh of the 3rd Battalion, 11th Sikh Regiment, handing a birthday gift to Churchill. The Sikh Regiment formed Churchill's guard at Teheran.

ABOVE Stalin raises his glass in a toast to Churchill at a reception held at the British Embassy on 30 November 1943 during the Teheran Conference. The British foreign secretary, Anthony Eden, stands on Churchill's right.

LEFT Roosevelt, Churchill and Stalin (left to right) at the British Embassy in Teheran on the evening of 30 November 1943 to celebrate Churchill's 69th birthday. Stalin became intoxicated and by the end of the evening was exchanging toasts with the surprised embassy servants.

RIGHT Stalin (left) and Roosevelt sitting together in Teheran. They established a good rapport during the conference, much to Churchill's irritation. Roosevelt aimed to involve Stalin in a postwar international order and hoped his personal relationship would help seal Soviet-American collaboration.

Soviet Union to join the war against Japan once Germany was defeated. On the evening of 30 November, Churchill hosted a lavish dinner in honour of his birthday at the British Embassy, where Stalin taunted both Churchill and Brooke for their hostile attitude to the Soviet Union. By the end of the evening Stalin was unusually intoxicated and the sour note he had introduced was finally overcome. The following day the three leaders signed a public communiqué on the strategy agreed for the defeat of Germany.

The Teheran Conference was regarded by Roosevelt as a possible starting point for a closer political relationship between the United States and the Soviet Union which might continue into peacetime. Churchill and Roosevelt returned to Cairo to complete the "Sextant" conference between 3 and 7 December, when Roosevelt announced his decision to appoint Eisenhower as supreme commander for the invasion of France. Churchill, who had not been well for much of the Teheran Conference, went on to Morocco to convalesce.

ABOVE German anti-partisan pin, awarded to those fighting groups of partisans in occupied Europe.

In some parts of Axis-occupied Europe resistance took the form of a violent armed campaign by guerrilla fighters, or partisans as they were generally styled during the war. The main areas in which they operated were in eastern and southern Europe, in Greece, Yugoslavia, Poland, the Soviet Union and, in the last years of the war, in German-occupied northern Italy as well. In all these regions, the occupying forces often had to deploy very substantial armed forces to combat a hidden enemy committed to the armed struggle for liberation.

Partisan warfare gave the Second World War a very different character from the war of 1914–18, stemming from the deep ideological conflicts that characterized the politics of interwar and wartime Europe, but also the sense that in total war civilians were just as much part of the fighting as the soldiers. Thousands of armed civilians, some of them former soldiers, died in pitched battles with the regular troops of Germany and her allies, who treated partisan war as terrorism and responded with a savage brutality against the partisan fighters and the civilian populations among whom they hid.

The largest and militarily most significant partisan movement developed in the Soviet Union, where Stalin summoned the population, civilian and soldier, to resist by every means possible against the German enemy. Small groups formed in the forests and swamps of Belorussia and Ukraine, at first isolated and poorly armed, but from May 1942, when a central organization was set up in

Moscow, they were supplied and often led by regular Red Army men infiltrated behind the lines. Linked by radio, it became possible to co-ordinate the efforts to cut German communications and to sabotage German rear areas. German forces imposed a savage retaliation, isolating the villages suspected of activity and burning them down and murdering the inhabitants. In Belorussia, an estimated 350,000 civilians were killed alongside 30,000 partisans in the German anti-partisan sweeps. But by 1943, there were an estimated 130,000 of them and in some areas Soviet rule had been re-established. German soldiers were confined more and more to pathways across Soviet territory where it was possible to retain control through terror.

In Yugoslavia, Greece and Italy, the partisan movements were different. They were divided, usually along political lines, but, in many cases, they were also involved in a

LEFT Women fighters of the Yugoslav royalist Chetnik partisans, 17 May 1944. Women played a role in all partisan and resistance movements, both fighting and organizing supplies or hiding partisans on the run.

ABOVE LEFT German soldiers and security forces burn down a village in Belorussia. Thousands of villages were destroyed to prevent partisans from getting access to food and to punish the population in retaliation for partisan attacks.

BELOW Greek soldiers from the ELAS (National People's Liberation Army) firing on a police station in 1944 during an armed uprising in Athens. The resistance in Greece was divided on ideological grounds and gave way to civil war after the Germans left.

TITO (JOSIP BROZ) (1892–1980)

Born of mixed Croat and Slovene parentage, Broz became a metal-worker and an active socialist. Imprisoned in 1914 for anti-war activities, he was then sent to the Russian front and captured in 1915. During the Russian Revolution he joined the Red Army, but eventually made his way back to Yugoslavia in 1920. There he became an active Communist, adopting the cover name Tito in 1934, and eventually general secretary of the Yugoslav Communist Party in 1937. In 1941, after the German invasion, he was declared military commander of the Communist resistance and was the most prominent figure on the Anti-Fascist Council. In 1944–45, Tito's movement liberated much of Yugoslavia, and in March 1945 he headed the Yugoslav provisional government. He was elected prime minister in November 1945 and was president from 1953 until his death in 1980.

PANTELEYEMON PONOMARENKO (1902–84)

The leader of the Soviet partisan movement appointed by Stalin on 30 May 1942 to head the Central Staff for Partisan Warfare, Ponomarenko acted as the chief-of staff of the guerrilla movement. He was a Red Army general and a senior party official, appointed in 1938 after the purges as first secretary of the Belorussian Communist Party. He played a part in "cleansing" the areas of Belorussia seized from Poland in 1939 of bourgeois and counter-revolutionary elements. He then helped to organize partisan resistance in the area after the German invasion before being summoned to Moscow. After the war, he was a member of the Politburo in 1952–53 and ambassador to Poland from 1955 to 1957. He was the co-founder of the Soviet National Jazz Orchestra based in the Belorussian capital, Minsk.

BELOW Ponomarenko (far left) in October 1939, in his role as Secretary of the Belorussian Communist Party at the Presidium of the First Conference of the People's Representatives of Western Belorussia.

political struggle against the old order, so that they targeted collaborators or prewar political enemies as much as the Axis enemy. In Yugoslavia a pro-monarchist Serb movement under General Draža Mihailovic fought against the Yugoslav Communist resistance led by Tito, and seldom confronted the Germans. Tito's movement was almost annihilated in 1941–42 but by the end of 1943 around 200,000 fighters had been organized, helped by the British, who decided that Tito's forces were the most likely to offer them serious military help. An estimated 1.2 million died in the conflicts in Yugoslavia from racial and political vendettas as well as Axis anti-partisan sweeps.

In Greece and Italy, the principal partisan groups were Communists. The Greek National People's Liberation Army (ELAS) and its political wing, the National Liberation Front (EAM), fought the Germans and the non-Communist National Republican Greek League. A truce was agreed in 1944 but EAM was the strongest organization, succeeding in controlling parts of rural Greece by 1944 when the Germans withdrew. Partisan war against the Germans was then followed by partisan war against the returning Greek government and its British allies, which developed into the Greek Civil War. In Italy the partisan movement emerged as a response to the harsh German occupation following Italian surrender in September 1943. A Committee for National Liberation was established, dominated by Communists, but there were also other partisan groups, including Justice and Liberty, representing the non-Communist Party of Action. An estimated 100,000 joined by 1944, based in the mountain areas of central and northern Italy, but fierce German retaliation, assisted by regiments of anti-Communist

Cossacks recruited from Russia, brought the Italian partisan movement to a point of crisis by early 1945.

Everywhere the Germans faced partisan activity they reacted with ferocity against what they regarded as an illegitimate form of warfare. In Italy, 40,000 died in retaliation raids and anti-partisan operations, including 560 men, women and children butchered by the SS 16th Panzer Division at the village of Sant'Anna di Stazzema in August 1944. In Slovakia, 25,000 were killed after an anti-German rising in August 1944 organized by Slovak partisans and a number of regular soldiers. Partisan activity often failed to dent the German war effort, but it gave the German army, frustrated and in retreat, a weaker enemy on whom they could vent their fury.

ABOVE A Serbian partisan hangs from a lampost after his execution by German forces, April 1943.

ABOVE Soviet poster – "Beat the enemy mercilessly, partisans!"

RIGHT Italian partisans in action in Venice in 1945. Fierce German counter-measures in the winter of 1944–45 decimated partisan numbers, but the movement revived in the spring of 1945 as the end of the war drew near.

BATTLE OF THE NORTH CAPE

The Battle of the North Cape, fought on Boxing Day (26 December) 1943, was the last engagement fought by the Royal Navy against a major battleship. The battle had its origins in the decision by the British government in November 1943 to recommence the Arctic aid convoys to the Soviet Union, which had been suspended in March 1943 because of the threat posed by German air and sea power and shortages of naval shipping. The two large German ships in Norwegian waters, the battleship *Tirpitz* and the fast battlecruiser *Scharnhorst*, had in fact done very little for most of the war and Hitler had decided that they should be scrapped. The resumption of northern convoys encouraged the German navy commander-in-chief Admiral Dönitz to order an attack so that Hitler could be shown that the large ships were not simply a waste of resources.

On 20 December, a large convoy, JW55B, left Loch Ewe in Scotland bound for the Soviet Arctic ports. An empty convoy, RA55A, was returning the other way. The two convoys would cross in the strait between Bear Island and the North Cape in northern Norway. The commander of the British Home Fleet, Admiral Fraser, suspected from intelligence evidence that the German navy would attempt to intercept the convoys, and on 23 December he took his flagship, the battleship *Duke of York*, with 360-millimetre (14-inch) guns, out to sea with a strong escort of one cruiser and four destroyers. To the east was a cruiser group under Vice Admiral Robert Burnett of *Belfast*, *Norfolk* and *Sheffield* which could also be used to defend the convoy and engage any German units.

The German commander of the *Scharnhorst*, Vice Admiral Bey, was a temporary appointment whose previous experience had been confined to destroyers. Encouraged by Dönitz to take action, the German headquarters at Kiel ordered Bey to take out his ships on Christmas Day 1943 and intercept a convoy, whose whereabouts were not known precisely, nor the position or strength of any Royal Navy force that might be protecting it. The weather

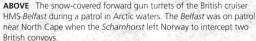

BELOW The German battlecruisers *Scharnhorst* and *Gneisenau* travel in a line with their guns firing, allegedly taken during their escape from Brest, known as the "Channel Dash" on 12 February 1942.

ABOVE The snow-covered forward gun turrets of the British cruiser HMS *Belfast* during a patrol in Arctic waters. The *Belfast* was on patrol near North Cape when the *Scharnhorst* left Norway to intercept two British convoys.

was atrocious, with heavy squally snow showers and high seas, but Bey left the safety of his fjord together with four destroyers. By the morning of 26 December, Bey had lost contact with his covering force and never regained it. Instead, the battlecruiser sailed on towards the convoy on its own, and into the path of the waiting British cruiser squadron. The *Scharnhorst* was detected by radar and then visibly and at 9.30 a.m. *Norfolk* began to engage, knocking out Bey's forward radar. The German ship made off to the north, towards the convoy.

The attack was a complete surprise for the German ship, but Bey relied on superior speed to reach the convoy ahead of the cruisers. Burnett took a shorter route and just after

VICE ADMIRAL ERICH BEY (1898–1943)

Erich Bey joined the German navy in 1916 and spent most of his subsequent career serving as an officer on destroyers. In the Norwegian campaign, as a junior captain, he commanded a four-destroyer flotilla which was among those destroyed when the Royal Navy attacked on 13 April 1940. On 10 May, he was promoted to full captain and commander of destroyers, a post he held down to his death in 1943. He was promoted to vice admiral and commanded the battleship *Scharnhorst* and a group of destroyers in the Battle of the North Cape. After the battleship was sunk he was seen badly wounded in the water, but drowned before he could be rescued.

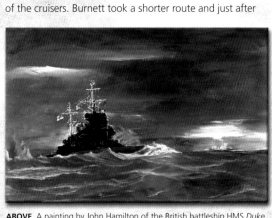

ABOVE A painting by John Hamilton of the British battleship HMS *Duke of York* engaging the German battlecruiser *Scharnhorst*.

midday contact was restored and the attack began again. This time the cruisers were damaged by the heavier shells of the battlecruiser, but Bey decided that the risk of attacking the convoy was now too great and turned for base, straight into the path of Fraser's force which was placed between the German ship and the Norwegian coast. Poor intelligence and reconnaissance left Bey in ignorance of the trap until, at 4.48 p.m., a salvo from the *Duke of York* straddled the *Scharnhorst*. The British battleship fired 52 salvos and damaged the German ship's boiler room, slowing it down to 8–10 knots. The other British ships closed in for the kill, but it took 11 torpedoes before the German ship sank at 7.45 p.m. with the loss of all but 36 of the 2,000-man crew.

The battleship *Tirpitz* stayed in Norwegian waters and, following 22 attacks by aircraft, was finally sunk on 12 November 1944 by two "Tallboy" heavy bombs with the loss of 1,204 men. Hitler's lack of confidence in battleships proved to have some foundation.

ADMIRAL BRUCE FRASER (1888-1981)

When Bruce Fraser was created a baron in 1946 he chose as his title 1st Baron Fraser of North Cape, the Arctic site where he commanded a notable Royal Navy victory in 1943. He joined the Royal Navy in 1904 and became an expert in gunnery, serving as a gunnery officer during the First World War. He fought in the intervention against the Bolshevik revolution, and briefly became a POW in 1920. In 1939, he was controller of the navy and third sea lord in the Admiralty. As commander-in-chief of the Home Fleet in 1943, he led the task force at the Battle of the North Cape. In November 1944, he was appointed commander-in-chief of the British Pacific Fleet, which took part in the invasion of Okinawa and the attacks on the Japanese home islands. He signed the Japanese Instrument of Surrender on behalf of the British forces on 2 September 1945. In 1948, he became first sea lord and chief of the Naval Staff, retiring in 1952.

ABOVE The German battleship *Tirpitz* at her berth on the Norwegian coast under air attack on 3 April 1943. Despite regular attacks from bombers the battleship remained resistant to all attempts to sink her until November 1944, though the bombing severely disabled the ship and prevented the remains of the German battle fleet fighting together.

ABOVE LEFT A scene aboard the *Scharnhorst*, one of a new generation of German fast battlecruisers with 280-millimetre (11-inch) guns which failed to fulfil the role intended for them as merchant raiders.

BELOW Blindfolded survivors of the sinking of the *Scharnhorst* are led ashore at the British naval base of Scapa Flow. Out of a crew of 2,000, only 36 survived.

THE BATTLE FOR ANZIO

CENTRE RIGHT (object)
German anti-tank mine used against the Allies in Italy.

ABOVE Badge of the 56th London Infantry Division.

Following the landings at Salerno, the Allies decided on a second coastal landing a little south of Rome around the port of Anzio as a way of turning the German Gustav Line, which by late December 1943 ran from Formia on the west coast to Ortona in the east, a mainly mountainous terrain with narrow river valleys, ideal for defensive purposes. The Anzio landings, strongly supported by Churchill and organized by General Mark Clark, were designed to trap the German 10th Army, which was resisting the advance of the British 8th Army and the US-led 5th Army towards the mountain stronghold around the ancient monastery of Monte Cassino. It was also hoped that the landings would open the way for an advance to Rome.

The operation, codenamed "Shingle", carried a considerable risk because the forces involved were modest. The 6th US Army Corps under Major General John Lucas comprised the British 1st Infantry Division and the US 3rd Infantry Division, supported by commandos and rangers, and a powerful element of air support. On 22 January 1944, over 370 ships arrived off the Italian coast to be met by no initial resistance. The Allied force landed and established a narrow beachhead, but Lucas, whose immediate objectives had not been made entirely clear in the planning, dug his forces in rather than exploiting the advantage of tactical surprise. Though often criticized for the decision, it almost certainly saved the operation from disaster, for within four days Field Marshal Kesselring succeeded in improvising a six-division 14th Army under General von Mackensen, which on 1 February began a sustained assault on the perimeter of the Anzio area after a number of smaller forays.

ABOVE United States troops of the 5th Army board landing craft for the voyage to the Italian coast at Anzio where it was hoped that the Allied landing would catch German forces in a pincer movement.

Although Lucas was soon reinforced, and was strongly supported by air and sea bombardment, the German forces succeeded in containing the bridgehead in five months of bitter fighting. By mid-February, the German counter-offensive threatened to drive a salient into the Allied line, dividing the British to the north of Anzio from the Americans to the south. Probing attacks by German armoured forces pushed back British and American troops, who had begun a cautious move out from their initial defensive line. A salient formed by the British 1st Division was attacked and on 9 February the 3rd Panzer Grenadier Division recaptured Aprilia and two days later the Scots Guards were expelled from the town of Carroceto, captured on 25 January. Von Mackensen was instructed by Kesselring to concentrate

ABOVE A Sherman tank and armoured personnel carriers on the beach at Anzio on 22 January 1944. The initial landings met almost no resistance but German forces soon regrouped and counter-attacked.

ABOVE A chaotic scene near an American medical post in the Anzio bridgehead in February 1944. After an almost unopposed landing, the fighting became fierce and losses high on both sides.

RIGHT Allied shipping unloading supplies in Anzio harbour in mid-February 1944. The bridgehead was held thanks to a regular flow of materiel and reinforcements which could be brought in by sea with a small level of risk.

his forces for a major offensive, codenamed "Fischfang" (Fish-catch) to divide the bridgehead and then expel it.

The Allies were pre-warned by ULTRA intelligence and a heavy air bombardment was directed at the German concentrations, but on 16 February von Mackensen launched a strong attack at the weak line between the British and American sectors which was only halted by a further ferocious barrage of fire from sea, air and artillery. The Germans established a salient eight kilometres (five miles) wide and three kilometres (two miles) deep but could progress no further. Six days later, Lucas was redeployed and his deputy, Major General Lucian Truscott, placed in effective command. His first action was to tour the battlefield, visiting every one of the Allied units in an effort to boost sagging morale. A second major German attack on 29 February was also repulsed. What followed was a war of attrition between the two sides: the German ring of armoured divisions was never quite powerful enough to push the bridgehead back into the sea, but the 6th Corps, despite continuous reinforcement, was too weak to break the cordon.

The trench stalemate was broken only by renewed pressure on the Gustav Line from Allied forces around Cassino. It became clear to Kesselring that the line would not hold, and German forces prepared to withdraw to defensive lines prepared further up the Italian peninsula. As the German grip weakened, Truscott prepared a fresh offensive and on 23 May Allied forces broke out of the Anzio bridgehead and drove east, intending to encircle the retreating Germans. Instead General Clark ordered a drive northwards, and Rome fell on 4 June to American forces. The costs of the Anzio campaign were high, 43,000 for the Allies, including 7,000 dead, and an estimated 40,000 for the Germans, with 5,000 killed.

FAR RIGHT Two captured German paratroopers carrying a wounded British soldier who has lost his foot in a landmine explosion, 22 May 1944.

ABOVE British soldiers shelter in a trench from German shelling on 22 May 1944, shortly before the breakout from the Anzio bridgehead which opened the road to Rome.

ABOVE Two black US servicemen from the 5th Army sitting at the entrance to an air-raid shelter in March 1944 during the defence of the Anzio bridgehead. Large numbers of black Americans served in the armed forces though they were still the victims of segregation when they returned home.

COLONEL GENERAL EBERHARD VON MACKENSEN (1889-1969)

A Prussian aristocrat, von Mackensen had a conventional soldier's career in the German army. He joined the army in 1908, served in the First World War where he was wounded and given a staff job, and remained in the army after 1919. By 1938, he was a major general and on the outbreak of war he was chief-of-staff of the German 14th Army. He served in France and in Army Group South in Russia, as commander of the 3rd Army Corps. In 1943, he was sent to command the 14th Army, and was retired in June 1944 after the failure to contain the Anzio bridgehead. After the war, he was tried as a war criminal and condemned to death. His sentence was commuted to 21 years in prison, but he was released in 1952.

MAJOR GENERAL JOHN LUCAS (1890-1949)

Lucas began his career in 1911 as a US cavalryman but then joined the field artillery and was wounded in service in the First World War. During the Second World War he saw service in North Africa before being selected to lead the Allied invasion of the Anzio beachhead in January 1944. He was critical of the operation and played a poor part in its execution, spending all his time as commander in an underground bunker. His relations with the British officers assigned to Anzio were strained. He was replaced in February 1944 by his deputy, Major General Truscott, and he was sent back to the United States to take command of an army.

THE BATTLE FOR MONTE CASSINO

11 JANUARY 1944
Former Italian Fascist foreign minister Count Ciano is shot for treason by Mussolini's new regime in northern Italy.

14 JANUARY 1944
Allied bombers attack Bulgarian capital Sofia from Mediterranean bases.

17 FEBRUARY 1944
US marines land on Eniwetok and Engei atolls in the Marshall Islands, securing both within six days.

6 MARCH 1944
Major American bombing raid on Berlin with 700 planes from 8th Air Force, resulting in losses of 69 aircraft.

2 APRIL 1944
Soviet forces begin the invasion of Romania, Germany's Axis ally.

17 APRIL 1944
Japanese army in China launches Operation "Ichi-Go" in Henan province, the start of seven months of fighting.

ABOVE A photograph of the Benedictine monastery of Monte Cassino taken c.1927. The site had been a monastery since the 6th century AD and was a building of exceptional architectural and religious significance. German forces promised not to occupy the building and did not do so until it had been destroyed by Allied bombing.

The key to breaking the German grip on southcentral Italy was the heavily defended area around Cassino and the valleys of the Liri and Rapido rivers. This was the setting for one of the most bitterly contested struggles of the war in the west which led to the complete destruction of the ancient Benedictine monastery of Monte Cassino, set high on an outcrop of mountainside above the town of Cassino.

The battle for Cassino lasted five months and involved four major operations. The German 14th Panzer Corps, under General von Senger und Etterlin, bore the brunt of the defence, dug in to the rugged landscape and valley sides that made up this part of the Gustav Line. The Allied plan, set out in a directive from Alexander's headquarters on 8 November 1943, was to destroy German forces in the Liri valley and to approach Rome from the south, in conjunction with a landing at Anzio designed to roll up the German front. Early attacks in December on the German defences showed how difficult the assault would be with Allied forces that were battle-worn after the hard drive up from Sicily.

The opening battle began on 17 January 1944 when British forces tried to cross the River Garigliano and the Americans the River Rapido three days later. Small bridgeheads were secured against fierce resistance and the US 5th Army began a slow ascent towards the monastery before heavy losses forced a halt on mountains to the

ABOVE Two German paratroopers fighting in the ruins of Monte Cassino monastery during April 1944. The destroyed monastery created a natural defensive position which was abandoned only after it was clear that German forces faced the threat of possible encirclement.

Map labels (Monte Cassino, 13–18 May 1944)

Germans withdraw to meet French flanking movement, 18 May

Mte. Cifalco
Mte. Abate
Mte. Belvedere
Terrelle
Rapido
Sant Elia
Mt. Cairo
Cairo
Viticuso
Mt. Castellone
Maiola Hill
Sant Angelo Hill
Piedimonte
Aquino
Piumarola
San Vittore del Lazio
San Pietro
Sant Angelo
Pignataro
San Giorgio a Liri
Sant Apollinare
Rocca
Mignano
Sant Ambrogio
Sant Andrea
Ausonia
Mte. Maio

XXX X McCREERY
XXX LI MTN VON SENGER UND ETTERLIN
XXXX 14 MACKENSEN
XXX XIV
to Rome

XX 5 POL
XX 3 POL
XXX II POL
XXXX 8 LEESE
1 Monte Cassino
Cassino
XX 6

Polish advance, 17 May
Polish troops enter empty monastery, 18 May

XX 44
XX 90
XX 4
XXX XIII
XX 78
XX 8 IND
Liri Valley
Dora Line
Gustav Line
Garigliano
Liri

18 May

XX 1
XXX EXP JUIN
XXXX 5 CLARK
XX 2 MOR
XX 4 MOR
XX 3 ALG
XX 71
XX 94

Aurunci Mountains

French advance over Aurunci Mountains, 13 May

Monte Cassino, 13–18 May 1944

GENERAL FRIDOLIN VON SENGER UND ETTERLIN (1891–1963)

The son of a German aristocratic family, von Senger und Etterlin joined the army in 1910 before going to Oxford University as a Rhodes Scholar. He served through the First World War and stayed on in the postwar army as commander of a cavalry regiment. He reached the rank of colonel by 1939 and fought in the Battle of France in command of his own mobile brigade. In October 1942, he commanded the 17th Panzer Division in southern Russia. As a lieutenant general he commanded German forces in Sicily in July and August 1943. On mainland Italy he commanded the 14th Panzer Corps and became a general of Panzer troops on 1 January 1944. He was opposed to Hitler but took no part in the assassination plot of July 1944. After the war he became a leading expert on German armoured forces and vehicles.

northeast while the French Expeditionary Corps made progress to the north. But on 11 February the first attack was called off, with total Allied casualties of 14,000, sustained in weeks of harsh weather and fierce fighting. A second assault was planned a week later using General Freyberg's New Zealand Corps, but Freyberg, anxious that German troops would use the monastery as a fortress, requested a preliminary bombing attack. Clark was unwilling, but he was overruled by Alexander, the Allied commander in Italy. On 15 February, 229 bombers pulverized the monastery into ruins.

It was only then that the German forces moved into the rubble, which provided good defensive positions. The only inhabitants of the monastery had been Italian civilians and a number of monks sheltering from the conflict, and between 300 and 400 were killed. On 15 February, the New Zealanders attacked the Cassino railway station while the 4th Indian Division attacked the monastery hill. After three days the offensive was called off after achieving almost nothing. Alexander then planned to wait until the spring to launch a more carefully prepared assault, but under pressure from London and Washington to give relief to the threatened Anzio beachhead, a third assault on Cassino was tried. After a massive air bombardment which turned Cassino into a ruin, the New Zealand Corps again tried to storm the town between 15 and 23 March, but after taking 4,000 casualties and battered by appalling weather, the attack was called off.

ABOVE A New Zealand anti-tank gun in action on 15 March 1944 during the attempt by the New Zealand Corps to seize the hill and monastery. After heavy casualties they were forced to withdraw.

BELOW Troops of the Polish 2nd Corps climbing the slopes of the monastery hill in May 1944. The Polish units took terrible casualties in the assault but fought with exceptional courage.

GENERAL WLADYSLAW ANDERS (1892–1970)

General Anders became famous in the Second World War as the leader of the Polish 2nd Corps which captured the monastery of Monte Cassino. The son of a German father, he was born in Russian-ruled Poland and fought in the tsar's army against the Germans during the First World War. After the war, he joined the army of the new Polish state as a cavalry commander. He was captured by the Red Army in September 1939 when Poland was invaded from the east, and imprisoned and tortured (though, unlike thousands of other Polish officers, not murdered). He was freed in July 1941 and then led a large force of Poles through Iran and Iraq where they met up with British forces and formed a Polish army corps. He fought in Italy and after the war stayed in Britain as a member of the Polish government-in-exile. He was buried in the cemetery at Monte Cassino among the soldiers he had led there.

The final assault was postponed until May. Alexander prepared a major operation, codenamed "Diadem", designed finally to unhinge the German line. The French forces in the south pushed across the Garigliano River and the Aurunci Mountains, threatening the whole south of the German line. The British 8th Army assaulted and finally captured Cassino, while on 17 May the Polish 2nd Corps under General Anders assaulted the monastery and after heavy hand-to-hand fighting, and losses of 3,500 men, occupied it on 18 May as German forces withdrew. The fourth Cassino battle persuaded Kesselring that his position was untenable and he began moving his forces back to the Gothic Line, north of Florence. Clark's 5th Army met up with Truscott's Anzio forces on 25 May. In the end, victory at Cassino was needed to rescue the Anzio operation, the opposite of what had been intended when the operations to break the Gustav Line were first launched late in 1943.

ABOVE Polish and British flags fly side by side above the monastery of Monte Cassino on 18 May 1944 after the German withdrawal. The capture of Monte Cassino paved the way for a rapid advance past Rome to Florence.

THE SECRET WAR: SPIES, CODES AND DECEPTION

The secret war of spying, deception code-making and code-breaking played an important part in the conduct of the Second World War for all the combatant powers. There were two main purposes behind the secret war: to shield from the enemy any knowledge of strategic and operational plans and force strengths, and to find out the plans and force strengths of the enemy. But there was also the possibility, exploited at times with remarkable success, of deceiving the enemy about operational intentions in order to maximize the chances of success and to get the enemy to dispose their forces at a disadvantage.

The most glamorous, but in many ways least successful, aspect of the secret war was spying. Most spies were caught if they operated in enemy country, and in many cases turned into double agents. In Britain a special double-cross organization, the XX-Committee, was set up under J C Masterman in September 1940 which succeeded in '"turning" a number of German spies and sending back misleading information to the German counter-intelligence organization, the Abwehr. Almost all German spies were caught, but so too were British agents in occupied Europe. The most successful spies were Soviet, but they spied on

ABOVE LEFT The US State Department official Alger Hiss was one of a number of high-ranking Soviet agents in the American administration. He was later accused by the House Un-American Activities Committee of working for Communism.

ABOVE RIGHT The chief of the German counter-intelligence organization (the Abwehr) was Admiral Wilhelm Canaris. He kept up the appearance of working enthusiastically for the regime but was in reality hostile to Hitler. After the July Plot in 1944 he was arrested and later hanged in April 1945.

their allies as well as their enemies. The Communist Red Orchestra spy ring was based in Göring's Air Ministry in Berlin until it was broken in 1942, but Soviet spies in Britain and the United States went undetected for years. The "Cambridge Five" worked at the heart of the British intelligence effort in MI6 and MI5, from where they fed a regular diet of information to their Soviet NKVD controller in London. In the Pacific War, the Allies made little use of spying, but Japanese spy networks in Hawaii and the United States supplied useful information before Pearl Harbor, though little thereafter.

Spying was a risky and unreliable source of information. During the war much more was expected from breaking enemy codes and ciphers. This was done routinely in most theatres, but the important point was to try to conceal from the enemy the fact that the codes had been broken. The Allies had a remarkable success in breaking German and Japanese codes and then preventing that knowledge from filtering back to the German and Japanese armed forces. The German Enigma coding machine, which was thought to be unbreakable, was first read in 1940, though very incompletely, but by the end of the war ULTRA traffic, as the British called it, could be read routinely and quickly. The effort to avoid giving any clue that the Allies could read their secret traffic was a major intelligence operation in its own right, but the Germans assumed that Enigma

BLETCHLEY PARK

Bletchley Park was a large Victorian country house northwest of London which became the home of the Government Code and Cypher School in 1939 under the codename Station X. It was the base for supplying secret codes and ciphers for use by British agencies but was also responsible for breaking enemy codes and ciphers. In 1942, it was renamed the Government Communications Headquarters. By 1945, around 10,000 people worked for the organization. It was famous for the work of Hut 6 where the German Enigma traffic was deciphered, and in June 1944 the first electronic computer, Colossus II, was introduced to help speed up the process.

RIGHT An inflatable dummy Sherman tank used in the deception Operation "Fortitude" to persuade the Germans that a large Allied army group was stationed in southeast England to attack the Pas-de-Calais in the summer of 1944.

was unbreakable and that the Allies got their information from other sources. The same was true in the Pacific where Japanese diplomatic traffic (PURPLE or MAGIC) and military traffic (ULTRA) was read by the Americans and the British, giving invaluable advance warning of Japanese moves after the disastrous failure at Pearl Harbor.

The third element of the secret war, deception, was perhaps the most important, because it could affect an entire campaign. The Allies had notable successes. The Soviet deception before the "Uranus" operation in November 1942 or Operation "Bagration" in summer 1944 was complete, and rapid victory in both cases owed a lot to the unpreparedness of Axis forces. The most famous was the "Fortitude" deception before D-Day, when an entirely fictitious army group (FUSAG) was set up in southeast England, with dummy tanks and bogus camps, to persuade Hitler that the assault would come across the narrowest part of the English Channel. A fake order-of-battle was also fed into German intelligence by double agents in Britain and the United States. So realistic was the deception that Hitler ordered large forces to remain in the Pas-de-Calais when they were desperately needed to repel the Normandy landings. British deception plans were carried out with particular skill and success, but this relied on the gullibility of the enemy. The German armed forces were less interested in playing deception games and so were an easy target for British ingenuity. The Allies in general made much greater use of intelligence as an arm of battle than did the Axis.

BELOW LEFT Four of the "Cambridge Five" who spied for the Soviets during the Second World War. Clockwise from top left: Anthony Blunt, Guy Burgess, Donald MacLean and Kim Philby. The fifth man, John Cairncross, was only exposed in the 1990s.

MAJOR GENERAL WILLIAM J DONOVAN (1883–1959)

Donovan, always known as "Wild Bill" after his early student exploits on the American football field, was a successful New York lawyer, who served as commander of a volunteer regiment in the First World War during which he won three Purple Hearts and the Medal of Honor. He was a US attorney for Western New York, and during the 1930s became a confidant of President Roosevelt, who sent him to Britain as an emissary in 1940 and 1941 to assess British chances of survival. Here he met intelligence chiefs and began to argue for a co-ordinated American intelligence effort. In June 1941, Roosevelt named him co-ordinator of information to try to bring together the many departmental intelligence agencies under a single umbrella. In 1942, his organization was renamed the Office of Strategic Services, with Donovan in charge, responsible for intelligence and sabotage in Europe and Asia (except for the Philippines). The office was terminated in September 1945, but two years later the CIA was founded, modelled on Donovan's plan for a single peace-time intelligence department.

ABOVE LEFT General Heinz Guderian in his command vehicle watches soldiers sending messages using the Enigma machine. Some of the Enigma codes were regularly read by Allied intelligence from the early stages of the war.

LEFT A nailbrush with a secret compartment carrying "escape aids" for SOE agents.

ABOVE The world's first computer was set up at the British code and cipher school at Bletchley Park to speed up the decrypting of the Enigma messages. Colossus II was in operation from June 1944.

BATTLE FOR INDIA: IMPHAL AND KOHIMA

4 JUNE 1944
US troops from Clark's
5th Army from the Anzio
beachhead enter Rome.

6 JUNE 1944
Allied forces mount largest-ever
amphibious operation against
German-occupied Normandy.

13 JUNE 1944
First German V-weapon lands
on British soil.

15 JUNE 1944
US air forces begin the
bombardment of the Japanese
homeland.

18 JULY 1944
General Tojo is removed as
Japanese prime minister.

ABOVE Badge of the British
14th Army formed in November
1943 to defend India and Burma.

The Japanese in Burma intended to hold the country defensively to prevent the Allies opening a supply route from India to the Chinese forces fighting in southern China. But the incursion of Chindit units in spring 1943 persuaded the Japanese commanders that Burma might be made more secure by seizing a frontier zone around Imphal and Kohima in Indian Assam. Lieutenant General Renya Mutaguchi, appointed to command the Japanese 15th Army in Burma in March 1943, used his friendship with the Burma commander-in-chief, General Kawabe, to persuade the Tokyo government to endorse an attack on India, despite strong criticism of an operation in which supply would prove a permanent obstacle.

The Japanese plan for what they called Operation "U-Go" was to seize the main supply depot at Imphal, cut the road from the north at Kohima and then to dig in on the new frontier while monsoon rains prevented an Allied counter-offensive. As the operation was being prepared, British and Indian forces attacked Arakan in southern Burma and routed a Japanese force there, while in northern Burma General Stilwell, using Chinese forces assisted by the British Chindits and the American "Merrill's Marauders", launched a protracted campaign to try to seize the northern town of Myitkyina. Both operations effectively weakened the Japanese forces prepared for the Imphal-Kohima offensive, but it was possible to organize a total force of between 80,000 and 100,000 men for an operation which opened on 7 March with an attack by the Japanese 33rd Division from the south towards Imphal.

Despite intelligence warnings, the opening of a southern offensive surprised General Slim's 14th Army which made

GENERAL MASAKAZU KAWABE (1886–1965)

In March 1943, General Kawabe was made commander-in-chief of the Burma Area Army. A graduate of the army college in 1907, Kawabe was an infantry commander and in 1929–32 military attaché in Berlin. He was involved in the Marco Polo Bridge incident that sparked the Sino-Japanese war in July 1937, and became chief-of-staff of the Central China Expeditionary Army in 1938–39 and again in 1942–43. In Burma in 1944, he approved plans to invade India despite opposition from other senior commanders, but following their failure he was replaced and sent back to Japan in August that year. He joined the Supreme War Council, was promoted to full general and commanded first the Central Army District then the Air General Army (made up from all remaining aircraft in Japan) for the defence of the home islands. After helping to demobilize the army after surrender, he retired at the end of 1945.

ABOVE LEFT Japanese soldiers in the ruins of a building during Operation "U-Go" against Kohima and Imphal. The Japanese forces were poorly supplied and took heavy losses during the campaign.

BELOW A Japanese position under fire on the Tamu Road. British Empire forces had a considerable advantage in tanks and aircraft over the Japanese attackers.

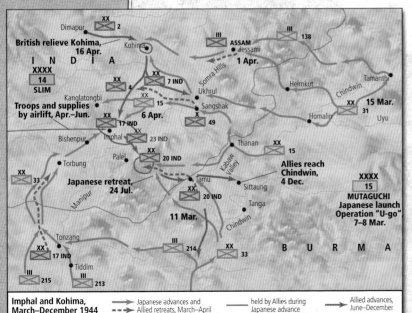

**Imphal and Kohima,
March–December 1944**

→ Japanese advances and
Allied retreats, March–April

— held by Allies during
Japanese advance

→ Allied advances,
June–December

(Map labels:) Dimapur · British relieve Kohima, 16 Apr. · Kohima · ASSAM · Jessami · 1 Apr. · 138 · INDIA · XXXX 14 SLIM · 7 IND · Somra Hills · Heirnkut · Tamanthi · Kanglatongbi · Ukhrul · Chindwin · 15 Mar. · Troops and supplies by airlift, Apr.–Jun. · 15 · Sangshak · 31 · Uyu · 6 Apr. · 49 · Homalin · Bishenpur · 17 IND · Imphal · 23 IND · Thanan · 15 · Palel · 20 IND · Allies reach Chindwin, 4 Dec. · Kabaw Valley · XXXX 15 MUTAGUCHI Japanese launch Operation "U-go" 7–8 Mar. · Torbung · Japanese retreat, 24 Jul. · Tamu · 20 IND · Sittaung · Manipur · 33 · Tanga · 11 Mar. · Chindwin · Tonzang · 214 · 33 · B U R M A · 17 IND · Tiddim · 215 · 213

ABOVE Men of the West Yorkshire Regiment clear a Japanese roadblock on the road between Imphal and Kohima during the Japanese offensive in 1944.

a rapid retreat towards Imphal, leaving the Indian 20th Division stranded and surrounded around Shenam, where it held out against Japanese attacks. Slim airlifted two divisions from Arakan to reinforce the Imphal area and by the time Mutaguchi released the 15th Division towards the town, Slim had been able to organize the first stages of an effective defence. The Japanese force succeeded in cutting the roads to Imphal and there followed a four-month siege during which Slim was supplied by the RAF Third Tactical Air Force, bringing reinforcements, oil, food and military equipment.

Further to the north, Mutaguchi sent the 31st Division under Lieutenant General Kotoku Sato to seize Kohima and open up the possibility of capturing the more distant British supply depot at Dimapur. Struggling through mountainous jungle territory, Sato succeeded in bringing his whole division to Kohima, surrounding the town on 5 April and fighting street by street to capture it. By 18 April, the defenders were confined to one small hill but a relief force sent down the road from Dimapur broke the siege and Sato found his forces pushed slowly back until, on 31 May, he ordered a general withdrawal of his exhausted and poorly supplied troops. The battle was hard fought, bringing 6,000 Japanese casualties but 4,000 British and Indian losses.

Mutaguchi's plan had been for Sato to seize Kohima and then send help south to reinforce the siege of Imphal. The failure further north left the Japanese facing a growing battle of attrition against a surrounded force too heavily armed to be decisively defeated. Slim's forces reopened the road from Imphal to Kohima on 22 June, breaking the siege, while the Japanese, short of food, ammunition and heavy equipment, and wracked with disease, fought an increasingly suicidal campaign. On 18 July, Kawabe and Mutaguchi agreed to terminate the operation and began a withdrawal that turned into a disastrous retreat as Slim's strengthened army pursued them across the Chindwin River. Japanese losses were 53,000, including at least 30,000 killed. The campaign broke the back of Japanese military strength in Burma and paved the way for the reconquest of the country in 1945.

ABOVE British soldiers search the long grass for Japanese snipers during the Battle of Imphal. They are covered by a Bren-gun unit in case of a sudden attack.

ABOVE RIGHT *Kukri* knives, a traditional Nepalese weapon used by the Gurkha divisions and also some Indian forces.

LEFT A Lee-Grant tank crosses a river north of the town of Imphal to meet the Japanese attack launched on 7 March 1944.

BELOW Units of Slim's 14th Army open the road between Kohima and Imphal in June 1944, breaking the Japanese siege. Troops from Imphal met forces advancing from Kohima on the northern edge of the Maniput plain after ten weeks of heavy fighting.

JAPAN'S WAR IN CHINA: OPERATION "ICHI-GO"

23 JUNE 1944
Start of the Soviet operation "Bagration" that destroys German Army Group Centre in a few weeks.

20 JULY 1944
Failed attempt by Colonel Claus von Stauffenberg to assassinate Hitler at his headquarters.

17 AUGUST 1944
Red Army units reach the German border in East Prussia.

25 AUGUST 1944
Paris is abandoned by the Germans after a week of fighting by the French resistance.

13 OCTOBER 1944
Red Army enters the Latvian capital Riga.

20 OCTOBER 1944
US 6th Army invades the island of Leyte in the Philippines.

11 NOVEMBER 1944
US Navy begins bombardment of Japanese island of Iwo Jima.

The military situation in China in the later stages of the war was one of great confusion. The Nationalists under Chiang Kaishek could see that Japan would be defeated and tried to conserve the strength of the Nationalist Kuomintang army for the expected postwar civil war with the Chinese Communists, who by 1944 had armed forces of around half a million men (and women), and a peasant militia estimated at two million. The Communists dominated parts of the northern countryside both inside and outside the Japanese area of occupation, but also avoided pitched campaigns against the Japanese. The most bellicose in China were the American commanders in the theatre, General Joseph Stilwell and the commander of the volunteer American air force, Major General Claire Chennault, whose "Flying Tigers" based in southern China organized the air supply of Chiang's forces over the "Hump" between India and China and flew missions against Japanese targets in occupied China.

It was the existence of the American air force bases in the southern provinces of Hunan and Guangxi, with the bombing threat they posed to the Japanese home islands, that prompted the Japanese commanders in China to undertake a renewed territorial offensive, the first since 1941. They also needed to open up a continuous rail link from Indo-China to Manchuria because the long sea routes had become dominated by American submarines and aircraft.

ABOVE President Roosevelt flanked by General Chiang Kaishek and his wife during a conference at Cairo in 1943. The Chinese leader hoped to get greater commitment from the United States for a campaign in Asia, but by the last years of the war it was evident that US forces could achieve Japan's defeat across the Pacific.

ABOVE Chinese workers in March 1944 build an airstrip with the help of American engineers. Here they can be seen taking stones to make the runways. The major US bases were overrun by Japanese forces during Operation "Ichi-Go".

Operation "Ichi-Go" (Number One) was launched in April 1944 when 150,000 Japanese troops seized the remainder of Henan province in central China and control of the Beijing–Hankou railway, meeting slight resistance.

The second phase began in late May 1944 with the drive to seize the southeastern provinces and eliminate Chennault's air bases. Stilwell warned Chiang and Chennault that unless adequate ground protection could be supplied by Chinese forces the air bases were not capable of defence. The Nationalist army numbered an estimated 3.5 million men, but many were loyal to local warlords and not reliable. Chiang organized a so-called Central Army of around 650,000 who were better armed and trained and loyal to him, but he was reluctant to commit them to pitched battle. The defence of the southeastern provinces

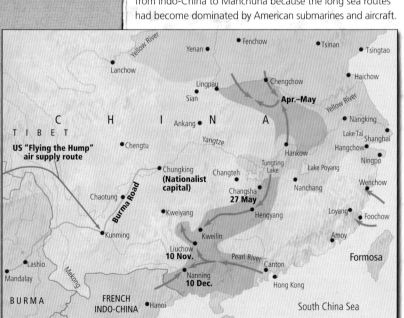

China, April–December 1944	
▨ Japanese occupied, early 1944	▨ Communist controlled areas
▨ Japanese occupied after Operation "Ichi-Go", April–December 1944	→ "Ichi-Go" advances

GENERAL JOSEPH STILWELL (1883–1946)

Stilwell was the leading American general in the Asian theatre of operations in China and Burma. He came from a strict Protestant background against which he was a natural rebel. Instead of Yale University he was sent to the Military Academy at West Point where he received demerits for laughing during drill. During the First World War he was intelligence officer for the US 4th Corps. In the interwar army his caustic style earned him the nickname "Vinegar Joe". He was military attaché to China, where he learned Chinese, from 1935 to 1939, and in 1942 he was selected to act as chief-of-staff to Chiang Kaishek and US commander-in-chief of the China-Burma-India theatre. In this role he found himself the victim of political intrigue and military rivalry and the corrupt exploitation of Lend-Lease supplies to China. In October 1944, after Chiang accused him of responsibility for failing to halt the Japanese "Ichi-Go" offensive, he was recalled to America, later serving as commander of the US 10th Army in Okinawa.

fell on the Cantonese forces of General Hsueh Yueh and Chennault's 200 aircraft. The city of Changsha, which had been defended by Nationalist forces earlier in the war, fell with little resistance on 18 June; then followed a drive by 350,000 troops through Hunan and Guangxi. Chinese resistance lasted six weeks but after that it crumbled and Chennault's air bases were overrun one by one. By November, Japanese troops had eliminated the last of them and linked up with forces coming from northern Indo-China to complete control of the rail link from Hanoi to Mukden in Manchuria. In the process Chinese forces suffered an estimated 500,000 dead or wounded.

"Ichi-Go" was then halted even though the road to the Nationalist capital at Chongqing, in central

China, was now open and poorly defended. Japanese ambitions had been confined to establishing a rail route and destroying the American threat from the air. The Japanese army in China was not large enough to risk undertaking major expansion into the central regions. In much of the occupied area Japan relied on an estimated one million Chinese troops and policemen recruited from local Chinese puppet warlords or from bandits. Over the remaining nine months of war, Japan held on to its railway lines but control over the rural hinterland in the south was often nominal. The Nationalist army was better supplied in 1945 when the road from Burma was reopened, but the corruption and incompetence of the commanders and the uncertain loyalty of many of the troops prevented Chiang from playing any significant part in the final defeat of Japan.

MAO ZEDONG (1893–1976)

Mao Zedong was the leader of the Chinese Communists in the struggle against Japanese occupation and the Nationalist Chinese under Chiang Kaishek. The son of peasants, Mao became an active Communist in the 1920s, espousing a popular democratic ideology in contrast to the Stalinist outlook of European Communism. He helped to establish a rural Communist community in Jiangxi Province but was driven from it in 1934 by the Nationalist Army. There followed the Long March to Shaanxi province in the far north where a new Communist area was established around the city of Yenan. Mao emerged during the war as the dominant figure, leading a popular Chinese Red Army against the Japanese. By 1945, much of the northern countryside was under Communist control and four years later Communism triumphed in China. In 1949, Mao became chairman of the new People's Republic.

BELOW A Japanese prisoner captured by Chinese Nationalist soldiers during the Japanese campaign in Hunan province in central China in March 1944. Despite early Chinese resistance the whole area was captured by the Japanese army in summer 1944.

ABOVE A Chinese man tortured and murdered by Japanese forces after the fall of the city of Changsha on 18 June 1944. Roped to a wall, he has had both his eyes gouged out. Japanese forces exacted a terrible revenge on Chinese civilians throughout the occupied area.

ABOVE The skulls of 5,000 Chinese murdered by the Japanese in June 1944 have been laid out as a memorial to the dead on a hillside near the Chinese city of Hengyang in Hunan province.

D-DAY

1 JUNE 1944
French resistance alerted to D-Day and begin guerrilla operations.

4 JUNE 1944
Allied forces enter Rome.

4 JUNE 1944
Poor weather forces postponement of D-Day from 5 June.

10 JUNE 1944
Red Army begins major operation against Finnish forces.

10 JUNE 1944
Waffen-SS forces destroy French village of Oradour and murder 642 men, women and children.

15 JUNE 1944
US forces land on the island of Saipan.

ABOVE A German heavy gun battery overlooking the English Channel, built in April 1942. It bears the name "Batterie Todt" in honour of Fritz Todt, leader of the Todt Organization which built the Atlantic Wall defences. He was also Minister of Munitions before his death in an air crash in February 1942.

The invasion of Normandy on 6 June 1944 was the culmination of years of strategic argument and operational preparation by the two Western Allies, Britain and the United States. In 1942, the US Army chief, General Marshall, wanted commitment to a cross-Channel Operation "Roundup" in the spring of 1943 following the build-up of American forces in Britain. British leaders were never enthusiastic about this plan and the decision to invade first North Africa (November 1942) and then Sicily (July 1943) made any major operation in northern Europe impossible. In the spring of 1943, a planning staff was finally established under the British Lieutenant General Frederick

Morgan to prepare for a possible invasion in May 1944. Over the course of 1943 this option hardened into a definite plan to invade on a narrow front in Normandy, but only at the Quebec Conference in August 1943 was the decision to launch what was called Operation "Overlord" finally confirmed. Over the winter of 1943–44 British leaders still harboured doubts and preferred a more peripheral strategy in the Mediterranean to a head-on collision with German forces in France.

The planning and preparation speeded up after Quebec. General Eisenhower was appointed the supreme commander for "Overlord" and General Bernard Montgomery was chosen as the army commander-in-chief in the field. Both men realized that the original plan to attack on a narrow front with a handful of divisions would not work. The eventual plan foresaw an attack on a broader front with five divisions

FIELD MARSHAL GERD VON RUNDSTEDT (1875–1953)

One of the most outstanding German army leaders of the war, von Rundstedt was the overall commander of German forces in the West at the time of the Normandy invasion. He came from a distinguished Prussian military family and was a successful and much-decorated soldier by the time Hitler came to power. He was made a full general in 1938 and commanded Army Group South for the invasion of Poland and Army Group A for the invasion of France. He was created field marshal in July 1940 and became commander-in-chief West until recalled to lead Army Group South in the Barbarossa campaign. He was sacked for retreating from Rostov in December 1941, but reinstated as c-in-c West from March 1942 to July 1944 and again from September 1944 to March 1945. Though a private critic of Hitler's strategy, he was publicly loyal throughout the war. He was arrested at the end of the war and was to be tried for war crimes but ill health led to his early release in 1949.

on five separate beaches, to be followed up with a force of 37 divisions which would break out and defeat the German armies in France. On 1 February, the staff planners agreed on the basis of the tides that 31 May would be D-Day, with an option for 5, 6 or 7 June if the weather proved difficult in May. The problem of supplying the beachhead was solved by the development of artificial harbours or "mulberries" that were to be towed in parts across the Channel and assembled close to the front line. The supply and transportation for D-Day was organized under the naval Operation "Neptune" commanded by the Royal Navy's Admiral Ramsay, who led 7,000 warships, transports and small boats towards the coast of France on the eventual day of the invasion.

To oppose the Allied invasion the German army had constructed a complex web of defences across northern France known as the Atlantic Wall. Command of the German armies in the field was given to Field Marshal Rommel but his view that the best way to repel invasion was on the beaches clashed with his immediate superior, Field Marshal von Rundstedt, who wanted the mobile forces instead held back from the coast to avoid Allied air and naval power but ready to launch an annihilating counter-offensive. Hitler intervened and divided the mobile forces so that neither strategy could work well, with too few mobile divisions on the coast yet too few in reserve. By June 1944, there were 58 divisions spread out over the whole of France. Rommel expected invasion in the Pas-de-Calais in northeastern France and a diversionary attack in Normandy. Hence, by June 1944 there were 14

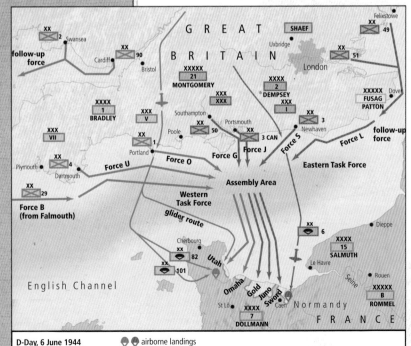

D-Day, 6 June 1944   airborne landings

ABOVE "Sword" Beach on the morning of 6 June 1944. Support troops of the 3rd British Infantry Division gather near La Breche under light artillery attack to prepare to move off the beach inland to secure a perimeter around the beachhead.

ABOVE A panorama of "Omaha" beach on D-Day after it had been secured by units of the US First Army. Tank-carrying landing craft can be seen drawn up on the beach unloading their vehicles directly onto the shore. By evening over 130,000 men had landed on the beaches with generous supplies of equipment

ADMIRAL BERTRAM RAMSAY (1883–1945)

Admiral Ramsay was the naval mastermind behind first the Dunkirk evacuations and then the naval component of the D-Day operations. He joined the Royal Navy in 1898 and served as a lieutenant commander in the Dover Patrol between 1915 and 1918. He retired as a rear admiral in 1938 after disagreements with his immediate superior but was recalled to active duty as flag officer, Dover between August 1939 and 1942. He was deputy naval commander for the "Torch" landings in November 1942, and commander of the Eastern Task Force for the invasion of Sicily before his appointment as Allied naval commander-in-chief for the invasion of France. He was a popular, efficient and tough-minded commander, who achieved remarkable success in organizing the naval back-up for the invasion. He died in an air crash on 2 January 1945.

ABOVE Badge of the Supreme Headquarters Allied Expeditionary Force – SHAEF.

BELOW American forces and trucks on the deck of an LST25 landing craft prepare to assault the beaches between St Laurent and Vierville in the western sector of "Omaha" beach on the morning of D-Day. German resistance here was strong and not until 10.00 a.m. had exits from the beach been secured, at high loss.

divisions in General Dollmann's 7th Army in Normandy, but 20 divisions along the coast around Calais. Thanks to a successful deception plan, planted in German minds by double-agents working in Britain, most German military planners, and Hitler too, expected the main weight of attack across the shortest stretch of Channel towards Calais. When Allied forces finally sailed for Normandy, the German defence was caught almost entirely by surprise.

After months of preparation the date for invasion was fixed in mid-May for 5 June. The United States First Army under Lieutenant General Omar Bradley was to attack two beaches codenamed "Omaha" and "Utah", while the British 2nd Army under Lieutenant General Miles Dempsey attacked "Juno", "Gold" and "Sword" beaches. Poor weather forced postponement until 6 June, but early that morning the huge armada of warships and smaller craft approached the French coast; there then began a ferocious bombardment, first with 2,856 heavy bombers, then with naval gunfire and finally with waves of fighter-bombers. So heavy was the bombardment that in the British sector the fight for the beaches was easily won and by the end of the day a bridgehead several kilometres deep had been captured and defended against limited German counter-attacks. American forces had the same success at "Utah", landing against only light fire and carving out a 10-kilometre (six-mile) bridgehead by the end of the day with only 197 casualties. On "Omaha" beach there was a harder battle, since the initial bombardment had failed to hit the defences effectively and high cliffs made rapid movement difficult. By the end of the day the beach was held, but little more; and with around 2,000 casualties. During the day a total of 132,000 men were landed successfully in Normandy for the overall price of around 10,300 casualties from all causes.

BATTLE FOR NORMANDY

19–20 JUNE 1944
Battle of the Philippine Sea results in heavy losses for the Japanese fleet and naval air power.

3 JULY 1944
Battle of Imphal on the Indian-Burmese border ends in a rout for the Japanese army.

18 JULY 1944
The Japanese prime minister, General Tojo, resigns following Japanese defeat at Saipan.

24 JULY
Soviet forces liberate the German extermination camp at Majdanek in their rapid advance across Belorussia and eastern Poland.

The lodgement in Normandy was secure enough by 7 June to prevent a strategic catastrophe, but the progress of the campaign over the following weeks was very much slower than the original plans for "Overlord" had envisaged. By 11 June, there were 326,000 men ashore supported by 54,000 vehicles; by the middle of the month more than 500,000 men, organized in 19 divisions, had been landed. But even with complete command of the air, Montgomery's forces failed to take the city of Caen, while in the western invasion area Bradley's First US Army finally seized the Cotentin Peninsula and captured the port of Cherbourg after more than three weeks of fighting against comparatively light German resistance.

Montgomery's plan was to force the Germans to concentrate most of their force, including the valuable Panzer divisions, on the front around Caen, so allowing Bradley to break out in the west and swing in a long encirclement behind German armies engaged against the British and Canadians. The operational skills of Rommel's forces combined with the difficult terrain (swampy in places or covered with thick, high hedgerows known as *bocage*) made it difficult for the Allies to bring their advantages to bear. When a fierce gale destroyed one of the floating "mulberry" harbours on 19/20 June, the supply of equipment and men temporarily dried up and Rommel took the opportunity to concentrate his armour

ABOVE (Welsh) 53rd Infantry Division.

ABOVE Cuff-band of the 9th SS Panzer Division.

ABOVE Vehicles drive ashore over the long pontoon bridges of the "mulberry" harbour at Arromanches in August 1944. Before a major port was secured much Allied equipment was shipped through the artificial harbours. The other harbour, at St Laurent, was damaged in a gale in June and could no longer be used, placing even greater strain on Arromanches.

ABOVE Royal Engineers' blue ensign flown from a "mulberry" harbour pierhead off Arromanches, Normandy.

for a counter-offensive around Caen which he launched on 1 July. The attack was repulsed in the heaviest fighting since D-Day, but the failure to secure Caen and speed up the collapse of German resistance led to strained relations between Montgomery and a frustrated Eisenhower, who had expected a quick break-out once the lodgement was sufficiently secure and reinforced.

On 7 July, Montgomery began a major operation of his own to seize Caen and break the German line. Following a massive aerial bombardment, which made progress through the rubble-strewn streets difficult, the town was captured, but Rommel withdrew to a series of five defensive lines constructed to the south, including a concentrated gun line

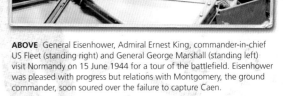

ABOVE General Eisenhower, Admiral Ernest King, commander-in-chief US Fleet (standing right) and General George Marshall (standing left) visit Normandy on 15 June 1944 for a tour of the battlefield. Eisenhower was pleased with progress but relations with Montgomery, the ground commander, soon soured over the failure to capture Caen.

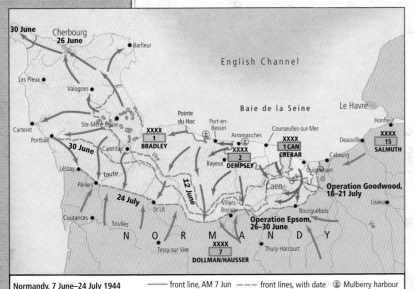

Normandy, 7 June–24 July 1944 — front line, AM 7 Jun --- front lines, with date ⊕ Mulberry harbour

GENERAL OMAR BRADLEY (1893–1981)

Omar Bradley became one of the most distinguished American army commanders during the Second World War. He did not see combat in the First World War but in the interwar years his qualities as an infantry commander brought him promotion to brigadier general by 1941. He was appointed deputy commander of Patton's Second US Corps in North Africa in 1943 and in April took over full command, playing an important role in completing the destruction of Axis forces there. He commanded the Corps in Sicily but then in September 1943 arrived in Britain where, thanks to his growing reputation as a cool-headed commander with considerable tactical flair, he eventually took over First US Army for the Normandy landings. During the campaign in France it was Patton (commander Third Army) who now played deputy to Bradley (commander of Twelfth US Army Group). Bradley commanded US land forces from Normandy to the final defeat of Germany and was promoted to four-star general in March 1945 and, eventually, to general of the army in 1950.

LEFT On 7 July 1944, 467 heavy bombers of the RAF made a devastating attack on the French town of Caen before beginning the operation to capture it from the German 7th Army. Here, on 10 July, a British soldier carries a small girl through the ruins of the city. The rubble made it harder for Allied forces to move through the streets, which were abandoned by the Germans on 9 July.

BELOW British Cromwell tanks assemble in preparation for the opening of Operation "Goodwood" on 18 July 1944. The operation was designed to break through the German line south of Caen but poor weather and stiff German defences forced a halt by 20 July.

GENERAL HENRY CRERAR (1888–1965)

As chief of the Canadian General Staff, Henry Crerar played an important role from 1941 in raising and organizing a large Canadian army for the campaigns in Europe. A career artillery officer who fought through the First World War, Crerar was appointed to command the 2nd Canadian Division and then the 1st Canadian Corps in the Italian campaign. At the end of 1943, he was appointed commander-in-chief of the 1st Canadian Army and led the Canadian component in the invasion of Normandy. Except for a brief period of medical leave, he commanded the Canadian armies for the liberation of France and the invasion of northern Germany. His reputation rested on his administrative and political skills rather than on his battlefield performance, which Montgomery rated poorly. After the war he held a number of diplomatic posts in Czechoslovakia, Japan and the Netherlands.

BELOW American servicemen from the US Seventh Corps pass a dead German soldier in the French port city of Cherbourg in early July 1944. The German garrison put up a stiff resistance until compelled to surrender on 26 June, but some units continued to fight for a further five days until they were overwhelmed by American forces.

of the formidable "tank-busting" 88-millimetre (3.5-inch) anti-aircraft guns along the Bourguebus Ridge. Urged on by Eisenhower, Montgomery then planned a second operation codenamed "Goodwood" to attack the German defensive zone. The operation was scheduled for 18 July; the day before, Rommel was severely injured when his car was strafed by British aircraft and his command was assumed by Field Marshal von Kluge. On 18 July, the attack began with the heaviest air bombardment of the campaign followed by fierce fighting all through the villages on the Bourguebus Ridge. Torrential rain two days later brought the operation to a halt with the German gun line still intact, but the German command had been forced to move two of the armoured divisions facing Bradley in the west to reinforce the eastern contest. This made it possible for the Americans to break out of Normandy a few days later.

Despite their defensive success, German commanders knew that they could not survive the rate of attrition of German forces. Between D-Day and "Goodwood" they had lost 2,117 tanks and 113,000 men and had been sent only 17 tanks and 10,000 men as replacements. Von Kluge wanted to move the front back in an orderly retreat across France, but Hitler insisted that the 7th Army should stand and fight where it was. Allied forces possessed around 4,500 tanks by late July against only 850 German, all but 190 of them facing Montgomery south of Caen. Allied air superiority was overwhelming, around 12,000 aircraft against a total of 1,000 German planes sent to France during June and July, which were shot out of the skies or destroyed at their bases. The defensive circle around the Allies in Normandy was a brittle one by the end of July. Montgomery's strategy had worked sufficiently to create conditions where a final push would produce a German collapse, but it operated too slowly for a supreme commander who wanted quick results. It was Eisenhower's sense of urgency against Montgomery's battlefield prudence that created the postwar myth that the British command failed in Normandy. In reality, the two months of attritional warfare had already broken the back of the German war effort in the West. Within a month almost the whole of France would be in Allied hands.

THE V-WEAPONS CAMPAIGN

8 MARCH 1944
First successful trial launch of the German "Wasserfall" remote-controlled ground-to-air missile at Peenemünde. The anti-aircraft rocket failed to see service.

17 JULY 1944
US forces using Napalm for the first time in attacks on German troops in Normandy.

29 JULY 1944
The Messerschmitt 163B rocket-powered fighter sees combat for the first time.

4 AUGUST 1944
The British Gloster Meteor jet fighter reports first successful shooting-down of V-1 missiles.

BELOW The young German rocket scientist Wernher von Braun in conversation with senior German officers at the rocket research centre in Peenemünde in 1944.

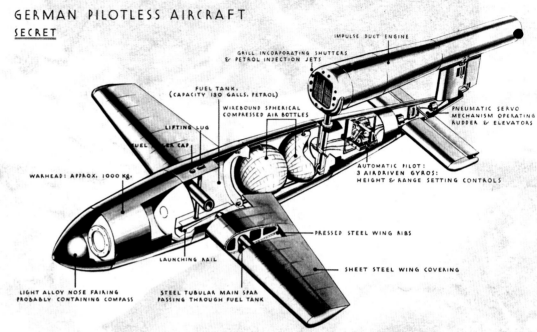

GERMAN PILOTLESS AIRCRAFT
SECRET

IMPULSE DUCT ENGINE

GRILL INCORPORATING SHUTTERS & PETROL INJECTION JETS

FUEL TANK. (CAPACITY 130 GALLS. PETROL)

WIREBOUND SPHERICAL COMPRESSED AIR BOTTLES

LIFTING LUG

FUEL FILLER CAP

PNEUMATIC SERVO MECHANISM OPERATING RUDDER & ELEVATORS

WARHEAD: APPROX. 1000 Kg.

AUTOMATIC PILOT: 3 AIRDRIVEN GYROS: HEIGHT & RANGE SETTING CONTROLS

LAUNCHING RAIL

PRESSED STEEL WING RIBS

SHEET STEEL WING COVERING

LIGHT ALLOY NOSE FAIRING PROBABLY CONTAINING COMPASS

STEEL TUBULAR MAIN SPAR PASSING THROUGH FUEL TANK

Under the impact of heavier Allied bombing attacks in 1942 and 1943, Adolf Hitler searched for some new weapon that could be used to attack British cities and perhaps force the Allies to end their bombing campaign. Two projects appealed particularly to Hitler as weapons of revenge (or Vergeltungswaffen): the first was a pilotless flying bomb, the Fieseler-Fi103, developed by the German air force; the second was the first successful ballistic missile, the A-4 rocket, developed by a team of scientists at the research station set up at Peenemünde on the north German coast. The two weapons were known as the V-1 and V-2, the "V" standing for vengeance (Vergeltung) in German.

The rocket first flew successfully in October 1942 but there were many technical problems to be overcome with the liquid-fuelled engine and the guidance and control systems. In the summer of 1943, Hitler ordered the manufacture of rockets and flying bombs in tens of thousands but technical difficulties in development, combined with British bombing of the research station on the night of 17/18 August 1943, postponed the introduction of V-weapons until the summer and autumn of

1944. The rockets were taken under the control of Heinrich Himmler's SS construction agency which set up a notorious underground facility at Nordhausen known as Mittelbau Dora; thousands of camp prisoners died in its construction and operation. The Fieseler flying-bomb was easier to produce and it came into operation in the summer of 1944 when, on 13 June, the first bombs were launched against London.

British intelligence had already identified the potential threat of new weapons and from December 1943 bomber forces based in Britain were ordered to attack the weapons'

ABOVE LEFT An infra-red image of a German V1 launch site taken with a 30-centimetre (12-inch) lens from 300 metres (1,000 feet) on 2 December 1944. The air campaign against the V-weapons, codenamed "Crossbow", saw 60,000 tons of bombs dropped between June and September 1944, by which time many of the original sites had been overrun.

ABOVE A cut-away drawing of the V-1 weapon, the Fieseler-Fi103 pilotless missile powered by an Argus pulse-jet engine. First tested in December 1942, around 10,000 of the missiles were launched against southern England causing widespread destruction. They had an approximate range of 200 kilometres (125 miles) and a maximum speed of around 670 kilometres (420 miles) per hour.

BELOW A group of V-1 weapons at a launch site somewhere in France. The wings were folded back during transport and the weapon prepared at the launching area before being fired from a small inclined launch ramp.

WERNHER VON BRAUN (1912–77)

Wernher von Braun was the most well-known rocket scientist of his generation. His teenage enthusiasm for rocketry led him to a position with the German army at the age of only 20 when he joined a research team working on ballistic missiles. He became technical director of the Army Ordnance Office in 1937 and continued his research on rocket propulsion at the Peenemünde research station set up on the Baltic coast. He led the team that developed the V-2 rocket (first used in September 1944), and in 1945 surrendered to the Americans, along with a cohort of German rocket scientists, plans and equipment. He was recruited to develop missiles for the US Army, including the Jupiter rocket. In 1960, he was transferred to NASA where he became director of the Space Flight Center and the mastermind behind the Saturn V rocket that took the first men to the moon. He retired in 1972 to work for private industry.

production facilities and launch sites in an operation codenamed "Crossbow". The campaign reached its height during the period June to September 1944, when 60,000 tons of bombs were dropped on V-1 targets. "Crossbow" succeeded in disrupting the V-weapons programme but not in halting it. Over 10,000 flying bombs were directed at London and a number of other British cities, but only 7,488 reached England and of these only 2,419 reached London. The death toll of 6,184 was nevertheless high in proportion to the tonnage of explosive and a more effective flying-bomb campaign might well have provoked a crisis in the capital. From October 1944 the V-1 was also directed at the Belgian port of Antwerp, which was a major supply base for Allied armies.

A high proportion of V-1s were shot down by aircraft or anti-aircraft fire before they reached their target, while misinformation fed from double-agents in Britain led the Germans to believe that their missiles were going too far north. The trajectory was readjusted and as a result many fell short of London on rural areas of the southeast.

Against the A-4 rocket there was less security. The first missile was fired on 8 September 1944. It was by its nature an imprecise weapon and the 517 rockets that hit London did so in no predictable pattern, causing the deaths of a further 2,754 civilians. The rocket was fired from small

BELOW A British policeman comforts a survivor of a V-1 attack near Gipsy Hill in London in 1944. The missile destroyed a street of houses, killing the man's wife and wrecking his house. Almost 9,000 people were killed in the V-weapons campaign.

ABOVE The test launch of a V-2 weapon, the A-4 rocket, from the SS troop training area near Cracow in Poland in 1944. The weapons were large and complex pieces of engineering but carried a warhead of just over 900 kilograms (2,000 pounds) in weight, a fraction of the payload carried by a single Allied bomber. However, the rocket's high speed gave the warhead added impact when it struck the ground.

easily-concealed silos and was difficult to attack from the air. Once in flight only technical malfunction would prevent its arrival at its destination. Of the 6,000 V-2s produced, only 1,054 rockets hit England between 8 September and 27 March 1945; a further 900 were directed at Antwerp in the last months of 1944. Hitler's plan to produce the weapons in tens of thousands was frustrated by the collapse of the German war economy, fatally damaged by the impact of Allied heavy bombing.

As well as the V-1 and V-2, other weapons were developed, but they failed to see service. The V-3 long-range gun, designed to fire special shells a distance of almost 160 kilometres (100 miles), was developed in 1943 and 1944 but had to be abandoned when bombers hit the two designated sites near Calais in November 1943 and July 1944. A further weapon, the so-called V-4, was a ground-to-air missile codenamed *"Wasserfall"* (waterfall) which was close to mass-production in 1944 but lacked the support of Hitler in the struggle for scarce resources. The ground-to-air rocket might well have played a vital role in the war against Allied bombers but the V-1 and V-2 did nothing to dent the combined bomber offensive.

THE MARIANAS: DEFENCE TO THE DEATH

15 JUNE 1944
US B-29 bombers attack the Japanese home island of Kyushu from Chinese bases.

23 JUNE 1944
Red Army begins Operation "Bagration" against Army Group Centre in Belorussia.

1 AUGUST 1944
First Soviet troops carve out a small bridgehead over the River Vistula.

4 AUGUST 1944
German armies pull back from Florence to man the Gothic Line in Italy.

15 AUGUST 1944
Allied Operation "Dragoon" mounted against occupied southern France.

After the island-hopping attacks on the Gilbert and Marshall Islands in the Central Pacific, Admiral Nimitz, commander-in-chief Pacific Ocean Areas, determined to capture the Marianas, a group of islands including Saipan and Guam, which were within air radius of the Japanese home islands for attacks by the new Boeing B-29 heavy bomber. Air attacks began on the island defences in February 1944, and in early June, Vice Admiral Spruance's Fifth Fleet, with a grand total of 530 ships, arrived in the seas off Saipan to undertake a massive bombardment of Lieutenant General Yoshitsugu Saito's Japanese forces, whose estimated 25–30,000 soldiers were dug in to resist the American invasion to the last man.

On 15 June, elements of Lieutenant General Holland Smith's V Amphibious Corps, the Second and Fourth Marine Divisions, attacked the southwestern beaches of Saipan through dangerous reefs and on beaches overlooked by high ground from which Japanese artillery could send a destructive barrage. Saito planned to contain the beachhead and then destroy it, but a steady flow of American reinforcements produced a breakout by day three and the seizure of Aslito airfield. Progress thereafter was slow against suicidal Japanese resistance and an operation planned for three days took three weeks to complete. On the night of 6/7 July the remains of the Japanese garrison in the north of the island undertook the largest *banzai* charge of the war. On 9 July, when the overall US commander Admiral Turner announced that Saipan was officially secured, Japanese soldiers and civilians leapt to their deaths from Marpi Point at the far northern tip of the island. The US forces suffered 3,500 dead but only 2,000 from the 32,000 of Saito's force were taken prisoner.

Two weeks later, on 21 July, Major General Roy Geiger's Third Amphibious Corps began the assault on Guam, an island ceded to the United States by Spain in 1898, which had been occupied by the Japanese navy at the start of the

Pacific War. The island was defended by 5,500 navy troops under Captain Yutaka Sugimoto and 13,000 army soldiers commanded by Lieutenant General Takeshi Takashima. They were dug in to prepared positions in the rugged mountainous district of the island around Mount Alifan. The beach landings on the west coast of Guam were less costly than on Saipan, though difficult to negotiate because of carefully constructed obstacles, but there followed a week of fierce fighting in which Japanese troops engaged in regular *banzai* charges, knowing full well that there was no prospect of reinforcement or fresh supplies. The island was finally secured by 10 August at the cost of a further 1,744 American dead. Only a handful of the Japanese garrison survived, retreating into the jungle areas where the last one surrendered in 1972.

RIGHT Japanese type 94 pistol. 70,000 of these were produced during 1935–45.

ABOVE An American battleship bombards the Japanese-held island of Guam on 20 July 1944, one day before the invasion. The bombardment by ships and aircraft was the heaviest and most co-ordinated of the Pacific War, leaving the Japanese garrison in a stunned state when the first wave of American marines reached the beaches.

BELOW US landing craft on the approach to the beaches on the west coast of Guam, 21 July 1944. The Third Marine Division and the Provisional Marine Brigade landed in two separate areas strongly supported by the ships and aircraft of Task Force 58. A destroyer can be seen in the distance.

LIEUTENANT GENERAL HOLLAND "HOWLIN' MAD" SMITH (1882–1967)

Holland Smith is generally regarded as the father of United States amphibious warfare. He joined the marines in 1905 and saw service in the Philippines (where he won the nickname "Howlin' Mad") and later in the First World War in France in 1917–18. He remained a marine officer after the war and by 1937 was in charge of operations and training at Marine Corps headquarters. In 1941, he became the first commander of the US 1st Marine Division and in June that year was chosen to train the first dedicated amphibious warfare divisions. In August 1942, he took command of the Amphibious Corps, Pacific Fleet, which became the V Amphibious Corps for the operations against the Gilbert and Mariana islands. He commanded the expeditionary troops for the invasion of Iwo Jima before returning to the United States in July 1945 to take over the Marine Training and Replacement Camp. He retired in May 1946 and died after a long illness in 1967.

KA·17·12

While Guam was under attack, a further American assault was made on the smaller island of Tinian, five kilometres (three miles) south of Saipan, by 15,000 men of the 4th Marine Division. The island was secured by 1 August, by which time American engineers (the famous Construction Battalions or "See-Bees") had already begun to construct the first B-29 airfields. The battles for all three islands had been very costly to both sides, but Japanese resistance in defence of the outer perimeter of the home island area was now almost entirely suicidal. The fall of Saipan was greeted with dismay in Tokyo and the Japanese prime minister, General Hideki Tojo, was forced to resign from all his military and administrative positions, to be succeeded by Lieutenant General Kuniaki Koiso. The fierce defence of the Marianas made it clear that even if the defeat of Japan was now inevitable, the invasion of the heart of the Japanese Empire was likely to exact a heavy, perhaps insupportable toll on the American forces involved.

LIEUTENANT GENERAL YOSHITSUGU SAITO (1890–1944)

A career cavalryman who saw his first service as a very young soldier in the last stage of the Russo-Japanese war of 1904–5, Saito rose to the rank of major general in the Kwantung Army in China as chief of cavalry operations. In April 1944, he was appointed to command the Japanese Army's 43rd Division which was moving to Saipan. He became overall commander of the island's forces and organized the final *banzai* charge against the US forces on 7 July, determined that everyone should die rather than surrender an island so close to the Japanese homeland. On 10 July, he committed hara-kiri and was given a final bullet by his adjutant.

ABOVE During the invasion of Saipan the defending forces of the Japanese 31st Army dug in to well-prepared positions, using the rough landscape to best advantage. Here marines can be seen throwing grenades into a cave on a rocky outcrop on the coast of the island. Over 30,000 Japanese died in the defence of Saipan.

BELOW US marines and tanks advance against the Japanese 31st Army across one of the few level areas of Saipan. General Saito withdrew into the high mountains in the centre of the island and three weeks were needed to finally dislodge him.

ABOVE A Japanese type 97 hand grenade. They were filled with TNT, with a time-delayed fuse of four or five seconds.

BELOW A tiny Japanese baby is carried down a mountainside on Saipan to a waiting ambulance jeep by a US marine. The baby was the only survivor found in an area of Saipan where Japanese resistance was being cleared. Many Japanese civilians committed suicide rather than fall into American hands.

BATTLE OF THE PHILIPPINE SEA

11 JUNE 1944
Task Force 58 begins bombardment of the Marianas.

15 JUNE 1944
US marines land on Saipan.

18 JUNE 1944
US 7th Corps reach west coast of France at Barneville, cutting off the Cotentin Peninsula.

20 JUNE 1944
Vyborg recaptured by the Red Army in the campaign against Finland.

26 JUNE 1944
launch of Operation "Epsom" in Normandy in unsuccessful attempt to outflank Caen.

ABOVE Shoulder title for a warrant officer in the Japanese navy.

Once it became clear that the United States was about to attack the Marianas, the Japanese navy launched Operation "A-Go", a further attempt to bring a large part of the US Pacific Fleet to battle and at the same time prevent the fall of Saipan and Guam. Two large Japanese task forces, Vice Admiral Ozawa's 1st Mobile Fleet and Vice Admiral Matome Ugaki's Southern Force, were to rendezvous in the Philippine Sea before moving to engage the US Task Force 58 commanded by Vice Admiral Marc Mitscher. Ozawa hoped that the prevailing trade winds would make it difficult for Mitscher's carrier aircraft to engage over long distances, while he could rely not only on his 473 aircraft and on nine aircraft carriers, but also on shore-based aircraft in the Marianas.

On 19 June, the stage was set for the largest carrier battle of the war. Ozawa had nine carriers, five battleships, 13 cruisers and 28 destroyers against Mitscher's 15 carriers and light carriers, seven battleships, 21 cruisers and 69 destroyers. The task for Admiral Spruance, in overall command of US forces, was more difficult because it was also essential to protect the difficult invasion of Saipan, which had begun on 15 June, but he had the advantage that intelligence sources had already identified the "A-Go" operation and reported the probable position of the Japanese fleets. Rather than seek combat, he and Mitscher waited for the Japanese to find them, confident that the much larger number of American aircraft, over 900 in total, would defend the fleet against attack. Even before the opening

VICE-ADMIRAL JISABURO OZAWA (1886–1966)

Jisaburo Ozawa was one of the Japanese navy's most experienced commanders and played a central part in the naval operations of the Pacific War. He was remarkably tall at two metres (6 feet 7 inches), and was later nicknamed "Gargoyle" by his men on account of his poor looks. He graduated as an officer cadet in 1909 and by 1919 commanded a destroyer. In the 1930s, he became a senior staff officer, serving as chief-of-staff of the Combined Fleet in 1937. Promoted to vice admiral in 1940, he became commander-in-chief of the Southern Expeditionary Fleet for the invasion of Malaya and the Dutch East Indies. In November 1942, he took over the 3rd Fleet and became commander of carrier forces and it was in this role that he suffered defeat in the Battle of the Philippine Sea. He tried to resign after the defeat but remained in post for the Battle of Leyte Gulf. On 29 May 1945, he became commander-in-chief of the Imperial Japanese Navy and, unlike many of his colleagues, did not commit suicide at the surrender, but survived to help with the demobilization of the navy.

BOTTOM LEFT The skyline is filled with anti-aircraft fire from the US fleet under attack from Japanese torpedo bombers on 19 June 1944 during the Battle of the Philippine Sea. The picture was taken from the deck of the USS *Alabama*.

BELOW A Curtiss Helldiver SB2C dive-bomber warms up on the deck of a carrier in Task Force 58, the carrier fleet assigned to support the island-hopping campaign in the Marianas in June 1944. Brought into service in 1943, the Helldiver had a radius of 1,440 kilometres (895 miles) and a top speed of 475 kilometres (295 miles) per hour.

of attacks. Another Japanese carrier was sunk and two badly damaged. Around 100 aircraft were lost during the battle, in the sea or in crashes on the carrier decks. But Ozawa was left with only 35 serviceable aircraft out of the 473 with which he had begun the battle.

The battle was a major victory for the US Pacific Fleet and it left the Japanese navy in a state from which it never effectively recovered. Ozawa was ordered on 20 June to disengage, having failed to sink a single American vessel or to prevent the final conquest of Saipan. His battered fleet retired to Okinawa, arriving on 22 June. Mitscher ordered further attacks on Japanese shore-based aircraft, over 200 of which were destroyed during the course of the naval battle. The gap that opened up between US and Japanese capability in the air spelt the end of any prospect that the heavy units of the Japanese fleet could engage and destroy the warships of the enemy. The Battle of the Philippine Sea, like the Battle of Midway in June 1942, was fought without a single engagement between surface vessels.

engagement, 17 out of 25 Japanese submarines were sunk, while land-based aircraft were destroyed on Saipan and Guam by heavy air attacks. When Ozawa's aircraft found Mitscher's fleet early in the morning of the 19 June, the Japanese plan was already compromised.

What followed went down in American airpower history as the "Great Marianas Turkey Shoot". Superior US aircraft, with radar and effective radio interception, destroyed the attackers at will. Japanese losses numbered 243 out of the 373 committed, while American losses were only 30. There then followed a further air battle over Guam which cost another 50 Japanese planes. During the battle, US submarines sank Ozawa's flagship carrier *Taiho* and the carrier *Shokaku*, both of which were lost in the mid-afternoon. On the following day, Ozawa was unclear about the extent of his losses, but sailed away from the US fleet hoping to re-engage. US aircraft found his ships early in the evening of 20 June and, although at the end of their range and with risk that the aircraft would have to be recovered to the carriers at night, Mitscher ordered a wave

LEFT The war ensign of the Japanese navy.

US SUBMARINE *ALBACORE*

The American submarine *Albacore* was a Gato class vessel laid down by the Electric Boat Company in April 1941 and launched in February 1942. The submarine played a part in much of the Pacific campaign, hunting for merchant vessels and warships. She sank her first naval vessel in December 1942, and on 19 June 1944 had the distinction of damaging the flagship of Vice Admiral Ozawa, the aircraft carrier *Taiho*, forcing him to transfer command to a destroyer and disrupting Japanese communications at a critical moment in the Battle of the Philippine Sea. The carrier blew up and sank a few hours later. The submarine sank four more vessels in 1944 before hitting a mine in Japanese home waters on 7 November 1944 with the loss of all the crew.

ABOVE FAR LEFT A photograph taken from the deck of USS *Birmingham* of a flight of 23 carrier-based fighters from US Task Force 58 during the Battle of the Philippine Sea on 20 June 1944. The aircraft are preparing to intercept Japanese dive-bombers and torpedo bombers attacking the US fleet west of the island of Guam. In the "Great Marianas Turkey Shoot" the Japanese lost 65 per cent of the air forces committed.

ABOVE CENTRAL The commander of Task Force 58, Vice Admiral Marc Mitscher, aboard his flagship, the aircraft carrier USS *Lexington*, on 19 June 1944, the first day of the battle which proved to be the largest carrier battle of the war.

ABOVE A Grumman Avenger pilot, Roland "Rip" Gift, has a drink in the ready room of USS *Monterey* after a successful night landing on the carrier, 20 June 1944. Around 100 aircraft were lost trying to get back to the US carriers at nightfall.

OPERATION "BAGRATION"

On the Eastern Front the success of the operations in the Ukraine in 1943 and early 1944 had left a large German salient, held by Army Group Centre under Field Marshal Busch, around the Belorussian capital of Minsk. Here was to be found the largest concentration of German forces, and it was the defeat of Army Group Centre that became the Soviet priority for the summer of 1944.

The plans were drawn up in great secrecy between March and May and with Stalin's agreement a series of five rolling offensives were planned: from the north of the front against Finland, designed as a feint to mislead the Germans; followed by two offensives towards Minsk by the 1st and the newly-created 2nd and 3rd Belorussian army groups; and then a heavy attack by Marshal Ivan Konev's 1st Ukrainian Army Group towards the Polish city of Lvov; and finally a blow in the far south towards the Romanian oilfields. In order to mislead the Germans, who expected a continuation of the attacks in the south, a whole deception operation was mounted with dummy tanks and bases and a simulated air defence system on the southern Ukrainian part of the front. The head of German intelligence in the East, General Gehlen, told Army Group Centre to expect "a calm summer". As a result of the deception, Busch found many of his tanks and much of his artillery transferred north or south against the anticipated summer offensives.

Stalin knew the summer offensive – which he codenamed "Bagration" after a fellow-Georgian and hero of the war against Napoleon – would coincide with the Allied invasion in the West, which was expected to contribute to German problems of reinforcement and priority. The date for the main assault was fixed for 19–20 June, but problems of

ABOVE A scene in Minsk, Belorussia, after its liberation on 3 July 1944. Houses in the background have been set on fire by the retreating German forces.

RIGHT A group of Russian partisans crossing a river in western Belorussia in 1944. By the time of Operation "Bagration" the guerrilla movement had more than 200,000 fighters, interrupting German communications and supplies in accordance with instructions from Moscow.

FIELD MARSHAL ERNST BUSCH (1885–1945)

Busch joined the Prussian Army in 1904 and served with distinction during the First World War. He remained in the army after the war and was made inspector of transport troops in 1925. He led the German 16th Army during the invasion of France and in the invasion of the Soviet Union in 1941, where his defence against Soviet counter-attacks around Leningrad earned him the rank of field marshal. He commanded Army Group Centre in 1943 and 1944, but after failure to stem Operation "Bagration", he was sacked by Hitler in June. He was recalled to command Army Group Northwest in March 1945 to try to stem the British attack in northern Germany, and surrendered to Montgomery on 4 May 1945. He died in a British POW camp at Aldershot in July 1945.

tank supply held up the launch until the anniversary of the German attack, 22 June. The first offensive against the Finns began on 10 June to distract the German defence. Then on the night of 19/20 June, partisans began the systematic destruction of transport targets, and two days later the Soviet air force launched a fierce bombardment of German positions and air bases in Belorussia. On 22 June, the full assault was launched with 2.4 million men, 31,000 guns, 5,200 tanks and self-propelled guns and 5,300 aircraft against the 1.2 million men, 9,500 guns, 900 tanks and 1,350 aircraft along the German central and northern front.

The element of surprise unhinged the German front. The attacks towards Minsk were spearheaded by special plough tanks to move the minefields, with infantry and tanks behind them, and searchlights used to dazzle the German defenders. On 24 June, Marshal Rokossovsky's 1st Belorussian Army Group, concealed at the edge of the Pripet Marshes, began a movement to encircle German forces from the south. In a week the German front collapsed, and the German 4th and 9th Armies and the 1st Panzer Army had been almost annihilated. On 28 June, Busch was replaced by Field Marshal Walter Model, regarded by Hitler as a trouble-shooting leader, but although he organized a more stable fighting retreat, by 4 July Minsk was captured and small pockets of German resistance, bypassed by the mobile Red Army, were subdued. The

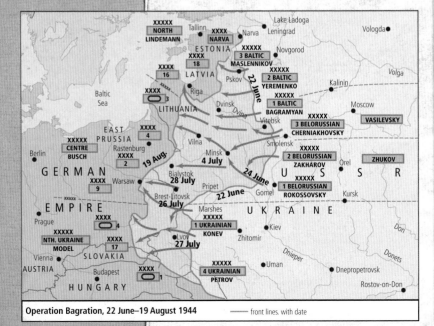

Operation Bagration, 22 June–19 August 1944 ——— front lines, with date

MARSHAL KONSTANTIN ROKOSSOVSKY (1896-1968)

Widely regarded as the best of the Red Army marshals during the Second World War, Rokossovsky led an adventurous and dangerous life. Born to Polish parents in the Russian-controlled area of Poland, he served in one of the premier Tsarist dragoon regiments during the First World War, first as a private, but ending the war as a commander. He joined the Red Army in 1917 and led a cavalry squadron in the Civil War, during which he was twice wounded. He became a cavalry commander in the 1920s and 1930s, rising to the rank of colonel before, as part of the purging of the Red Army, he was arrested in August 1937 on charges of sabotage and spying. Despite torture, he refused to be broken and was given only a three-year sentence. In March 1940, he was rehabilitated into the army. By June, he was a major general in command of the 5th Cavalry Corps and in October 1940 the newly-formed 9th Mechanized Corps, which fought against the German invasion in the Ukraine. Rokossovsky played a key role in the defence of Moscow and later of Stalingrad. At Kursk, he was responsible for organizing the deep defensive system around the salient. He led the 1st Belorussian Front against Army Group Centre in summer 1944 and the 2nd Belorussian Front against East Prussia in 1945. He was appointed commander-in-chief of Soviet troops in Poland from 1945 until 1949, when he was appointed Polish defence minister and made a Polish national. In 1956, he was brought back to the Soviet Union, where he held a number of senior posts before retiring in 1962.

contrast with the slow progress of Western forces in Normandy was complete.

Over the following weeks the rolling offensives continued. The 1st Belorussian Army Group moved towards Warsaw, while the 2nd and 3rd Belorussian army groups moved north towards the Baltic states and East Prussia. Further south, unable now to mount an effective defence, German armies fell back before Konev's 1st Ukrainian Army Group. Brest-Litovsk fell on 26 July, Lvov a day later. By 29 August, after two months of gruelling fighting, the Red Army had cleared the Germans from Belorussia, southern Poland and

part of the Baltic states, capturing over 200,000 German soldiers and destroying Army Group Centre. Soviet losses – dead, missing and POWs – amounted to 179,000, but German losses between June and August in the east amounted to a remarkable 589,000. On 17 July, captured Germans, including no fewer than 19 generals, were paraded through Moscow. "Bagration" was the largest defeat ever inflicted on German armed forces.

ABOVE A moment's relaxation for Red Army men and women as they fought their way across Belorussia in the summer of 1944. By the end of the war there were 246,000 women in the Soviet armed forces, though few concessions were made to them by their male colleagues.

BELOW A group of Red Army infantry, part of the 2nd Belorussian Army Group, leap out of a trench in the operations in Belorussia in August 1944 in pursuit of the retreating German Army Group Centre.

ABOVE Captured German soldiers are marched from the Belorussian station in Moscow through the streets of the capital after the conquest of Belorussia in July 1944. They were sent on to POW camps and Stalin ordered the streets they had marched along to be disinfected afterwards.

DEFEAT OF THE LUFTWAFFE

14 OCTOBER 1943
US Eighth Air Force attacks Schweinfurt ball-bearing factories, losing 60 out of 291 aircraft.

NOVEMBER 1943
P-51 Mustang long-range fighters begin flying with Eighth Air Force bombers.

1 JANUARY 1944
US Strategic Air Forces in Europe formed under command of General Spaatz.

20 FEBRUARY 1944
Start of "Big Week" attacks on German aircraft industry.

24 MARCH 1944
Last RAF attack in the "Battle of Berlin" launched the previous November.

26 JULY 1944
First kill by a Messerschmitt Me 262 jet fighter.

At the start of the Second World War, the German air force was second in size only to the Soviet air force, and was the most advanced in terms of the quality of equipment and the training of its pilots. The air force played an important part in securing the rapid victories in 1939–41, and, though smaller in size, it destroyed the Soviet air force on the ground and in the air during the opening stages of "Barbarossa". By 1944, however, the force faced serious crisis and during the course of the year was effectively defeated, contributing to the collapse of German resistance on all fronts in the last year of the war.

The major problem facing the German air force was the impact of the Combined Bomber Offensive, launched by the British and US bomber forces from the spring of 1943. The bombing by day and by night forced the German air force to keep more and more of its fighter aircraft in Germany to defend the home economy and population, and to distort German aircraft production in favour of fighters rather than bombers and dive-bombers. In January 1943, 59 per cent of the fighter force was in the Reich, by January 1944 68 per cent, and by September 1944 some 80 per cent. By 1944 bomber output, so essential for the support of the front-line campaigns, constituted only one-fifth of German aircraft

ABOVE A squadron of German Messerschmitt Bf 110 night-fighters flying over Germany in the summer of 1944. Because of its heavy armament of guns and rockets the Bf 110 could inflict heavy damage on Allied bombers. By day they were easy prey for the long-range Allied fighters.

LEFT The Messerschmitt Me 262 jet-fighter prototype on trial in 1943. The aircraft would have been the fastest fighter aircraft in service but Hitler insisted on converting it to a fighter-bomber role, delaying its introduction until well into 1944. Before mass-production could begin the German war economy was brought to collapse.

production, as compared to over half at the start of the war. The decline in the numbers of aircraft at the fighting fronts meant a high level of attrition against more heavily armed opponents. On D-Day, only 170 German aircraft were available in northwest France against the 12,000 aircraft of the Western Allies. Air superiority passed to the Allies in France, in Italy and on the Eastern Front.

Bombing also disrupted the production of aircraft, aero-engines and components. Germany was outproduced in aircraft by each of its major adversaries over the course of the war. In 1944, against the 39,807 aircraft produced in Germany and the satellite territories, the Allies produced 163,079. In 1944, the Combined Bomber Offensive was directed at German aircraft output and oil production in order to undermine the efforts still being made to combat

GENERAL JAMES DOOLITTLE (1896–1993)

General Doolittle earned fame in the Second World War for leading a daring raid on Japanese cities in April 1942 in carrier-borne aircraft, but he was also a senior commander who played a major role in the Combined Bomber Offensive. He had an unusual prewar career, achieving a doctorate in aeronautical science in 1925 while a serving officer, winning all three major international air-speed trophies and then retiring his commission to work for the oil industry, where he pioneered the development of high-quality aviation fuel. In January 1942, he was called back to service, was promoted to lieutenant colonel and volunteered to lead the raid on Japan, his first and only combat mission. He was immediately promoted to brigadier general and in September 1942 took command of the Twelfth Air Force in North Africa, and then in November 1943 leadership of the Fifteenth Air Force in Italy. From January 1944 to September 1945, he commanded the Eighth Air Force in England for bombing raids over Europe, where he inaugurated the strategy of allowing escorting fighters to attack the enemy air force at will. After the war, he became a director of Shell Oil and special advisor to the US Air Force chief-of-staff until he retired in 1959.

Allied bombing. For six days, starting on 20 February, bomber forces launched Operation "Argument", better known as "Big Week", against the German aircraft industry. Altogether RAF Bomber Command and the US Eighth Air Force dropped 20,000 tons of bombs on air production targets. This did not destroy production, but forced an improvised dispersal and held back the expansion of German output. More damaging was the attack on oil installations during 1944, which reduced the supply of oil by September to 31 per cent of what it had been in January, while the output of aviation fuel was temporarily reduced to just five per cent of requirements. The lack of oil made it difficult to train pilots, and contributed to the high loss rates of German aviators during 1944.

The most important factor was the Anglo-American development, late in 1943, of an effective long-range fighter to contest German air space. The P-51 Mustang fighter began as a design produced for the British using a Rolls Royce Merlin engine, but even loaded with extra fuel tanks, its fighting capacity was little impaired. It was chosen to accompany Eighth Air Force bombers and in December 1943 made its first fighting appearance over the German port of Kiel. In March 1944, Mustangs flew 2,900 kilometres (1,800 miles) to Berlin and back.

ABOVE A US Consolidated Liberator B-24 bomber after bombing a German airfield near St Dizier in occupied France in June 1944. Allied air power was directed at German air bases, supply depots and factories, making it difficult for the Luftwaffe to regain the initiative.

GENERAL ADOLF GALLAND (1912–1996)

Adolf Galland became one of Germany's best-known fighter aces, with 104 "kills" credited to him during the war. He was a keen student of aviation in the 1920s and in 1933 was taken into the German armed forces, secretly trained and in 1935 became a pilot in Fighter Squadron 2 "Richthofen". An injury in October that year almost cost him his career, but he flew again with the Kondor Legion in the Spanish Civil War. He recorded his first kills in May 1940 during the invasion of France and fought as commander of 3rd Fighter Group in the Battle of Britain. In November 1941, he became a major general, at 30 years old the youngest general in the German armed forces, designated as "general of fighters". He became increasingly critical of Hermann Göring, commander-in-chief of the German air force, and in January 1945 he was sacked. Hitler employed him to lead an elite formation of pilots armed with the new Me 262 jet fighter. After the war he was imprisoned for two years and on his release became an advisor for the Argentine air force and later an industrial director in Germany. He became a leading spokesman for the fighter veterans he had commanded during the war.

A crash production programme was pushed through and during the spring and summer of 1944 the Mustang, together with other fighters converted to operate at long-range, contested German air space for the first time. The attrition rate for the German fighter force increased sharply, from around 20 per cent losses per month late in 1943 to more than 50 per cent every month in the spring and summer of 1944. Although German production rose to more than 3,000 fighters a month, they were destroyed piecemeal at the factories, at their bases or in the air, flown by pilots who had been trained for much of the time on simulators for lack of fuel. During 1944, the RAF resumed occasional daylight bombing because the risk from German fighters was so reduced. Not even the development of the first jet fighter, the Messerschmitt Me 262, could reverse the outcome, because far too few were available. The massive bombing attacks of the last year of war on the German homeland were made possible by the neutralization of the Luftwaffe.

ABOVE LEFT Long-range fuel tanks being fitted on an RAF Hawker Typhoon Mark 1B fighter-bomber to enable it to carry out strikes on distant targets in Germany. The introduction of extra fuel capacity transformed the air war over Germany in a matter of months.

ABOVE A still from a film shot from an RAF Avro Lancaster bomber on 25 July 1944 of an attack on a German airfield and depot at St Cyr, outside Paris, carried out by aircraft of No. 5 Group, Bomber Command. The large bomb is a 1,800-kilogram (4,000-pound) high-capacity bomb, and beneath it a 230-kilogram (500-pound) medium-capacity bomb is just visible.

STALEMATE IN ITALY

When the US Fifth Army entered Rome on 4 June 1944
there was hope that the campaign in Italy might now
be decided by the autumn. German forces under
Field Marshal Kesselring, together with a small number of
Italian Fascist forces still loyal to Mussolini, pulled rapidly
northwards, towards other prepared lines of defence. What
followed was a long and gruelling campaign that did not
see Allied victory until the very end of the war in Europe, in
May 1945.

The decision to divert forces to Rome opened up a gap
between American and British armies and allowed the
German army to extricate itself from a potential trap. No
real effort was made to pursue the retreating enemy, and
Kesselring was able to draw his forces north to the Arno
Line running through Pisa and Florence to the Adriatic coast.
Behind this line was the more heavily defended Gothic Line,
running from just south of La Spezia through the Apennine
Mountains to the coast at Pesaro. Allied forces in Italy under
General Alexander followed the Germans to the Arno
river, all but one of whose bridges had been blown up, but
Kesselring declined to fight for the Arno Line. Livorno was
captured on 19 July, Florence on 13 August. By mid-August,
both the British 8th Army and the US Fifth Army were
approaching the Gothic Line.

The 8th Army commander, Lieutenant General Oliver
Leese, persuaded Alexander to allow him to launch
Operation "Olive" to break the Gothic Line along the
Adriatic coast where it was thought that armour could
deploy more easily. The loss of six divisions for the

ABOVE A photograph of a British soldier, "Gunner Smith", taken from
a guidebook to Rome produced in June 1944 by the British Fine Arts
Sub-Commission for troops in Italy granted leave from the front. In the
background is the Colosseum.

FIELD MARSHAL HENRY MAITLAND WILSON (1881–1964)

Maitland Wilson, better known
as "Jumbo" Wilson on account
of his size, had a long army
career spanning the Boer War
to the early years of the Cold
War. He joined the army in 1900
and was already a major in 1914
when war broke out. He served
briefly on the northwest frontier
between India and Afghanistan in the interwar years, and in
June 1939 became commander-in-chief of the British army in
Egypt. He commanded British forces in Greece in 1941, and
then commanded the successful Iraq-Syria campaign. In 1943,
he was appointed commander-in-chief in the Middle East,
and in January 1944 succeeded Eisenhower as supreme Allied
commander in the Mediterranean, in overall command of
the war in Italy. In December 1944, he was promoted to field
marshal and sent to Washington as chief of the British Joint
Staff Mission, retiring from the post in 1947. In retirement he
was appointed constable of the Tower of London.

BELOW American troops of the US Fifth Army make their way along a
muddy track in the Apennine Mountains during the autumn battles along
the Gothic Line in 1944. Mules were widely used in the Italian campaign
to bring supplies and men across otherwise impassable mountain terrain.

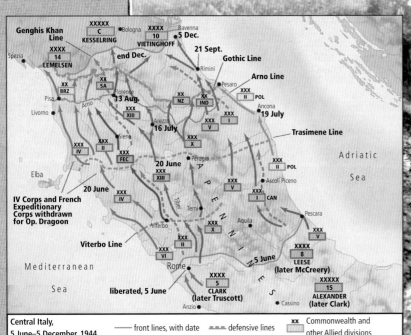

Central Italy,
5 June–5 December. 1944

— front lines, with date ▪▪▪ defensive lines ☒☒ Commonwealth and other Allied divisions

ABOVE An Italian partisan poses for the camera in the Tuscan city of Florence on 14 August 1944. Partisan units occupied the Di Basso fortress and fought against German snipers left in the city as the Axis army vacated it. Allied forces had been told to avoid fighting in the city itself to preserve its architectural heritage.

LEFT Higher formation badge for the headquarters of the 15th Army and headquarters Allied Armies Italy (AAI).

invasion of southern France forced a temporary halt in preparations. The 8th Army attacked on 25 August and, despite the difficulty of crossing the rivers along the coast, was by 4 September fighting for the coastal town of Rimini, which fell on 21 September. Kesselring moved his reserves to blunt the British attack and against the now weakened centre the US Second Corps attacked towards Bologna, breaching the Gothic Line again. German reserves were moved again and poor weather together with determined German defence halted General Clark's attack only 14 kilometres (nine miles) from Bologna, while the 8th Army, facing heavy rain and poor terrain, moved slowly towards Ravenna, which was reached in December.

The German 10th and 14th armies held what was now called the Genghis Khan Line from Bologna to Argenta on the east coast. The Allied attack faltered and in an exceptionally bad winter a stalemate descended over the front. For the Germans and their remaining Italian Fascist allies this was the opportunity to deal with the threat posed by an estimated 82,000 Italian partisans in the German-occupied north who had already embarked on a major confrontation with the German army as the Allies moved north. Around six of the 26 German divisions were forced to combat the Italian resistance. In northwestern Italy the Alpine passes had been freed from Axis control and small areas of partisan rule established.

The end of the Allied advance allowed the Germans to turn their full attention against the partisans, even more so when Alexander had it broadcast on the radio on

13 November that the Allies would stay where they were for the winter, advising the partisans to stop fighting and await further orders. The result was disastrous. The Voluntary Freedom Corps under General Raffaele Cadorna, which co-ordinated partisan operations, found itself subject to large sweeping operations by German forces and two Cossack cavalry divisions fighting for the Axis. The anti-partisan campaign was conducted with extraordinary brutality against the civil population, and much of the area controlled by the partisans was seized back again. By the end of the campaign the resistance was down to around 20,000 men and women, reviving again only later in 1945 when the Allied advance began once again. Around 40,000 partisans perished in the fighting.

TOP Italian civilians pick their way through the rubble of the Ponte all Grazie over the Arno river in Florence in August 1944, returning to the northern part of the city after the German evacuation on 11 August. The only bridge not destroyed was the Ponte Vecchio.

ABOVE American gunners from the US Fifth Army load a massive 240-millimetre (9.5-inch) Howitzer near Bologna on 26 October 1944. Efforts to reach the city and break through the German line ended on 20 October and a stalemate ensued between the two sides as the front line consolidated.

THE SALÒ REPUBLIC

After Mussolini was overthrown and imprisoned in July 1943 Hitler authorized a dramatic rescue bid, organized by Otto Skorzeny, in September 1943. Mussolini moved into German-occupied northern Italy and set up the Italian Social Republic (RSI) with its base at Salò on the shores of Lake Garda. The new regime rallied remnants of the Fascist movement as well as young nationalists reluctant to abandon Italy to the Allies. In reality, the new state was dominated by German interests: Italian industry worked for the Germans, Italian workers were shipped to the Reich and four divisions raised from the local Italian population were trained in Germany and fought alongside the German army.

LEFT Benito Mussolini, head of the Italian Social Republic set up in 1943, at his regime's headquarters on the shores of Lake Garda in northern Italy, in conversation with the commander-in-chief of Fascist forces, Marshal Rodolfo Graziani.

JULY PLOT: THE COUP THAT FAILED

8 NOVEMBER 1939
Bomb placed by Georg Elser in the Munich beer hall where the Hitler *Putsch* was annually commemorated explodes 13 minutes after Hitler's unexpectedly premature departure.

13 MARCH 1943
Bomb smuggled onto Hitler's plane by resisters in the German army fails to explode.

15 JULY 1944
Stauffenberg takes bomb into Hitler's headquarters but has no opportunity to detonate it.

24 JULY 1944
"*Heil* Hitler" salute introduced into the German armed forces.

14 OCTOBER 1944
Field Marshal Rommel commits suicide after he is implicated in the July Plot.

BELOW Badge awarded to those injured during the assassination attempt on Hitler.

ABOVE On the day of the assassination attempt Hitler's Italian ally Benito Mussolini was due to make a visit to headquarters. He arrived and was shown the wreckage of the room where Hitler had been standing some hours before.

BELOW Hitler gives a radio broadcast from the bunker in his "Wolf's Lair" headquarters shortly after the failed assassination attempt on 20 July 1944. He was bruised and shaken but suffered no serious injury.

COLONEL CLAUS SCHENK GRAF VON STAUFFENBERG (1907–1944)

Claus von Stauffenberg was the most important figure among the army plotters in 1944 in the plans to assassinate Hitler. The son of south German aristocrats, he joined a cavalry regiment in 1926, and later became an officer in the 6th Panzer Division in France. He fought on the Eastern Front and in 1943 was sent to be first general staff officer to the 10th Panzer Division in

ABOVE Stauffenberg in 1934 on his horse Schwabenherzog during a cavalry regiment parade.

Tunisia. Here he was wounded by a British aircraft, losing his left eye, right hand and the fourth and fifth fingers of his other hand. After recovering, he was posted to the staff of the Home Army, from which he had ample opportunity to see Hitler on a regular basis. He was a German patriot, keen that Germany should not be occupied or lose territory after the war but he feared Hitler would destroy Germany entirely, which was why he decided to kill him. He returned to Berlin after the bomb exploded at Hitler's headquarters, but was arrested that evening, summarily tried and executed at 1.00 a.m. on 21 July 1944. His last words were "Long live our holy Germany!"

H itler was in the unusual position among the leaders of the combatant powers during the war as the only one whose own army leaders regularly plotted to assassinate him. As early as 1938 a group of senior generals, including the then chief-of-staff of the army, Ludwig Beck, planned to overthrow Hitler rather than risk war over the Czech crisis. The Munich settlement ended this plan, but in 1939 it was revived, only to collapse again because of the evident popularity of the regime. During the invasion of the Soviet Union, a group of conspirators, unwilling to let Hitler destroy Germany or compromise the reputation of the army, began to explore the possibility of killing their supreme commander and seizing control of the German state.

This proved far more difficult to do than might have been expected. Hitler had elaborate security but some of the plotters had regular and close access to him. In March 1943, General Henning von Tresckow, one of the leading conspirators, placed a time bomb on Hitler's aircraft using British plastic explosive and a fuse picked up from Allied parachute drops to the resistance, but the bomb failed to explode. Another plan to blow Hitler up with a suicide bomber at a review of new uniforms was abandoned after Hitler failed to appear. In July 1944, frustrated by the failure to act, the young Colonel von Stauffenberg, badly injured

in 1943 during the Tunisian campaign, volunteered to take a time bomb to Hitler's daily briefing conference at the "Wolf's Lair" headquarters in Rastenburg in East Prussia. Twice during July he arrived with the bomb in his briefcase, but Hitler left early on one occasion and on the other Himmler and Göring, also targets of the assassins, were not present.

Finally, on 20 July 1944, Stauffenberg determined to do the deed. The whole operation was codenamed "Valkyrie", borrowed from an earlier security plan in the event of a domestic political upheaval, but now to be used to secure army control of Germany after Hitler's death. As soon as news arrived that Hitler was dead, army units in Berlin and other centres were to take over key buildings and arrest leading party members. Stauffenberg arrived, primed one of two bombs in his briefcase, and in the meeting room pushed the case as close to Hitler as possible. After a few minutes, Stauffenberg left on the pretext that he needed to make a telephone call, and he and his adjutant watched the explosion. Convinced that Hitler must be dead, Stauffenberg bluffed his way out of the compound, flew to Berlin and prepared to stage a *coup d'état*. Late that afternoon, news arrived that Hitler had survived. The local commander,

ABOVE Hitler greets a gathering of party leaders (*Gauleiters*) after the failed attempt on his life on 20 July 1944. Over the days that followed demonstrations of loyalty were organized by local party officials, but there were also spontaneous expressions of relief among a public which still hoped that Hitler might find a way out of the looming defeat.

BELOW The German resistance member Elisabeth Charlotte Gloeden stands before the People's Court in Berlin accused of sheltering General Fritz Lindemann, one of the participants in the July Plot. She was found guilty and executed on 30 November 1944 along with her mother and her husband.

JUDGE ROLAND FREISLER (1893–1945)

Freisler was the notorious judge of the People's Court where the conspirators in the July Plot were tried and convicted. He served in the First World War, was captured on the Russian Front and imprisoned in Siberia. When released after the Revolution, he briefly became a Bolshevik commissar. On his return to Germany, he became a successful lawyer, joined Hitler's party in 1925 and defended National Socialists in court. In 1934 he was appointed state secretary in the Justice Ministry where he helped to undermine the justice system by setting aside the principle "no punishment without a law". In August 1942, he was appointed president of the People's Court in Berlin where treason trials were held; the court handed down 5,000 death sentences between 1942 and 1945, including a number for the July plotters. On 3 February 1945, he was killed by a bomb splinter during a bombing attack on Berlin.

BELOW In 1964 the Federal Republic of Germany issued a block of commemorative stamps to mark the twentieth anniversary of the July Plot. The stamps bear portraits of some of the most prominent German resisters including Sophie Scholl, the Munich student executed after her part in the White Rose resistance circle.

General Erich Fromm, himself compromised by contact with the plotters, arrested Stauffenberg and a number of other officers, tried them quickly and shot them in the courtyard of the War Ministry early in the morning of 21 July.

Hitler exacted a terrible revenge on his enemies. He had survived because another officer had moved the briefcase further under the heavy oak conference table, shielding Hitler from the blast. The Gestapo already had a good deal of information on the military conspirators and in the weeks following the attempted assassination, hundreds of leading German soldiers and aristocrats were arrested, tortured into admitting other names, and either put on trial or sent to concentration camps. They included some of the most prominent names in the armed forces: General Franz Halder, the former army chief-of-staff, Field Marshal von Witzleben, Admiral Wilhelm Canaris, head of German counter-intelligence. Three important suspects, General von Tresckow and field marshals von Kluge and Rommel, committed suicide. The first trials were held on 7–8 August 1944 at the People's Court in Berlin and a total of around 200 people executed. Some 5,000 were arrested during the hunt for resisters and many of these were murdered in camps towards the end of the war as the security forces took savage revenge on anyone who was thought to have undermined the German war effort.

BREAKOUT: OPERATION "COBRA"

BELOW Badge of the US Third Army.

The slow progress made in the Normandy campaign in June and early July was dramatically reversed when, on 25 July 1944, the US First Army under Lieutenant General Bradley began Operation "Cobra", designed to create the conditions for a final breakout from the Normandy bridgehead into France. The original plan was for a sharp blow against the German line around St Lô with a strong force of aircraft and tanks, but the German army was so drained after 45 days of continuous combat and air attack that when "Cobra" was launched the line quickly collapsed.

Bradley had at his disposal 15 fully equipped divisions with four in reserve and an overwhelming number of tanks and aircraft. The German 7th Army had only nine weakened divisions, including the armoured Panzer Lehr Division, and 110 tanks. An air attack by heavy bombers on 24 July almost disrupted the Allied plan when aircraft hit the forward American units in error, but on 25 July "Cobra" started with a pulverizing attack by 1,500 heavy bombers on the unfortunate Panzer Lehr Division. Resistance rapidly crumbled and instead of a preparatory forward move, Bradley found his forces racing towards the Brittany coast and the open country beyond. The speed of the attack was made possible by the development of the "Rhinoceros Tank", a Sherman tank with large steel teeth welded to the front to allow it to cut through and remove the thick hedgerows that made progress otherwise so slow. German forces were compelled to fight in the narrow roads, but the US forces could now deploy at speed across country.

On 28 July, the US Eighth Corps reached Coutances, near the Atlantic coast, while the Fourth Armored Division raced through a gap in the line to seize the town of Avranches on 30–31 July and open the way to the occupation of

LEFT A French family carrying what they can on bicycles return to the village of Marigny, recently liberated by the US on 26 July 1944 during Operation "Cobra". Thousands of French people were caught in the crossfire of war and an estimated 60,000 were killed by Allied bombing.

BELOW An enthusiastic French crowd greets troops of the US Thirtieth Assault Unit as they enter the town of Granville on the French Atlantic coast on 31 July 1944 during the early stages of Operation "Cobra".

ABOVE The Allied commanders pose for the camera during a conference in a hayfield in northern France during the rapid Allied advance following Operation "Cobra". General Montgomery, centre, is flanked by (left to right) Lieutenant General Hodges of the US First Army, General Crerar of the Canadian 1st Army, General Bradley, commander of the US Twelfth Army Group and Lieutenant General Dempsey, commander of the British 2nd Army.

Brittany. Montgomery, whose British and Canadian forces were still pinned down around Caen, saw the opportunity to turn the German line and ordered Bradley to use light forces to occupy Brittany, while taking the bulk of his army eastwards to encircle von Kluge's whole army group. On 1 August, Bradley became commander-in-chief of the newly formed Twelfth Army Group, leaving Lieutenant General Hodges in command of First Army and bringing in General George Patton as commander of the new US Third Army. Patton, who had been chafing at the bit in Britain, needed no second chance. He drove his forces forward towards Le Mans and Chartres, with Paris now a distant prize. The German 7th Army and 4th Panzer Army faced the imminent prospect of complete encirclement and von Kluge asked to be allowed to retreat.

Hitler characteristically refused, ordering von Kluge not only to stand fast but to scrape together his remaining armoured units and mount a counter-attack from the town of Mortain, 48 kilometres (30 miles) from the Atlantic coast, designed to cut off the thin US line at Avranches and restore the initiative. Hitler was entirely out of touch with the reality of the campaign. Against the protests of his officers, von

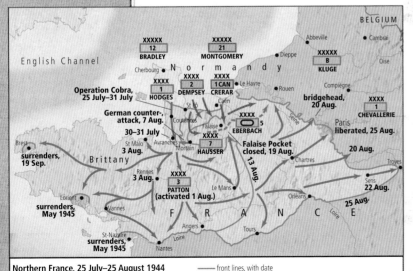

Northern France, 25 July–25 August 1944 ——— front lines, with date

Map labels:
English Channel
BELGIUM
Abbeville • Cambrai
Cherbourg
XXXXX 12 BRADLEY
XXXXX 21 MONTGOMERY
Dieppe
XXXXX B KLUGE
Oise
Normandy
XXXX 1 HODGES
XXXX 2 DEMPSEY
XXXX 1 CAN CRERAR
Le Havre
Rouen
Compiègne
Operation Cobra, 25 July–31 July
German counter-attack, 7 Aug.
30–31 July
St Lô
Caen
bridgehead, 20 Aug.
XXXX 1 CHEVALLERIE
Coutances
Falaise
XXXX 5 EBERBACH
Seine
Paris liberated, 25 Aug.
Brest
surrenders, 19 Sep.
St Malo 3 Aug.
Avranches
Mortain
XXXX 7 HAUSSER
Falaise Pocket closed, 19 Aug.
13 Aug.
Chartres
20 Aug.
Troyes
Brittany
Rennes 3 Aug.
XXXX 3 PATTON (activated 1 Aug.)
Le Mans
Sens 22 Aug.
Lorient
surrenders, May 1945
Vannes
Angers
Orleans
25 Aug.
Loire
St-Nazaire
surrenders, May 1945
Nantes
Tours
FRANCE

COLONEL GENERAL JOSEF "SEPP" DIETRICH (1892–1966)

"Sepp" Dietrich, a senior Waffen-SS officer, became notorious for the so-called Malmédy massacre of American POWs in 1944. He volunteered for the Bavarian army in 1914 and became one of the first members of a German Panzer unit in 1918. He fought in the postwar Freikorps and was one of the participants in the Hitler *Putsch* in 1923. He joined the party in 1928 and the SS the same year, becoming a parliamentary deputy in 1930. He rose rapidly through the SS ranks and in 1933 took over responsibility for guarding Hitler. During the war he led the newly-formed Waffen-SS (armed SS) division *Leibstandarte* and later became commander of the 1st SS Panzer Corps and then commander-in-chief of the 6th SS Panzer Army. He served in Normandy against the Allied breakout, and again in the Ardennes offensive in December 1944. In 1946, he was tried for the murder of 70 US servicemen and sentenced to life imprisonment. He was released in 1955, sentenced again for his role in murdering SA stormtrooper leaders in June 1934, and finally freed in 1959, still a convinced enthusiast for National Socialism.

ABOVE Exhausted American infantrymen take a rest during the 10-day, 155-kilometre (96-mile) advance through Normandy to the port of Avranches, which opened up a swift advance into Brittany over the following week. After weeks of static fighting, the rapid breakout made heavy demands on the troops involved.

BELOW Men from the US Twentieth Corps move through the battle-scarred countryside around Chartres on 17 August 1944 on the way to the first crossings of the River Seine. By this time the German army was in frantic retreat towards the German borders.

Kluge reluctantly did what Hitler wanted, making defeat even more certain. ULTRA decrypts alerted the Allies, who prepared solid anti-tank defences and large-scale air attacks. The Mortain offensive began on 7 August under cover of night, but when the early-morning mists had cleared, air attacks destroyed the advance and Bradley counter-attacked, driving the weakened German divisions back to where they had come from. To mount the offensive, von Kluge had taken armoured divisions away from Caen, and this finally allowed Montgomery to push south to try to create a pocket which would trap the entire German force around the town of Falaise.

Hitler replaced von Kluge with Walter Model, hero of the fighting retreat in the East, but Model saw at once that the situation was hopeless. The jaws of the Allied pincers were closing by the hour; Model ordered a retreat, which became a rout. Fighting a desperate rearguard action, large numbers of German soldiers escaped with all their equipment gone. Even so, 45,000 were captured when the pocket was sealed on 19 August. The defeated army fled towards the Seine, but Patton's Third Army had already reached the river, and made two crossings on 19–20 August, north and south of Paris. Model's force improvised their own river crossings, but on the far side he could organize only four weak divisions and 120 tanks against an Allied force of more than 40 divisions. Little now lay between the Allies and the German border.

GENERAL COURTNEY HODGES (1887–1966)

Courtney Hodges failed his officer training at the West Point Academy and joined the army as a private in 1906, but rose to officer status within three years. He served in the Philippines and Mexico, then in the army in France in 1918. His success as a soldier brought him appointment as an instructor at West Point despite his earlier failure. By 1941, he was commandant of the Infantry School, then chief of infantry. In 1942, he took over command of US Tenth Corps, and was sent to Britain in March 1944 to serve under Bradley. He was deputy commander of the US First Army on D-Day, and in August became its commander. His forces reached Paris first, and also crossed the Rhine first over the Remagen bridge, finally meeting the Red Army in April 1945 at Torgau on the River Elbe. He was promoted to full general in April 1945, only the second man to have moved from private to general in the US Army.

LEFT Badge of US Twentieth Corps.

BELOW The bloated carcasses of dead horses fill the highway near the town of Falaise in northern France where the German 7th Army was faced with encirclement. Allied air power and artillery blasted the area, destroying vehicles and horses but around as many as 100,000 German soldiers managed to escape eastwards.

THE WARSAW UPRISING

6 AUGUST 1944
US First Army captures French city of Nantes.

9 AUGUST 1944
Japanese resistance on island of Guam finally ended.

19 AUGUST 1944
Allied armies close the neck of the Falaise pocket, trapping 50,000 German soldiers.

23 AUGUST 1944
Romania agrees to an armistice with the Soviet armies after the fall of Marshal Antonescu.

17 SEPTEMBER 1944
Allied forces begin Operation "Market Garden".

26 SEPTEMBER 1944
British 8th Army crosses the River Rubicon in northern Italy.

LEFT A Jewish resister is captured by German SS men – a photograph from the album of SS leader Jürgen Stroop who was charged with suppressing the first uprising in Warsaw in the Ghetto, during April and May 1943. Around 14,000 Jews were killed and 56,065 deported for slave labour or extermination.

BELOW A German machine-gun unit in a street battle with the Polish Home Army during the Warsaw uprising in the late summer of 1944. The Poles had few heavy weapons and relied on what they could capture.

As the Red Army approached Poland in 1944, the Polish underground forces, first organized in 1940 as the Union for Armed Struggle, then renamed the *Armia Krajowa* (Home Army) in 1942, planned to launch a major operation codenamed "Tempest" to disrupt German supplies and to harass retreating German forces. The campaign began in January 1944 when Polish partisan units began systematic attacks on German communications. The operation was also part of an attempt by the Polish government-in-exile in London to

ensure that the liberation of Poland was carried out not only by the Soviet Union but also by the Polish people themselves.

The political issue was a major explanation for the decision taken by the London-based Polish commander-in-chief of the Home Army, General Kazimierz Sosnkowski, to include a rising in the Polish capital, Warsaw, as part of Operation "Tempest" in August 1944. The London Poles were now competing with a pro-Communist Moscow-based organization, the Union of Polish Patriots, set up in March 1943, which established a Polish Communist armed force under Lieutenant Colonel Zygmunt Berling to fight alongside the advancing Soviet army. The Moscow Communists had contact with the Communist Polish Workers' Party and its armed wing, the People's Guard, a pro-Soviet resistance movement in Poland. Stalin authorized these groups to set up what was known as the Lublin Committee in July 1944 which became a government-in-waiting, opposed to the London Polish government.

Marshal Rokossovsky's 1st Belorussian Army Group reached the riverbank opposite Warsaw in late July. On 1 August 1944, General Komorowski, commander-in-chief of the Home Army in Poland, ordered his forces in Warsaw to seize the capital from the German garrison before the Red Army arrived. Around 37,000 Poles joined in the uprising; poorly-armed, they nevertheless succeeded in seizing large parts of the residential areas, but they failed to take over the main communications centres or any of the bridges straddling the River Vistula which divided the city.

RIGHT The Red Army reached the River Vistula near Warsaw at the beginning of August 1944 but stopped short of crossing the river in strength because of growing German resistance and heavy Soviet losses. A transport of wounded Soviet soldiers can be seen near the river front.

Descended from Polish nobility, Erich von Zelewski (who changed his surname in 1925 to the more German-sounding "von dem Bach-Zalewski") volunteered for the Prussian army after the outbreak of the First World War even though he was only 15. After the war he joined the German border guards *(Grenzschutz)*, but left in 1930 when he joined the National Socialist Party. He joined the SS in 1931, took part in the Night of the Long Knives in 1934, and became police and SS chief in Silesia in 1937. In 1939 he organized units to resettle Poles forcibly and secure the newly conquered areas. It was his suggestion that led to the establishment of a camp at Auschwitz. In 1941, he became SS and police chief for the rear area of Army Group Centre, and in July 1943 was appointed overall commander of the anti-partisan units. In this capacity his security forces were responsible for the murder of over 235,000 people. He was chosen to command all forces for the suppression of the Warsaw uprising, which he did with extraordinary brutality. Despite his ruthless pursuit of mass-killings, he was not put on trial at Nuremberg, and was imprisoned in the 1960s only on account of his role in murdering opponents of Hitler in the early 1930s. He died in a Munich prison.

LEFT Polish Home Army fighters run for shelter in a Warsaw street during the fighting against the German army. Using guerrilla tactics, they succeeded in holding out for two months against a ruthless and heavily-armed enemy.

The Germans immediately decided to contest the rising. Strong armoured forces staged a counter-attack against the approaching Soviet units to prevent them crossing the Vistula in support, while Heinrich Himmler, head of the SS, organized 21,300 troops and security men under the notorious SS commander Erich von dem Bach-Zalewski to put down the rising. Himmler ordered the massacre of the civilian population and in the first few days 40,000 were murdered. Bach-Zalewski used two of the most bloodthirsty units available to him for the task: the Dirlewanger Brigade made up of ex-prisoners and the renegade Soviet Kaminsky Brigade which perpetrated atrocities too hard for even the SS to stomach. Kaminsky was shot on Himmler's orders.

On 25 August, German forces began a major offensive to retake insurgent-held areas, but the Polish defenders fought for every street and house. By the end of September, the Home Army held only part of central Warsaw, and to avoid further suffering Komorowski negotiated a surrender on 1 October, which came into force a day later. During the uprising, the Western Allies made attempts to drop supplies by air, the first as early as 4 August, but the Polish capital was too far from their bases and the Soviet Union was unwilling to allow British or American aircraft to land at Soviet bases. In September, Stalin allowed Berling's Polish army to try to attack across the Vistula to aid the rising but the attempt was beaten back. On 13 September, Soviet aircraft began low-level supply drops, but much of the parachuted material fell into German hands. It suited Stalin that the anti-Communist Home Army was destroyed, but it is not clear that the Red Army, after a gruelling summer campaign across Belorussia, was in any condition to make a crossing of the Vistula in sufficient strength to withstand German counter-attacks.

For Warsaw the collapse of the rising was a disaster. An estimated 250,000 civilians died and the remainder were forced to leave the city in October 1944 while German demolition squads destroyed Warsaw, block by block. Bach-Zalewski estimated German casualties at 17,000, but this is an unlikely figure. 15,000 of the Polish insurgents were killed in the campaign. Later, in early 1945, when Warsaw had finally fallen to the Red Army, the Soviet-backed Lublin Committee was installed as the first provisional government of postwar Poland.

ABOVE Hungry and ill Polish survivors in October 1944 leave the sewers and cellars where they had been hiding during the Warsaw uprising. Thousands were killed during the fighting and the rest sent to concentration camps or work camps. The city was then systematically destroyed.

BELOW Polish women fighters in the Polish Home Army trudge into captivity at the end of Polish resistance in Warsaw in October 1944. The German SS commander agreed to give them POW status, which was not usually granted to partisan units.

GENERAL TADEUSZ BÓR-KOMOROWSKI (1895–1966)

Tadeusz Komorowski was a Polish soldier who led the Polish Home Army in the rising against German occupation in August 1944. He added his wartime codename "Bór" to his surname after the war. He served in the Austrian army during the First World War, joined the new Polish army and became commander of the Polish Cavalry School. After Poland's defeat in 1939, he went underground and became first deputy commander of the clandestine Home Army in July 1941, then its commander in March 1943. He led the Warsaw uprising but surrendered in October 1944 after persuading the Germans to treat his army as regular prisoners-of-war. After the war he moved to London, where, during 1947–49, he became prime minister of the anti-Communist Polish government-in-exile.

THE END OF VICHY FRANCE: OPERATION "DRAGOON"

17 AUGUST 1944
Red Army reaches the old German border of East Prussia.

23 AUGUST 1944
Coup in Romania overthrows pro-Axis Marshal Antonescu.

4 SEPTEMBER 1944
British and Canadian armies capture Antwerp in Belgium and secure a major port for future operations.

5 SEPTEMBER 1944
Finns agree to sign a ceasefire with the Red Army and formally surrender five days later.

8 SEPTEMBER 1944
British 8th Army breaks through the Gothic Line in northern Italy.

12 SEPTEMBER 1944
"Octagon" conference convenes in Canadian city of Quebec to discuss Western strategy.

When plans for "Overlord" were being completed, in 1943 the Anglo-American Combined Chiefs-of-Staff decided that a subsidiary landing, codenamed Operation "Anvil", should be made in southern France at the same time. The decision was taken at the Cairo Conference in November 1943, but during the early months of 1944, Eisenhower insisted that it be postponed to ensure enough men and landing craft were available for D-Day, while in Italy the Allied commanders opposed the diversion of resources from an Italian campaign which threatened to descend into stalemate. Only Roosevelt remained fully committed and insisted, against Churchill's call for an alternative attack through southeastern Europe towards Austria, that the operation should take place.

Forces for what became known as Operation "Dragoon" were diverted from Italy. Under the overall control of the supreme commander in the Mediterranean, the British General Henry Maitland Wilson, the US Seventh Army under Lieutenant General Alexander Patch and the French Army B under General de Lattre de Tassigny were assigned to the operation, a total of 11 divisions, backed by large air and naval forces. They were opposed by 10 divisions of General Blaskowitz's 19th Army, but most were not stationed near

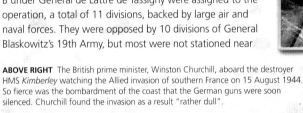

the coast and only one, the 11th Panzer Division, was a first-class unit. The landings, supported by 887 warships and 1,370 landing craft, took place on 15 August 1944 and were largely unopposed. The German army began to withdraw, since prospects for serious defence were limited. French forces, renamed the 1st French Army on 19 September, took Toulon and Marseilles by 28 August, while the Sixth Corps of Seventh Army, led by Major General Lucian Truscott, pursued the retreating enemy up the Rhone valley towards Alsace-Lorraine.

Progress was swift, for by 3 September Lyons was liberated, and by 10 September the city of Dijon was reached, where Patch's army met up with units of General Patton's US Third Army coming from the northwest. Much of the region was liberated by the French Forces of the Interior which tried to slow down the German retreat, but Blaskowitz succeeded in avoiding a trap and withdrew his forces to the Vosges region. On 15 September, the southern armies were brought under Eisenhower's command and formed into a 6th Army Group for the expected advance

BELOW Allied troops and tanks from the US Seventh Army land on the southern coast of France on 15 August 1944 somewhere between Toulon and Cannes in the early stages of Operation "Dragoon". The beach landings were lightly opposed after 126 warships and 2,000 aircraft had pounded the defences.

ABOVE RIGHT The British prime minister, Winston Churchill, aboard the destroyer HMS *Kimberley* watching the Allied invasion of southern France on 15 August 1944. So fierce was the bombardment of the coast that the German guns were soon silenced. Churchill found the invasion as a result "rather dull".

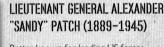

LIEUTENANT GENERAL ALEXANDER "SANDY" PATCH (1889–1945)

Better known for leading US forces in the campaign for the Pacific island of Guadalcanal, Alexander Patch was commander of forces for the invasion of southern France in August 1944. He joined the army in 1909 and served as an infantry officer in the First World War. In 1940, he was promoted to brigadier-general and helped to train the expanding US army under General Marshall. He went to the south Pacific in 1942, where he formed what he called the "Americal Division" out of a number of smaller units stationed there. He led the division on Guadalcanal in October 1942, and in December took over command of all forces on the island, leading some operations himself. He was transferred to Europe, where he took over the US Seventh Army from Mark Clark. He led the army in the invasion of southern France and on into southern Germany by the end of the war. He returned to the United States in August 1945 to command the US Fourth Army but died of pneumonia three months later.

MARSHAL JEAN DE LATTRE DE TASSIGNY (1889–1952)

Jean de Lattre was descended from a Franco-Flemish aristocratic family. He joined the French army in 1908, and as a young officer in the 12th Dragoons was wounded twice in the first month of the First World War. He had become an infantry captain by the end of the war and pursued an army career in the interwar years, rising to the rank of brigadier general in March 1939, when he was chief-of-staff of the French 5th Army. He commanded the 14th Infantry Division in the Battle of France and then became a general in the Vichy French army. Arrested late in 1942 after the German occupation of the whole of France, he escaped from prison and made his way to London. He was promoted to full general by General de Gaulle and put in command of French Army B. He led the force in the landings in southern France, liberated Toulon and Marseilles, and then entered Germany in 1945 alongside the Allies. He represented France at the German surrender in Berlin in May 1945. He was created a marshal of France shortly after his death in 1952.

ABOVE A Sherman tank manned by men of the Free French Army B in the port city of Marseilles on 29 August 1944 after the city had fallen to a French attack the previous day. Although Hitler had designated Marseilles and Toulon as "fortress cities" they fell quickly to determined French assault.

ABOVE Badge of the 1st French Army.

LEFT Badge of the French Commando Brigade.

ABOVE Paratroopers dropped from the C-47 transport aircraft of the Twelfth Air Force Troop Carrier Air Division on 15 August 1944. The troops of the First Airborne Task Force were dropped early in the morning west of Cannes to support the beach invasion.

into Germany. The whole campaign had cost only 4,000 French and 2,700 American casualties, while 57,000 Germans were captured, more than the number ensnared in the Falaise pocket by Montgomery in August. Eisenhower now had a major port in Marseilles which could be used to bring in supplies and men for the next stage of the campaign to enter and occupy the German homeland.

The invasion of southern France hastened the end of the Vichy regime which by the summer of 1944 was dominated by pro-German French Fascists under the premiership of Pierre Laval. On 19 August, the head of the Vichy regime, Marshal Pétain, resigned and was taken by the Germans first to Belfort then to Sigmaringen. In April 1945, he was allowed to leave for Switzerland, but volunteered to return to France where he stood trial and was condemned to death (later commuted to life imprisonment). Laval followed Pétain to Belfort and Sigmaringen with the remnants of the Vichy government. He was captured in July 1945, sentenced to death for treason and executed.

The government of France was now taken over by General de Gaulle's French Committee for National Liberation which became the de facto provisional government. The Third Republic, which had been replaced by Vichy in 1940, was not reconstituted. Instead, a new republican constitution for the French Fourth Republic was agreed in 1946 following national elections in October 1945 that gave overwhelming support to the parties of the left, and to the legacy of the resistance against German occupation and the authoritarian Vichy system.

ABOVE LEFT Members of the Vichy French *Milice* (militia) are executed by Free French forces at Grenoble, 2 September 1944. Thousands of French collaborators with Vichy or with the Germans were executed in the weeks following liberation.

THE LIBERATION OF PARIS

GENERAL JACQUES-PHILIPPE LECLERC DE HAUTECLOQUE (1902–1947)

Philippe, count of Hautecloque, changed his name in 1945 to Jacques-Philippe Leclerc in order to incorporate his wartime resistance alias. He graduated from the Saint-Cyr military academy in 1924, and was an army captain by 1937. After the defeat of France in June 1940, he went to London and joined de Gaulle's Free French army. He saw service in West and North Africa before joining in the Normandy invasion with the French 2nd Armoured Division. He was allowed to enter Paris to liberate the city, and then led his unit to liberate Strasbourg. His forces ended the war at Hitler's Bavarian residence at Berchtesgaden. He then commanded French forces in Indo-China (Vietnam) in the civil war there in 1945, but was replaced because he favoured negotiation. He died in a plane crash in 1947, and was awarded the posthumous rank of Marshal of France in 1952.

ABOVE During the liberation of Paris in August 1944 two soldiers from the 2nd French Armoured Division, in the shadow of the Arc de Triomphe, fire at German snipers and French *Milice* trying to rescue German prisoners, who lie dead on the Champs Elysées.

As Allied forces broke out of the Normandy bridgehead, the population of Paris began to prepare for their liberation. However, General Eisenhower did not initially give Paris priority, preferring to bypass the capital while Allied forces chased the German army to the German frontier. General Patton's US Third Army reached and crossed the Seine at Mantes-Gassicourt on the night of 19/20 August, some 60 kilometres (37 miles) north of Paris, and followed that with crossings south of Paris at Melun and Fontainebleau on 24 August. American forces then raced on across France in pursuit of around 250,000 German soldiers retreating towards the German frontier.

The Allied assumption was that the Germans would abandon Paris, and they detailed General Leclerc's 2nd Armoured Division as the unit with the honour of entering the city first when it was finally free of German forces. The population of Paris reacted to the news of the American advance by starting the liberation of their capital themselves. The starting point was a strike movement, beginning with railway workers on 10 August but followed, when news came of the Allied landings in the south, by a large part of the Paris police force on 15 August. The liberation movement in Paris was divided between the Gaullists and the Communists, led by Henri Tanguy, who was head of the local Committee of Liberation, but on 19 August, following a call for general mobilization by the French Forces of the Interior the day before, the two groups finally worked

ABOVE The Croix-de-Guerre.

ABOVE French resistance fighters behind a makeshift barricade in Paris with an assortment of weapons and helmets. The rising against the German garrison began on 19 August and lasted until the city was liberated by Allied armies six days later.

together when they launched a rising in the city against the German garrison commanded by General Dietrich von Choltitz.

There was still an element of risk in mounting a rising, for at the same time German forces were brutally suppressing a similar revolt in Warsaw. Hitler, who had visited Paris in June 1940 and respected it as a centre of architectural splendour, now ordered Choltitz to defend Paris at all costs and to destroy what could not be defended. All over the city sporadic fighting broke out, while in the main Communist districts barricades were set up. The Gaullist leader, Alexandre Parodi, tried with the help of the Swedish consul general to calm the fighting down. What followed were six days of confusion until Choltitz, a Prussian officer

of the old school rather than a National Socialist fanatic, finally decided to ignore Hitler's orders and surrender. On 23 August, Eisenhower had given permission for Leclerc to leave pursuit of the German army temporarily and to secure Paris. The first French armoured columns reached central Paris on the evening of 24 August and the following day the whole of the capital was liberated amidst scenes of wild celebration. Some 3,200 Germans were killed in the rising and 1,500 French; a further 12,800 German soldiers were taken prisoner.

On 26 August, General de Gaulle entered Paris in triumph. He rekindled the flame on the tomb of the unknown warrior at the Arc de Triomphe and then marched at the head of Allied forces down the Champs Elysées. He later went to Notre Dame where he was shot at by a sniper concealed in the cathedral. That evening the German air force made a final retributive attack on Paris, the heaviest raid of the war. Around 500 houses were destroyed and the huge wine warehouse the Halle aux Vins was set on fire, illuminating the whole of central Paris.

The experience of Paris was not universal in France. Around 85 per cent of French communes waited for the arrival of Allied forces and did not risk German revenge. The liberation of Paris was a necessary and symbolic act, which was why de Gaulle chose it as the site for his first major speech on French soil when he talked of a city that had "liberated itself" in order to liberate France. The Committee for National Liberation moved from Algiers to Paris and set about reconstituting a unitary and democratic country.

FAR LEFT The German commander in Paris, General Dietrich von Choltitz, signs the act of surrender on 25 August 1944. Though ordered by Hitler to leave nothing in Paris standing, Choltitz had no desire to be remembered as the man who destroyed the city.

BELOW General de Gaulle, leader of the Free French, and soon to be head of a provisional French administration, walks down the Champs Elysées to the cathedral of Notre Dame where a service of thanksgiving was to take place on 26 August 1944. In the cathedral a sniper fired at de Gaulle. Sporadic fighting continued for some days.

Henri Rol-Tanguy (1908–2002)

Henri Tanguy was a French communist who became commander of the resistance French Forces of the Interior in Paris in June 1944. He was the son of a sailor who became an active Young Communist in Paris in the 1920s and 1930s. In 1937, he joined the International Brigades fighting against Franco's uprising in Spain and was wounded at the Battle of Ebro. He went underground after French defeat in 1940. Under the pseudonym "Colonel Rol" he organized the resistance group Francs-Tireurs et Partisans in Paris. He was one of the leaders of the uprising in the city in August 1944. He joined the French 1st Army fighting its way into Germany and then remained a regular army officer until 1962. He became a member of the French Communist Party central committee, on which he served until 1987. He was made an honorary Spanish citizen in 1996 for his role in the Spanish Civil War.

BELOW Overjoyed Parisians greet a tank of the French 2nd Armoured Division commanded by General Leclerc as it arrives at Place Michel-Ange-Auteuil on 24 August 1944.

OPERATION "MARKET GARDEN"

The sudden collapse of German resistance in France in August 1944 opened up the prospect that the war in the West might be brought to a rapid conclusion if Allied armies could penetrate into Germany fast enough. Montgomery's 21st Army Group and Bradley's Twelfth Army Group pushed on into eastern France and Belgium during September. On 4 September, the port of Antwerp was captured, but not the Scheldt estuary to the north, which was still defended by scattered German units, making it impossible to use the major port for supplying Allied armies. The sheer speed of the advance had produced a crisis of supply which threatened to undermine the ambition to destroy German resistance by the winter.

It was in this strategic context that Montgomery now suggested a daring operation to try to accelerate the Allied advance. "Market Garden" was designed to drive a salient into the German line towards the Dutch city of Arnhem, force a crossing of the lower Rhine and create the conditions for Allied forces to sweep down towards the industrial region of the Ruhr. It was an ambitious plan, and left the estuary around Antwerp still in enemy hands, but on 10 September Eisenhower approved it and agreed to make available the First Allied Airborne Army led by US Lieutenant General Lewis Brereton, but under the tactical command of the British Lieutenant General Frederick Browning. The three airborne divisions were allocated different tasks. The US 82nd and 101st Divisions were to seize the Nijmegen and Eindhoven bridges over the River Waal and the Wilhelmina canal, while the British 1st Airborne Division was to capture the bridges at Arnhem and create a narrow bridgehead across the Rhine. While the airborne forces fought for the

ABOVE An aerial view of Airspeed Horsa and GAL Hamilcar gliders on Landing Zone "Z" near Wolfheze woods, northwest of the Dutch city of Arnhem on 17 September 1944. Operation "Market Garden" depended on the successful transport of airborne forces and equipment, including the operation's headquarters staff and commander.

LIEUTENANT GENERAL FREDERICK BROWNING (1896–1965)

Generally regarded as the father of the British airborne forces, Frederick Browning began his career in the First World War with the Grenadier Guards. He was a Guards commander in the early years of the Second World War until appointed in October 1941 to command the British 1st Airborne Division. He designed the distinctive maroon beret for the force and played a key part in their organization and training. In April 1943, he became airborne advisor to Eisenhower in the Mediterranean theatre where he helped to plan the Sicily invasion, and in December 1943 was commander of Headquarters Airborne Troops under Montgomery. After the Normandy invasion, he became deputy commander of the 1st Allied Airborne Army and in this capacity helped to organize and lead Operation "Market Garden". After its failure he was sent as chief-of-staff to the Southeast Asia Command. After the war, he became comptroller of the Royal Household.

RIGHT Badge worn by Montgomery during his command of US airborne forces during the Normandy campaigns and Operation "Market Garden".

bridges, Lieutenant General Horrocks was to bring his 30th Corps forward through the narrow passageway carved out of the German line to strengthen the Allied grip on Arnhem.

The operation began on 17 September with mixed fortunes. The 19,000 troops were dropped into the combat zones more accurately than was often the case, but the attempt to cross eight water barriers was in itself a challenge. Browning insisted on taking part in the operation personally, taking the whole headquarters staff by glider to Arnhem, but he found it difficult to hold together the scattered airborne units with poor radio communications. The American divisions succeeded in taking their objectives in Eindhoven and Nijmegen, but further north the 1st Airborne Division met stiff German resistance and failed to take the bridges over the Rhine. The 9th and 10th SS Panzer Divisions were refitting at Arnhem and although Browning had been warned by his intelligence officers that the divisions had been detected, he chose to launch the operation regardless. The result was strong German counter-attacks in and around Arnhem that forced the British 2nd Parachute Battalion to surrender on 21 September. The expected help from the 30th Corps did not materialize.

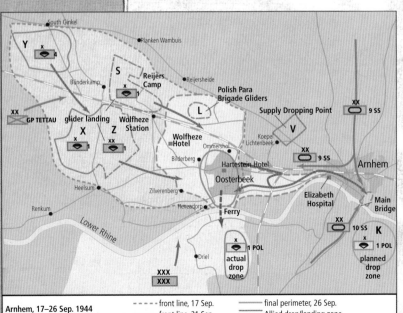

Arnhem, 17–26 Sep. 1944

- - - - - front line, 17 Sep.
––– – front line, 21 Sep.
––––– final perimeter, 26 Sep.
░░░ Allied drop/landing zone

ABOVE A Lloyd carrier of the anti-tank platoon of the 3rd Battalion, Irish Guards explodes on the road towards Eindhoven as the British 30th Corps begins its advance to meet up with forces in Arnhem on 17 September 1944.

LEFT A German infantry battalion hunting for British troops in the suburbs of Arnhem during the battle for the river crossings in the town. German resistance was heavier than anticipated.

BELOW Mark V Sten gun of the type issued to airborne troops for use during the Arnhem operation.

LIEUTENANT GENERAL BRIAN HORROCKS (1895–1985)

Brian Horrocks was one of the most popular and well-regarded British generals of the Second World War whose long army career was spiced with incident. He almost failed his cadet course at Sandhurst, but the outbreak of the First World War gave him the opportunity to prove himself in battle. He was wounded and captured in October 1914 and spent four years trying to escape; in exasperation the Germans put him in a Russian POW camp, where he learnt fluent Russian. On repatriation in 1919 he volunteered to serve with the British intervention in Russia where he was captured again in January 1920 and held as a prisoner for 10 months. He had become a career soldier and by the outbreak of war was an instructor at the staff college. He commanded a machine-gun battalion in France, and a division in Britain in 1941. He was sent to North Africa to command the 13th Corps under Montgomery in 1942, where his unit defended the Alam Halfa ridge in the battle in early September 1942. He played a key role in Tunisia and accepted the surrender of Rommel's Afrika Korps. In June 1943 he was severely wounded, but in August 1944 was back in command of 30th Corps which he led in Operation "Market Garden". At the end of the war he was promoted to lieutenant general and in 1949 he was appointed gentleman usher of the Black Rod in the House of Lords.

Horrocks's units were held up by the slow process of bridge-building and by bad weather and reached the River Waal only on 21 September. They crossed it the following day, only to find that the British position was now hopeless. Airborne forces were ordered to make their way back across the Waal on 25 September and the operation was abandoned.

Montgomery's gamble failed to pay off and involved a heavy cost. The 1st Airborne Division suffered 7,842 casualties, including 6,000 prisoners. The two American divisions, which held the salient they had formed for a further two months, suffered total casualties of 3,532. Browning took much of the blame for the failure, but he

had famously warned Montgomery early in September that Arnhem might be "a bridge too far". In October and November 1944, Montgomery concentrated instead on clearing the Scheldt estuary and freeing Antwerp as a supply base, a campaign that was only completed on 8 November with the capture of Walcheren at the mouth of the river. By late November, the port could at last be used, but Allied armies had been brought to a halt along the German frontier where months of bitter fighting still lay ahead.

RIGHT Four British paratroopers move cautiously through a ruined house in Oosterbeek where they had been forced to retreat after abandoning Arnhem. The picture was taken on 23 September 1944 by a photographer of the Army Film and Photographic Unit sent to accompany the 1st Allied Airborne Army during the operation.

BELOW RIGHT A line of British paratroopers captured by the German defenders of Arnhem. After months of Allied success in Western Europe, Arnhem was a sharp reminder of the remaining fighting-power of the German enemy. Around 6,000 Allied soldiers were taken prisoner.

BELOW The bridge at Arnhem which had been the focus of the struggle between 1st Airborne Army and the 9th and 10th SS Panzer Divisions. The photograph was taken after 20 September when Allied forces gave up the attempt to capture it. This was, as the commander of the operation said, "a bridge too far".

YUGOSLAVIA: LIBERATION FROM WITHIN

Two wars were fought in Yugoslavia during the last years of the Second World War. The first was a guerrilla war against the German occupiers, led largely by the Communist partisans under Tito (Josip Broz); the second was a vicious civil war fought between rival ethnic groups and rival political factions. The main conflict was between the Serb nationalist Chetniks (Army of the Homeland) led by Mihailovic, who remained loyal to the exiled monarch, Peter II, and the Communist partisans who wanted to overturn the monarchy and establish a communist republic.

The civil war weakened the attempt to fight against the German occupiers and led to the deaths of hundreds of thousands of Yugoslavs. The Chetniks murdered Croats and Bosnian Muslims – an estimated 30–50,000 – and killed Communists in the areas they controlled in Serbia and central Yugoslavia. They were in turn murdered by the Communist partisans when they were caught. In Italian-occupied Yugoslavia, the Chetniks collaborated with Italian forces in attacking Communist resistance until Italy withdrew from the war in 1943. The German occupiers succeeded in playing the different groups off against each other. A rival Chetnik leader, Kosta Pecanac, collaborated directly with the Germans until he was caught and executed in 1944 by Mihailovic's forces. The Chetniks were wary of attacking the Germans directly for fear of retaliation against the civilian population and remained an army-in-waiting for the defeat of the Axis and the return of the king. Their cause was weakened further in 1944 when the exiled Peter finally switched his support to Tito.

ABOVE Tito (centre), leader of the Yugoslav Communist partisans, in discussion at his headquarters on the island of Vis in 1944. By the end of the war the Communist resistance had become the most important element of the partisan movement, and Tito became premier of the provisional government.

BELOW An armed German police unit near the Italian-Croatian border in late 1944 defend a strongpoint against partisan attack. German forces held out in northern Yugoslavia until the end of the war. The Croatian capital, Zagreb, was liberated on 8 May 1945.

The fighting against the Germans and, until September 1943, the Italians was largely sustained by Tito's partisan army. By 1944, they numbered more than 300,000, based not in Serbia but in the Dinaric Alps in Croatia. At the peak they were confronted by around 35 Axis divisions. Despite major operations mounted in 1943 by the Germans and their Croat allies, codenamed "White" and "Black", the partisans survived in their mountain stronghold. When the British,

who had supported the Chetniks, changed to supporting and supplying Tito because of the Communist strategy of direct military confrontation with the enemy, the partisans became the major force in Yugoslavia. Late in 1944, Hitler decided to abandon the Balkans and German forces withdrew from Greece, Albania and southern Yugoslavia. The partisans attacked the retreating forces, and on 20 October 1944 captured the Serb capital of Belgrade, aided by Red Army units which had entered Romania in August,

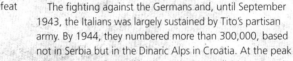

COLONEL DRAGOLJUB "DRAŽA" MIHAILOVIC (1893–1946)

When Yugoslavia was occupied by the Germans and Italians in 1941, Draža Mihailovic led the non-Communist arm of the Yugoslav resistance movement. He joined the Serbian army in 1910, fought in the Balkan wars of 1912–13 as a young cadet and then in the First World War against Austria-Hungary. He became a staff officer in the interwar years and achieved the rank of colonel by 1941. After the conquest of Yugoslavia he set up a resistance group loyal to the exiled king known as the Chetniks, but insisted that they should not fight the Germans and Italians directly for fear of reprisals, though they did fight against other partisan movements and the Bosnian Muslims. In 1942, he was made a general and minister of war by the government-in-exile, but the Allies abandoned support for him in late 1943 in favour of Tito. In 1946, he was arrested by the new Communist secret police, sentenced for treason and executed.

occupied Bulgaria the following month and had by 28 September reached the Yugoslav border.

Between October 1944 and the end of the war, Tito's partisan army pursued the retreating Germans to their last line of defence in Hungary and northern Yugoslavia, where Army Group G was finally defeated only in May 1945. The port of Trieste was reached by the partisans on 30 April, and occupied by them the following day, shortly before the arrival of British forces from Italy, while the Croat capital Zagreb finally fell on 8 May. In March 1945, a new national government had been formed, dominated by Tito's Anti-Fascist Council of National Liberation, and with Tito as prime minister. Although it initially included pro-royalist elements to create the image of a united political front, the Communists quickly moved to dominate the liberated state and to take savage revenge on the Chetniks and pro-German Croats who had fought against them during the war. The battle-lines of the savage civil war were papered over, only to reappear 45 years later with the breakup of Yugoslavia and the renewal of violence in the wars of 1991–95.

ABOVE LEFT Yugoslav partisans from Tito's Anti-Fascist Army of National Liberation march through the Serb capital, Belgrade, after its capture by Yugoslav and Soviet forces on 20 October 1944.

ABOVE Yugoslav partisans in action in Slovenia, northern Yugoslavia on 17 November 1944. They are approaching the Litija bridge held by a German garrison from Army Group C.

KING PETER II OF YUGOSLAVIA (1923–1970)

The last king of Yugoslavia, Peter II came to the throne in 1934 at the age of 11 following the assassination of his father, Alexander, on a visit to France. A regent, Prince Paul, was appointed because Peter was too young to rule. Regent Paul agreed to the join the Axis pact in 1941 before the invasion of Russia, but in March 1941 Peter, supported by a group of senior military officers, overthrew Paul and rejected the Axis alliance. He fled following the German invasion and, after a brief exile in the Middle East, went to London in June 1941. He went to Cambridge University, then served with the RAF. In 1946, Peter was formally deposed by Tito's Communist government and moved to the United States, where he died of cirrhosis of the liver, aged 47. He is the only monarch buried on American soil.

RIGHT A Bosnian Muslim volunteer fighting on the German side in Yugoslavia in 1944. Conflict between religious and ethnic groups in Yugoslavia created divisions which were exploited by the German occupiers. Thousands of Muslims were murdered by other partisan groups.

THE RECAPTURE OF THE PHILIPPINES

10 MARCH 1945
Destruction of central Tokyo in a firestorm following heavy attack by US B-29 bombers

3 MAY 1945
Allied forces capture Rangoon in Burma from the Japanese

30 JUNE 1945
Japanese resistance ends on the island of Okinawa

14 AUGUST 1945
Japanese emperor announces surrender

ABOVE US 43rd Division.

LEFT Ships of US Task Force 38 sail into Lingayen Gulf on the western coast of the Philippine island of Luzon shortly before the landings scheduled for 9 January. Japanese positions were subjected to a heavy and continuous bombardment. The lead ship is the battleship USS *Pennsylvania*.

BELOW LEFT One of the most famous photographs of the Pacific War shows General Douglas MacArthur wading ashore at Leyte Gulf in the southern Philippines in mid-October 1944 to redeem the promise he made when he left in 1942 that "I shall return". The photograph was deliberately staged; MacArthur had come ashore less ostentatiously a little while before.

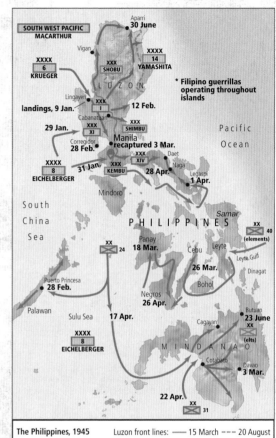

The Philippines, 1945   Luzon front lines: —— 15 March --- 20 August

In July 1944, American commanders met in Hawaii to decide on the future course of the war against Japan. The navy favoured a direct approach to the Japanese home islands, supported by air power, while the army, represented by General MacArthur, wanted to liberate the Philippines, first to establish secure bases for further operations, second as a point of honour to free the islands from Japanese rule. Roosevelt ruled in MacArthur's favour and in September 1944 carrier-borne aircraft began a systematic destruction of Japanese airpower on the islands.

The American planners chose the island of Leyte, in the more weakly defended central area of the islands, as the starting point for the invasion. In mid-October, 700 ships and approximately 174,000 men sailed into position. On 17 October, US Rangers landed on the smaller islands of Suluan and Dinagat to secure the approaches to Leyte Gulf. Three days later, on the morning of 20 October, four divisions landed on Leyte against minimal resistance. While a major naval battle developed in and around the landing area on 24 and 25 October, the Japanese 35th Army was pushed back and airfields were secured. The Japanese commander in the Philippines, General Tomoyuki Yamashita, the conqueror of Malaya, decided to make Leyte the point at which to contest the American campaign and 45–50,000 reinforcements were sent over the following two months. By mid-December, however, the Americans had landed some 200,000 men on the island, and

ABOVE American civilian prisoners of the Japanese at the Santo Tomas University prison camp in Manila welcome US troops after liberation on 6 February 1945. Conditions at the camp, as in all Japanese camps, led to high levels of death from mistreatment and debilitation.

ABOVE The port of Manila under heavy artillery bombardment on 23 February 1945 as the US Sixth Army fought for the capital. Caught in the crossfire are thought to have been around 100,000 Filipinos killed, many by the Japanese occupiers.

RIGHT US 37th Division.

organized Japanese resistance ended on 19 December with over 80,000 Japanese dead, although sporadic fighting continued for a further week.

While the grip on Leyte was consolidated, MacArthur ordered assault forces to seize the island of Mindoro as a stepping stone to the conquest of the main island of Luzon. On 15 December, Mindoro was invaded and, by the middle of January 1945, secured. On 9 January, two corps of Lieutenant General Krueger's Sixth Army landed at Lingayen Bay on the west coast of Luzon and rapidly advanced across the central plain to the capital, Manila. Yamashita decided not to contest the advance but to hold his sizeable army in the mountains, forcing the Americans to fight a protracted and costly campaign. Although the Japanese High Command had decided to abandon Luzon, and sent no further reinforcements from mid-January, the surviving garrison decided to fight to the death as had many others during the island campaign. Rear Admiral Sanji Iwabuchi retreated with a force of sailors into Manila and held out in the city between 3 February, when the Sixth Army arrived, and 3 March when the Japanese force was all but annihilated. During the siege around 100,000 Filipinos were killed by artillery fire, conflagrations and the deliberate violence by the desperate Japanese forces. The battle for Manila cost US forces around 1,000 dead against 16,000 Japanese.

While Manila was secured, US forces captured the Bataan Peninsula and the fortress of Corregidor, scene of the final American defence three years before. Before the fortress fell, Japanese forces ignited a large munitions dump, creating a colossal explosion, a fitting finale to the eclipse of Japanese power in the islands. Over the following months, some 38 separate landings were made to clear the southern and central islands by Lieutenant General Eichelberger's Eighth US Army in collaboration with Filipino guerrillas. In June, Krueger's Sixth Army was withdrawn. Over the course of the whole campaign the Japanese garrisons, some of which continued to exist in mountains and jungles until the end of the war, endured overwhelmingly high losses. In the conquest of the islands the American forces lost 10,381 killed, 36,631 wounded and over 93,000 casualties from sickness and accident.

While American forces were securing the Philippines, a less glamorous campaign was waged further to the west, as Australian troops cleared Japanese positions in Borneo and the Dutch East Indies to secure the oil supplies there, while the remaining Japanese soldiers, beyond any prospect of reinforcement or assistance, spent the rest of the war in a vicious conflict with local anti-Japanese guerrillas organized by the Special Operations Australia units infiltrated onto the island in March and April 1945. The last Japanese only surrendered in October 1945.

ABOVE Two soldiers of the US 37th "Buckeye" Division in the fighting for Manila on 14 February 1945 stand on top of a wall in an effort to flush out a Japanese machine-gun nest. The Japanese naval troops fought almost to the last man before the city fell.

ABOVE Troops of the 9th Australian Division land from a US landing ship on the island of Labuan off the coast of the island of Borneo on 10 June 1945. Australian and Dutch forces, supported by Australian and US ships, re-occupied key areas in the East Indies in the last months of the war.

RIGHT Japanese General Tomoyūki Yamashita, commander of Japanese forces on the island of Luzon, washes his hands after surrendering to the Americans on 2 September 1945. He was later tried for war crimes and executed.

213

THE BATTLE OF LEYTE GULF

LEFT The Battle of Leyte Gulf saw Japanese suicide attacks by aircraft for the first time. Here a Japanese Mitsubishi Zero-Sen "Zeke" fighter prepares to dive on the USS carrier *White Plains*. The US Navy lost just six ships during the battle. Suicide tactics became significant only in 1945 in the approach to the Japanese home islands.

BELOW The *Independence*-class carrier USS *Princeton* on fire during the Battle of Leyte Gulf following an attack by a land-based Japanese dive-bomber in the morning of 24 October. Hosepipes are directed from the cruiser USS *Birmingham* in an attempt to bring the fire under control, but an explosion on the stricken ship badly damaged *Birmingham* before the carrier sank in the late afternoon.

The naval battle off the Philippine island of Leyte was the largest naval engagement of the war and it led to the final decisive defeat of the Japanese Combined Fleet. For once the balance of intelligence between the two sides tilted in favour of Japan. When Admiral Halsey's Third Fleet and Vice Admiral Thomas Kinkaid's Seventh Fleet arrived off the island of Leyte to launch the first landings, the Japanese naval High Command, under Admiral Soemu Toyoda, planned a final showdown with the American navy codenamed "Sho-Go" (Operation "Victory"). This time the American commanders did not know the nature of the Japanese plan and the final assault on the American invasion forces in the Philippines achieved a large measure of surprise.

Toyoda's plan was to lure Halsey's powerful Third Fleet into an engagement off the north of the Philippines with what remained of the Japanese carrier force while two other naval groups, Centre Force under Vice Admiral Takeo Kurita and Southern Force commanded by Vice Admiral Kiyohide Shima, sailed through narrow straits on either side of Leyte to attack and destroy the American landings in a powerful pincer movement. The whole plan relied on Halsey taking the bait of an attack on the Japanese carriers, allowing the battleships and cruisers of the other two elements of the Japanese navy to overwhelm the forces left behind.

The battle plan worked better than might have been expected, since both the Southern Force and Centre Force were detected and attacked when they sailed into position on 23 October. Centre Force lost two cruisers on passage from Brunei, and a further battleship and destroyer to air attack in the Sibuyan Sea, west of Leyte, forcing Kurita to withdraw temporarily. The first branch of Southern Force arrived at the Surigao Strait, leading to the landing area,

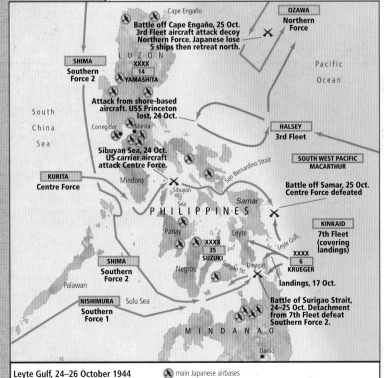

Battle off Cape Engaño, 25 Oct. 3rd Fleet aircraft attack decoy Northern Force. Japanese lose 5 ships then retreat north.

OZAWA Northern Force

Cape Engaño

SHIMA Southern Force 2

LUZON
XXXX
14
YAMASHITA

Pacific Ocean

Attack from shore-based aircraft. USS Princeton lost, 24 Oct.

South China Sea

Corregidor · Manila

HALSEY 3rd Fleet

Sibuyan Sea, 24 Oct. US carrier aircraft attack Centre Force.

KURITA Centre Force

Mindoro

San Bernardino Strait

SOUTH WEST PACIFIC MACARTHUR

Sibuyan Sea

Samar

Battle off Samar, 25 Oct. Centre Force defeated

PHILIPPINES

Panay · Leyte

Leyte Gulf

KINKAID 7th Fleet (covering landings)

XXXX 35 SUZUKI

SHIMA Southern Force 2

Negros

Surigao Str.

Dinagat

XXXX 6 KRUEGER

landings, 17 Oct.

Palawan

NISHIMURA Southern Force 1

Sulu Sea

Battle of Surigao Strait, 24–25 Oct. Detachment from 7th Fleet defeat Southern Force 2.

MINDANAO

Davao

Leyte Gulf, 24–26 October 1944   ⚙ main Japanese airbases

VICE ADMIRAL JESSE B OLDENDORF (1887–1974)

Jesse "Oley" Oldendorf commanded the last victorious fleet engagement fought exclusively by surface vessels unsupported by aircraft when his task force defeated the Japanese Southern Force off Leyte in the Philippines. He joined the US Navy in 1909 and commanded his first ship by 1922. In the early stages of the war he was posted to anti-submarine duty in the Caribbean and then commanded the Western Atlantic escort forces from May to December 1943. Posted to the Pacific in January 1944, Oldendorf commanded Cruiser Division 4 in the Marshall islands, the Marianas and the invasion of the Philippines. In December 1944, he was promoted to vice admiral and was wounded during the invasion of Okinawa. He commanded the Western Sea Frontier after the war and retired in 1948.

LEFT A Japanese *Zuiho*-class carrier under attack on 25 October 1944 by aircraft of Air Group 20 from the carrier USS *Enterprise*. The photograph was taken from a torpedo-bomber a few seconds before the torpedo hit the carrier, which later sank.

BELOW LEFT A line of American landing craft moves towards the beach on Leyte on the 20 October 1944 as the US Sixth Army, heavily protected by the US Third Fleet, begins the invasion of the Philippines.

VICE ADMIRAL SHOJI NISHIMURA (1889-1944)

Shoji Nishimura joined the Japanese navy in 1911, and became a navigation specialist, getting his first command, a destroyer, in 1926. In the 1930s, he was commander of the 26th Destroyer Group and entered the war as a rear admiral, commanding the 4th Destroyer Squadron. His squadron played an important role in the Battle of the Java Sea, which made him briefly famous in Japan. He then commanded the 7th Cruiser Division in the battle for Guadalcanal. He was appointed commander of the Southern Force for "Sho-Go", but his small force was annihilated and he was killed during the battle.

BELOW Troops from the US Sixth Rangers battalion march to their embarkation point at Finschafen on the eastern coast of New Guinea before arriving at Dinagat Island in Leyte Gulf, which they attacked and captured on 17 October.

but was spotted by American motor torpedo boats and subjected first to torpedo attacks by destroyers, then, as it sailed in a straight line towards its destination, Rear Admiral Jesse Oldendorf's force of battleships and cruisers performed a classic crossing of the "T", subjecting the Japanese force to a thunderous broadside that sank all but two ships in the space of two hours. As the remaining ships retreated, the cruiser *Mogami* collided with a ship from the second part of Southern Force and was sunk by American aircraft during the morning of 25 October. Shima withdrew from the battle, leaving Kurita to attack with only one arm of the pincer still intact.

On the afternoon of 24 October, however, Halsey's aircraft had spotted the northern decoy force of carriers. Halsey ordered the bulk of his fleet, based around Task Force 38 (commanded by Vice Admiral Marc Mitscher) to steam north to engage. Kurita recovered his nerve and steered through the San Bernardino Strait with Centre Force. There were only escort carrier groups available to protect the US landings, with some 500 aircraft. They engaged Kurita's force when contact was made in the early morning of 25 October, sinking two cruisers, while a third was severely damaged by a torpedo attack, but the superior firepower of the Japanese force sank two escort carriers and with the first use of "kamikaze" suicide planes, threatened to overwhelm the American covering force. But after three hours Kurita, uncertain perhaps of Kinkaid's true strength, withdrew.

By this time, frantic messages to Halsey had forced the Third Fleet to turn back towards Leyte. All four Japanese carriers had been sunk, but the miscalculation of Japanese intentions meant that the remnants of both Kurita's Centre Force and the Northern Force were able to escape. Nevertheless, the separate actions proved a disaster for the Japanese navy, which lost 28 out of 64 warships committed and 10,500 sailors and pilots. The American naval forces lost six vessels out of the 218 sent to the Philippines. The superiority of American sea power, already proved in the island-hopping campaigns, now made the conquest of Japan's southern empire inevitable.

1929
Third Geneva Convention for protection of POWs signed. USSR and Japan failed to ratify it.

JUNE 1941
USSR asks Germany to agree to Red Cross supervision of POWs. Germany refuses.

1946–51
Far Eastern War Crimes Trials of Japanese soldiers accused of mistreatment of POWs.

1949
Fourth Geneva Convention signed.

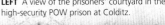

ABOVE POW armband worn by those held captive by the Japanese in Java.

Of the many millions of men and women mobilized to fight the Second World War, a substantial proportion became prisoners of the enemy. Their treatment and survival rates varied a great deal between the different combatant powers. In many cases, in contravention of the Geneva Convention, they were used as forced labour for war-related purposes. In some cases, most notably the German efforts to recruit a Russian Liberation Army from captured Red Army soldiers, prisoners became soldiers fighting against their former comrades.

The number of prisoners caught reflected the pattern of victory or defeat. Around 5.2 million Soviet soldiers were captured in the period of German victories in the east, when great encirclement operations ensnared whole Soviet armies. From 1944, it was the turn of the Soviet side to capture large numbers of Germans, while Soviet POW losses declined sharply. The British captured 600,000 Italian (including Italian colonial) soldiers in Africa, many of whom had no stomach for the contest; in Sicily, too, Italian soldiers surrendered in large numbers. German soldiers were captured in millions only in the last weeks of the war when American, British Commonwealth and French forces defeated the German army in Germany and Italy. In the Asian and Pacific wars, Japan took large numbers of prisoners in the first weeks of the war in 1941–42, but thereafter relatively few; Japanese soldiers were ordered not to surrender, and around 1.7 million Japanese soldiers, sailors and airmen died in the war, fighting suicidally rather than give in.

Once captured, the fate of prisoners was highly variable. In the war in the West both sides respected as far as they could the 1929 Geneva Convention (though on both

COLDITZ CASTLE

The eleventh-century German castle at Colditz, in Saxony, was used during the Second World War as a prison camp for officers who were either inveterate escapers or regarded as a security risk. The castle had been used as a mental asylum between 1829 and 1924, and during the early years of the Third Reich housed political prisoners and so-called "asocials". In 1939, designated Oflag IV-C, it became a camp for Polish and French officers, then a high-security camp for escapers, including Wing Commander Douglas Bader. The nature of the prison population made further escape attempts inevitable. There were around 300 attempts, and 30 successful escapes. The war ended before a glider, under construction in an attic area, could be used to mount yet another escape bid.

LEFT A view of the prisoners' courtyard in the high-security POW prison at Colditz.

ABOVE German POWs working in the vegetable garden at Glen Mill POW camp in Oldham, Lancashire on Christmas Eve 1940. Few German prisoners had yet been captured and not until 1942 were significant numbers in British hands.

LEFT A Soviet POW tries to revive a collapsed comrade under the gaze of indifferent German soldiers. The picture was taken on 21 November 1941 by which time around three million Soviet soldiers were in German hands. The great majority perished of disease and malnutrition.

BELOW Italian POWs load sacks of sugar destined for liberated Europe at Falcon Spinning Mill, Bolton, Lancashire in March 1945. Although Italy was now one of the Allied co-belligerent states, many Italian POWs continued to work for the Allies until after the end of the war.

sides there were cases where prisoners were killed on the battlefield) and camps were visited by the Red Cross. In most camps, the NCOs were responsible for keeping the discipline of their own rank and file, which in the case of some POW camps for SS soldiers in Britain led to kangaroo courts and the murder of anti-Hitler Germans. For servicemen caught in the West, there was an endless round of camp sports, entertainment, camp newspapers and journals and occasional attempts at escape. Since many Axis prisoners were sent to the United States, Canada and Australia, escape was pointless. But British and American servicemen regularly tried to escape from German prison camps and, once free, to contact underground escape organizations which could help them reach Switzerland, Sweden, Spain or Portugal. Around 35,000 escaped or evaded capture during the war. In Britain, prisoners were recruited to work on farms and building projects, and after the war, German POWs were kept back from repatriation until 1947–48, despite protests, because they provided a necessary contribution to British economic recovery.

On the Eastern Front, the prisoner regime was much harsher. Neither Germany nor the Soviet Union had been prepared for the scale of the prisoner population. Red Army soldiers were herded into makeshift enclosures in the summer and autumn of 1941 and typhus became endemic.

Lack of food, shelter and sanitation decimated the prisoner population and an estimated 2.4 to 3 million died. Eventually, in response to labour shortages in Germany, Hitler agreed to allow Soviet prisoners to be transported west to work, predominantly on essential military building projects and in agriculture.

Prisoners of the Japanese were also forced to work, usually in debilitating conditions and subject to savage punishments, inflicted in part because the Japanese despised soldiers who surrendered or were captured. Captured Chinese soldiers were often murdered, and occasionally recruited to fight for the local Japanese militia.

Many POWs continued to suffer once the war was over. German soldiers died in the makeshift camps set up by the Western Allies, who had simply nowhere to house them and no plan to supply them with food. Red Army prisoners returned to the Soviet Union were all interrogated by SMERSH, the anti-spying organization set up in 1943, and many were sent to labour camps from fear that they had been contaminated by fascism. For prisoners free to return home there were ambiguous feelings provoked both by defeat and also by victory in which they had been unable to take part.

ABOVE A view of the German POW camp for air force prisoners Stalag Luft III, at Sagan in Silesia, Germany, 1944. This camp was the site of a major escape attempt which was later made famous by the Hollywood film *The Great Escape*.

RIGHT An American interment camp for German women who had been members of National Socialist organizations. Many supporters of the Hitler regime, men and women, found themselves imprisoned in the months after the end of the war as a slow process of "de-Nazification" was carried out. This image dates from 1 April 1946.

BELOW A picture of American POWs taken in Bilibid prison in the Philippines capital of Manila on 8 February 1945 shortly after their liberation. Thousands of prisoners died in Japanese captivity from murder, hunger and disease.

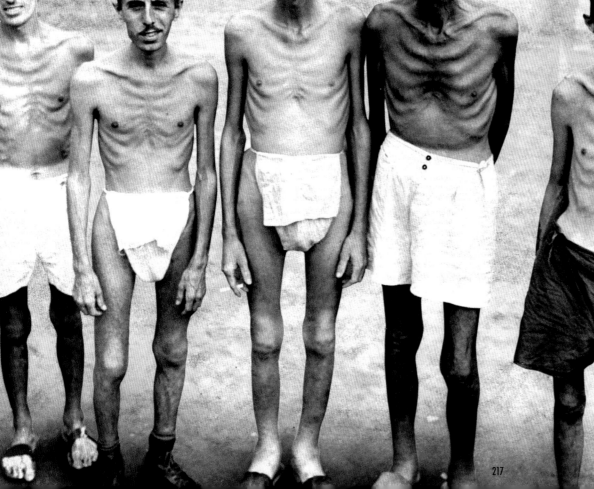

GERMAN POWS IN THE SOVIET UNION

In the early days of the German–Soviet war, only small numbers of Germans were captured by the Red Army. From Stalingrad onwards, more and more were captured, though some died on the way to prison camps or were killed when they were captured. German sources calculate that 3,155,000 German soldiers ended up in captivity, while Soviet records show only 2,730,000. There are also very wide differences in the calculation of how many prisoners died, principally from cold, hunger and disease. The German figure suggests that 1,186,000 died or were killed while Soviet security records show only 380,000 deaths. After the war, German POWs were forced to help rebuild the shattered towns and infrastructure of the Soviet Union and were repatriated slowly to Germany, 1.4 million by 1948, the last prisoners only in 1956, by which time they had played an important part in Soviet reconstruction.

BATTLE OF THE BULGE

ABOVE 101st Airborne Division – "The Screaming Eagles".

As the Allied armies pushed towards the German frontier in September 1944, Hitler argued for a fresh campaign to try to stem the tide in the west and to divide the Western Allies, both literally, by driving a heavily armed wedge between the American and British Commonwealth armies, and psychologically, by sowing confusion and argument between them. Although his senior commanders in the west, field marshals von Rundstedt and Model, were both reluctant to undertake too ambitious an operation given Germany's weakening position, Hitler got his way by insisting on an operation that later came to be known as the Battle of the Bulge.

The initial German codename for the spoiling action was Operation "Watch on the Rhine", chosen to mislead the Allies by suggesting a defensive intention. The plan, later renamed "Autumn Mist", was to use two large Panzer armies to drive through the very same Ardennes woodland that had been exploited so successfully in the invasion of France in May 1940, with the aim of crossing the River Meuse and capturing the Allies' major supply port at Antwerp. Preparations involved the strictest secrecy and a radio silence so absolute that Allied ULTRA intelligence detected nothing of the build-up and plan. The 6th SS Panzer Army under SS General Sepp Dietrich was to spearhead the drive to Antwerp; on his left was General Hasso von Manteuffel's 5th Panzer Army, which

ABOVE A briefing meeting at Hitler's headquarters to discuss Operation "Bodenplatte", the air support for the Ardennes offensive in December 1944. Hitler is unusually photographed wearing glasses. On his extreme right is the German air force commander-in-chief, Hermann Göring; on Hitler's far left the army chief-of-staff, General Heinz Guderian.

ABOVE Two officers from the 1st SS Panzer Division pause by a signpost to the Belgian towns of St Vith and Malmédy, scenes of some of the toughest fighting in the Battle of the Bulge. At Malmédy on 17 December 1944, 86 US prisoners were massacred by troops of SS Colonel Joachim Peiper's battle group.

was to cross the Meuse and swing north to the coast; both were to be protected from flank attack by General Erich Brandenberger's 7th Army to the south. A total of 500,000 men, almost 1,000 tanks and 1,000 aircraft, most of them fighters, were gathered together to strike at the weakest point of the Allied line, held by 83,000 American troops, some of them new units, some resting from fighting elsewhere.

The operation was nonetheless a gamble. Overall the Allies were much stronger and the drive to the coast carried the same risk it had run in 1940 of exposing long and vulnerable flanks to possible counter-attack. Success relied on speed, surprise and poor weather, which would limit Allied air action. On 16 December, in winter conditions

too poor for air action, the German armies attacked. The front line gave way under the sheer weight of the assault, but did not crack entirely. Eisenhower sent the US Seventh Armored Division to strengthen defences around the small Belgian town of St Vith against the 6th SS Panzer units, while the 101st Airborne arrived in Bastogne to prevent the road junction from falling easily into enemy hands. German paratroopers and a special unit, dressed in American uniforms and led by SS Lieutenant Colonel Otto Skorzeny, infiltrated Allied rear areas to cause panic and disruption, but their impact on the battle was also less than had been hoped. Those caught were shot.

The Allied response was rapid. As it became clear just how large the German assault was, Eisenhower ordered all

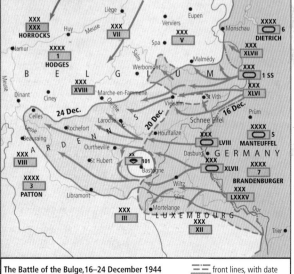

The Battle of the Bulge, 16–24 December 1944 ‑‑‑ front lines, with date

FIELD MARSHAL WALTER MODEL (1891–1945)

Walter Model was one of the most successful of German field generals and a staunch supporter of the Third Reich. He joined the German army in 1909 and fought in the First World War until severely wounded in 1917, after which he held a number of staff appointments. He stayed in the army after the war, rising to the rank of colonel by 1934. He became chief of the Technical Office of the General Staff in 1935 and was promoted to major general three years later. He was chief-of-staff of the IV Corps in Poland and of the 16th Army in France and commander of the 3rd Panzer Division in the invasion of the Soviet Union. In October 1941, he became a general of Panzer troops and commander of the 41st Army Corps, and in 1942 commander of the 9th Army, which he led in the key battle of Kursk in July 1943. In 1944, he took over Army Group North in Russia and was promoted field marshal, but during Operation "Bagration" he took over Army Group Centre and stabilized the German front. Hitler regarded him as someone who could perform miracles in a difficult situation. After halting the Russian advance, he was rushed to France in August 1944 to try to prevent disaster there. He withdrew the German army to western Germany, where his Army Group B was finally overwhelmed in the Ruhr pocket in April 1945. He killed himself on 21 April 1945 in a forest near Duisburg.

Battle of the Bulge, 25 December 1944–7 February 1945 — front lines, with date

ABOVE Can of US Army rations used throughout the campaign in northwest Europe.

THE BASTOGNE POCKET

During the Battle of the Bulge, the advancing German army failed to capture the small Belgian town of Bastogne, held from 19 December by the men of the US 101st Airborne Division and elements of the Ninth and Tenth armored divisions. The town was a vital road centre which the German Panzer armies needed, and time and effort had to be devoted to besieging it which could have been diverted to speeding up the advance. Low on ammunition and supplies, but hopeful of relief from advancing US forces, the commander, Brigadier General Anthony McAuliffe, famously replied to German demands to surrender on 22 December with the single word "Nuts!". Despite desperate German efforts to break the defending circle, Bastogne held out until the counter-offensive arrived on 26 December to relieve it.

ABOVE An American force held out at Bastogne, although surrounded and outnumbered.

LEFT German infantry move forward during the Ardennes offensive which opened on 16 December 1944 under heavy cloud. Helped by the wintry conditions, German troops punched a hole 95 kilometres (60 miles) deep into the Allied line.

BELOW LEFT A grim relic of the failed German assault. A German Panther tank with its turret blown off by anti-tank fire in a photograph taken on 3 January 1945. The destruction of most of the 1,000 tanks dedicated to the campaign fatally weakened the German defence of the homeland.

BELOW A German medical corps officer holds an improvised white flag as he is approached by an American tank towards the end of the failed German offensive in January 1945.

other fighting to stop so that Patton could swing his Third Army north to attack the south of what was now a large "bulge" (hence the name) in the American line; Montgomery took command of US forces in the north and co-ordinated Lieutenant General Hodges's US Seventh Corps and Lieutenant General Horrocks's Thirtieth Corps to blunt the German attack and then began to assault the northern flank. Dietrich's SS troops were held at St Vith until 23 December, while Manteuffel's forces, despite their inability to take Bastogne, pushed on rapidly until they were within five kilometres (three miles) of the Meuse at Celles, where the Seventh Corps forced them to halt. At its greatest extent the Bulge was 65 kilometres (40 miles) wide and between 95 and 110 kilometres (60 and 70 miles) long. By this stage, the weather had cleared and thousands of British and American fighters and fighter-bombers were unleashed on the German units. Unable to capture additional oil stocks as planned, Manteuffel's tanks and vehicles also ran out of fuel. Both shoulders of the Bulge held, and by late December, counter-offensives began to create the danger of another encirclement like the one at Falaise. Rundstedt asked Hitler for permission to withdraw which was refused, but by 8 January, with the neck of the Bulge rapidly closing, Hitler relented. Fighting a punishing rearguard campaign, German forces by 7 February were back where they had started.

The cost to both sides was high. Out of the half-million men committed, the German forces lost 100,000 casualties, around 850 tanks and almost all the 1,000 aircraft involved. This represented the end of serious German resistance in the west. US forces committed around 600,000 men to the contest and had casualties of 81,000, including 19,000 dead. British losses were 1,400, with 200 dead. The Battle of the Bulge was the costliest operation of the whole war in Western Europe.

SOVIET ADVANCE ON GERMANY: VISTULA–ODER OPERATION

The German High Command knew that the Red Army, after its long pause in the autumn of 1944, would undertake a major operation aimed at the German capital. The head of German military intelligence in the east, General Gehlen, accurately predicted the date (mid-January) and the massive destructive effect that the Soviet army would have. Hitler ordered a series of defensive lines to be set up across Poland, with major cities designated as "fortress" strongpoints, to be defended to the death. Soviet planning took final shape in November with Marshal Zhukov, released from his work in Moscow as Stalin's deputy, appointed to command the 1st Belorussian Army Group at the centre of the whole operation. To his left was Marshal Konev's 1st Ukrainian Army Group, and to the north Rokossovsky's 2nd Belorussian Army Group. Konev was to drive to Silesia and to capture its rich industrial resources, if possible intact; Rokossovsky was to drive towards East Prussia and Pomerania; Zhukov's armies aimed directly towards Berlin.

By January 1945, the disparity between the strength of the two sides had become a chasm. Along the whole Eastern Front the Red Army could field six million men against two million Germans and 190,000 from their Axis partners. For the Vistula–Oder Operation there were 2.2 million Red Army troops, 33,500 guns and mortars, 7,000 tanks and self-propelled artillery and 5,000 aircraft. The German Army Group A (renamed Army Group Centre on 26 January) could field only 400,000 men, 270 aircraft and 1,136 tanks and self-propelled guns, while in East Prussia and Pomerania there were a further 580,000 troops, 700 tanks and 515 aircraft. The speed and completeness with which this force was defeated in January and February 1945 owed a good deal to the sheer weight of weaponry available to the Soviet side.

The operation unfolded in waves, like the "Bagration" campaign in Belorussia in summer 1944, designed to unhinge the German defences. Konev's 1st Ukrainian Army

T he operation that brought the Red Army from the River Vistula in eastern Poland across prewar Polish territory to the River Oder in eastern Germany was a victory almost as swift and comprehensive as the earlier German invasion of Poland in September 1939. In a little over two weeks, the German army in the east was finally broken and pushed back into Germany for the final defence of Berlin.

ABOVE LEFT Soviet engineers working in freezing water in the Oder river oversee the construction of a bridge to ensure that the small bridgehead on the western bank of the river near Küstrin can be supplied.

RIGHT German rocket fire from the Baltic coast directed at the approaching Red Army, 8 March 1945. After the success of the Vistula–Oder operation Stalin ordered the Baltic coast to be cleared of German forces before the final assault on Berlin could take place.

MARSHAL IVAN KONEV (1897–1973)

Next to Marshal Zhukov, perhaps the best known of Soviet generals from the Second World War was Ivan Konev. The son of poor peasants from northern Russia, Konev worked as a lumberjack before being conscripted into the Russian army in 1916. He was still in training when Lenin's revolution took place in October 1917 and he became a keen and lifelong supporter of Communism. He became a military commissar during the Russian Civil War and stayed in the army after it was over. He was one of many young officers who were helped by the purges of 1937–38. By 1941, he was commander of the 19th Army in the Ukraine and was among the leading units to be hit first by the German invasion. Despite the disasters that overtook his forces, Konev survived Stalin's displeasure and was a key figure in the defence of Moscow, in charge of the Western Army Group. He was a major commander in the battles of 1942 and 1943 and led the 2nd Ukrainian Army Group for the drive across Ukraine to the frontiers of Eastern Europe. He was created a marshal in February 1944. After the war he became commander of Soviet land forces, and later commander-in-chief of Warsaw Pact forces, helping to repress the Hungarian revolution in 1956. He retired in 1963, and was buried in the Kremlin Wall on his death in 1973.

The Vistula-Oder Operation, 12 January–2 February 1945 ——— front lines, with date

Map labels:
Baltic Sea; Gdynia; Danzig; Königsberg; 9 Apr.; EAST PRUSSIA; LITHUANIA; Grodno; Allenstein; Marienwerder; POMERANIA; Stettin; XXXXX VISTULA HARPE; 2 Feb.; Chelmo; 12 Jan.; Bialystok; Lomza; G E R M A N Y; Oder; Berlin; Warta; Torun; Vistula; Modlin; 12 Jan. XXXXX 2 BELORUSSIAN ROKOSSOVSKY; Küstrin; Poznan 23 Feb.; Frankfurt; Kutno; Warsaw 17 Jan.; Brest-Litovsk; P O L A N D; Cottbus; Glogau; XXXXX A HARPE; Lodz; 12 Jan. XXXXX 1 BELORUSSIAN ZHUKOV; Bug; Dresden; Breslau; Radom; Chelm; 17 Jan.; 14 Jan.; XXXXX B SCHÖRNER; Elbe; Oder; Katowice; Cracow; 19 Jan.; Vistula; XXXXX 1 UKRAINIAN KONEV; Gorlice; Jaroslaw; Lwów

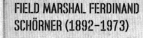

FIELD MARSHAL FERDINAND SCHÖRNER (1892–1973)

Notorious as one of the most brutal of German army commanders, Schörner fought in a Bavarian regiment in the First World War in France, Italy and the east and was severely wounded three times. He remained in the army after 1919 and took part in suppressing the Hitler *Putsch* in Munich in November 1923. By the outbreak of war, he was a colonel in command of the 98th Regiment of Mountain Troops. In May 1940, he took over command of the 6th Mountain Division, which he led in France and the Balkans. From January 1942, he commanded the 19th Mountain Corps and was promoted to lieutenant general. He was noted for his National Socialist sympathies and tough leadership style (he liked the phrase "More fear of what is behind than what is in front!") and on 1 February 1944 was named chief of the newly created National Socialist Army Leadership Staff. He led army groups in the east in 1944, and in January 1945 took command of Army Group Centre in Poland. In April, he was made a field marshal. After the war he was sentenced to 25 years' hard labour in the Soviet Union, but released in 1955.

ABOVE Soviet T-34/85 tanks on the road towards Königsberg in late January/early February 1945. To save on vehicles and fuel, Soviet infantry assigned to armoured formations travelled on top of the tanks. The mixed-arm units introduced gradually from 1943 gave the Red Army the flexibility and fighting power enjoyed earlier by Germany's Panzer divisions.

ABOVE The Silesian city of Breslau, encircled by Marshal Konev's 2nd Ukrainian Army Group on 15 February, held out until 6 May 1945. Here Soviet scouts search for the German positions in the battered city.

Group attacked on 12 January, and Zhukov's 1st Belorussian Army Group on 14 January. On the day in between, the northern Soviet army groups began the operation to clear East Prussia, a move that brought the Red Army into German territory and with it a regime of atrocity and terror directed at the civilian population, including the mass rape of German women. Within two weeks, Konev had driven deep into Silesia and began a long siege of Breslau, which lasted from 15 February until 6 May, shortly before the German surrender. In the centre of the operation, Zhukov's armies finally seized Warsaw on 17 January from determined German defence of the ruined capital. Included among the attackers was the Polish 1st Army, recruited from among Poles sympathetic to communism. General Schörner was sent to take over Army Group A to try to steady the front line, but with little effect. Over the next two weeks, Zhukov pushed his forces forward, his faster motorized units pushing deep into the German rear. By 31 January, his first units reached the Oder near the fortified town of Küstrin, only 65 kilometres (40 miles) from Berlin, and by 2 February a small bridgehead had been forged across the Oder by troops who crossed the treacherously thin ice.

Slower progress was made in East Prussia and Pomerania, where the German army fiercely defended German soil. In front of the advancing Red Army flowed a stream of German refugees, terrified of Soviet vengeance. They arrived at the Baltic coast and a slow evacuation began, but for many German civilians the only way to escape was on foot through the narrow slice of territory that still divided Rokossovsky's forces from the sea. Everywhere small pockets of German resistance remained in the fortress zones. They were bypassed by the Red Army, to be picked off one-by-one when the campaign was over. The stage was now set for the final advance on the capital of Hitler's New Order.

ABOVE German refugees taste the reality of war. Here they are pictured crossing the frozen lagoon Frische Haff in East Prussia to escape the approaching Red Army. The Soviet troops looted whatever they found and raped hundreds of thousands of German women as they moved into German territory.

THE YALTA CONFERENCE

5 JANUARY 1945
Soviet Union recognizes the Lublin Committee as the government of Poland.

27 JANUARY 1945
Soviet forces cross the Vistula river in the drive across Poland.

13 FEBRUARY 1945
The 35,000-strong German garrison in Budapest surrenders.

By the last stages of the war, the three major Allies found it necessary to stage another major summit meeting to try to resolve some of the remaining issues exposed by the rapid collapse of German resistance and the expected defeat of Japan. Stalin suggested the Crimean city of Yalta, but Roosevelt, now terminally ill, preferred Athens or Malta. When Stalin said he was unable to travel outside the Soviet Union, his alliance partners reluctantly accepted and Roosevelt was forced to travel 7,750 kilometres (4,800 miles) by sea and a further 2,200 kilometres (1,375 miles) by air. Churchill later complained that 10 years of research could not have found "a worse place".

The conference, codenamed "Argonaut", met from 5 to 11 February. Roosevelt and Churchill had met beforehand in Malta and flown on to the Crimea. Both men wanted to be able to maintain what they saw as a good working relationship with Stalin in the hope that the postwar world order could be constructed through co-operation. However, most of the issues discussed at Yalta could not be resolved

BELOW The "Big Three" seated during the conference in the Crimean town of Yalta outside the Livadia Palace. By this stage of the war Churchill complained that he was marginalized, while Roosevelt remained confident that the three states could continue to co-operate after the war was over.

ABOVE The assembled delegates at the Dumbarton Oaks Conference which opened at the Washington DC mansion on 21 August 1944 and continued until 7 October. The conference of representatives from the major Allied states discussed the formation of the United Nations as a means to keep the peace in the postwar world.

ABOVE An ill and ageing Roosevelt confers with Churchill aboard a warship off the coast of Malta during "Argonaut I" (30 January–3 February), the first stage of the discussions between the leaders of the Grand Alliance. The two men met twice before making the final trip to Yalta.

at once. From the United States' point of view, the war with Japan still featured prominently and in a secret agreement, undertaken without Churchill's knowledge, Roosevelt made concessions to the Soviet Union in exchange for their participation in the Asian war once Germany was defeated. The Soviet Union was guaranteed a pro-Soviet Mongolia, the return of the southern half of Sakhalin Island and annexation of the Kurile Islands.

The political discussions covered the fate of defeated Germany and the future of Poland, as well as the creation of the United Nations Organization, which Roosevelt hoped

MARSHAL ALEXEI ANTONOV (1896–1962)

Alexei Antonov was one of the most influential figures on the Soviet General Staff in the last three years of the war. The son of a Russian artillery officer, Antonov was conscripted into the Russian infantry in 1916 and fought in the last major campaign of the eastern war, the failed Kerensky Offensive, in July 1917. He joined the new Red Army in late 1918 and soon rose to command positions thanks to his clear intelligence and military skills. He joined the Communist Party in 1928 and attended the Frunze Military Academy. In the 1930s, he spent most of his time as student then teacher at the Academy. In 1937, during the purges, he was appointed, aged 41, as chief-of-staff of the Moscow Military District. He was a major general by 1940, and in 1941 was sent as deputy chief-of-staff for the Kiev Military District in the path of Army Group South in the subsequent German invasion. His brief successes in the battles around Rostov and in the Caucasus in 1942 earned him promotion to chief of operations in Moscow. In this role, he discussed campaigns with Stalin directly and offered him advice. He attended the Yalta and Potsdam conferences. He was promoted to deputy chief-of-staff and served in this role until 1948. In 1955, he became chief-of-staff of the Warsaw Pact and died of a heart attack at his desk in 1962.

ABOVE The Polish "Lublin Government", a provisional administration of pro-Soviet Poles set up after the liberation of eastern Poland by the Red Army. Poland became the sticking point in many of the discussions at Yalta. The West wanted guarantees that all Polish parties would be represented in the new regime.

RIGHT Winston Churchill in Scotland on 23 October 1940, inspecting Polish troops who had escaped to Britain from Europe after Polish defeat, accompanied by General Wladyslaw Sikorski, prime minister of the Polish government-in-exile in London. Churchill later complained that Polish intransigence over their prewar frontiers had soured relations with Stalin.

FAR RIGHT US poster, 1943, celebrating the United Nations (UN), those states fighting the Axis powers who had signed the UN Declaration. The first signatories were the USA, the USSR, Britain and China on 1 January 1942, followed by a further 41 nations. The postwar development of a UN organization was discussed at Yalta.

THE UNITED NATIONS FIGHT FOR FREEDOM

would pave the way for genuine co-operation after the war. The Soviet side had the advantage that the whole of the Livadia Palace, where Roosevelt was staying, was bugged. The secretly recorded conversations were reported each day to Stalin by Sergo Beria, son of the NKVD police chief, Lavrenti Beria. Stalin used this information in his negotiations, appeasing the Western leaders when it cost him little, manoeuvring round them when it was something he wanted. It was agreed that France would be one of the occupying powers in Germany. Stalin asked for a bill of $20 billion of reparations from Germany, and although Churchill and Roosevelt demurred, they did not reject the demand out of hand. For defeated Germany it was agreed to establish an Allied Control Commission to oversee the transfer to peace.

The greatest stumbling block was Poland. Although neither Roosevelt nor Churchill was opposed to the idea of moving Poland westwards at the expense of German territory and giving the Soviet Union the conquests of 1939, both were concerned that the new Poland, at that point very recently conquered by the Red Army, should remain independent and democratic. Stalin was reluctant to accept a broadening of the political base by allowing the leaders of the Polish government-in-exile a place in the newly

reconstituted government, and after a considerable degree of argument he acquiesced in the principle of a "free, independent and democratic" Poland, in the knowledge that political reality dictated a future Communist takeover. Soviet bugging had revealed to Stalin just how important this principle was to the British and Americans and his concession of a broader-based regime in Poland was entirely expedient.

The Yalta Conference was also the setting for a decision that sealed the fate of the German city of Dresden. In discussions with General Antonov, chief of operations, the Soviet side requested the bombing of Germany's eastern cities to help ease the path of Soviet forces. The Western air forces had already been ordered to begin attacks before Yalta to help prevent the movement of German soldiers to the mountainous regions of southern Germany where it was feared they might make a last stand. There remains dispute about whether the name Dresden was actually voiced, but other eastern German cities were mentioned, Leipzig in particular, and duly bombed by the Western Allies' bomber forces. Dresden was destroyed on 13/14 February 1945 in a bombing firestorm, with the death of an estimated 25–35,000 people.

ABOVE President Roosevelt waves to supporters on election night 7 November 1944 from the porch of his Hyde Park estate in New York. Eleanor Roosevelt stands to his left. He was elected for an unprecedented fourth term, but his terminal illness led to his premature death on 12 April 1945.

IWO JIMA

4 MARCH 1945
Allied forces capture Meiktila in Burma (Myanmar).

5 MARCH 1945
US armies reach the River Rhine in Germany and capture Cologne.

30 MARCH 1945
Red Army captures Danzig where the war began in 1939.

ABOVE Badge of a Japanese superior private.

As American forces closed in on the Japanese home islands in 1944, a choice had to be made between invading Formosa (Taiwan) or other islands closer to Japan. The Formosa plan was finally abandoned in October in favour of attacks on the Bonin and Ryukyu Islands. On 3 October 1944, Admiral Nimitz was instructed to choose an island for attack which could be used by fighter aircraft to support the bombers flying from the Marianas. He chose Iwo Jima, an eight-kilometre- (five-mile-) long volcanic island 1,060 kilometres (660 miles) south of Tokyo where Japanese aircraft were based for attacks on American air bases in the Marianas.

The Japanese High Command guessed that the United States would try to find bases closer to the home islands. The local garrisons were strengthened and complex networks of tunnels and bunkers constructed. On Iwo Jima, Lieutenant General Tadamichi Kuribayashi commanded 22,000 troops dug in to well-prepared positions. The Japanese plan here, as elsewhere, was to allow the Americans to land and then to wear down their will to continue the fight in a brutal war of attrition. The 72 continuous days of aerial bombardment prior to the invasion of the island seem to have done little to dent the fighting power of the hidden defenders.

ABOVE Landing craft filled with marines of the Fifth Amphibious Corps speed towards the landing beaches on the southeastern coast of the Japanese island of Iwo Jima on 19 February 1945. After a brief period of calm on the beaches, the force was subjected to heavy fire which took a large toll on the first day.

BELOW Troops from the Fourth Marine Division land on "Blue" beach on Iwo Jima in the morning of 19 February 1945. They had to cross a high bank of soft black volcanic ash with full equipment. By the end of the day over 30,000 marines were ashore and the beachhead secured.

GENERAL HARRY SCHMIDT (1886–1968)

Harry Schmidt was Marine commander of the Fifth Amphibious Corps in the battle for Iwo Jima. He joined the Marine Corps in 1909 and had his first posting to Guam in the Pacific in 1911. After a long career on and off water he was head of the Paymaster Department of the Marine Corps when war broke out in 1941. In January 1942, he became assistant to the Marine Corps commander and in August 1943 commanding general of the Fourth Marine Division. His forces took part in the capture of Saipan and Tinian, by which time he was commander of the Fifth Amphibious Corps. His corps distinguished itself in the capture of Iwo Jima and went on to become part of the occupying force in Japan after the war was over. In February 1946, he took over the Marine Training Command and retired in 1948, when he was promoted to four-star general.

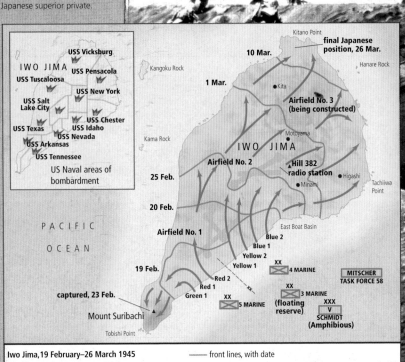

Iwo Jima, 19 February–26 March 1945 —— front lines, with date

almost 30,000 men. Most of Kuribayashi's force remained concealed in the defensive lines built further inland in deep bunkers and pillboxes carved into the soft volcanic rock. The first airstrip was captured on 20 February and Mount Suribachi four days later. By 27 February, the other completed airstrips had been captured, but it took another month before the island was declared secure.

Japanese resistance so close to the home islands increased in intensity and the marines took exceptionally heavy casualties. On Hill 382, nicknamed the "Meat Grinder", the marines had to fight for every yard against defenders who fought until they were killed. Each defensive position in the gorges and caves of the rocky island had to be captured using flamethrowers and explosives to kill or flush out the defenders. Even when forced into the open, many Japanese soldiers hurled themselves at the attackers rather than surrender. The sheer weight of American firepower from sea, air and land drove the Japanese defenders back to the north of the island where they made their last stand in "Bloody Gorge" at Kitano Point which took ten days to clear and ended with a final suicidal *banzai* charge. Even though the island was declared secure on 26 March, a further 2,409 Japanese soldiers were killed in the period up to June as defenders fought almost literally to the last man. The Japanese suffered a total of 23,300 killed, with nearly no prisoners taken. Marine losses totalled 5,931 dead and 17,372 wounded, over one-third of the original force committed.

Fighter aircraft began to operate from Iwo Jima even before it was secured and the first B-29 "Superfortress" bomber landed on the island on 4 March, the first of 2,251 which made emergency landings on the island on the way to or from the Japanese home islands. At a high cost in lives, the air route to Japan was finally secured and the last stages of the heavy bombing of Japan's cities could be undertaken.

ABOVE Marines on Iwo Jima crouch behind a rock to avoid the blast from a heavy explosive charge laid in a cave connected to a three-tier Japanese block-house. The Japanese defenders were hidden in caves and deep shelters and had to be forced out in a long drawn-out campaign which did not end until 26 March.

The invasion force comprised the Fourth and Fifth Marine Divisions of Major General Harry Schmidt's Fifth Amphibious Corps, backed up by a reserve division, a total of 60,000 marines. There were 800 warships eventually committed to the battle. The invasion had to be postponed because of the slow progress in capturing the Philippines, but on 19 February, supported by the first naval "rolling barrage" of the Pacific War, the marines went ashore. The thick volcanic ash and steep shoreline made progress slow, and after 20 minutes the force was suddenly subjected to heavy flanking fire from hidden defences; some 519 marines were killed on the first day. Nevertheless. the first marines ashore succeeded in establishing a beachhead which soon housed

MOUNT SURIBACHI

One of the most famous images of the Second World War is the raising of the flag on top of Mount Suribachi, a small extinct volcano at the southern tip of Iwo Jima. The photograph was a staged replay of the first flag-raising by Company E of the 28th Marines on the morning of 23 February 1945, who seized the summit even though the mountain was still occupied by Japanese units. The first small flag was attached to a piece of waste pipe, but later that day a second patrol unit arrived at the peak with a larger flag and a war photographer, Joe Rosenthal. He photographed the men raising the second flag and created an iconic image.

ABOVE A small group of Japanese prisoners out of 20 taken alive on Iwo Jima from the garrison of 23,000. These prisoners were taken during mopping-up operations in the weeks following the defeat of organized resistance. They have been issued with cigarettes by their American captors.

RIGHT Naval medical corps doctors and assistants at an emergency frontline dressing station. The poles have been stuck in the sand to support plasma bottles for blood transfusions. More than 17,000 marines were wounded, almost one-third of the attacking force.

ABOVE The US Seventh Fighter Command base on Iwo Jima on the former Japanese Airfield No 1 in the shadow of Mount Suribachi (right). Among the squadron of P-51 Mustangs is a Boeing B-29 heavy bomber, forced to land on Iwo Jima on the shuttle to and from bombing the Japanese mainland.

THE FIREBOMBING OF TOKYO

14 FEBRUARY 1945
Firebombing of the German city of Dresden.

23/24 FEBRUARY 1945
First firebombing raid on Tokyo destroys one square mile.

8 MARCH 1945
First efforts made by German emissaries to bring about an armistice in northern Italy.

14/15 MARCH
B-29 bombers attack the city of Osaka, inflicting further heavy casualties.

ABOVE Badge of Twentieth US Army Airforces which included Twenty-first and Twentieth Bomber Command.

The bombing of Japan, like the bombing of Germany in Europe, began slowly and with mixed results. Because of the long distances involved, the bombers then in use in the European theatre were unable to reach mainland Japan from existing bases. Only when the first B-29 "Superfortress" bombers became available from the summer of 1944 – the first 130 arrived in India in May – was it possible to mount long-distance attacks against targets in the Japanese Empire in Manchuria, Korea or Thailand; the Japanese home islands were still difficult to reach for aircraft at the limit of their range. The capture of the Marianas was essential for the planned campaign of precision bombing against Japanese steel production and the aviation industry.

The first major B-29 raid was against the Thai capital of Bangkok on 5 June 1944. From then until early 1945, the Twentieth Air Force operated from bases in India and China against distant targets with very limited success. Operation "Matterhorn", as it was codenamed, achieved little and when the Japanese army overran the Chinese airfields the operation was wound up. Instead General Arnold, the USAAF chief-of-staff, decided to deploy the B-29s from the Marianas using Twenty-first Bomber Command under General Haywood Hansell, one of the planners of the air war in Europe. The first B-29 landed in October 1944 on Saipan, but a combination of slow delivery of aircraft, regular harassing attacks by Japanese aircraft, now using ramming techniques against enemy bombers, and the exceptionally long flights to mainland Japan in generally poor weather once again led to very limited achievements. In the first three months of operations, only 1,146 tons of

LEFT Japanese children being evacuated from Ueno station in Tokyo. Around 8 million Japanese moved from threatened urban areas to the overcrowded countryside, placing a severe strain on an already overstretched rationing system.

BOTTOM A Boeing B-29 heavy bomber at a base in China as it prepares to take off for a bombing mission over Japan. Most B-29 attacks were later made from the Mariana Islands in the central Pacific but from June 1944 attacks were made from China until the main airfields were overrun by Japanese armies later in the year. The B-29 had a range of 6,500 kilometres (4,000 miles) and could carry 5,500 kilograms (12,000 pounds) of bombs.

GENERAL HENRY "HAP" ARNOLD (1886–1950)

As chief-of-staff of the United States Army Air Force throughout the Second World War, Arnold played a central role in the American war effort. He became an army airman in the First World War, and by 1918 was assistant commander-in-chief of the Air Service, though he arrived too late in Europe to see combat. In September 1938, he was chosen to head the Army Air Corps with the rank of major general, and when the corps was turned into the Army Air Forces in June 1941, Arnold became its chief. He sat on both the American Joint Chiefs-of-Staff Committee and the Anglo-American Combined Chiefs Committee. In March 1942, his official title became commanding general of the US Army Air Forces. He was an energetic, hardworking and sociable commander ("Hap" was short for "Happy"), with a clear understanding of technical development and high managerial skills. He suffered from poor health towards the end of the war, when he became the air force's first five-star general.

GENERAL CURTIS LEMAY (1906–1990)

Curtis E LeMay masterminded the bombing of Japan and went on to play a central role in creating the US Strategic Air Command after the war. He joined the US Army Air Corps (later the Army Air Forces) in 1928 and had risen by October 1942 to the rank of colonel in charge of a bomber group of the Eighth Air Force based in England. A commander who flew with his men to experience combat, and a thoughtful tactician, LeMay was rapidly promoted. He was already a major general, the youngest in the army, when in August 1944 he took over command of Twentieth Bomber Command based in India for attacks from Chinese bases on Japanese targets in Manchuria and the home islands. He moved in January 1945 to take command of the Twenty-first Bomber Command on the Marianas and from here organized the bombing of Japan's cities. In July, he took command of Twentieth US Army Air Forces (which included Twenty-first and Twentieth Bomber Command) and later the same month became chief-of-staff to the newly formed Strategic Air Forces in the Pacific. After the war he became commander of the Strategic Air Command from 1949 to 1957, and in 1961 chief-of-staff of the US Air Force.

ABOVE US carrier-based aircraft on a bombing raid against Tokyo on 2 March 1945. Aircraft from Task Force 58 and Task Force 38 bombarded Japanese cities and defences from March to August 1945 against light Japanese resistance. Aircraft also engaged in the heavy mining of Japanese coastal waters, bringing trade almost to a halt.

bombs were dropped on a range of precision targets. The first raid on Tokyo took place on 24 November 1944 but the effects were slight.

The disappointing nature of the bombing campaign led Arnold to sack Hansell and replace him with the more aggressive Major General Curtis LeMay, who arrived on Saipan in January 1945. After more weeks of unspectacular high-altitude precision attacks, LeMay was arguing with senior commanders for a radical change in tactics. He advocated using the newly available and highly effective M-69 firebomb in large quantities in low-level night-time attacks on Japan's urban areas. The subsequent fires would destroy local industry, demoralize the population and perhaps accelerate surrender. Uncertain whether Arnold would approve "area bombing", LeMay planned an experiment against Tokyo on the night of 9/10 March. A total of 334 B-29s were launched from three island bases carrying over 1,600 tons of incendiaries and 279 reached their destination.

The aircraft arrived over Tokyo in the early hours of 10 March, flying at between 1,200 and 2,800 metres (4,000 and 9,200 feet) where they met little resistance from the air defences. Pathfinders marked the area to be

bombed with napalm, and the bombers released their loads indiscriminately within the designated zone. The attack quickly provoked a firestorm which burned out 41 square kilometres (16 square miles) of the city and killed an estimated 100,000 people in a single night, the highest death toll of any single air attack. One million people were rendered homeless and a quarter of all residential buildings were destroyed. Over the next six months, LeMay's force destroyed 58 Japanese cities and inflicted an estimated 500,000 deaths. The new tactics of fire-bombing at low altitude proved grimly effective. An attack, for example, on the northern Honshu town of Aomori on the night of 28/29 July destroyed 88 per cent of the built-up area. By this time there were 3,700 B-29s available, more than the Marianas could accommodate. There remains much argument over whether the urban attacks were responsible for reducing Japanese war production, since the loss of the merchant marine and attacks on communications played an important part in this, but there is no doubt that the bomb attacks quickly demoralized the home population and accelerated the efforts of those Japanese leaders who could see the war was lost to try to find some acceptable formula for surrender.

ABOVE An aerial view of central Tokyo following the firebombing of the city on the night of 9/10 March 1945. Only the concrete structures remain among the ruins of a highly flammable city where more than 100,000 lost their lives. The heat became so intense that people fleeing into the Sumida River (top) were boiled alive in the water.

THE WESTERN ADVANCE INTO GERMANY: FROM THE RHINE TO THE ELBE

19 MARCH 1945
Hitler issues his "scorched earth" directive ordering Germans to destroy everything in the path of the advancing Allied armies.

27 MARCH 1945
Argentina finally declares war on Germany and Japan.

12 APRIL 1945
Death of President Roosevelt. Vice President Truman takes his place.

13 APRIL 1945
Vienna captured by the 2nd and 3rd Ukrainian army groups.

ABOVE US Ninth Army formation badge.

LEFT British troops of the Gordon Highlanders fighting in the Reichswald forest in northwest Germany, 9 February 1945. Fighting here was fierce against five defensive lines and in heavy mud. The forest was finally cleared by 9 March.

BELOW The bridge at Remagen over the Rhine River captured intact on 7 March by a surprise assault of the US Ninth Armored Division. Here vehicles and troops are crossing the Hindenburg Bridge on 17 March while German soldiers trudge into captivity from the other direction.

BELOW LEFT A landing craft helps to tow a bridge section in the Reichswald sector of the River Rhine, 25 March 1945. A Taylorcraft Auster spotter aircraft flies above, while the engineers construct a crossing for British Commonwealth armies.

At the end of 1944, the Western Allies were poised to begin the assault on Germany when the Battle of the Bulge interrupted their preparations. The effect was not entirely negative, for the final fling of German forces in the west removed the last major reserves of tanks and aircraft and left the three German army groups – General Student's Group H in the north in the Netherlands, Group B under Field Marshal Model in the Ruhr and Group G under General Blaskowitz in the south – well under strength and devoid of serious air support.

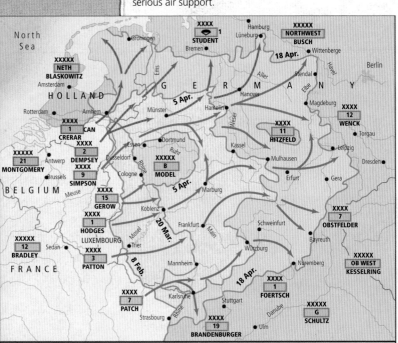

The western advance into Germany, 8 February–18 April 1945   —— front lines, with date

Eisenhower favoured an approach on a broad front, as the Red Army was doing in the east. By 3 January, he had 73 divisions, 20 of them armoured and the rest well-equipped, supported by overwhelming strength in the air, both tactical and strategic. The campaign to bring the war to an end involved three stages: clearing the territory on the west bank of the Rhine, effecting a series of Rhine crossings to establish solid bridgeheads on the eastern bank, and finally a general break-out to bring Western armies to the River Elbe and into Austria and Czechoslovakia, where they would meet up with the Soviet armed forces. Although Montgomery would have preferred a breakthrough on a narrower front and rapid deployment towards Berlin, Eisenhower accepted the decision agreed at Yalta that Berlin would be in the Soviet zone of operations.

The first series of operations was launched on 8 February 1945 when Montgomery's Twenty-first Army Group, under the codename "Veritable", began an attack to clear the area between the River Meuse and the Rhine. The British 2nd Army and Canadian 1st Army encountered fierce resistance

GENERAL JACOB DEVERS (1887–1979)

A career field artillery officer, who joined the US Army in 1909, Devers was an outstanding administrator. As the army's youngest major general, he oversaw the expansion of the American Armored Force from just two divisions to 16 by 1943. In May 1943, he was appointed overall commander of US Army forces in Europe where he helped to organize and train units for the D-Day landings. At the end of the year, he became deputy supreme commander in the Mediterranean and in September 1944 he was posted to active command of Sixth Army Group, which was moving through southern France towards Alsace. He led the army group across the Rhine and accepted the surrender of German forces in Austria on 6 May 1945; he was shortly thereafter promoted to full general. He retired from the army in 1949.

from the German 1st Paratroop Army in the Reichswald forest and not until 21 February was the northern area west of the Rhine cleared. The US Ninth Army, mounting Operation "Grenade", was held up by flooding and could only begin on 23 February, but weak German resistance brought them to the bank of the Rhine near Düsseldorf on 1 March. Further south, Bradley's Twelfth Army Group, in Operation "Lumberjack", cut rapidly through the defences of the Westwall, the main frontier fortifications, to reach the river by 7 March, while Operation "Undertone", led by Lieutenant General Jacob Devers's Sixth Army Group, pushed forward into the Saarland to reach Mannheim on the southern Rhine.

It was during the "Lumberjack" operation that the US Ninth Armored Division surprised German troops trying to demolish the Hindenburg railway bridge over the river at Remagen. They captured the bridge intact on 7 March and established a small bridgehead on the far side. Despite efforts to destroy the bridge with V-2 rockets, it survived until 17 March, when it finally collapsed. Eisenhower insisted on maintaining a broad front nevertheless, and Montgomery

planned a massive assault across the river between Rees and Duisburg. German forces had been reduced to a mere 26 divisions, by contrast with more than 200 facing the Red Army in the east. To cope with the expected assault, Hitler replaced the faithful von Rundstedt with Field Marshal Kesselring, the defender of Italy. There were simply too few soldiers and too little equipment to hold up the assault for long. When the Rhine was crossed in force on 24 March in the north a broad bridgehead was easily secured. Ever mindful of the opportunity to get the better of the British, General Patton made his crossing further south at Oppenheim two days before, on the night of 22/23 March.

Unequal though the contest was, it would be wrong to see it as a straightforward campaign. German forces often fought with fanatical determination and great tactical skill and high casualties were exacted in the last month of the conflict, but the final outcome was not in doubt. On 1 April, Model's forces were trapped in the area of the Ruhr, and on 21 April the encircled German armies surrendered, an estimated 350,000 men in total. Meanwhile, Montgomery's Twenty-first Army Group reached the ruins of Lübeck on the Baltic coast. Further south, resistance crumbled. The US Ninth Army reached Magdeburg on the Elbe river on 12 April, while forward units of Lieutenant General Hodges's US First Army reached the Elbe on 25 April near the town of Torgau where they experienced a historic meeting with units of Konev's 1st Ukrainian Army Group. The US Sixth Army Group, which included the French 1st Army under General de Lattre de Tassigny, cleared southern Germany and moved into Austria. It was now only a matter of time before Germany was utterly defeated.

ABOVE Hundreds of German POWs herded into a makeshift camp, 25 March 1945. Millions of soldiers fell into Allied hands in the last weeks of the war in Europe but arrangements for housing and feeding them were slow to materialize and many were left at first on the bare ground with little food.

BELOW American Stuart VI light tanks advance past vehicles of the 15th Scottish Division during the advance to the Elbe river on 13 April 1945. Once German resistance was broken progress was swift across Germany towards the oncoming Red Army.

RIGHT Soviet and US servicemen fraternize on the banks of the Elbe river at Torgau on 25 April 1945 where elements of the US First Army and the Soviet 1st Ukrainian Army Group joined forces. First contact had been made a few hours earlier at the village of Stehla, but the heavily photographed gathering at Torgau has become popularly accepted as the initial meeting.

ABOVE RIGHT Montgomery's beret, with field marshal's badge, worn through the northwest Europe campaign.

RIGHT Winston Churchill lunching with Field Marshal Montgomery and Field Marshal Alan Brooke, chief of the Imperial General Staff, on the east bank of the Rhine on 26 March 1945, two days after the British assault across the river.

GENERAL JOHANNES BLASKOWITZ (1883–1948)

The son of a Prussian priest, Johannes Blaskowitz joined the army as a cadet at the age of 10, and was a lieutenant by the time he was 19. He was a company commander and staff officer on four different fronts during the First World War, stayed in the postwar army and was a major general by 1932. He was commander of Army Group 3 in Dresden from 1938 and in this capacity his forces helped occupy Austria and the Sudetenland in 1938, and Czechoslovakia in March 1939. He commanded the 8th Army in Poland and took the surrender of Warsaw. He was afterwards commander of the German army of occupation, during which time he protested regularly about the atrocities being perpetrated against Poles and Jews. He was removed by Hitler in May 1940 and posted as commander of the German 1st Army of occupation in France in October. In 1944, he took over Army Group G in southern France and successfully withdrew his forces northwards following Operation "Dragoon". In January 1945, he commanded Army Group H in the Netherlands, finally surrendering to the British on 5 May 1945. He was imprisoned after the war and committed suicide at Nuremberg in February 1948.

OKINAWA

While the final battles were waged for Iwo Jima, a huge task force was made ready to invade Okinawa, largest of the Ryukyu Islands, on the edge of the Japanese home islands. The battle was the largest of the Pacific War and the costliest for the American and Japanese forces involved. Okinawa was chosen as a potential base for heavy air attacks on Japan, but it could also be used as a staging post for the eventual invasion of the main islands.

The preparations matched the scale of the "Overlord" landings in France the previous year. Under the overall command of Rear Admiral Raymond Spruance, Operation

"Iceberg" eventually involved half-a-million men and 1,213 naval vessels. Lieutenant General Simon Buckner's recently activated US Tenth Army, made up of two marine and four regular army divisions, was given the task of clearing the island, but this time it was defended by approximately 100,000 Japanese troops, including 20,000 Okinawan militia, a much larger concentration than on Iwo Jima or Saipan. The invasion was supported by Vice Admiral Marc Mitscher's Task Force 58, which began a heavy naval bombardment of the island on 23 March.

The Japanese commander, General Mitsuru Ushijima, decided, against the instructions of the High Command, to adopt the same tactics used on Iwo Jima, despite their evident failure. Most of the long, thin island was difficult to defend except for the limestone outcrops at the south end. Ushijima concentrated most of his forces in the hilly region of the south with a defensive line across the island from its chief town, Naha. Other forces were based on the Motobu Peninsula further up the west coast. The Japanese hoped to benefit from the decision, taken some months before, to use aircraft on kamikaze missions, employing the aircraft itself as a weapon to sink American shipping.

The campaign began with the seizure of the outlying Kerama and Keise islands between 23 and 29 March.

ABOVE LEFT A Marine 155 Howitzer shells Japanese defences in the south of Okinawa in the early hours of the morning. The crew turn away from the blinding muzzle blast which illuminates the camouflage net stretched over the gun.

LEFT A concealed Japanese artillery piece on the island of Okinawa, part of the network of deep bunkers and shelters constructed in the mountainous southern tip of the island where the Japanese 32nd Army concentrated its forces.

FAR LEFT US marines laden with equipment clamber down ladders into waiting landing craft on 10 April 1945 during the early stages of the three-month campaign on Okinawa. Over 170,000 US servicemen saw action in the capture of the island.

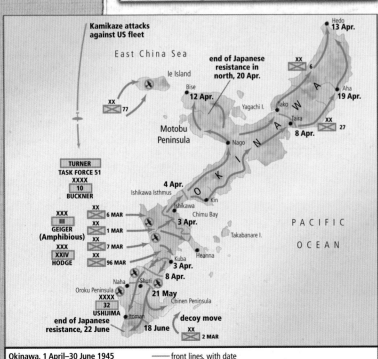

Okinawa, 1 April–30 June 1945 ——— front lines, with date

Kamikaze attacks against US fleet
East China Sea
Ie Island
Bise
Hedo 13 Apr.
XX 6
end of Japanese resistance in north, 20 Apr.
12 Apr.
XX 77
Yagachi I. Tako
Taira
Aha 19 Apr.
Motobu Peninsula
Nago
XX 27 8 Apr.
OKINAWA
TURNER
TASK FORCE 51
XXXX
10
BUCKNER
4 Apr.
Ishikawa Isthmus
Kin
Ishikawa
Chimu Bay
3 Apr.
PACIFIC
XXX
III
GEIGER
(Amphibious)
XX 6 MAR
XX 1 MAR
Takabanare I.
OCEAN
XXX
XXIV
HODGE
XX 7 MAR
XX 96 MAR
Heanna
Kuba 3 Apr.
Naha
Oroku Peninsula
Shuri 8 Apr.
21 May
Chinen Peninsula
XXXX
32
USHIJIMA
end of Japanese resistance, 22 June
Itoman
18 June
decoy move
XX 2 MAR

ABOVE The carrier USS *Bunker Hill* on fire after being hit by two Japanese suicide planes off Okinawa on 11 May 1945. The Japanese aircraft crashed onto the carrier's aircraft which were preparing to take off for an attack on Okinawa.

KAMIKAZE

In October 1944, the Japanese navy authorized the formation of a force of suicide pilots who would crash their aircraft deliberately into enemy ships in an effort to sink or disable them. The term chosen, *kamikaze* (divine wind), was a reference back to a medieval Chinese–Japanese war in which the Chinese fleet was dispersed by a fierce gale and Japan saved from invasion. The first official suicide attack was made on 25 October 1944 against the US escort carrier *St Lo*. Large numbers were used in the Battle of Leyte Gulf and the peak of suicide attacks came during the invasion of Okinawa in April 1945. The aircraft were fighters or trainer aircraft, loaded with bombs; the pilots were volunteers initially, then supplemented by conscripts. They flew a total of 2,314 sorties and hit 322 Allied ships, sinking 34. The effect of the campaign was to destroy much of what was left of the Japanese air force for a very limited tactical gain.

FAR LEFT A US flame-thrower tank in action on 21 June 1945 in southern Okinawa towards the end of the campaign to seize the island. Flame-throwers were used to flush out hidden Japanese snipers. A US infantryman crouches behind the tank to fire at Japanese soldiers escaping the flames.

BELOW LEFT Marines of the Second Battalion, Twenty-ninth Marines, Sixth Division flush out Japanese resisters on the Oruku Peninsula at the far southwest of the island on 27 June 1945, shortly before the island was declared secured. The Japanese soldier standing is holding a white flag, an unusual act among Japanese troops, most of whom fought to the death on the island.

BOTTOM An officer of the US Tenth Army shares his rations with two Okinawan children found hiding in an abandoned tomb on the island. Thousands of civilians perished in the fighting or committed suicide.

LEFT Japanese open-faced flying helmet.

The main attack came on the morning of 1 April on the west coast of Okinawa. The invasion force faced little opposition and moved inland to seize the airfields. By the following day, the island was split in two as US forces reached the east coast. The marine units moved northwards against weak resistance, reaching the north of the island by 15 April. Only on the Mobotu Peninsula was there heavy fighting, but the Marine Sixth Division secured it by 20 April.

The four army divisions faced a much more formidable obstacle when they reached the southern defensive line on 9 April. The terrain favoured the defenders and the American assault stalled. On 4 May, in torrential rains that turned the ground to mud, the Japanese launched a powerful counter-attack which produced a prolonged hand-to-hand battle with high casualties on both sides.

From 6 April, the invasion fleet was also subject to repeated kamikaze attacks launched by the commander of the Japanese 1st Mobile Fleet under the codename "Ten-Go". From then until 22 June, the fleet was subjected to 1,900 suicide attacks which caused high casualties among

the crews, sank 38 naval vessels and damaged a further 368. The Japanese navy also launched a suicide mission when the giant battleship *Yamato*, together with a single cruiser and eight destroyers, set out to attack the US fleet. The ship was sighted on 7 April in the East China Sea and sunk in an attack by 380 carrier aircraft, a dramatic end to what had been in 1941 one of the most powerful navies in the world.

Not until 21 May did the Japanese line begin to break. Naha was captured on 27 May and Ushijima retreated with his remaining forces to the Oroku Peninsula where a final ferocious encounter brought an end to Japanese resistance on 22 June. Buckner was killed on 18 June; Ushijima killed himself four days later. These were two of a high toll of casualties. Only 7,400, mainly Okinawan militia, survived from the 100,000 strong Japanese garrison, while total American deaths amounted to 12,520 with 36,631 wounded. The very high cost of securing a tiny island made the invasion of the home islands seem an increasingly hazardous and costly undertaking and played a part in the decision, taken a month later, to drop the atomic bomb.

LIEUTENANT GENERAL SIMON BOLIVAR BUCKNER (1886–1945)

Lieutenant General Simon Buckner was the highest-ranking US officer to be killed by enemy fire during the Second World War. The son of a Confederate general of the same name, Buckner joined the army in 1908, serving in the Philippines during the First World War. He was a tough trainer of men and was commandant of cadets at West Point in the early 1930s. He was sent to command the defence of Alaska in 1941 and was then promoted to brigadier general. In 1943, he seized back the two Aleutian islands captured by the Japanese in 1942. In July 1944 he organized the US Tenth Army for the conquest of Taiwan, but their destination was then changed to Okinawa and it was here, on 18 June 1945, towards the end of the campaign, that he was hit by shells from a Japanese battery and killed instantly.

LIBERATION OF THE CAMPS

24 JULY 1944
Red Army soldiers liberate the extermination/labour camp of Majdanek.

11 APRIL 1945
Red Army liberates the Buchenwald concentration camp.

29 APRIL 1945
Dachau concentration camp is liberated by the United States Army.

5 MAY 1945
Arrest of Hans Frank, former governor-general of German-occupied Poland.

23 MAY 1945
Heinrich Himmler, head of the SS and organizer of the camp system, commits suicide in British custody.

11 MARCH 1946
Rudolf Höss, disguised as a farm worker, arrested by the British.

When the Allies finally advanced towards the German homeland, they began to uncover clear evidence of the atrocious nature of the regime Hitler's Germany had imposed on political prisoners, on so-called "asocials" (vagrants, the workshy, homosexuals, recidivist criminals etc.), on Gypsies and above all on the Jews of Europe. These many groups had been transported to one of a number of different kinds of camp. By 1944, there were 20 major concentration camps, with 165 sub-camps. Here prisoners were expected to work in difficult conditions. The death rate was exceptionally high, from disease and malnutrition as much as deliberate murder, but the object was to make the prisoners labour. There were also seven main extermination camps – where Jews and other prisoners were sent for immediate murder in purpose-built centres with gas chambers and crematoria – at Majdanek, Sobibor, Chelmno, Belzec, Treblinka, Auschwitz-Birkenau (by far the largest) and a smaller facility at Maly Trostenets. At least 3.5 million people died in these camps. Majdanek and Auschwitz also served as concentration camps.

These two, Auschwitz and Majdanek, were the first major camps to be liberated, both uncovered by the Red Army as it marched through Poland. In Majdanek in July 1944, the Red Army found 1,000 emaciated prisoners and warehouses full of hair, cases, clothing and children's toys. Auschwitz-Birkenau, half slave camp, half extermination centre, was occupied on 27 January 1945 after many of the prisoners had been forced to leave on foot 10 days earlier on one of the many "death marches" of the last months of war. Here the Soviet soldiers found around 3,000 prisoners in the main camp, many close to death. They also found more evidence of German scrupulousness – stores of 380,000 men's suits and 836,000 women's coats and dresses, and

ABOVE The former commandant of Auschwitz is handed over on 25 May 1946 at Nuremberg airport to Polish policemen to stand trial in Cracow.

RUDOLF HÖSS (1900–1947)

Rudolf Höss was the notorious commandant of the Auschwitz-Birkenau complex for much of the war period. From a strict Catholic Bavarian family, he was destined at first for the priesthood, but turned against religion and joined the German army at the age of only 15. He fought in Turkey, Iraq and Palestine and, at 17, became the youngest German NCO. He served in the Freikorps after the war, became a member of the National Socialist Party in 1922, and joined the SS in 1933. He took over duties as a block commander in Dachau Concentration Camp and stayed in camp administration thereafter. He took over a camp for Polish POWs and political prisoners at Auschwitz in May 1940, and remained its commandant as it was turned into an extermination camp. He left the camp in late 1943, but returned to supervise the killing of Hungarian Jews in 1944. After the war he hid away disguised as a farmer, but was caught in March 1946 and handed over to the Polish authorities in May. He was tried, sentenced to death and then executed at the camp where he had helped to murder at least one million people.

LEFT Jewish prisoners at a German concentration camp demonstrate to the liberating forces how the bodies were loaded into the crematorium ovens for disposal. The gruesome work was carried out by a work detail taken from the prison population. By the end of the war most of the dead were victims of starvation and disease.

7.7 tons of human hair, packed and ready to transport. But the other evidence of mass killings had been destroyed and the crematoria ovens blown up. The true horror of the camp was revealed by Soviet prisoners found there, who were interrogated by SMERSH, the military security organization, in the same buildings where they had been prisoners shortly before. The Soviet authorities had allowed some visits to Majdanek by foreign representatives, but the liberation of Auschwitz was not announced until 7 May, after the German surrender.

ABOVE On 24 April 1945, nine days after the camp was liberated, a British army chaplain holds a brief service over a mass grave in the German concentration camp of Bergen-Belsen before it is covered over.

In the West, no extermination camps were uncovered, for these had been built on occupied Polish or Belorussian territory. British Commonwealth and American forces came across concentration camps instead, where by April 1945 conditions were lethal in the extreme. Lack of food, the absence of any form of hygiene or effective medical care, coupled with the growing brutality of the guards as the war drew to a close, created conditions in which huge numbers of prisoners died. As the German boundaries contracted, thousands of prisoners were marched from overrun camps to the few that remained in operation. It was this final migration of prisoners that caused the terrible scenes found by the British 8th Corps when units entered the camp at Bergen-Belsen in northwestern Germany on 15 April 1945. The camp had held 15,000 prisoners in December 1944, but by April there were between 40,000 and 50,000, many of them Jews forced to march on foot to the camp from sites further east. The piles of corpses and the hollow-eyed, starving prisoners became the standard images of German atrocity and were sent to newspapers in the West immediately after liberation.

The prisoners in Bergen-Belsen, where the camp was infected with typhus, continued to die in large numbers after liberation. In the end 14,000 of the 40,000 prisoners died. German civilians from the locality were brought in to view the camp on 24 April 1945, and it was burned down on British army orders in June. Further south, the American army liberated Dachau camp on 29 April. As a unit of the US 45th Division approached the camp, they found 39 rail cars filled with dead and decomposing bodies. As the soldiers approached the camp, SS guards opened fire. They were rushed by the prisoners and beaten to death. Around 70,000 prisoners were found in the Dachau system. The liberation of the camps provoked horror and outrage among the troops that first arrived on the scene, but in many cases it took years before the perpetrators were finally brought to trial.

LEFT Former SS camp guards at Bergen-Belsen take a break from clearing the bodies of the dead in the camp in April 1945. As a punishment they have been made to lie face-down in one of the empty mass graves excavated at the camp.

BELOW LEFT In May 1945 at Nanning, near the German town of Passau, US soldiers force the local population to view the remains of concentration camp prisoners who died or were murdered while being transported from Buchenwald camp to Dachau in April 1945. Scenes like these were repeated all across occupied Germany.

ABOVE A machine found in a German concentration camp near the Polish city of Lvov in 1945 used for sifting the ashes of victims whose bodies had been cremated in search of gold teeth. The gold was then boxed up and sent to Berlin.

NAZI GOLD

During the war the German state needed all the gold it could get to buy materials and equipment abroad from suppliers who would not accept payment in marks. One of the sources exploited was the gold in dental fillings taken from murdered Jews, and also from dead Soviet prisoners-of-war. The gold was packed into special containers alongside gold spectacle frames, rings and gold jewellery, and sent by rail to the German central bank in Berlin. The fillings were then melted down into ingots and transferred abroad, mainly through Swiss banks, to assist in war purchases. By the end of the war, 76 shipments had been sent from the camps, mixed in with other sources of looted gold. Only in the 1990s did the full extent of the gruesome trade become clear when a conference on Nazi gold was held in London in 1997.

VICTORY IN BURMA

After the failure of the Japanese offensive in northern India against Imphal and Kohima, Lieutenant General Slim's 14th Army began to plan the reconquest of Burma. Allied forces moved forward to the Chindwin River in western Burma, while in the north a combination of Indian forces and General Stilwell's Chinese divisions cleared the last Japanese forces and finally opened the Ledo Road (renamed at Chiang Kaishek's suggestion the Stilwell Road) in January 1945 to transport supplies to the Chinese army facing the Japanese in southern China.

Slim's plan, codenamed Operation "Capital", followed by "Extended Capital", was to drive across the Chindwin into the central Shwebo Plain, across the River Irrawaddy and on to the Burmese capital of Rangoon (Yangon). This operation involved first capturing Akyab on the coast of the Bay of Bengal, which could be used as an air base. A mixed British-Indian force captured the town on 4 January and moved on down the coast, driving the Japanese 28th Army towards the Arakan Mountains. In the central plain, Slim's forces captured Shwebo by 8 January, but then faced growing Japanese resistance from the Japanese 33rd Army stationed to defend Mandalay and the path to the south.

Slim undertook an elaborate deception plan which involved persuading the Japanese command in Burma, under Lieutenant General Hyotaro Kimura, that Mandalay was the main objective for the northern Allied force, while the rest of 4th Corps went south through the mountains to outflank the Japanese and cross the Irrawaddy at Pakokku. The strategy worked almost perfectly. Against light resistance, the British and Indian forces crossed the river further south and drove for the communications centre at Meiktilan where a fierce battle took place against the Japanese 15th Army commanded by Lieutenant General Shihachi Katamura. The Japanese were caught between two forces and were not strong enough to contain both. Mandalay fell on 20 March to the northern forces, while

ABOVE A wounded West African soldier of the 82nd West African Division is carried from an L-5 aircraft at a landing strip near Kantha in February 1945. One East African and two West African divisions took part in the fighting around the Arakan Mountains in Burma.

RIGHT Airpower was a critical dimension in the Burmese campaign, not only in combat but also for essential transport and liaison operations. Here a Consolidated B-24 Liberator bomber takes part in a joint RAF/USAAF attack on Japanese stores in the Rangoon area on 17 March 1945.

BELOW American-built Sherman tanks and trucks of the 62nd Motorised Brigade drive along a road in March 1945 between the bridgehead over the Irrawaddy River at Myaungyu and the key communications centre at the town of Meiktila, captured on 3 March.

MAJOR GENERAL AUNG SAN (1915–1947)

Aung San was the leading figure in the Burmese independence movement. He attended Rangoon (Yangon) University where he helped to organize student strikes. Strongly anti-British, he joined the nationalist Our Burma Union and became general secretary until 1940. That year, to avoid arrest, he fled to China, where he was caught by the Japanese and persuaded to go to Japan. In Bangkok, in December 1941, he set up the Burma Independence Army with Japanese support and became its first chief-of-staff. When it moved to Burma after the Japanese conquest it was renamed the Burma Defence Army and later, when Burma was granted "independence" by the Japanese in August 1943, the Burma National Army. In March 1945, he changed sides and helped the British drive out the Japanese. He became a key figure in negotiating Burmese independence, but was assassinated six months before the transfer of power by a rival political group. His daughter, Aung San Suu Kyi, went on to lead the pro-democracy movement in modern Burma (Myanmar).

positions around Meiktila, briefly surrounded and besieged by the Japanese, were abandoned on 29 March. There was now little between Slim's force and the city of Rangoon further to the south.

Two separate attacks were made towards the capital, one led by Lieutenant General Stopford down the Irrawaddy valley, the other by Lieutenant General Messervy along the Sittang river. His flank was protected by the Burma

Independence Army of Aung San, which changed sides in March to help end Japanese domination in Burma. Slim was anxious that Rangoon should be captured before the onset of the monsoon rains in May, and in order to be certain of it he organized a further operation, codenamed "Dracula", for the 26th Indian Division on the Arakan Coast to be taken by ship to the coast below Rangoon to take it from the sea. When the division arrived on 3 May, the Japanese had already abandoned the struggle and retreated east across the Sittang river. The forces from the north met up with the southern invasion force on 5 May and the whole of central Burma was in Allied hands.

The Japanese army was never defeated entirely in Burma. The 28th Army in the hills of Arakan tried in July 1945 to break out eastwards from its encirclement. Forewarned by intelligence sources, the British Commonwealth forces imposed 17,000 casualties at the cost of only 95 of their own. Intermittent fighting continued along the Sittang river until on 28 August the Japanese surrendered formally in Rangoon. The whole operation to reconquer Burma cost only 3,188 Allied dead; Japanese dead totalled 23,000. Throughout the Burma campaign, the great weight of responsibility had fallen on the Indian Army and some 17,000 Indians lost their lives between 1941 and 1945 in what was the longest single British and Commonwealth land campaign of the war.

BELOW Indians of the 6/7 Rajput Rifles mop up remaining Japanese resistance in Pyawbwe, north of Rangoon on 11 April 1945. The Burmese capital was occupied by 5 May as the Japanese army withdrew eastwards.

LIEUTENANT GENERAL FRANK MESSERVY (1893-1974)

A career Indian Army officer, who joined the army in 1913, Frank Messervy played a key part in the reconquest of Burma. He fought in the First World War in France, Syria and Palestine, and in the Second World War was posted to East Africa where he commanded Gazelle Force, a fast-moving reconnaissance and strike force to support the campaign against Italian forces. In the desert war, he was the only Indian Army officer to command a British division, initially 1st Armoured then 7th Armoured. He was a poor tank commander and returned to India in 1943, where he played a part in the battles at Imphal and Kohima before taking command of the 4th Corps for the invasion in Burma in 1945, entering Rangoon in May. He was nicknamed "bearded man" because he chose not to shave during battle. After the war, he became briefly commander-in-chief of the Pakistan Army on independence in 1947, but retired in 1948.

ABOVE LEFT British Commonwealth soldiers look at a line of Japanese dead after an unsuccessful Japanese counter-attack during the operations around the key town of Meiktila in March 1945. Japanese soldiers continued to fight to the end. For every Allied soldier killed in the reconquest of Burma, there were eight Japanese dead.

LEFT Indian engineers construct a wooden bridge over a shallow stream during the advance southwards from Meiktila to Rangoon. The final drive against the Japanese down the Irrawaddy and Sittang valleys was carried out by four Indian divisions.

BELOW US 11-millimetre (.45-inch) liberator pistol, a cheaply-produced weapon supplied to resistance groups.

BELOW RIGHT Men of the 2nd York and Lancaster Regiment search the ruins of a railway station for Japanese snipers during the advance of the 14th Army to Rangoon along the railway corridor, 13 April 1945.

BATTLE FOR BERLIN

18 APRIL 1945
Field Marshal Model surrenders 225,000 soldiers trapped in the Ruhr pocket, then kills himself.

3 MAY 1945
The German port city of Hamburg is captured by the British 21st Army Group.

ABOVE Armshield worn by volunteers from Turkistan serving with the German army.

The end of the massive Vistula–Oder operation left the Red Army only 65 kilometres (40 miles) from Berlin by the beginning of February 1945. But the drive for the capital, first planned the previous November, had to be postponed because of Stalin's anxiety about the remaining substantial pockets of German resistance in Königsberg, Breslau, Poznan and the fortress of Küstrin. Further north in Pomerania, scattered German units were gathered together

under Army Group Vistula, briefly commanded by the head of the SS, Heinrich Himmler. Stalin also worried about the intentions of his Western allies, who were rapidly crossing Germany from the west and his fears were only allayed when Eisenhower finally told him in March that he would move southeast and north, leaving Berlin to the Red Army.

The German strongpoints were gradually reduced during February and March, but the fortress at Küstrin, besieged by General Chuikov's 8th Guards Army, was only captured on 29 March. Rokossovsky's 2nd Belorussian Army Group reached Danzig, on the Baltic coast, a day later. Detailed planning for the final Berlin operation began in mid-March. Stalin was keen that the final operation should be a clear success, since it would take place in full view of his allies. Over two million men, in 29 armies, supported by 3,155 tanks and 7,500 aircraft, crowded into a wide semi-circle around the German capital. Opposing them were the forces of Army Group Centre under General Ferdinand Schörner and Army Group Vistula, now under General Gotthard Heinrici, which together could muster around one million men, many of them irregulars of the recently-created Volkssturm made up of over-age men and boys. They could muster 1,519 tanks and very few aircraft.

The battle plan was for a frontal assault on Berlin by Zhukov's 1st Belorussian Army Group across the Seelow Heights on the far bank of the Oder straight towards the heart of Berlin while some units swept westwards, encircling the city; in the south Konev's 1st Ukrainian Army Group, which had fought a draining campaign to pacify Silesia, was to attack towards the Elbe with orders to swing northwards towards Zhukov if help were needed or asked for; in the

ABOVE LEFT A dead German soldier lies on the roadside in the battle for Berlin in late April 1945. Although the German army had few resources left to defend the city, the Soviet forces sustained heavy casualties.

LEFT On 3 April 1945 German grenadiers lie in wait on the Seelow Heights above the Oder river in small pits from where they will oppose the Soviet bridgehead over the river using the *Panzerfaust* hand-held anti-tank weapon. The attack came 13 days later.

LIEUTENANT GENERAL HELMUTH WEIDLING (1891–1955)

Karl Weidling was the last commander of the Berlin Defence District, and surrendered the city to the Red Army on 2 May. He joined the army in 1911, and served as an artillery commander in the early stages of the Second World War. He then commanded the 41st Tank Corps in the Soviet Union, rising by 1943 to the rank of general of artillery. In April 1945, he was appointed commander of the 56th Tank Corps facing the Soviet campaign against Berlin. He was condemned to death by Hitler for withdrawing his force, but reprieved just before his execution after the reasons for the retreat were explained. On 23 April, he was appointed defender of Berlin and negotiated its surrender with General Chuikov on 2 May. "I think every unnecessary death is a crime," he told Chuikov. He was arrested and died in a Soviet prison in 1955 during a 25-year sentence for failing to surrender Berlin sooner.

Map labels:
Rostock · Stralsund · Baltic Sea · Berlin Centre · Lübeck · Wismar · XXXXX 21 MONTGOMERY · Hamburg · night, 28/29 Apr. · Moltke Bridge · Gestapo HQ · XX 171 · Reichstag 30 Apr. · Stettin · XXXXX VISTULA HEINRICI · 18 Apr. · XXXXX 2 BELORUSSIAN ROKOSSOVSKY · theatre · anti-tank barrier Brandenburg Gate · Wittenberg · G E R M A N Y · Stendal · 25 Apr. · Berlin 2 May · Küstrin · XXXXX 1 BELORUSSIAN ZHUKOV · Potsdam · Frankfurt an der Oder · XXXXX 12 BRADLEY · Magdeburg · Elbe · POLAND · Dessau · XXXXX CENTRE SCHÖRNER · Cottbus · Torgau · XXXXX 1 UKRAINIAN KONEV · 26 Apr. · 18 Apr. · Leipzig · Bautzen · Neisse · 16 Apr. · Chemnitz · Dresden · 25 Apr.

Berlin, 16–2 May 1945 —— front lines, with date ▬▬ defensive lines

dazzled by Soviet searchlights which reflected back from the accumulated smoke of battle on to advancing Soviet soldiers, Zhukov's forces took more than two days to clear the Heights, and then found a third defensive zone lying just beyond. Only by 20 April did the advance units of Chuikov's 8th Guards Army, part of Zhukov's army group, reach the eastern suburbs of Berlin and begin the bombardment of the central areas. North of the city, the remnants of Heinrici's Army Group Vistula crumbled and Zhukov's armies swept round Berlin to encircle it.

On the morning of 25 April, the first of Zhukov's units crossed the River Spree, close to the centre of the city. When Chuikov's army approached Schönefeld airfield they were met not by Germans but by forward units of Konev's 3rd Tank Army. While Zhukov had struggled to reach the capital, Konev's armies had swept easily through eastern Germany into Saxony so that Konev was free to order some of his army to march northwards and attack Berlin from the south. After the first encounter, Chuikov deliberately drove for the centre of Berlin across the path of Konev's forces. Konev bowed to reality and allowed Zhukov to seize the prize. By 29 April, Chuikov began to storm the Tiergarten, west of the government zone, and on 30 April the first units fought their way into the Reichstag building. German resistance, at times fanatical and suicidal, crumbled away. Two days later, the remains of the Berlin garrison surrendered. The final campaign for the city cost the Soviet forces 78,000 dead; German losses have always been difficult to calculate, but are believed to run into hundreds of thousands for the last weeks of fighting.

ABOVE Soviet JS-II heavy tanks roll through the centre of Berlin on 2 May 1945 while the Red Flag flutters from the roof of the Reichstag building in the background. The tank in the foreground has the name "Combat Girlfriend" written on it.

north Rokossovsky would clear German resistance to ensure that Zhukov's flank was secure. On 1 April, Stalin summoned the commanders to a conference where he asked, "Well, who is going to take Berlin?" Although the honour was supposed to be Zhukov's, Stalin left it open, in case circumstances changed on the battlefield and Konev could move faster.

As the campaign unfolded, it became clear that Zhukov might be beaten to the target by Konev. The assault on the Seelow Heights, even with overwhelming strength, proved one of Zhukov's few disasters. On the morning of 16 April, he sent his forces forward for a direct assault on the hills, crammed in a narrow salient, bombarded endlessly by hidden German defences. Caught in swampy ground, and

RIGHT A Soviet poster by Ivanov shows a smiling Red Army soldier and the words "Raise the Banner of Victory". The Red Army went on the rampage in Berlin as elsewhere, responsible for the rape of as many as 100,000 German women.

BOTTOM German prisoners-of-war are marched through the Brandenburg Gate past a JS-II tank on their way to captivity on 2 May 1945. The last prisoners returned to Germany in 1955.

BELOW A Volkssturmgewehr VG-1-5 rifle used by members of the Volkssturm.

ГЕРМАНИЯ

ВОДРУЗИМ НАД БЕРЛИНОМ ЗНАМЯ ПОБЕДЫ!

RED FLAG OVER THE REICHSTAG

The photograph taken by the Soviet photographer Yevgeni Khaldei of the Red Flag flying over the Reichstag, the German parliament building, in May 1945 is one of the most famous pictures of the war. The story behind the flag is nonetheless confusing. The first Red Flag was raised at approximately 10.40 p.m. on the evening of 30 April after a small group of Soviet soldiers fought their way to the roof and placed the Red Banner of the 3rd Shock Army on one of the statues. The flag was photographed by a Russian aircraft the following day before German fire dislodged it. It was retrieved two days later and in June sent to Moscow. Khaldei's flag was made from three red tablecloths, allegedly sewn with the hammer and sickle by his uncle, which he took to Berlin and then had hoisted onto the roof on 2 May by two soldiers, after the Germans in the building had surrendered. This photograph had to be doctored to remove the two watches on the soldiers' wrists and to add more smoke in the background, but it remains among the most heavily used images of the European war.

LAST DAYS IN HITLER'S BUNKER

1 APRIL 1945
US Tenth Army invades the Japanese island of Okinawa.

4 APRIL 1945
Slovak capital at Bratislava falls to Soviet forces.

7 APRIL 1945
Red Army begins the assault on Vienna which falls six days later.

26 APRIL 1945
American and Soviet forces meet at the Elbe village of Torgau.

28 APRIL 1945
Mussolini and other Fascist leaders executed by Italian partisans.

2 MAY 1945
Burmese city of Prome falls to the Indian army.

It was from this underground base that Hitler forlornly controlled the last vestiges of his shrinking empire. By April 1945 almost 2,000 people worked for him in and around the bunker, among them the minister of propaganda and commissioner for total war, Joseph Goebbels, whose family lived in the the bunker too. The daily military briefings were also held in the bunker, in a small room three by four metres (10 by 13 feet), where as many as 18 people would gather, pressed around a small map table at which Hitler sat, moving forces around that in reality had melted away or were so weakened as to be incapable of achieving the orders relayed to them from the bunker. On 9 March, Hitler issued the order for the final defence of Berlin, which was to be held street by street. The inner defensive zone was the government sector, with the bunker at the core, an area codenamed "The Citadel". On 23 March, following the bombing of Berlin's airports, Hitler ordered that an east–west axis for aircraft should be created along a road next to the government sector, and until almost the last days of the war small army liaison aircraft landed and took off from this improvised landing ground.

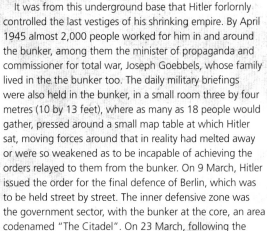

During these last weeks, Hitler's mood swung between despair, apathy and a euphoric belief in final victory. When the Soviet operation against Berlin began, Hitler issued an order for

As the Reich collapsed around him in Berlin in the late spring of 1945, Hitler retreated to the large complex of rooms built for him beneath the garden of the new Reich Chancellery. The exact date is not known, and for much of January and February, Hitler seems to have continued to inhabit the Chancellery rooms above ground, where the daily military briefings were also held. It is likely that he finally abandoned the building in late February or early March, and thereafter lived in the bunker, with occasional moments in the open air.

ABOVE The last press photographs of Adolf Hitler were taken on 20 March 1945 when he left the bunker to review a group of Hitler Youth and present them with medals. By the end of the war thousands of young Germans found themselves fighting alongside regular soldiers.

ABOVE RIGHT The German celebrity pilot Hanna Reitsch in the cockpit of a glider. She flew to Berlin to be with Hitler at the end but he insisted that she escape. On 28 April, accompanied by her companion Colonel General Ritter von Greim, she flew her Fieseler Storch light aircraft out of Berlin, the last flight from the city.

RIGHT Empty jerrycans of petrol reportedly used to burn the bodies of Adolf Hitler and Eva Braun on the afternoon of 30 April in the garden of the Reich Chancellery building. Their bodies were wrapped in carpets, carried out to the garden by SS men and Hitler's closest aides, and placed in a small shell crater. Petrol was poured over them and then set alight. The bodies were burned beyond recognition.

EVA BRAUN (1912–45)

Eva Braun briefly became Hitler's wife shortly before their joint suicide in the bunker. The daughter of a Bavarian schoolteacher, Eva worked in 1929 for Heinrich Hoffmann, the National Socialist Party's official photographer at whose studio she first met Hitler. After attempting suicide, she eventually became his companion, concealed from the wider population and forced to live a humdrum routine of films, parties and occasional visits from Hitler. Thanks to Eva Braun there is also cine-film footage of Hitler at Berchtesgaden. She had no apparent influence on his policies, but he enjoyed relaxing in her company when he could. In April 1945, she drove from Munich to Berlin in order to be with him in the bunker and on the night of 28 April the two were married. Two days later she committed suicide by swallowing cyanide.

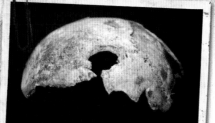

HITLER'S REMAINS

When the Soviet army reached Hitler's bunker there began a desperate search for his body. A collection of dental remains found in the Chancellery gardens was made and shortly afterwards the technician of Hitler's personal dentist, Käthe Heusemann, helped to identify from the fragments she was shown Hitler's upper dental bridge, lower jawbone and bridge, and Eva Braun's resin bridge and gold crown. These remains

ABOVE The skull fragment with bullet hole, alleged to be from Hitler's corpse.

were taken to Moscow and locked away. The papers surrounding the dental research have still not been released and the jawbone itself is in the former KGB archive in Moscow. Instead, in 1995 a box containing skull fragments was revealed in the state archives in Moscow which it was claimed were Hitler's remains. No convincing evidence has been found to show that the skull was Hitler's and the dental evidence is still the clearest proof of Hitler's death.

LEFT Armband worn by military staff of Hitler's supreme headquarters.

BELOW Winston Churchill, in Berlin for the Potsdam Conference, sits on one of the damaged chairs from Hitler's bunker surrounded by British and Soviet soldiers.

Führer-Hauptquartier

ABOVE In the Reich Chancellery building on 2 May 1945 Soviet soldiers found a dead man with a strong resemblance to Hitler. The body was photographed but it was soon identified as that of a man with a Hitler moustache, not Hitler himself. When the picture was first released in the West 19 years later it was claimed as the last photograph of the dictator after his suicide.

the day calling on all German soldiers to stand fast so that "the Bolshevik attack will drown in a sea of blood". On 20 April, as Soviet heavy artillery began to bombard the centre of Berlin, Hitler celebrated his 56th birthday. It was the last occasion on which the senior figures of the regime gathered together; the group included Göring, Himmler, Bormann, von Ribbentrop and Field Marshal Keitel. At the end of the celebration most of them made their way out of Berlin along with the major ministries, which were evacuated on 21–22 April. Hitler, too, thought about flying to the south, but on 22 April he decided to stay in his capital and to kill himself if Berlin fell to the enemy. On the following day, Albert Speer, his armaments minister, landed on the road-airstrip and came to say his farewell to Hitler before leaving for the north of Germany. The same day Göring wrote from Berchtesgaden that he would take over the functions of leadership. Hitler ordered his arrest and stripped him of his many offices. On 28 April, news arrived that Himmler too was trying to negotiate surrender to the Western Allies. Hitler stripped him of his offices and ordered his arrest.

During the last week of April, Berlin was gradually occupied by the Red Army. On the night of 28 April, Hitler and Eva Braun were married. Hitler dictated his final testament and, with the noise of battle thundering above, made arrangements for his suicide and cremation. On 30 April, shortly before 4.00 p.m, Hitler shot himself in the head and Eva Braun took cyanide. Their bodies were wrapped in carpets, taken to the Chancellery garden and burned beyond identification. Goebbels and his wife also committed suicide having first poisoned their six children. Two days later, the war in Berlin ended and Soviet soldiers searched for Hitler's remains. Although the Soviet authorities later claimed to have found the body, and eventually to have disposed of it years later, only some fragments of dental work were recovered which revealed clearly that Hitler was dead. Stalin knew of this evidence by the end of May, but so suspicious was he of his Western allies and of Hitler's guile that he told Truman at the Potsdam Conference that Hitler had escaped. Months of investigation by British intelligence finally established beyond any reasonable doubt that Hitler had taken his own life, but fantasies about his survival continued long after the end of the war.

VICTORY IN ITALY

16 APRIL 1945
Launch of the Red Army's major campaign against Berlin by Konev's 1st Ukrainian and Zhukov's 2nd Belorussian army groups.

20 APRIL 1945
US forces enter the Bavarian city of Nuremberg where the prewar Nazi Party rallies were staged.

25 APRIL 1945
Opening of the San Francisco Conference for founding of the United Nations.

1 MAY 1945
New German government under Grand Admiral Dönitz following Hitler's suicide the day before.

5 MAY 1945
German forces surrender in Norway.

LEFT A British Churchill Crocodile flamethrower tank supports infantry of the 2nd New Zealand Division during the assault across the Senio River south of Ravenna on 9 April 1945 at the start of the final campaign in northern Italy.

BELOW CENTRE British 8th Army Royal Artillery troops on 28 April 1945 complete work on a searchlight to illuminate the first pontoon Bailey bridge built across the Po River so that traffic across it can be continuous. Once across the river, Allied armies rapidly occupied the rest of northern Italy.

ABOVE Formation badge of the 46th (West Riding) Infantry Division.

A s a result of the winter weather and the diversion of resources to other fronts, the campaign in Italy did not begin again until spring 1945. Allied forces amounted to 17 well-resourced divisions (British, American, Polish, Brazilian, South African, Indian and the New Zealand Division) and substantial airpower. Kesselring, who was replaced in March by Colonel General von Vietinghoff, had 23 divisions, most very under-strength, with an average of 1,700 soldiers in each, little air power and the assistance of two Italian divisions of Marshal Graziani's Army of Liguria, all that was left of the Fascist armed forces.

Alexander planned a major campaign to complete the destruction of Axis forces. Operation "Grapeshot" aimed to encircle the German 14th and 10th armies south of the River Po, almost all of whose bridges had been destroyed long before by Allied air power. The US Fifth Army would attack west of Bologna and then swing eastwards, while the British 8th Army under Lieutenant General McCreery was to force the Argenta Gap on the coast and then swing westwards. After a number of small preliminary operations to tidy up the Allied line, the operation was launched on 9 April when waves of heavy bombers, followed by 200 medium bombers and 500 fighter-bombers, attacked the German line. Already dispirited, and with German commanders trying to

GENERAL RICHARD McCREERY (1898–1967)

Richard McCreery was commander of the British 8th Army in its last years in the Italian campaign. He joined the army in 1915 and served for most of the First World War in France with the 12th Royal Lancers, whose commander he became in the 1930s. He commanded the 2nd Armoured Brigade in the Battle of France, then moved to North Africa as adviser on armoured vehicles and then Chief-of-Staff, 18th Army Group. He was posted to Italy in July 1943 to command 10th Corps, and towards the end of 1944 took over command of the 8th Army from Lieutenant-General Leese. He led it to a famous victory over German forces in the Po Valley. After the war he commanded occupation troops in Austria, and in 1946 became Commander-in-Chief of the British Army of the Rhine. He retired from the army in 1949 with the rank of general.

negotiate a secret armistice, the German army crumbled quickly and by 17 April Argenta was captured and the way opened to exploit westwards and north towards Venice.

The US Fifth Army opened its part of the offensive on 14 April, moving quickly through the mountains and reaching the outskirts of Bologna by 20 April. Hitler refused von Vietinghoff's request to withdraw and growing numbers of German prisoners were taken as Bologna was encircled by the two Allied armies, who met on 25 April at Finale nell'Emilia. The Po valley provided a much easier battlefield and with little serious opposition remaining the US Fifth Army reached Verona on 26 April, swinging west to take Milan. The 8th Army moved rapidly north, crossing the Po unopposed on 24 April, liberating Venice on 29 April and reaching Trieste on 2 May, just after the arrival of Tito's forces. A German delegation arrived at Alexander's headquarters at Caserta on 28 April and an armistice was agreed the next day to come into effect on 2 May.

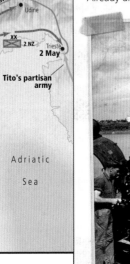

Victory in Italy, 1 April–2 May 1945

LIEUTENANT GENERAL KARL WOLFF (1900–1984)

Karl Wolff was a high-ranking SS man who negotiated the armistice on the Italian front in the spring of 1945. He joined the army in 1917 and saw action on the Western Front, but was demobilized after the war. He became a businessman in the 1920s, but during the slump of 1929–32 he became convinced that only radical politics held the answer. He joined the National Socialist Party in 1931 and the SS the same year. He joined Himmler's staff and by 1935 was chief of the personal staff of the Reichsführer-SS. He became the SS representative at Hitler's headquarters, and in July 1943 was sent to Italy as supreme SS representative. It was here that he began secret negotiations for an armistice in February 1945, which led to an end of hostilities on 2 May. He was arrested and served several short periods of imprisonment before being sentenced by a West German court to 15 years in jail in 1964. On account of poor health, he was released in 1971.

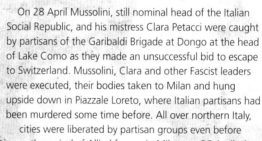

ABOVE The corpse of the Italian dictator Benito Mussolini (centre) hangs upside down next to his mistress, Clara Petacci, shot by partisans while trying to escape to Switzerland on 28 April 1945. Other Fascist leaders were killed at the same time and hung up in Piazzale Loreto next to their dead leader.

RIGHT Sherman tanks and army vehicles in the Piazzale Roma in Venice on 30 April 1945 following the liberation of the city by the British 8th Army the previous day. On 29 April the German army had agreed an armistice.

BELOW The war over, a group of British 8th Army soldiers enjoy a period of leave with a traditional gondola ride along the canals of Venice. Privilege leave was granted to troops serving with the 8th Army, and Venice was a popular destination, hosting a cinema and club for British forces and information offices and guided tours run by the army welfare organization.

BELOW Lieutenant General von Senger und Etterlin, commander of the 14th Panzer Corps, meets General Mark Clark, Lieutenant General McCreery and Lieutenant General Truscott at 15th Army Group headquarters on 4 May 1945 to discuss the instructions for the unconditional surrender of German troops, which had come into force on 2 May.

On 28 April Mussolini, still nominal head of the Italian Social Republic, and his mistress Clara Petacci were caught by partisans of the Garibaldi Brigade at Dongo at the head of Lake Como as they made an unsuccessful bid to escape to Switzerland. Mussolini, Clara and other Fascist leaders were executed, their bodies taken to Milan and hung upside down in Piazzale Loreto, where Italian partisans had been murdered some time before. All over northern Italy, cities were liberated by partisan groups even before the arrival of Allied forces. In Milan, on 26 April, the local partisans established their own government before the Americans arrived. What followed was a period of great confusion as the pro-Allied Italian government in Rome tried to co-operate with partisan groups, many of whom were Communists distrustful of other Italian political groups. A coalition was formed in June 1945 under the democrat and anti-Fascist Feruccio Parri which brought together all the groups involved in the struggle to liberate Italy from German rule.

The cost of the long campaign in Italy was very high. The US Fifth Army suffered 188,746 casualties, the 8th Army 123,993. German casualties amounted to at least 435,000. Around 60,000 Italians were killed by bombing attacks, most of them in the last year of the war. The war and the bombing destroyed important parts of Italy's cultural heritage while the divisions between Fascists and partisans left a long residue of bitterness and hostility in Italian society and politics.

THE GERMAN SURRENDER

2 MAY
Axis forces in Italy surrender unconditionally.

4 MAY 1945
German forces surrender in northern Germany and the Netherlands.

6 MAY 1945
The 82-day Soviet siege of Breslau comes to an end.

7 MAY 1945
German submarine U-2336 sinks last two merchantmen of the war.

8 MAY 1945
Reich Marshal Hermann Göring gives himself up to the Americans, the highest-ranking German prisoner.

The final surrender of remaining Axis forces in Europe was an uncoordinated and messy process. Though victory in Europe was proclaimed on 8 May, resistance still continued in some parts, while the Soviet Union announced victory on 9 May and declared 11 May as a day of celebration. Evenw the formal signing of a surrender document had to be done twice to satisfy Soviet sensibilities.

The first surrender came in Italy where a ceasefire, negotiated by General Heinrich von Vietinghoff on 29 April, came into effect on 2 May, the same day as the surrender in Berlin. Some 490,000 German and Axis soldiers were taken prisoner. The surrender of forces in Germany and Austria took place as each area was encircled or captured. On 4 May, German forces in northern Germany and the Netherlands surrendered to Field Marshal Montgomery's 21st Army Group; on 5 May German forces in Bavaria surrendered. Also on 5 May, the new German government in Flensburg ordered Hitler's wartime chief of operations, General Alfred Jodl, to proceed to the French city of Rheims to surrender to the Western Allies, still hoping perhaps that a division could be opened up between the West and Stalin. Eisenhower insisted on unconditional German surrender, as had been the case in all the subsidiary theatres. At 2.40 in the early morning of 7 May, a brief ceremony took place in a schoolhouse in Rheims, which Eisenhower had made his temporary headquarters. Surrounded by Allied officers and

ABOVE General Alfred Jodl, chief of operations at the German Supreme Command during the war, signs the instrument of unconditional surrender at a schoolhouse in the French city of Rheims, 7 May 1945.

RIGHT Air Marshal Arthur Tedder, deputy supreme Allied commander to Eisenhower at SHAEF, signs the German unconditional surrender document at Soviet headquarters in Berlin during the second surrender ceremony held on 8 May to satisfy Stalin.

BELOW BACKGROUND Thousands of German soldiers wait to be transported to POW camps after crossing a ruined bridge over the Elbe to surrender to the Western Allies and avoid Soviet captivity, May 1945.

FIELD MARSHAL WILHELM KEITEL (1883–1946)

Wilhelm Keitel, nicknamed "Lakaitel" (lackey) by his critics, was chief-of-staff at Supreme Headquarters. He joined the army in 1901, and served in the Field Artillery in 1914 until severely wounded. He served the rest of the war in staff positions and in 1919–20 helped to organize Freikorps activity against Poland. From 1924, he became a senior administrator in the army and in 1935, as a lieutenant general, was promoted to run the Armed Forces Office in the War Ministry. When the ministry was replaced in February 1938 by the Supreme Headquarters, directly under Hitler's control, Keitel continued his job as the senior administrator, now designated "chief-of-staff", and ran the headquarters from then until the end of the war. Though he did not always approve of what Hitler planned, Keitel earned his nickname by following orders. He signed numerous documents on Hitler's behalf, including the notorious "commissar order" for murdering Soviet commissars attached to the Red Army. He was arrested in May 1945, tried at Nuremberg and hanged on 16 October 1945.

After the suicide of Hitler and Goebbels in the bunker, the government of Germany was temporarily assumed by Grand Admiral Karl Dönitz, Hitler's appointed successor as Reich president. Dönitz had his headquarters at Flensburg near the Danish border and for two weeks after the end of the war was allowed to operate freely, with a cabinet of ministers and a small defence force. The government in reality ruled nothing, but did authorize the German surrender on 7 May and the second surrender in Berlin a day later. There was some confusion among the Allied powers as to what to do with the new regime, which hoped to become a German provisional government. In the end, on 23 May, a unit of British soldiers was sent to Flensburg and arrested the whole government, except for the former minister Himmler, who was caught a day earlier and committed suicide after he was recognized.

LEFT Grand Admiral Karl Dönitz leads the remnants of the German government in Flensburg following their arrest by British soldiers on 23 May 1945. Behind him are Albert Speer and Alfred Jodl.

LEFT Thousands of jubilant Britons crowd into London's Piccadilly Circus on VE Day, 8 May 1945. At 3.00 p.m. Churchill broadcast to the nation from 10 Downing Street ending with the words "Advance Britannia!". His speech was relayed by loudspeakers across central London.

BELOW A Czech propaganda poster from May 1945 declares victory over Fascism and the triumph of the working class under the Red Flag. Much of the resistance to German rule in the Czech lands had been undertaken by communists and socialists.

ABOVE Crowds in New York's Times Square on 42nd Street celebrate VE Day on 8 May 1945 overlooked by a giant model figure of the Statue of Liberty.

17 invited newsmen, Jodl signed the act of surrender. The Soviet representative, General Susloparov, caught unawares by the capitulation and uncertain about what his instructions from Moscow would be, signed in a way that suggested the possibility of a second ceremony. A little later a directive from Stalin arrived ordering him to sign nothing.

Stalin deeply distrusted his Allies for agreeing to a full German surrender without proper Soviet participation. At a meeting in the Kremlin that night he accused the West of organizing a "shady deal" with the defeated Germans. He refused to accept the Rheims document and pressed his allies to agree to a formal, public ceremony in Berlin, the heart of the enemy war effort. His allies agreed and a second surrender document was prepared in Moscow, which had to be reconciled during the course of 8 May with the Western version. A power failure left the typists completing the draft by candlelight. Exactly at the stroke of midnight, Field Marshal Keitel led the German delegation into the room in the former German military engineering school. He signed for the Germans, Marshal Zhukov for the Soviet Union, Air Chief Marshal Arthur Tedder for the British Empire, General Carl Spaatz for the Americans and General de Lattre de Tassigny for the French.

By this time the British and American people had already been told about the surrender and 8 May was designated Victory in Europe (VE) Day and a public holiday. Scenes of jubilation, widely photographed in London, were more modest in other parts of the country. During the course of the day, Churchill appeared next to the royal family on the balcony at Buckingham Palace to an ecstatic welcome. The Soviet population were only told about the surrender early in the morning of 9 May, and only two days later was there a formal day of celebration. In central Europe Soviet forces were still fighting against the remnants of Field Marshal Schörner's Army Group Centre which had retreated for a last stand in Czechoslovakia. It was overwhelmed by Konev's 1st Ukrainian Army Group and Malinovsky's 2nd Ukrainian Army Group and finally surrendered on 11–12 May 1945. Elsewhere, news of the surrender was brought to German garrisons in Lorient and St Nazaire on the French Atlantic coast, in the Channel Islands and at the port of Dunkirk, which had all been bypassed in earlier campaigns and never freed. Local documents of surrender had to be signed in Denmark and Norway. It had taken almost a week from Jodl's original instructions for the cumbersome process of unconditional surrender to be completed.

THE ATOMIC BOMBS

19 JULY 1945
600 B-29 bombers drop 4,000 tons of bombs on Japan in a single raid.

28 JULY 1945
Last US ship sunk by a kamikaze plane off Okinawa.

30 JULY 1945
The USS *Indianapolis* is sunk by a Japanese submarine after delivering vital parts for the atomic bombs at Tinian island.

2 AUGUST 1945
6,600 tons of bombs, the highest wartime total, dropped on Japanese cities.

9 AUGUST 1945
President Truman ratifies the United Nations Charter, making the USA the first state to do so.

BELOW Glass bottle distorted by the efects of the effects of the atomic explosion, Hiroshima, 6 August 1945.

RIGHT The centre of the Japanese city of Hiroshima after the atomic bomb attack on 6 August 1945. The large building in the centre is the Industry Promotional Hall which was retained in its ruined state as a war memorial.

The final defeat of Japan was long expected to be a costly and lengthy campaign and the determination with which the Japanese forces defended Iwo Jima and Okinawa reinforced this conviction. A campaign plan for what was called Operation "Olympic" was drawn up, but unofficial estimates suggested that there would be between 500,000 and one million American casualties in an invasion of the home islands, and although military chiefs thought this exaggerated, they knew that Japan would be defended with more than usual ferocity. The sea blockade and the bombing of Japan's cities would, it was hoped, produce the defeat of Japan without a full invasion.

It is against this background that the decision to use the atomic bomb was made. Since 1942, under the codename of the "Manhattan Project", a large team of scientists in the United States had worked to produce a useable bomb. The physics necessary to understand how a bomb might be developed and what its possible effects would be was pioneered in the 1930s, and by 1939 the theoretical feasibility of such a bomb was established. The problem lay with production. In 1940, a high-level committee of scientists in Britain, known as the Maud Committee, was set up to report on the bomb. In July 1941 the committee concluded that a bomb could be made in the probable period of the war from enriched uranium and in October Churchill's government gave the go-ahead. The British did not recommend using plutonium, a new element derived from uranium, but this was developed later in the United States and used for one of the bombs.

The economic effort of making the bomb proved beyond British capabilities, and in June 1942 the United States took over full responsibility for the whole project. British scientists moved to America and worked with a scientific team under Robert Oppenheimer. The whole project cost $2 billion and employed 600,000 people, and by the summer of 1945 enough plutonium and bomb-grade uranium-235 had been produced to test and use atomic weapons. On 16 July 1945, at the Alamogordo air base in New Mexico, a plutonium bomb was detonated successfully. News of the explosion was sent to Roosevelt's successor President Truman, who was attending the inter-Allied conference at Potsdam. He approved the use of two bombs on Japanese cities. Whether this decision was taken principally to avoid an invasion of Japan, or to test the new technology or to impress the Soviet Union has been argued over ever since.

ROBERT OPPENHEIMER (1904–1967)

Robert Oppenheimer was the physicist who led the research on the atomic bomb as scientific director at the laboratory at Los Alamos. The son of a textile merchant, Oppenheimer was marked out from an early age as a scholar and intellectual of extraordinary power and range. He studied theoretical physics in Germany in the 1920s before returning to America as professor of physics at Berkeley, California. It was his pioneering work on nuclear research in the United States together with his charismatic personality and driving energy that made him a natural choice to run the scientific side of the Manhattan Project. His flirtation with American Communism did not prevent his work at the time, but after the war, as chairman of the General Advisory Committee of the Atomic Energy Commission, he made powerful enemies who disliked his radicalism. In 1954, his security status was revoked when he was investigated by Senator McCarthy's UnAmerican Activities Committee. He moved to Princeton as director of the Institute of Advanced Study and died of throat cancer in 1967.

ABOVE The Los Alamos research facility in the New Mexico desert where Robert Oppenheimer led his team of scientists in the development of the first nuclear weapons.

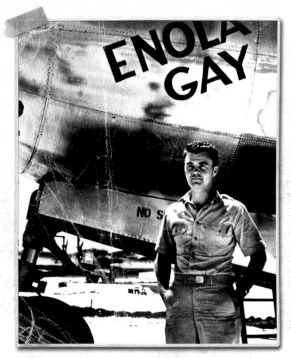

ABOVE Colonel Paul Tibbets standing in front of his B-29 Superfortress bomber *Enola Gay* which carried the first atomic bomb for the attack on Hiroshima, August 1945. He helped to train and organize the 509th Composite Group which was to undertake the atomic attacks in the summer of 1945.

Some Japanese cities had not been bombed by LeMay's Twenty-first Bomber Command so the atomic weapons could be tried out on them. The first bomb was used against Hiroshima on the morning of 6 August 1945. Nicknamed "Little Boy", the 4,000-kilogram (8,800-pound) uranium bomb was carried in a B-29 bomber from Tinian. It caught Hiroshima's workforce on its way to work. Thirteen square kilometres (five square miles) were utterly destroyed and an estimated 120,000, about 40 per cent of the city's population, died either immediately or within a few days from the effects of radiation. The second bomb, carried from Tinian on the morning of 9 August, was destined for the city of Kokura but it was obscured by cloud and the crew dropped the 4,600-kilogram (10,200-pound) plutonium bomb – dubbed "Fat Man" – on the secondary target, Nagasaki. The city was sheltered by hills and the blast effects less damaging, but an estimated 74,000 people were killed and 74,000 injured from a population of 270,000. Tens of thousands suffered the long-term after-effects of exposure to high levels of radiation.

The effect in Japan was one of disbelief at first, turning rapidly to terror at the prospect of further attacks. In reality, the United States was not yet in a position to drop a further atomic bomb, but the same day as the Nagasaki attack the Japanese prime minister asked Emperor Hirohito to decide on the issue of surrender. The effect on the Soviet Union of the atomic attacks was less startling than the Americans had hoped, since spies had already supplied extensive information on the Manhattan Project. Stalin ordered a high-speed programme of nuclear development and the Soviet Union detonated its first atomic test in August 1949, by which time the United States had a further 298 bombs.

ABOVE A photograph of suburban Nagasaki in September 1945 after the second atomic bomb was dropped on 9 August 1945. This scene was eight kilometres (five miles) from the epicentre of the explosion.

LEFT A Dutch medical officer examines two Javanese POWs who were caught in the atomic attacks on Japan. They were among tens of thousands of victims of the after-effects of radiation and blast.

RIGHT Commemoration of the 60th anniversary of the dropping of the atomic bomb on Nagasaki by the B-29 bomber *Bock's Car*. Here shrine maidens attend the memorial ceremony on 9 August 2005 at the Atomic Bomb Hypocenter in Nagasaki.

LIEUTENANT GENERAL LESLIE GROVES (1896–1970)

Leslie Groves is best remembered for two things. He was a senior military engineer who supervised the building of the Pentagon building in Washington, and also military head of the Manhattan Project for constructing the atomic bomb. He joined the army in 1918 after education at the Massachusetts Institute of Technology, and became an officer in the US Corps of Engineers. In 1940, promoted to lieutenant colonel, he joined the General Staff as chief of operations, Corps of Engineers, and deputy to the chief of construction. He was an energetic and ruthless administrator who played a major part in organizing the huge construction projects made necessary by the expansion of the US military between 1940 and 1942. In September 1942, he was appointed as military director of the bomb project which he codenamed "Manhattan". He was one of the leading advocates of bombing the ancient Japanese capital of Kyoto, but was overruled. He retired in 1948 with the rank of lieutenant general, unhappy about the transfer of the nuclear programme to the civilian Atomic Energy Commission.

THE JAPANESE SURRENDER

The Allied demand for the unconditional surrender of Japan presented a more difficult process than was the case in Europe. Surrender was deeply dishonourable for the Japanese military, which was why so many Japanese soldiers and sailors fought literally until the last, or committed suicide. The military domination of decision-making in Japan and the prevailing ethos of sacrifice for the sake of the Emperor impeded any attempt by civilian leaders during 1945, faced with the inevitability of defeat, to find a formula that would satisfy both the Allies and the Japanese military.

The Japanese leadership also shared many illusions about the invincibility of Japan and the defensibility of the Empire. Only with the heavy destruction of Japanese cities in 1945 and the bombardment of the homeland by Allied ships and carrier aircraft was it evident to the wider population that the propaganda of victory had been a cruel deception. Yet in the face of defeat the military decided that the Japanese homeland would be defended at all costs under the slogan "The Glorious Death of One Hundred Million". In January 1945, a Homeland Operations Plan was formulated and in March a law passed to enforce the creation of People's Volunteer Units, followed in June by the creation of People's Volunteer Combat Corps. These people's militia were poorly armed and supplied, but the assumption among Japan's military was that death must always be preferable to dishonour.

In April 1945, a new prime minister, Admiral Kantoro Suzuki, was installed. While some efforts were made to see if there was an acceptable formula for an end to hostilities, Suzuki continued to work with military plans for a final defence. On 26 July, the Allies announced the Potsdam

ABOVE The Japanese General Yoshijiro Umezu signs the instrument of unconditional surrender on behalf of the Japanese army aboard the battleship USS *Missouri* on 2 September 1945.

Declaration which re-affirmed the demand for unconditional surrender and committed the Allies to the democratic reconstruction of Japan. The stumbling block remained the question of the Emperor: unless the Allies would guarantee the survival of the monarchy, the government would not be able to endorse surrender. Hirohito had already let it be known through the Japanese ambassador in Moscow (Japan and the Soviet Union were not yet at war) that Japan wished to end the war, but his own position made it difficult to deliver what the Allies wanted.

ABOVE Admiral Lord Louis Mountbatten, supreme commander Southeast Asia Command, reads out the terms of unconditional surrender to Japanese military leaders at a ceremony in Singapore on 12 September 1945.

ABOVE RIGHT Badge of the US Forty-first Division. This division was one of those to occupy the Japanese mainland following the end of the war in 1945.

BELOW Troops of the 25th Indian Division searching Japanese POWs in the Malayan capital Kuala Lumpur after they had been disarmed in September 1945.

EMPEROR HIROHITO (1901–1989)

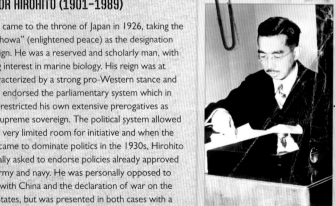

Hirohito came to the throne of Japan in 1926, taking the name "Showa" (enlightened peace) as the designation of his reign. He was a reserved and scholarly man, with a lifelong interest in marine biology. His reign was at first characterized by a strong pro-Western stance and Hirohito endorsed the parliamentary system which in practice restricted his own extensive prerogatives as Japan's supreme sovereign. The political system allowed Hirohito very limited room for initiative and when the military came to dominate politics in the 1930s, Hirohito was usually asked to endorse policies already approved by the army and navy. He was personally opposed to the war with China and the declaration of war on the United States, but was presented in both cases with a *fait accompli* which he could not easily reverse. He was nevertheless unwilling for Japan to abandon its empire or to accept dishonour and as a result was a reluctant partner in the military imperialism of his cabinets. In 1945, he played a key part in finally forcing the military to accept surrender. He remained on the throne from 1945 until his death in 1989, helping to adapt Japan to modern democracy.

The changed circumstances of early August forced the hand of the Japanese government. On 6 August, the first atomic bomb was dropped and on 8–9 August, before the bomb on Nagasaki, Soviet forces opened up a major offensive against the Japanese Kwantung Army in Manchuria. The Soviet army expected a hard fight in difficult terrain, but so weakened was Japanese capability that the million men, 5,000 tanks and 5,000 aircraft of the Far Eastern army groups overwhelmed Japanese opposition within six days, with the deaths of 80,000 Japanese. On 9 August, Suzuki finally asked the Emperor to decide on surrender or a final fight to the death and the Emperor, who had already had secret intimations from the Americans that the throne would be protected, opted for surrender. He had to repeat his decision at an imperial conference on 14 August, and the following day, despite continued opposition from the military, he made an unprecedented broadcast to his people that Japan would surrender.

The final process proved as messy as it had been in Europe. Some Japanese soldiers continued to fight on weeks after the decision to surrender. Many could not be reached in distant outposts and garrisons and the Allied troops had great difficulty in persuading them that the surrender was actually true. In Manchuria, formal surrender came only on 21 August and fighting continued in some areas until September. On 2 September, aboard the battleship USS *Missouri* in Tokyo Bay, Japanese representatives met with General MacArthur to sign the formal instruments of surrender. Japanese forces surrendered in China on 9 September, in Burma on 13 September and in Hong Kong on 16 September. Japan was occupied by American and British Commonwealth forces; the Emperor was not deposed and played an important part in the democratic reconstruction of his country.

ABOVE Jubilant Manchurians greet the Soviet army as it enters Port Arthur on 22 August 1945 after a lightning victory over the occupying Japanese Kwantung Army. The Manchurian territory was ceded to China in 1946 and became part of the new Communist People's Republic in 1949.

ABOVE LEFT A Japanese doctor attempts to staunch the blood from a self-inflicted wound sustained in a suicide attempt by the former prime minister General Hideki Tojo in Yokohama, September 1945. Tojo, who survived, was later tried and hanged as a war criminal in 1948.

BELOW LEFT The US First Cavalry Division parading down a main street in Tokyo on 4 July 1946 during Independence Day celebrations. The commanders of the First Cavalry Division and the US Eighth Army took the march-past in front of the Imperial Hotel.

MARSHAL KIRIL MERETSKOV (1897–1968)

Kiril Meretskov was not one of the stars of the Soviet military leadership, but he played a major part in the swift destruction of the Japanese army in Manchuria in 1945. He was also one of the few marshals not to have had military experience in the First World War. He joined the Bolshevik Party in May 1917, and was appointed chief-of-staff of a Red Guard unit despite his lack of any military experience. It was as a staff officer that he made his subsequent career, and he served briefly in the 1st Cavalry Army, of which Stalin was military commissar. His first major command was the war against Finland, where his troops failed again and again to break the Mannerheim Line. He nevertheless survived several bouts of Stalin's displeasure and for the whole of the European war commanded forces on the far-northern front against Finland and in defence of Leningrad. After forcing the Finns to sue for an armistice in September 1944, he was promoted to marshal. The following year he moved to the Far East for the brief war against Japan.

THE CASUALTIES

Unbekannter englischer Soldat

LEFT A crude grave for a soldier of the British 1st Airborne Division at Arnhem, photographed by liberating forces on 15 April 1945. The German inscription simply reads "Unknown English soldier".

STATISTICAL CHART

	Military dead	Civilian dead
ALLIED POWERS		
USSR	8,670,000	c.16,900,000 **
USA	292,000	n/a
France	250,000	170,000 **
UK	240,000	65,000
Yugoslavia	300,000	1,400,000 **
China	3,400,000	c.10,000,000
India	48,000	n/a
Poland	600,000	6,000,000 **
Belgium	10,000	90,000 **
Canada	40,000	n/a
Australia	34,000	n/a
Netherlands	10,000	240,000 **
Czechoslovakia	7,000	310,000 **
Greece	17,000	400,000 **
New Zealand	12,000	n/a
South Africa	9,000	n/a
Norway	5,000	8,000 **
Denmark	4,000	3,000
AXIS POWERS		
Germany	3,250,000	2,000,000 **
Japan	1,700,000	500,000
Italy*	380,000	180,000 **
Romania	200,000	460,000 **
Bulgaria	10,000	7,000 **
Hungary	140,000	610,000 **
Finland*	80,000	10,000

* Italy and Finland had losses while co-belligerents with Germany, but in the Italian case some losses occurred after 1943 when Italy joined the Allies while Finnish losses come from the two wars with the USSR in 1939–40 and in 1941–44.

** Civilian losses here include Jewish victims who were murdered during the Holocaust. In Poland around 3,000,000 Jews were killed. The total Jewish losses have been estimated at 5,700,000.

The exact number of people killed during the Second World War, either directly as a result of battle, or indirectly through genocidal violence, or terror, or deliberate starvation, will never be known with certainty. The figure most commonly used is between 50 and 55 million, but, as more information becomes available about losses in the Soviet Union or China, this is a figure that is likely to change either up or down. There is no doubt that the death toll from the Second World War was the largest in history, dwarfing by millions the losses sustained in the First. It was also a war in which there were more civilian deaths than military, an estimated 33.35 million against 19.8 million.

The greatest number of casualties suffered was by the Soviet Union and China, victims of the savage wars of expansion waged by German and Japanese forces. The totals of estimated civilian dead, 16 million in the Soviet case, 10 million in China, have never been fully verified since in many cases both prewar census material and postwar investigations were unreliable. It is also the case that a proportion of the dead in both cases were victims of Soviet or Chinese actions, and not killed by the enemy. In the Soviet Union, tens of thousands were killed or died in the forced deportations carried out during the war, or from life in the camps where 2.1 million were sent between 1941 and 1944, or as a result of the decision that ration cards would only be given to those who worked, leaving many older or disabled people to starve. In China, conflict between Nationalists and Communists left many dead in its wake, while warlords fighting on the side of the Japanese

ABOVE A group of "Displaced Persons" (DPs) in a camp in Hamburg Zoo on 18 May 1945. The camp had formerly housed forced workers for the Blohm & Voss shipbuilding company but was taken over by the British on 5 May 1945. DPs were processed before being sent to camps for different nationalities and then repatriated. Estimates ranged between 45,000 and 120,000 for the number of DPs in Hamburg alone.

ABOVE Berliners at a main railway station in October 1945. Hundreds of thousands of German civilians were homeless, or orphaned, while some 13 million Germans were driven from the countries of Eastern Europe to try to find new homes in bomb-damaged Germany.

RIGHT The war produced thousands of psychiatric casualties. Here a US serviceman is being given an injection of sodium amytal as part of his psychiatric care at the Mason General Hospital. For traumatized civilians there was little formal psychiatric help.

also indulged in routine atrocities against the population.

There was also a remarkable disparity in the scale of military losses between the different combatants. Britain and the United States lost only 532,000 military dead, while Germany and Japan between them lost almost 5 million. This is partly explained by longer periods of continuous combat on the Axis side, and the fanatical nature of the final period of resistance, but it also reflected the priority for the Western Allies, both of them democracies, of keeping losses to a minimum. The emphasis in the West on air power as a war-winning weapon also meant that large armies of vulnerable infantry were not needed when much of the necessary force on the battlefield could be exerted by aircraft. Soviet military losses, at almost 8 million, reflected both the primitive nature of early Soviet battlefield tactics and the high death rate among prisoners in German hands, but also the constant propaganda, laced with coercion, about fighting to the last. The different death rates reflected in most cases the different nature of the societies that suffered them.

There were many other forms of casualty besides the dead. Millions were maimed or psychologically disorientated by the war, including those who survived the bombings, and particularly the atomic bombs, whose after-effects continued through genetic transfer to future generations. Millions more were rendered homeless by bombing and land war, forced to live in huts and cellars or pre-fabricated buildings years after the war. In Hamburg over 21 square kilometres (eight square miles) of the city were destroyed completely, in Tokyo over 13 square kilometres (five square miles). A quarter of the urban housing in Britain was destroyed or damaged by the German bombing and V-weapons

offensive. Many people suffered complete dispossession, a reality for millions of those affected by war, not only as a result of bombing but also from forced takeover of land or goods, the requisitioning of wealth and, in the case of Europe's Jewish population, the deliberate seizure of everything they possessed.

At the end of the war, Europe and Asia also faced a major refugee crisis. So-called Displaced Persons numbered perhaps 30 million in 1945; around 13 million Germans were expelled from Eastern Europe in 1945–46; millions of Chinese and Koreans had been forced to move as labourers for the Japanese or fled as refugees during the war. The newly formed United Nations set up a Relief and Rehabilitation Administration (UNRRA) to cope with the displaced populations, and in December 1946 a separate administration for children (UNICEF) to help cope with orphaned or displaced children in Europe, who had numbered an estimated 11 million in 1945.

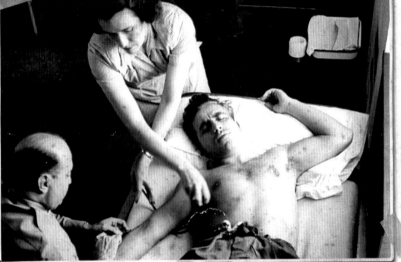

BELOW A small group of surviving Polish Jews arriving in the American sector of Berlin on 22 January 1946 from the Soviet Zone. Over three million Polish Jews were murdered during the war, but in 1945 the small number who returned to Poland found themselves the victims of Polish anti-Semitism. Thousands made their way to Palestine in the years after the war.

THE WAR CRIMES TRIALS

23 JULY 1945
Trial of Marshal Philippe Pétain begins in France. His eventual death sentence is commuted to life imprisonment.

9 OCTOBER 1945
Former Vichy-French head of government Pierre Laval is sentenced to death by a French court.

16 JULY 1946
43 Waffen-SS soldiers are condemned to death for the Malmédy massacre.

15 OCTOBER 1946
Hermann Göring commits suicide by swallowing cyanide the night before he is due to be executed.

RIGHT German SS-Brigade Leader Otto Rasch was commander of Einsatzgruppe C on the southern front in the Soviet Union where his killing squad was responsible for killing at least 80,000 Jews. He was tried with others in the Einsatzgruppen trial in 1948 but developed Parkinson's disease and died in November 1948. He is seen here being photographed at Nuremberg for his file record.

Even while the war was being fought and won, the Allies declared that those responsible for starting the war and for perpetrating atrocities on a large scale would face punishment for violating both the laws of war and the laws governing international conduct. The first declaration was made in 1942, and in September 1943 the United Nations, the term already used to describe the Allied nations fighting the Axis, established a War Crimes Commission to draw up a list of those likely to be indicted for major breaches of international law and the laws of war. However, not until May 1945, at the founding conference of the United Nations Organization, was agreement reached on the establishment of an International Military Tribunal for the major war criminals.

A clear distinction was made between war crimes committed in particular locations (the murder of POWs, the destruction of a village etc.), which were in general to be sent to trial under the jurisdiction of the state whose citizens had been the victims, and crimes "that have no special geographical location", such as waging aggressive war, or the deliberate perpetration of genocide (a crime introduced for the first time in the postwar trials). The most important case was the trial of the major war criminals at Nuremberg in 1945–46. Here the defendants, drawn mainly from the surviving leadership group of the Third Reich, were charged with conspiracy, crimes against peace, crimes against humanity and war crimes. Many of the charges involved crimes defined retrospectively, since the concept of crimes against peace or crimes against humanity did not yet exist in international law. After much argument about who was or was not to be regarded as a major criminal, 23 names were submitted for indictment, including Martin Bormann, Hitler's Chancellery chief, *in absentia*. Robert Ley, head of the German Labour Front, hanged himself in his cell and eventually 22 defendants were tried, 12 of whom

(among them Bormann) were found guilty and condemned to death, three found not guilty and seven sent for long periods of imprisonment.

At Nuremberg, subsequent tribunals were established for military commanders, leading businessmen (most prominently the directors of the chemical giant I G Farben) and the bureaucratic apparatus responsible for the genocide of the Jews, the employment of slave labour and supporting aggression. The trials petered out in 1947–48, but a long series of subsequent trials were then organized by the West German government, including the Frankfurt Auschwitz trial in 1963–65 of those who had managed to evade punishment at Nuremberg. Alongside the trials the Allies undertook a process of so-called "de-Nazification", which involved the official screening of millions of Germans, some of whom were removed from their posts, while many more returned to civilian life in the 1940s, rising in many cases to senior positions in the new democracy.

In Japan, an International Military Tribunal for the Far East was announced in January 1946 by General MacArthur,

LEFT The major defendants in the dock before the International Military Tribunal at Nuremberg in November 1945. Robert Ley committed suicide before the trial and Martin Bormann was tried *in absentia*.

BELOW General Hideki Tojo, the wartime Japanese prime minister, on trial for war crimes and crimes against peace at the Far Eastern International Military Tribunal in the former Japanese Army Ministry in Tokyo. The trial was even longer than the Nuremberg Tribunal, lasting from 3 May 1946 to 4 November 1948. Tojo was found guilty of crimes against peace and was hanged.

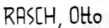
RASCH, Otto

JUSTICE ROBERT JACKSON (1892–1954)

Robert Houghwout Jackson was the chief United States prosecutor at the Nuremberg trials of the major war criminals in 1945–46. He also played a key part in deciding on the terms of the indictment and formulating the new crimes against peace and against humanity first used at the trial. He began his career in law in 1913 in New York State, where he came to the attention of the Democrat politician Franklin Roosevelt. He was appointed to federal office by Roosevelt in 1934, first as counsel for the Treasury Department, then in 1938 as solicitor general, and finally in 1940 as attorney general. In 1941 he became a US Supreme Court justice. He was appointed by President Truman in May 1945 to head the US prosecution team for the major war crimes trial. After the trials, he considered a political career, but ill-health prevented him and he died in Washington in 1954, aged 62.

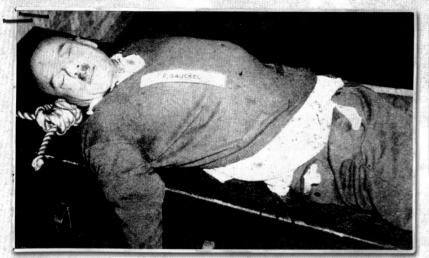

RAFAEL LEMKIN (1901–1959)

Rafael Lemkin is best remembered for coining the term "genocide" (literally the killing of a people). He was a senior Polish lawyer and academic who in the 1930s was already working on his theory of genocide when the war forced him to flee from Poland. He arrived in the United States in 1941, and in 1943 first used the term "genocide", which was then borrowed by the International Military Tribunal at Nuremberg. He played an important part in drafting the United Nations Convention on Genocide adopted in December 1948. Ironically in his first discussion of genocide he argued that it could not apply to the Jews, because they did not constitute a clear national group.

LEFT The body of Fritz Sauckel after he was hanged at Nuremberg on 16 October 1945. Photographs were taken as a record of each of the hanged defendants. Sauckel was responsible for the supply of forced labour from German-occupied Europe, thousands of whom died in German work camps and construction sites.

BELOW LEFT The trial of the directors of the German chemical trust I G Farben in September 1947. Trials of businessmen, bureaucrats and soldiers were designed to show the German people the nature of the elites that had collaborated with Hitlerism. I G Farben was accused of supplying war material and seizing foreign assets from captured firms.

ABOVE A German skinhead sports a tee-shirt with the face of Rudolf Hess at a neo-Nazi rally on 21 August 2004 in the Bavarian town of Wunsiedel. Hess, who committed suicide in Spandau prison in 1987, has become a hero for the extreme right.

LEFT Adolf Eichmann on trial in Jerusalem, 22 June 1961. The former head of the Jewish department IV B4 of the Gestapo in Berlin, he stood trial for helping to organize the genocide of almost six million European Jews. He fled to Argentina after the war where he was snatched by Israeli security police. Although he argued that he was only a transport official doing his job, the court remained unconvinced and he was sentenced to death.

supreme commander, Allied Powers. A trial was held in Tokyo in 1946–48 of 28 major war criminals, including the former prime minister, General Tojo. They were charged, like the defendants at Nuremberg, with the new categories of crimes against peace and crimes against humanity. Twenty-five were found guilty, and seven, including Tojo, were hanged on 23 December 1948. Sixteen were sentenced to life imprisonment, but those still imprisoned were released on amnesty in 1958. Around 2,000 other trials took place of soldiers and civilians accused of specific war crimes, lasting until 1951. At these smaller trials, 5,700 were tried, approximately 3,000 found guilty and 920 executed.

Although there has been continued argument since 1945 about the legitimacy of trials where the charges were in the most important cases based on crimes not defined as such at the time they were committed, the decision to hold the international tribunals was based on the belief that the public exposure of the aggressive and atrocious nature of the war efforts of Germany and Japan would encourage the development of a postwar international order based on greater respect for international law and human rights.

FROM WORLD WAR TO COLD WAR

24 OCTOBER 1945
The United Nations Charter is ratified by the five principal powers, Britain, France, the USA, the USSR and China.

3 NOVEMBER 1946
New Japanese constitution is authorized by Emperor Hirohito excluding war and military service overseas for the Japanese state.

3 APRIL 1948
Marshall Plan for US aid to Europe becomes law.

4 APRIL 1949
The North Atlantic Treaty Organization (NATO) is established.

29 AUGUST 1949
A Soviet atomic bomb is tested in the desert of Kazakhstan.

1 OCTOBER 1949
The People's Republic of China is founded.

BELOW Churchill, Stalin and the new American president, Harry Truman, stand hand-in-hand outside the Cecilienhof palace in Potsdam on 23 July 1945. It was to be their last summit. In the middle of the conference Churchill heard that he had been defeated at the polls and Labour prime minister Clement Attlee took his place.

The end of the Second World War between May and August 1945 left many issues unresolved and the immediate postwar years saw a further wave of civil wars, political conflict, anti-colonial struggle and the onset of a major confrontation between the former wartime Allies defined by the term coined by the veteran American journalist Walter Lippmann as the "Cold War".

The most violent postwar areas were Southeast Asia and the areas taken under direct Soviet rule in Eastern Europe. In Asia, the wartime defeat of the colonial powers encouraged growing demands for independence. In the Dutch East Indies, the returning colonial administration, assisted by British and Australian forces, fought against nationalist insurgents, but by 1949 independence was conceded to what was now called Indonesia. In Malaya and French Indo-China, Communist insurgency provoked growing violence and in the latter the onset of what became later the Vietnam War. Nationalist pressure in India led to independence and partition into India and Pakistan in 1947, and Burma (Myanmar) and Ceylon (Sri Lanka) achieved independence a year later. Within a matter of years, the colonial presence in South Asia had come to an end.

In the borderlands of Eastern Europe, a guerrilla war was waged against the Soviet state by irregular forces in Latvia, Estonia, Lithuania, Belorussia and Ukraine. The post-1945 civil war was shielded as far as possible from the outside world, but the conflict was large-scale and conducted with

brutality on both sides. In Lithuania, an estimated 20,000 Soviet soldiers were killed fighting 30,000 nationalists. In Ukraine, the nationalist People's Army kept up its war against Communism and was not fully suppressed until the early 1950s; the Polish Home Army revived after the destruction of Warsaw and this, too, was not finally rooted out until 1948. Around 300,000 people suspected of nationalist sympathies were deported to the camps in Siberia and the Russian interior. Civil war continued in Greece until 1949, when the Communist insurgents were finally defeated. In Italy and France, the lines of conflict defined in the war between partisans, resistance and the extreme right persisted into the postwar years when old scores were settled between the two sides.

The major change in the international order came with the onset of growing hostility between the Western states and the Soviet bloc. The roots of the Cold War lay in prewar distrust of Communism, and renewed tension was already evident before 1945 in the arguments over the fate of Eastern Europe and Germany. In 1946, Churchill famously defined the division in a speech at Fulton, Missouri, as an "Iron Curtain". Between 1945 and 1948,

LEFT Soviet prisoners at the Buchenwald camp, liberated by the US Third Army on 30 April 1945, cheer an improvised portrait of Stalin. They faced a grim future when they returned to the Soviet Union. Regarded as contaminated by fascism, they were processed and interrogated and in thousands of cases sent to Gulag camps.

BELOW Berliners watch as a man paints the words "British Sector" across Potsdammer Strasse to demarcate the zone of Berlin assigned to British occupation in August 1945. The capital became a battleground of the Cold War because it was deep in Soviet-controlled territory but divided into British, Soviet, American and French sectors.

the Soviet Union increased its political domination of Pola..., Czechoslovakia, Romania, Bulgaria, Hungary and the eastern zone of Germany, all of which were effectively under Communist control by 1948. The poor state of Europe's economy raised fears that Communism might move westwards with economic hardship and in 1947 President Truman announced that his government would support any state resisting external

HARRY S TRUMAN (1884–1972)

Harry S Truman was Roosevelt's vice-presidential running mate in the 1944 election. On Roosevelt's death on 12 April 1945, Truman assumed the presidency. He started life as a farmer in Missouri, served in the field artillery in the First World War, and returned home to open a haberdashery shop in Kansas City. He was elected a judge in 1922, and Democratic senator in 1934. Although Roosevelt was in poor health in 1945, he made little effort to involve Truman in the war effort, with the result that Truman suddenly found himself in the international limelight with almost no experience of international affairs or military strategy. He became a firm advocate of democracy in Europe and accepted as inevitable the growing Cold War with the Soviet Union. In 1947, he formulated what became known as the "Truman Doctrine", which stated that the United States would defend any state trying to resist external political and ideological pressure. He was re-elected in 1948 and oversaw American involvement in the Korean War. He retired from political life in 1953.

Es geht vorwärts

ACHTUNG!

BAUARBEITEN

durch den Marshallplan

Andrei Zhdanov (left) was a close political ally of Stalin and the author of the postwar idea of "two camps", one capitalist, one communist. He joined the Bolshevik Party in 1915, and after a modest early career, was chosen by Stalin to run the Leningrad party machine in 1934. He was best-known for his role as the arbiter of Soviet cultural production after 1945, when he imposed a rigid censorship. In 1947, he played a leading part in founding Cominform, an international communist organization designed to co-ordinate Communist rule in Eastern Europe and to provide a common ideological approach to the growing conflict with the West. Zhdanov died in 1948, and Stalin later accused Jewish doctors of deliberately killing him, but he was an inveterate heavy drinker who almost certainly killed himself.

LEFT A 1950 West German poster advertising the benefits of the Mashall Plan. It reads "Building Work – It's Moving Forward with the Marshall Plan".

RIGHT A small child is placed on board an RAF Dakota transport aircraft for evacuation during the Berlin Airlift of 1948–49. Berlin was cut off by road and rail but Stalin could not risk an armed confrontation and the air lifeline stayed open.

BELOW Chinese Communist supporters in the city of Peiping raise their fists in welcome for Communist forces who drove out the Guomindang Nationalists on 5 February 1949. The central portrait is of Mao Zedong, soon to become Chairman of the new People's Republic.

BOTTOM RIGHT Greek government commandos wearing British-style berets and American combat jackets during the Greek civil war in May 1948. The Greek Communists were finally abandoned by Stalin. Government forces won the war and imposed a harsh regime on those who had resisted. Greece, like Berlin, became one of the first sites of Cold War conflict.

political aggression. In 1948, the wartime US Army chief-of-staff, George Marshall, who was now Truman's secretary of state, established a major economic rescue package for Europe known as the Marshall Plan. Stalin insisted that the Eastern European states reject it, and the division between the two sides became completely evident. From June 1948 to May 1949, the Soviet Union blockaded Berlin (which was divided into four occupation zones). The population of the three zones comprising West Berlin was supplied by an airlift organized by air forces that only four years before had been pounding Berlin to rubble. The Soviet Union avoided a direct confrontation and the blockade was lifted, but Germany

was divided into two separate states in 1949.

The same year, Chinese Communism under Mao Zedong triumphed and founded a new Communist republic. The threat posed by international communism now prompted the West to organize a military alliance, the North Atlantic Treaty Organization, which came into being also in 1949. The division between the wartime Allies was now unbridgeable and the Cold War confrontation persisted for a further 40 years.

INDEX

Page numbers in *italic* refer to picture captions.

CREDITS

PHOTOGRAPHS

The vast majority of photographs reproduced in this book have been taken from the collections of the Photograph Archive at the Imperial War Museum. The museum's reference numbers for each of the photograph is indicated below, giving the page on which they appear in the book and location indicator. Key: t = top, b = bottom, l = left, r = right and c = centre.

IWM: 2 (Hitler, MH 11051), 2 (Churchill MH 26392), 3 (Dunkirk NYP 68075), 3 (Gen. Sir Archibald Wavell & Lt. General Richard O'Connor E 1549), 3 (Dunkirk COL 294), 3 (Australian troops E 1570), 8c (UNI 1280), 10bl (OMD 64), 12bl (MH 11051), 12bl (HU 2411), 13tl (MH 11040), 13bl (ART PST 3183), 14bl (PST 2504), 15cl (O 227), 15tc (ATP 8231 B), 15tr (Army Training 06/08), 16cl (MED 914), 17bl (NYP 22525), 18tr (OMD 6444), 19tr (CH 1297), 19cr (FIR 1130), 20c (HU 39964), 20br (MH 6081), 21l (PST 3159), 22bl (OMD 6446), 22br (HU 5358), 23c FIR 7278), 25tr (D 2597), 26tl (INS 7974), 26bl (INS 7972), 26cl (HU 39620), 28cl) UNI 12861), 28bl (A 2), 28tc (HU 204), 28tr (A 14906), 29tl (HU A20791), 29cl (HU 90420), 30cl (HU 55640), 30cr (HU 809), 30bl (INS 7979), 30br (A 42), 30bc (NYP 68074), 31tc (HU 28737), 31c (N 229), 31br (A 29155), 32br (H 4367), 33tl (HU 55578), 33tr (MH 26392), 33b (H 15384), 34cl (FEQ 870), 35tr (F 2036), 36l (HU 1135), 36c (NYP 41240), 36tc (NYP 68075), 36bc (HU 2286), 36br (F 4849), 37tl (O 177), 37tr (COL 294), 37c (HU 2280), 37b (H 1647), 38c (MUN 3286), 38tr (FIR 6058), 39tl (MH 10412), 39cr (D 1966), 39cl (HU 3266), 39b (HU 2283), 40tc (DEU 503409), 40b (PST 9199), 41tc (MISC 17435), 41tr (PST 8358), 42tc (INS 7997), 42br (INS 7991, 7993, 8012), 42bc (CH 1398), 43t (CH 74), 43tr (HU 4481), 43cl (CM 3513), 43cr (CH 1827), 43b (CH 1827), 44tr (CM31), 44c (E 1968), 44cl (INS 8043), 45tl (E 6661), 45tr (K 325), 45c (E 6064), 45b (E 892), 46tr (H 3096), 46cr (H 667), 46bc (H 3233), 47tl (no.35 Operation Sealion), 47cr (A 10296), 47br (H 3640), 47bc (HU 95927), 47bl (MH 10132), 48tc (HU 1129), 47tl (97471), 48bl (Exhibits and Firearms), 48br (HU 44272), 49tc (D 5984), 49bc (H 5593), 50c (HU 75995), 51tr (HU 2791), 52tr (CM 164), 52c (A 9760), 52cr (CM 294), 53tr (A 3532), 53bc (A 20659), 54br (E 2298), 54cl (E 1549), 54tr (E 1570), 54cr (CM 354), 55tr (E 7392), 55b (E 1766), 55cl (E 1579), 56l (INS 8045), 56cl (E 446), 56br (HU 39455), 58tr (E 3265), 58cr (E 3020), 58bc (MH 6100), 58bl (INS 8060), 58cl (HU 52264), 59tl (HU 1997), 59bl (E 3282), 59cr (E 3039), 60tr (HU 374), 60c (HU 381), 60br (A 4217), 61bl (ART LD 284 HMS Ark Royal in Action by Eric Ravilious, 1940), 61c (A 4100), 61br (A 4386), 64tc (HU 75533), 64br (HU 10180), 64l (INS 8051), 70tl (RUS 1206), 70cr (RUS 1191), 72tc (E 2887), 72br (E 2478), 72c (HU 5625), 73bc (E 6390), 73tr (E 8263), 74tc (CM 774), 74tr (E 3154E), 74c (E 3464), 74bl (INS 6662), 75tl (E 3989), 75cl (E 4087), 76br (H 12719), 77c (A 3869), 78bl (E 6577), 78br (CM 1500), 79tl (E 6839), 79c (CM 1561), 79br (E 9569), 81bl (EN 21474), 81c (NYP 68079), 82bl (NYP 45042), 82c (INS 7204), 82tl (HU 2779), 83b (NY 7343), 84bc (V 60), 85tl (HU 63768), 88tr (K 757), 88bl (K 652), 89bc (HU 2770), 90tr (D 8896), 90c (F 492), 90bl (N 459), 91tl (N 481), 91c (D 12870), 91r (H 17365), 92tr (A 8166), 92br (A 8701), 92bl (GM 786), 93tl (A 11155), 93tr (A 11186), 93cr (CM 3697), 93bc (GM 1765), 97 (SE 3310), 101tl (FL 740), 101tr (MAD 294), 102tr (C 3246), 102bl (CH 13020), 102br (TR 11), 103tl (CH 3337), 103c (C 2615), 104bl (MH 2104), 107tr (B 7188), 111tl (E 12789), 112bc (A 13363). 123tc (E 8487), 123tr (E 15223), 123bl (TR 2283), 126cl (E 18474), 127tr (E 18971), 127cr (E 21333), 127tc (E 18980), 128cl (A 12661), 128bc (A 12649), 128tc (TR 285), 136tc (NY 6082), 137br (K 5870), 138tr (SE 7946), 138br (HU 6643), 138cr (MH 7877), 138br (SE 7910), 139bc (SE 7921), 139tr (IND 2290), 139br (HU 6643), 141br (NA 2876), 142cl (C 3717), 142bl (HU 92132), 143tl (CH 11047), 143cl (CH 18005), 143bc (HU 4594), 143r sequence top to bottom (FLM 2339), (FLM 2340), (FLM 2342), 144tr (D 8463), 144cr (PST 8105), 145bl (D 2894), 145tr (PST 696), 148cl (CAN 902), 148tr (A 17916), 148cr (EA 38785), 148br (NA 4940), 149tl (NA 5854), 149bl (A 18492), 149r (NYF 9892), 150cr (C 3677), 151tl (CL 3400), 151r (BU 5077), 152tl (ZZZ 11837E), 156tl (A 19246), 156c (NA 6157), 156tr (NA 6630), 157tr (CNA 1700), 157bc (NA 142), 157br (NAM 57), 160br (NYF 11281), 162bl (E 26634), 162br (TR 153), 163tl (A 20731), 163tr (A 20744), 164bl (MISC 60756), 165tr (PST 3075), 166tr (A 20687), 166br (ART LD 7424), 167b (A 21200), 167tr (A 22633), 167c (A 16489), 168tr (AI 13229), 168c (IA 19828), 168bl (NA 11041), 168br (NA 12136), 169br (NA 15295), 169tc (NA 15306), 170cr (MH 6352), 170tc (MH 11250), 171br (MH 1680), 171bl (MH 1978), 171tc (NA 12810), 172bc (H 42531), 174br (IND 3331), 174bc (IND 3430), 175cl (IND 3468), 175tl (IND 3479). 175 (BU 1098), 180tl (HU 40203), 180tr (MH 10132), 180b (B 5114), 181tl (EA 26941), 181tr (TR 2626), 181bc (A 23997), 182tc (B 8441), 182tr (FLA 5499), 182bc (FRA 200371), 183tl (B 6781), 183tr (HU 64137), 183c (B 7649), 184tl (COL 34), 184tr (C 4431), 184br (CL 3430), 185bl (D 21213), 186c (FIR 1745), 187cl (MUN 3433), 189cr (FLA 5500), 192c (MH 24073), 193tr (HU 4128), 193bl (CL 1725), 193br (C 4525), 194tc (TR 1959), 194tr (TR 1763), 195tl (TR 2282), 195tr (TR 2287), 196tl (MH 2111_B), 196bl (NS 8086), 198tc (B 9473), 199br (B 9668), 199tr (B 13169), 199bl (EA 34627), 202tc (A 25247), 204tl (EA 37079), 205cr (HU 66477), 206tc (CL 1173), 206br (B 10124_A), 206tr (TR 174), 207tl (HU 2126), 207tr (E 16462), 207cr (BU 1121), 207bl (HU 2127), 207br (HU 2129), 209br (CM 5648), 213cr (NYF 57021), 214tr (H 6293), 214bl (H 20288), 214br (V 170), 215tc (H21013), 216tr (EA 47958), 216bc (MH 12850), 217c (EA 48015), 217bc (EA 48447), 217bl (EA 49104), 220c (EA 52870), 220bl (NAM 23), 221c (H 4969), 221tl (HU 31076), 226tl (B 14413), 226c (A 27813), 226br (IA 13766), 227tl (BU 2332), 227cr (BU 3421), 227bl (BU 3421), 228bc (HU 51237), 230br (BU 4269), 231tr (BU 4094), 231cr (NYP 49945), 232tc (SE 3006), 232tr (C 5149), 232c (SE 3071), 232cr (OMD 2550), 233tr (IND 3143), 233tc (IND 4592), 233b (SE 3773), 233br (SE 3804), 233c (SE 3891), 235br (HU 68178), 236tl (NYP 62569), 236c (HU 59474), 238tl (NA 23837), 238cr (TR 2377), 238bc (TR 2846), 239tl (HU 50242), 239cr (NA 24683), 239br (NA 24791), 239br (TR 2891), 240tr (EA 65715), 240bl (FRA 203385), 241c (EA 65879), 242bl (MH 29427), 243tl (HU 44878), 244tc (A 30427 A), 244tr (A 30492), 244bl (HU 53442), 244br (IND 4848), 246bl (BU 3646), 247tr (BU 6629), 248tc (MH 24088), 250bl (BU 9195), 251cr (HU 36829). All badges, armaments and other artefacts © Imperial War Museum.

Photographs from sources outside the Imperial War Museum, with the kind permission of the following:

AKG-Images: 8br, 11cr, 21tr, 23br, 32tr, 38bc, 50tr, 55tc, 57tr, 57bl, 57cr, 57br, 64bc, 65tl, 65tr, 67c, 67bc, 67r, 70tr, 70br, 73bl, 84tr, 89l, 93br, 104tc, 104br, 125bl, 132c, 132tr, 133cl, 134c, 134br, 135br, 137tr, 141c, 142tr, 143c, 146tr, 147bc, 152br, 154tr, 155c, 155tr, 167tc, 174tc, 176c, 191tc, 197tl, 198c, 200bc, 201tl, 201br, 202b, 204c, 209tl, 219bl, 234bc, 240tc, 251tl; /Florian Profitlich: 197cr; /RIA Novosti: 124tr, 125tr, 154bl, 164tc, 205cl, 245br; / Ullstein Bild 16cl, 67l, 110cl, 110c, 114tl, 146cl, 247tl, 195bc, 196tr, 200c, 208tr, 231bl, 234c, 245tr, 249cr; /**The Aerial Reconnaissance Archives:** 41tl; /**Alinari:** 126tc, 127bl; /**Australia War Memorial:** 158br (016422), 158tr (042999), 158r (127965), 158c (REL34921), 159bl (070242), 159br (042740), 159tr (P00554_002); /**Bildarchiv Preussischer Kulturbesitz**: 105tl, 105br, 110tr; /Corbis: 67tl, 83tr, 107cr; /Bettmann: 76tc, 77cr, 78tr, 81tr, 83tc, 83cr, 84c, 84bl, 85tc, 85cr, 100tc, 107tc, 111bc; /The Dimitri Baltermants Collection: 70tc; /Hulton-Deutsch Collection: 65br, 75bc, 76bl, 97bl, 106cl, 106–7c; /Yevgeny Khaldel: 115br; /Visuals Unlimited: 106bl; /**Cody Images:** 152bc, 155r; /**Corbis** (HMS Illustrious under attack) 27cr, 35br, 35c, 103bl, 135tl, 136cl, 140br, 147tc, 149tr, 150bl, 160l, 160tr, 161br, 243br, 248bl; /Archivo Icongrafico, S.A. 11bc; /Austrian Archives 19bc; /Bettmann, 1, 3 (Japanese forces advance), 3 (Death Cart), 6tr, 7c, 8tr, 9tr, 10c, 10bc, 14tr, 27br, 32l, 34tr, 34bl, 41cl, 41br, 44bc, 50bl, 51tc, 51bc, 53cl, 132br, 135bl, 136br, 137cl, 137tl, 145bl, 145tc, 150tr, 161tl, 164tc, 169cr, 174tr, 176tr, 177bl, 182cr, 189cr, 190tc, 195cr, 197bc, 202bl, 208br, 215bl, 216cr, 230tr, 245bl, 247br, 248bc, 249tr, 250br; /The Dimitri Baltermants Collection: 133tr, 134tc; / DPA: 184bl, 197tr, 217tr, 230c; /Hulton-Deutsch Collection 2 (Germans cross Rhine), 9br, 12tl, 13br, 15bc, 18bl, 20bl, 26–27, 27tl, 30tr, 34br, 40r, 128tr, 163br, 183bc, 247tl, 250cr, 251tr; / Michael Nicholson: 241br; /Swim Ink 2, LLC: 221r; /Underwood & Underwood 11bl; /**Getty Images:** 2 (Newspaper vendor), 2 (Mounted Polish Brigade), 6br, 6c, 6bl, 7tc, 7cr, 7br, 7bl, 8cl, 10tc, 16c, 17tr, 18c, 20tc, 22c, 23cr, 24tc, 24cr, 24bc, 25bl, 29bc, 33c, 35tl, 35tc, 38cl, 38tr, 46c, 48tr, 48c, 49cr, 49c, 56tr, 56bl, 57tl, 60tl, 60bl, 65bl, 68cl, 69r, 70c, 71bc, 76c, 77br, 79tr, 80tr, 82tc, 84tc, 85br, 87c, 87tr, 88tr, 89br, 92tc, 102tc, 106c, 114br, 115tl, 115tc, 115tr, 191tl, 192b, 193tc, 200tl, 201cr, 201bc, 203tr, 203cl, 203cr, 204tl, 204cl, 209tr, 214tc, 218br, 224tc, 224cr, 232bl, 234tl, 235bl, 237tr, 239tr, 243cr, 243c, 246tl, 249br, 251br; /AFP 22tr, 77tr, 124bc, 125tl, 129tr, 130c, 131r, 133bc, 141tl, 144bl, 147cr, 145bl, 153tr, 161cl, 162tr, 163bl, 164br, 167bc, 172cl, 172bl, 248cr; /National Geographic: 134bl; /Popperfoto: 124tl, 171tr, 225tr, 237tl; /Time Life Pictures 10tr, 13tr, 16bc, 17tl, 17br, 23tl, 34bc, 68tr, 69tr, 76bc, 86bl, 96tc, 96tr, 96bl, 96br, 106bc, 111tr, 112tc, 133tc, 139tl, 161tl, 161bl, 165c, 196bc, 215cr, 215tr, 216tc, 220tr, 224bc, 236br, 236bl, 240bc, 243tr, 249tl, 249cl; /**The Granger Collection:** 144cl; /**Library of Congress, Washington:** 169bl, 173tr; /**Mary Evans Picture Library**: 25cr, 31tr, 122br; /**National Archives and Records Administration, Washington:** 81tl, 81cr, 94tr, 94bc, 98br, 99br, 98tr, 98tc, 98bl, 99tl, 99c, 99bc, 108c, 108tc, 108br, 108bl, 109bl, 109br, 109tc, 109cr, 112tr, 112cr, 112br, 113bl, 113tr, 113cr, 113br, 113tl, 116tc, 116tr, 116bc, 116bt, 116cr, 117tl, 117br, 186tr, 186bl, 186r, 187tl, 187bl, 187br, 188tl, 188bc, 189tl, 189tc, 189bl, 194bc, 210tl, 210bl, 210br, 211tl, 211tr, 211bl, 211cr, 211br, 211bc, 212tl, 212cr, 213tl, 213tr, 213br, 222tc, 222bc, 222tr, 223tl, 223tr, 223cr, 223bl, 223br, 228cl, 228c, 228tc, 229tl, 229bl, 229bc, 229cr, 229br; /Office of War Information: 95br; /US Army: 94tc; /US Navy: 80tc, 80bc; /US Signal Corps: 94c, 95tl, 95bl, 95tr, 95cr; / USMC: 95br, 117cr; /**PA Photos:** 35bc, 103br; /AP Photo 21tc, 66tr, 130tl, 130br, 131cl, 131tl, 154br, 177br, 221tl, 225tl, 225br, 240cr, 241tl, 250tc, 251c; /DPA: 153b; /**Photo12. com:** Bertelsmann Lexiko 52cr; Collection Bernard Crochet: 66c; /Coll-DITE-USIS: 129l, 153cr, 198tr, 199tl, 203tl, 205bc; /Hachédé 17c, 24bl; /Oasis: 152tr; /Photovintages: 204tr; /Ullstein Bild: 68br; /**Private collection:** 8cl, 85tr, 117tr, 130bl, 166bl, 187br, 191cr; /**Rex Features:** Snap: 136bl; /Scala Archives 124cl, 147tr, 150br, 151cl, 173tc; /**RIA Novosti Photo Library**: 21c, 27bc; /**Roger-Viollet:** 169tr; /Ullstein Bild: 125tc, 126bc, 127c, 135cl, 140tr, 140bc, 144br, 157bl, 170br; /**SAMNH:** 100tr, 101cl; /Science & Society: Science Museum: 112bl; / **Scala Archives, London:** © De Agostini Picture Library, Scala, Firenze 11tr; BPK: 201tr, 219tr; /**Topfoto.co.uk:** 14c, 52bl, 68tl, 82cr, 86cr, 91bl, 91tr, 97tc, 100bc, 127c, 135cl, 140tl, 146bc, 147c, 149cr, 165br, 173bl, 175bl, 177cr, 190tr; /Alinari Archives 44bl; /HIP: 198cr; / RIA Novosti: 68–9, 114bl, 165cl, 235tl, 235tr; /Roger-Viollet: 86tc; /Ullstein Bild: 74c, 87tc; / **Ullstein Bild**: 3 (Tri-Partite Pact), 19tl, 20bl, 28br, 29tc, 50tl, 51cr, 81tr, 83tl, 77tl, 79cr, 88br, 103tr, 104tr, 110br, 111br, 114tr, 115cr, 190bc, 191bc, 207bl, 209bc, 218tl, 218cr, 219tl, 219br, 221br, 227bc, 230bl; /SV Bilderdie: 82br; /Walter Frentz: 66b, 185tl, 185tr; /**United States Holocaust Memorial:** 87bc; /**US Naval Historical Society:** 109tr

Every effort has been made to acknowledge correctly and contact the source and/or copyright holder of each picture, and Carlton Books apologizes for any unintentional errors or omissions, which will be corrected in future editions of this book.

PUBLISHING CREDITS

Editorial Director: Piers Murray Hill
Executive Editor: Gemma Maclagan
Additional Editorial work: Philip Parker and Cathy Rubenstein
Design Director: Russell Porter
Art Director: Russell Knowles
Design: Russell Knowles, Drew McGovern, Brian Flynn and Chris Gould
Cartography: Martin Brown
Picture Research: Steve Behan
Photography: Russell Porter and Karl Adamson
Production: Rachel Burgess